"Chris de Ploeg's book stands out fron the Ukraine's crisis, even by highly e careful work with the facts, which is amidst the conscious propaganda and information war from all the sides of the conflict. It is also the best left-wing analysis so far. Being critical to a problematic Maidan uprising and the neoliberal-nationalist government it helped to bring to power, the author does not take equally wrong Putin-versteher position and shows how the rivalry of competing imperialisms and nationalisms brought Ukraine into the current political and economic disaster."

—**Volodymyr Ishchenko**
Deputy director
Center for Social and Labor Research in Ukraine and lecturer at the Department of Sociology Kyiv Polytechnic Institute

"A meticulously documented interpretation of the Second Maidan that focuses on the darker side of Ukraine's Revolution of Dignity. By weaving together the role of the Far Right and western governments, the emergence of resistance in Donbass, and the reasons why Kiev responded to it with military force, De Ploeg provides the sort of compelling narrative that is typically missing in the media. An impressive achievement."

—**Nicolai N. Petro**
Professor of political science at the University of Rhode Island (USA)
formerly U.S. Fulbright Research Scholar in Ukraine

"a splendid little book"

—**Kees van der Pijl**
Emeritus Professor of international relations University of Sussex

"A highly informative and forcefully argued analysis of the contradictions of the Ukrainian revolution and Western reactions. The informational war over the Ukraine crisis demonstrates not just the limits to our understanding of these complex events but above all the tensions generated by the failure to establish an inclusive peace after the Cold War. Chris Kaspar de Ploeg brilliantly dissects the resulting dilemmas, and provides a convincing analysis of where we went wrong."

—**Richard Sakwa**
Professor of Russian and European politics
University of Kent
Author of *Frontline Ukraine: Crisis in the Borderlands*

"This book is the best analysis in the Dutch language to date of the complexity, the conflicting interests, the cynical power games that the EU, the US and Russia play there, and the one-sided reporting on this in the European and American media."

—**Lode Vanoost,** *De Wereld Morgen*

"Every now and again readers with a particular interest in international politics find a gem served on a silver platter, which you would hope gains a readership that extends to the inner circles of political decision making. Especially when that book is written by a Dutchman and follows an informed, rational, left, principled line that is rarely if ever observed in the mainstream media. *Ukraine in the Crossfire* ... is such a book, one that you also finish rapidly and with delight.

... [De Ploeg] follows the American dissident Noam Chomsky and his method of promoting peace, security and democracy by creating a discourse in which the facts speak for themselves but argue against the powers-that-be. ... The force of the book by Chris de Ploeg lies in the clear, logical structure, whereby the reader gains layer for layer insights into the meaning of the conflict in Ukraine on every political level."

—**Hector Reban,** *Ravage Webzine*

UKRAINE IN THE CROSSFIRE

CHRIS KASPAR de PLOEG

Clarity Press, Inc

© 2017 Chris Kaspar de Ploeg
ISBN: 978-0-9972870-8-0
EBOOK ISBN: 978-0-9978965-4-1

In-house editor: Diana G. Collier
Cover: R. Jordan P. Santos

ALL RIGHTS RESERVED: Except for purposes of review, this book may not be copied, or stored in any information retrieval system, in whole or in part, without permission in writing from the publishers.

Library of Congress Cataloging-in-Publication Data
Names: De Ploeg, Chris Kaspar, 1994- author.
Title: Ukraine in the crossfire / by Chris Kaspar de Ploeg.
Other titles: Oekraïne in het kruisvuur. English
Description: Atlanta, GA : Clarity Press, Inc., 2017. | Includes
  bibliographical references and index.
Identifiers: LCCN 2017005277 (print) | LCCN 2017008103 (ebook) | ISBN
  9780997287080 (alkaline paper) | ISBN 9780997896541
Subjects: LCSH: Ukraine--Politics and government--1991- | Ukraine--Foreign
  relations--Western countries. | Western countries--Foreign
  relations--Ukraine. | Ukraine--History--Euromaidan Protests, 2013-2014. |
  Political violence--Ukraine--History--21st century. |
  Nationalism--Ukraine--History--21st century. | Donets Basin (Ukraine and
  Russia)--History, Military--21st century. | Russia (Federation)--Foreign
  relations--Western countries. | Western countries--Foreign
  relations--Russia (Federation)
Classification: LCC DK508.848 .D43 2017 (print) | LCC DK508.848
(ebook) | DDC
  947.7086--dc23
LC record available at https://lccn.loc.gov/2017005277

Clarity Press, Inc.
2625 Piedmont Rd. NE, Ste. 56
Atlanta, GA. 30324 , USA
http://www.claritypress.com

TABLE OF CONTENTS

Acknowledgments / 7

Prologue / 9

Chapter One
    A Divided Country / 12

Chapter Two
    The Return of the Wolfsangel / 21

Chapter Three
    The Militarization of Maidan / 29

Chapter Four
    Far Right-backed Regime Change / 36

Chapter Five
    Oligarch-backed Regime Change / 45

Chapter Six
    Western-backed Regime Change / 54

Chapter Seven
    Imposing Austerity / 69

Chapter Eight
    Condoning Corruption / 87

Chapter Nine
    Dismantling Russophone Ukraine / 104

Chapter Ten
    The East Responds / 115

Chapter Eleven
> Civil War Darkens the Ukrainian Landscape / 123

Chapter Twelve
> The Ravages of War / 137

Chapter Thirteen
> Dehumanizing the Donbass,
> Embracing the Far Right / 154

Chapter Fourteen
> Beyond Populism: Assessing the Influence
> of the Far Right / 162

Chapter Fifteen
> Repression and Diversion in Divided Ukraine / 171

Chapter Sixteen
> Obstructing Peace / 191

Chapter Seventeen
> The Imperial Desire for War / 198

Chapter Eighteen
> Western Military Doctrine and the
> Normalization of War Crimes / 224

Chapter Nineteen
> Seeing Beyond the Imperial Divide / 236

Chapter Twenty
> Divisions on the Western Front? / 277

Chapter Twenty-One
> Cold War Politics in the Age of Trump / 295

Glossary of Acronyms / 344

Index / 348

ACKNOWLEDGMENTS

I would firstly like to thank Volodymyr Ishchenko for his extensive feedback throughout all stages of the writing process; his thoughtful comments have greatly improved the quality of the work. I would also like to thank Oleksandr Kravchuk for his feedback on the economic parts of the book. My gratitude also goes out to Clarity Press, not least for their willingness to publish a significantly expanded edition of the initial manuscript. I would in particular like to thank my editor Diana Collier, whose patience and careful work has been very much appreciated. My praise also goes out to my former colleagues at Platform Authentieke Journalistiek—Jilles Mast, Bas van Beek and Sophia Beunder—who were very understanding as I wrote the manuscript and granted me the time I needed to finish. Most of all, I am grateful to my brother and my parents who, like always, supported me through all the troubles that came on my path. Finally, I would like to thank Dean Muraya, Abulhassan Al-Jaberi, Menno Grootveld, Samuel Igelnik, Darya Nicolson, Josua Münch and everyone I have forgotten to mention. You have all made this book possible. Of course, it goes without saying that any errors that remain are mine.

PROLOGUE

It is the 19th of April, 2014. The printing presses are hot and running, and soon every American can buy the newest issue of *The New York Times* for a couple of dollars at their local news stand. The front-page headline: "In Cold War Echo: Obama Strategy Writes Off Putin."[1] This is the day that Obama, after a quarter century of decreasing wars, democratization and diminishing weapon expenditures, has divided the world once again into a frightening dichotomy. The American president used journalist Peter Baker to inform his country about his new long-term approach to Russia that rests on the cold war strategy of containment: "isolating ... Russia by cutting off its economic and political ties to the outside world ... and effectively making it a pariah state". It was a measure of historic proportions that was implemented without any debate: none of the 535 congressman publicly expressed any doubt, and the established media response was laudatory.[2] In light of the recent imaging this is somewhat unsurprising. If you have followed the mainstream news, you will have been advised that Putin is a dangerous dictator who intends to restore the former Soviet Union in its full glory, starting with Ukraine. Indeed, mutual demonization was a fundamental pillar for the cold war. Perhaps a critical reconstruction of the current conflict can help to prevent a potentially more catastrophic one.

Many believe the origins of the current conflict lie in the negotiations between George H. W. Bush and Mikhail Gorbachev, during the disintegration of the Soviet Union in 1990.[3] Gorbachev had agreed to let go of East Germany, under the condition that NATO would not move "an inch to the East".[4] This was a sensitive issue; during the Yalta conference of 1945, the allied forces had agreed to give the eastern bloc to the Soviet Union as a buffer-zone, because, with 25 million fatalities, it had made the biggest sacrifice in the history of mankind. Russia had already suffered a long history of hostile relations with the West, including the devastating invasion of Napoleon and another by the United States, Japan, Turkey and multiple European countries in their effort to roll back Communism in 1918-1921. Since the hostile relations between the two power blocs had just started to improve, Gorbachev's demand was very understandable—even more so if you consider his commitment to considerable demilitarization.[5] But in spite of all this, the Czech Republic, Hungary and Poland (1999), Bulgaria, Estonia, Latvia, Lithuania, Romania, Slovakia, Slovenia (2004), and Albania and Croatia (2009) are now all NATO members.

In 2008 a prophetic memo was sent with direct precedence to Washington by the US ambassador in Russia. The WikiLeaks cable was titled: "Nyet means Nyet: Russia's NATO enlargement redlines".[6] The ambassador stated that "Foreign Minister Lavrov and other senior officials have reiterated strong opposition, stressing that Russia would view further eastward expansion as a potential military threat. In Ukraine ... there are fears that the issue could potentially split the country in two, leading to violence or even, some claim, civil war, which would force Russia to decide whether to intervene." These prophetic assessments echoed those of a US intelligence report in 1994, which warned that regional divisions in Ukraine would eventually lead to civil war.[7] Regardless, two months after the 2008 memo, a NATO summit was held in Bucharest, where they "agreed ... that these countries [Ukraine and Georgia] will become members of NATO".[8] Putin reportedly warned the attendees that this would lead to an annexation of Crimea, home to an important Russian military base.[9]

Endnotes

1   Baker, P. (2014). In cold war echo, Obama strategy writes off Putin. *The*

2. Heuvel, K., Van den, & Cohen, S. (2014, May 01). Cold War Against Russia—Without Debate. Retrieved from http://www.thenation.com/article/cold-war-against-russia-without-debate/
3. Mearsheimer, J. J. (2014). Why the Ukraine Crisis is the West's Fault. *Foreign Affairs*, 93(5), 77-89.
4. The reality is slightly more complicated and will be explored in chapter twenty. Some balanced accounts of the diplomatic affair are provided by M. E. (2014). A Broken Promise?. *Foreign Affairs*, 93(5), 90-97; Shifrinson, J. R. I. (2016). Deal or no deal? The end of the cold war and the US offer to limit Nato expansion. *International Security*, 40(4), 7-44; *Der Spiegel*. Klussmann, U., Schepp, M., & Wiegrefe, K. (2009). Did the West Break Its Promise to Moscow?. Spiegel. de, 26.
5. As stipulated in the Treaty on Conventional Armed Forces in Europe. CSCE Commission. (1997). Treaty on Conventional Armed Forces in Europe (CFE). Briefing. Washington, DC: Commission on Security and Cooperation in Europe (US Congress), February.
6. Burns, W. J. (2008, February 01). Nyet Means Nyet: Russia's NATO enlargement redlines. Retrieved from https://wikileaks.org/plusd/cables/08MOSCOW265_a.html
7. D'Anieri, P. J. (1999). *Economic interdependence in Ukrainian-Russian relations*. SUNY Press, p. 173.
8. NATO. (2008, April 03). Bucharest Summit Declaration - Issued by the Heads of State and Government participating in the meeting of the North Atlantic Council in Bucharest on 3 April 2008. Retrieved from http://www.nato.int/cps/en/natolive/official_texts_8443.htm
9. NEWSru. (2008, April 07). Путин пригрозил аннексировать Крым и Восточную Украину в случае принятия Украины в НАТО. Retrieved from http://www.newsru.com/russia/07apr2008/annex.html

| Chapter One |

A DIVIDED COUNTRY

For centuries, Ukraine has been split between Russia, Poland and Austria and ever since Ukraine regained its independence in 1991, the country has been a fertile soil for interference by its neighboring powerhouses. This is partially because Ukraine has, throughout its post-soviet history, been a country divided by political, economic, religious and ethno-linguistic lines.[1] In the Southern and Eastern provinces, a big Russian-speaking proletariat works in an industry that largely exports to the Russian market. Many have relatives right across the border. In West and Central Ukraine, most people speak Ukrainian at home, and their diaspora is rather aimed at Europe and the United States. The precise number of ethnic and linguistic Russians in Ukraine is subject to interpretation, and often downplayed or inflated based on the political whims of the commentator at hand. In this respect, a literature review by the prominent Polish Center for Eastern Studies (OSW) is enlightening.[2] According to the official 2001 census, 17 percent of Ukrainians considered themselves ethnic Russians, while 29 percent considered Russian their native language. Surveys reveal, however, that the term 'native language' carries its ambiguities. A third of Ukrainians considered their best mastered language 'native'; another third considered it to be the language of their nation; a quarter equated 'native' with the language of their parents; 9 percent considered it to be the language they spoke most often.[3] Therefore, different survey questions give different results. When asked which language people felt most comfortable speaking, there has been a stable roughly 50/50 split in Ukraine.[4]

In turn, these ethno-linguistic divisions are correlated with religious affiliations.[5] The majority of practicing Christians in Central and Western Ukraine are either affiliated with the Greek Catholic Church, or the Kyiv patriarchate of the Ukrainian Orthodox Church. On the other hand, nearly all churches in Southern and Eastern Ukraine are affiliated with the pro-Russian Moscow patriarchate of the Ukrainian Orthodox Church. Southern and Eastern Ukraine are also much less religious in general; most provinces count less than 10 percent as practicing believers. For the most provinces in Central Ukraine this fluctuates around 25 percent, while the majority of Western Ukrainians are practicing. Indeed, the Western Ukrainian provinces were the last to be incorporated into the Soviet Union, dodging 25 years of atheist imposition.

Addressing pro-Western and pro-Russian cultures, however, masks the fluidity of Ukrainian identities and overemphasizes cultural divisions. As of 2003, for example, 23 percent of Ukrainians identified as both Ukrainian and Russian, while 31 percent of the country's citizen's identified as Ukrainian yet spoke Russian.[6] In fact, many Ukrainians speak Surzhyk, a mixture of both Russian and Ukrainian. Ukraine also contains other ethnic, linguistic and religious minorities that fit neither categories. Indeed, the territory of modern Ukraine has historically been populated by major Ukrainian, Russian, Jewish, Polish, Belarussian and German communities, among others. There was no dominant ethnic group, and if one could speak of a common identity then this was certainly a multicultural one.[7] In fact, even as of 2005, a mere three percent of Ukrainians identified primarily as a member of an ethnic or national group. Thirteen percent considered themselves to be citizens of the former USSR, 41 percent citizens of Ukraine, and 43 percent identified primarily with their local region.[8]

Regardless, cultural issues still remain contentious. A good example is the language law of 2012. This long-awaited bill allowed government institutions to adopt bilingualism if a minority language was spoken by more than 10 percent of the region's population. In practice, this meant that, among other things, every Eastern and Southern region would adopt Russian alongside the Ukrainian language. This was not irrelevant: 22 percent of Ukrainian citizens indicated that their mastery of the Ukrainian language was 'low.'[9] The bill, however, provoked a fist-fight in parliament and was followed with riots on the streets by Ukrainian nationalists, who saw the retention of the Russian language as a dangerous post-colonial legacy.[10] The 2012 language law itself had largely developed as a response to state language policies formulated under the previous nationalist administration, which intended to promote Ukrainian as the universal language of the country. In the words of the former president Yushchenko: "only occupants, slaves and fools do not speak the national language."[11] This back-and-forth conflict was nothing new. In fact, the language issue had been a major electoral topic for nearly two decades. Predictably, the support for bilingualism had a clear regional split.[12] There was, however, one commonality: few Ukrainians actually saw the language issue as a top priority. In 2011, 70 percent of respondents did not even notice it as a problem.[13] Rather, what seems to have happened, is that both Ukrainian and pro-Russian nationalists successfully politicized a rather fluid cultural diversity that exists in Ukraine.

There is, however, more to this story. The reason that cultural differences could so easily become politicized is partially because their geographical distribution strongly correlates with material realities. The historical roots can be traced to the soil. When the country industrialized under the Soviet Union, the transformations primarily took place in Eastern and Southern Ukraine, where plenty of natural resources were hidden underground. These regions are now characterized by urbanization and heavy industries that were integrated in the post-Soviet economy, and therefore reliant on exports to the Russian market. In Central and Western Ukraine, on the other hand, most people still live in rural areas where the economy is driven by agriculture, and they have practically no economic stakes in their Eastern neighbor.[14] Since Ukraine's first elections in 1991, the voting behavior of Ukraine has neatly correlated with this economic, ethno-linguistic and religious framework. In turn, one

A Divided Country 15

of the most important policy issues during most election debates revolves around the question: More Europe, or more Russia?

More Russia formed the basis of Yanukovych's election campaign.

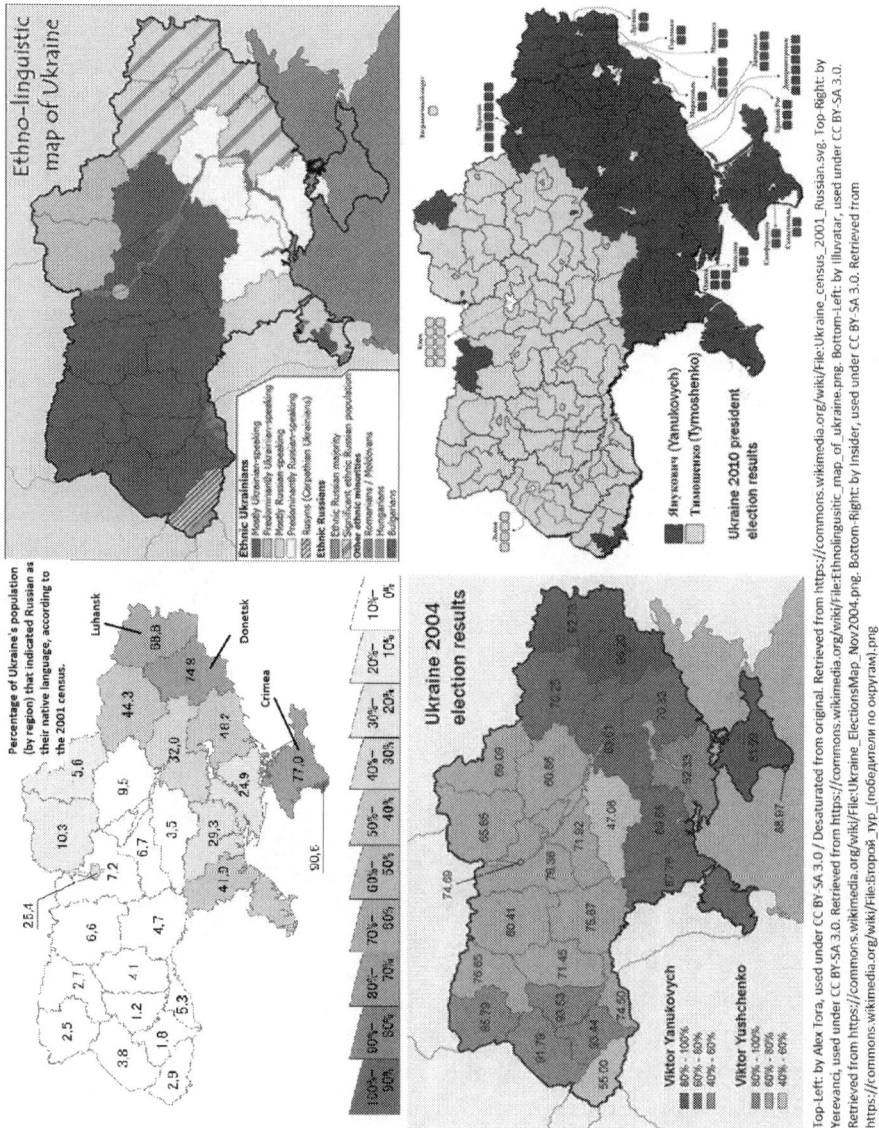

Ukraine was hit hard in 2009 when the economy, under the reign of Yushchenko's pro-European cabinet, plunged into a crisis with a 15% contraction (the largest in Europe bar Latvia).[15] With the entry of Yanukovych in 2010 the economy recovered that same year with a growth of 4%, pushing through with another 5% in 2011.[16] But halfway through 2012 the economy started to stagnate again. Yanukovych promised to accelerate the negotiations for a trade agreement with the EU that were started by Yushchenko in 2008. On the other hand, he tried to gain access to the Eurasian Economic Union (EEU)—a customs union between five post-Soviet states, including Russia. This way he sought to break down trading barriers with Ukraine's two most important trading partners and, supposedly, stimulate economic growth and balance the passionate foreign aspirations of the Ukrainian people. Indeed, according to the polls, support for both agreements hovered at around 40%.[17] However, a vast majority of Ukrainians thought the country's course on foreign policy integration ought to be decided through a national referendum.[18]

The plan of Yanukovych—to strive for both agreements—sounds very politically neutral. But the European association agreement is more than just a trade agreement. The treaty contains provisions on a wide range of topics, from immigration to combating terrorism. Pro-European politicians like to point at the chapters dedicated to human rights, corruption and justice. But the provisions concerning security are no doubt a thorn in the flesh of Putin. Under the heading "foreign and security policy" the treaty states that "the parties shall intensify their dialogue and cooperation and promote gradual convergence in the area of foreign and security policy, including the Common Security and Defense Policy (CSDP)", which is the successor of the European Security and Defense Identity (ESDI) that served as the European division of NATO.[19] Indeed, in a WikiLeaks cable US Secretary of State Hillary Clinton "emphasized that the United States envisioned multiple pathways to NATO membership."[20] To make matters worse, in early 2013 the president of the European commission, Manuel Barroso, made clear that "one country cannot at the same time be a member of a customs union and be in a deep common free-trade area with the European Union".[21] Regardless, in March Yanukovych adopted a plan for European integration that was issued by the national security and defense council of Ukraine.[22] The agreement would be signed on the 21st of November, 2013. The same year a Gallup poll found that nearly twice as many Ukrainians considered NATO a threat rather than offering protection.[23]

But in August 2013 Russia hit back. The Ukrainian employers' federation, whose members account for 70% of the economy, stated that they have to conform to such extensive quality checks at the Russian border that it practically amounts to an import ban. A close economic advisor of Putin publicly stated that this was just a taste of what's to come if Ukraine follows the "suicidal path" of the EU association agreement.[24] In Eastern Ukraine the first lay-offs were already taking place and the entire economy fell back into a recession.[25] The EU agreement and the accompanying costly reforms were approaching. Yanukovych stated that Ukraine needed a loan of $27 billion. The EU offered him $833 million, and referred to the IMF for the remaining sum. But the IMF made harsh demands: a 40% rise in gas prizes, freezing of wages and budget cuts. This ran contrary to Yanukovych's election promise to lower gas prices. In addition, the Russian sanctions would hit the eastern industry, while the unpopular budget cuts of the IMF had the potential to drag the economy back into a deep recession. Understandably, Yanukovych announced that he would delay signing the agreement, and asked the EU to help negotiate better terms with the IMF.[26]

The story that follows is well known. With the taste of an EU-agreement on their lips, disappointed demonstrators took to the streets in Lviv and Kiev. It already started forcefully when, with a peak of 40.000 people on the streets on the 24th of November, the Berkut resorted to batons and tear gas. The images were spread on a large scale through both social and conventional media, and the protests soon grew into the hundreds of thousands. When images of snipers shocked the world on the 20th of February, the days of

Yanukovych were numbered. He fled Kiev the next day and soon a new interim government, consisting of the former opposition, took over. According to the polls, however, the Maidan protests did not enjoy a clear majority support in Ukraine.[27] In addition, as expected, support for Maidan was heavily skewed, with especially low rates in Southern and Eastern Ukraine. In fact, one third of Ukrainians described the culmination of Maidan as a 'coup d'état;' only slightly more Ukrainians referred to the movement as a 'conscious struggle of citizens who get united to protect their rights.'[28]

The nature of the Maidan uprising is perhaps best illustrated with systemic protest data from the Center for Social and Labour Research in Kiev.[29] Before Maidan, for four consecutive years, the most frequent demands were of a socio-economic nature and this trend was increasing. In 2013, before the start of Maidan on the 20th of November, 3419 protests had already occurred, 56 percent of which had socio-economic demands, including 40 worker strikes. This was almost the same amount of protest activity as the entire year of 2012 and nearly twice the amount of the preceding two years. During Maidan, however, socio-economic protest reduced to a mere seven percent. Two-thirds of the protests were of a political nature, a question of which party seizes power, and were the most frequent demands during Maidan. Half of the protests raised issues of civil liberties and a third pressed ideological demands, such as Ukrainian nationalism It is this latter trend to which we will now turn.

Endnotes

1 Karácsonyi, D., Kocsis, K., Kovály, K., Molnár, J., & Póti, L. (2014). East-West dichotomy and political conflict in Ukraine - Was Huntington right? Hungarian Geographical Bulletin, 63(2), 99-134. A good overview of the different divisions, their relevance and their historical roots.
2 Olszański, T. A. (2012). The Language Issue in Ukraine: An Attempt at a new Perspective. OWS Studies, 40.
3 Ibid, pp. 14-15.
4 Ibid, p. 19.

5	All the figures surrounding religious affiliations in Ukraine can be found in Karácsonyi, *et al*. East-West dichotomy and political conflict in Ukraine - Was Huntington right?, pp. 177-120
6	Polese, A. (2011). Language and identity in post-1991 Ukraine: was it really nation-building?. Studies of Transition States and Societies, 3(3), 36-50, p. 43.
7	Scheijen, S. (2015, September 30). Oekraïne, wie? Hoezo? Retrieved from http://www.groene.nl/artikel/oekraine-wie-hoezo
8	Olszański. The Language Issue in Ukraine: An Attempt at a new Perspective, p. 18.
9	Ibid, pp. 21-22.
10	Stern, D. (2012). Ukrainians Polarised Over Language Law. BBC News.
11	Cited in Olszański. The Language Issue in Ukraine: An Attempt at a new Perspective, p. 39.
12	Ibid, p. 23
13	Ibid, p. 22.
14	The differences in regional economies are extensively explored in Adarov, A., Astrov, V., Havlik, P., Hunya, G., Landesmann, M., & Podkaminer, L. (2015). How to Stabilise the Economy of Ukraine. wiiw and United Europe, April, pp. 64-73.
15	World Bank Data.
16	Ibid.
17	Which way Ukraine Should go - Which Union should Ukraine join? (2013, November 26). Retrieved from http://www.kiis.com.ua/?lang=eng&cat=reports&id=204
18	Thoughts population of Ukraine regarding who should decide what course to choose for Ukraine's foreign policy integration. (2013, October 10). Retrieved from http://www.kiis.com.ua/?lang=eng&cat=reports&id=195&page=19
19	Article 4 of the Association agreement between the European Union and its Member States, of the one part, and Ukraine, of the other part (2014, September 25). Retrieved from http://eeas.europa.eu/ukraine/docs/association_agreement_ukraine_2014_en.pdf
20	Gordon, P. (2009, December 18). Secretary Clinton's December 9, 2009 meeting with Ukrainian foreign minister Petro Poroshenko. Retrieved from https://wikileaks.org/plusd/cables/09STATE129520_a.html
21	EU Tells Ukraine That Reforms Are Necessary for Trade Pact. (2013, February 25). Retrieved from http://www.themoscowtimes.com/news/article/eu-tells-ukraine-that-reforms-are-necessary-for-trade-pact/476058.html

22	Presidential Decree number 127/2013. Retrieved from http://web.archive.org/web/20130317113744/http://www.president.gov.ua/ru/documents/15520.html
23	Ray, J., & Esipova, N. (2014, March 14). Before Crisis, Ukrainians More Likely to See NATO as a Threat. Retrieved from http://www.gallup.com/poll/167927/crisis-ukrainians-likely-nato-threat.aspx
24	Trading insults. (2013, August 24). Retrieved from http://www.economist.com/news/europe/21583998-trade-war-sputters-tussle-over-ukraines-future-intensifies-trading-insults
25	Decline in industrial production in Ukraine in October 2013 slows to 4.9 percent. (2013, November 18). Retrieved from http://www.kyivpost.com/content/business/decline-in-industrial-production-in-ukraine-in-october-2013-slows-to-49-percent-332016.html
26	Ukraine 'still wants to sign EU deal.' (2013, November 29). Retrieved from http://www.aljazeera.com/news/europe/2013/11/ukraine-still-wants-sign-eu-deal-20131129111345619208.html
27	Kiev International Institute of Sociology (KIIS). (2014, February 28). Attitude of Ukrainians and Russians towards protests in Ukraine. Retrieved from http://kiis.com.ua/?lang=eng&cat=reports&id=231; Research & Branding Group. (2013, December 10). EuroMaydan 2013. Retrieved from http://rb.com.ua/eng/projects/omnibus/8840/; Poll: More Ukrainians disapprove of EuroMaidan protests than approve of it. (2014, February 07). Retrieved from http://www.kyivpost.com/content/ukraine/more-ukrainians-disapprove-of-euromaidan-protests-than-approve-of-it-poll-336461.html
28	Poll cited in Pogrebinskiy, M., Alshaer, A., Bahceci, S., Eiran, E., Tabachnik, A., Kedem, N., ... & Onuch, O. (2015). Russians in Ukraine: Before and After Euromaidan. Ukraine and Russia: People, Politics, Propaganda and Perspectives, 90, p. 95.
29	Center for Social and Labour Research. (2015, December). Repressions against protests April-August 2015. Retrieved from http://cslr.org.ua/wp-content/uploads/2015/12/ProtestRepressionsApril-August2015-ecj-edits.pdf

| Chapter Two |

THE RETURN OF THE WOLFSANGEL

A more sinister side of the revolution has remained undiscussed. Undoubtedly, the Berkut and government sponsored thugs have used disproportionate violence. But equally violent footage emerged of demonstrators attacking the police with gas and batons.[1] Indeed, these were no ordinary hooligans. On the first of January, the streets of Kiev hosted a 10,000-strong torch-lit march in memory of the ultranationalist Stepan Bandera, the largest Bandera march known to post-Soviet Ukraine.[2] The aforementioned Center for Social and Labor Research, which has been monitoring protests and repressions since 2009, notes that the far-right was present in, at the very least, 25% of the protests nationwide, which were violent or confrontational in 36% of the cases.[3] On the other hand, a third of the Maidan protests were met with repression by the state (which includes the courts and government-sponsored thugs).

But before we examine in closer detail the escalations at Maidan, it is important to realize that the Ukrainian ultranationalists are the product of a long and brutal history. In Soviet Ukraine, approximately three million civilians starved in 1932-33. At the time, West Ukraine had been a part of Poland and had remained unscathed. But in 1939 this part was annexed as well. Stalin sought to subdue the population using political repressions and deportations to Siberia. On the other hand, the Organization of Ukrainian Nationalists kept organizing for an independent and ethnically pure Ukraine, their founding goal since 1929.[4] When the Nazis invaded in 1941, Ukrainian nationalists attempted to declare an independent Ukrainian state. This idea was not supported by the Nazis and the leader of the OUN, Stepan Bandera, was subsequently imprisoned. Nevertheless, due to their virulent anti-communism and racism, the Ukrainian ultranationalists maintained ambiguous relations with Nazi Germany. At the insistence of the OUN, for example, the 14th Waffen SS division was created to fight alongside the Germans.[5] By 1945, nearly a million Jews had died in Ukraine. The OUN participated in the Holocaust.[6] In addition, they founded and led the Ukrainian Insurgent Army (UPA) that slaughtered some 35,000 Poles, mainly women and children and some unarmed men, in Volyn, and approximately 25,000, more in Eastern Galicia.[7]

This history has left its footprints. During the Perestroika several Ukrainian far-right movements started to emerge. In 1991, an ultranationalist movement was founded in Lviv that later culminated in the Social-National Party of Ukraine, according to experts a direct reference to Hitler's national socialism.[8] Their symbol was a variant on the Wolfsangel, the logo of several SS divisions. In 1999, they created the paramilitary organization, Patriot of Ukraine. But in 2004 the party decided to moderate its image under the leadership of Tyahnybok. The name changed into "all-Ukrainian union" Svoboda, the Wolfsangel symbol into a variant on the coat of arms of Ukraine, and the formal ties with Patriot of Ukraine were terminated. This way Svoboda made its first major electoral gains, winning local elections in Ternopil province in 2009 and securing two more Western provinces the year afterwards. In 2012, Svoboda made a sweeping entrance into the national parliament with 10 percent of the votes, presenting themselves as the most radical opposition to Viktor Yanukovych.

Nevertheless, it doesn't take much effort to see through Tyahnybok's public image. Shortly after his change of course he praised the UPA for fighting against "Moscovites, Germans, Jews and other scum who wanted to take away our Ukrainian state" and called for the country to be redeemed from a "Muscovite-Jewish mafia".[9] One year later he sent an open letter to several political leaders, including the president, in which he pleaded for state intervention against the "criminal activities" of "organized

Jewry".[10] Other members assaulted MPs in the middle of parliament for speaking Russian.[11] Yet other colleagues describe the Holocaust as a "bright period" in European history.[12] This is why the EU in 2012 justly adopted a resolution calling Svoboda a "racist, anti-Semitic and xenophobic" party.[13]

The moderation of Svoboda's image was, however, not the sole reason for its emergence from marginality. The western-backed Orange revolution of 2004 played a crucial role as well. UNA-UNSO, the para-military wing of the Ukrainian National Assembly (UNA), had provided Yushchenko's supporters protection during the Orange revolution.[14] A 2008 wikileaks cable from the US embassy in Kiev notes that the UNA is "a coalition of nationalist groups that venerated Mussolini," adding that "UNSO fighters were reported to have participated in the 1992 Moldova-Tranistria conflict against Moldovan forces, the 1993 Georgia-Abkhazia war on the side of Georgia, the 1995 conflict in Chechnya on the side of the Chechyens, and in the 1999 Kosovo conflict on the side of the Serbs."[15] The cable also confirms that "UNA-UNSO supported Yushchenko in the 2004 elections." These ultranationalists supported Yushchenko because, like most pro-European politicians in Ukraine, his liberalism was combined with a strongly anti-communist and monist nationalism. Indeed, the ultranationalist support for Yushchenko bore fruits. Svoboda's leader, Tyahnybok, for example, entered parliament as part of Yushchenko's Our Ukraine voting bloc. So did Andriy Parubiy, co-founder of Svoboda's predecessor, the Social-National Party of Ukraine, as well as the former leader of its paramilitary wing, Patriot of Ukraine. Yushchenko's support was not, however, unconditional. Indeed, the new president expelled Tyahnybok from his electoral bloc after the Svoboda leader made public statements about "Moscovites, Germans, Jews and other scum," as previously cited.

Nevertheless, Yushchenko's relation with the far-right was ambiguous at best. In the recent past, he had sat on the board of directors of MAUP, a private university which, in the words of the US state department, "is one of the most persistent anti-Semitic institutions in Eastern Europe."[16] In a 2006 peer-reviewed paper, Professor Per Anders Rudling documented that, among other things, former KKK leader David Duke taught a history and international relations course at MAUP, and that the university prints anti-Semitic publications in numbers far greater than the entire Jewish population, which had gone from 487,000 to 103,600 Jews between 1989 and 2001.[17] He also noted that the university "operates a well-connected political network that reaches the very top of the Ukrainian society. (...) It has educated more government officials, diplomats and administrators than any other university."[18] Indeed, Yushchenko's foreign minister Tarasiuk had also served on the board of directors of MAUP, and so did the first president of Ukraine, Kravchuk.[19]

Another noteworthy connection to MAUP was Levko Lukianenko, elected as MP for the Yulia Tymoshenko Bloc, which formed a coalition with president Yushchenko and delivered its prime-minister. Levko Lukianenko has written, among other things, that the Ukrainian famine under Stalin was a "satanical" plot concocted by Jews.[20] In 2005, president Yuschenko awarded him with the most prestigious order of the republic, Hero of Ukraine, "in recognition of his civic valor, selfless dedication in championing the ideals of freedom and democracy, and meritorious contribution to the building and development of the Ukrainian state."[21] Another noteworthy MP elected for the Yulia Tymoshenko Bloc was Andriy Skhil, a former member of the aforementioned UNA who had been arrested a few years earlier due to violent clashes with the police.[22] This is not to say that Tymoshenko and Yushchenko sought to actively promote anti-Semitism. Indeed, the reason Yushchenko dubbed Lukianenko Hero of Ukraine was primarily due to his credentials as a former political prisoner, Soviet dissident and leader in the movement for Ukrainian independence during the 1980s. Nevertheless, it is clear that the Orange president was willing to ignore certain racist connections in service of his vision for a new nationalist identity for his country.

Indeed, Yushchenko would go on to initiate an enormous propaganda campaign to revise the history of Ukraine. He established an Institute of National Memory and a Museum of Soviet Occupation in Kiev. Volodymyr Viatrovych was appointed as director of the former and granted access to the archives of the SBU (Ukrainian Secret Service). This nationalist historian was simultaneously the director of the Center for the Study for the Liberation Movement, characterized by Rudling as an "OUN(b) front organization."[23] In addition, the director of the SBU (Ukrainian Secret Service) under Yushchenko, Valentyn Nalyvaichenko, stated that the task of his agency was to disseminate "the historical truth of the past of the Ukrainian people" and to "liberate Ukrainian history from lies and falsifications and to work with truthful documents only."[24]

Rudling goes on to note, quite unsurprisingly, that "Ignoring the OUN's antisemitism, denying its participation in anti-Jewish violence, and overlooking its fascist ideology, Nalyvaichenko and his agency presented the OUN as democrats, pluralists, even righteous rescuers of Jews during the Holocaust."[25] The Great Famine of 1932-33, which saw millions of people starve across multiple Soviet republics, was characterized as an ethnic genocide uniquely aimed at Ukrainians. Its fatalities in Ukraine—with an estimated three million possibly Stalin's gravest crime against humanity—were severely inflated. The aforementioned SBU director, Valentyn Nalyvaichenko, even claimed to know the exact count: 10,063,000.[26] Rudling explains that "The 'memory managers' juxtaposed the genocidal Soviet rule with the self-sacrificial heroism of the OUN-UPA, producing a teleological narrative of suffering (the famine) and resistance (the OUN-UPA) leading to redemption (independence, 1991)."[27]

Across the country, a plethora of monuments arose that honoured the former fascists.[28] Criticizing this trend was not always easy. A Jewish journalist who covered the aforementioned MAUP, which published about 85% of anti-Semitic literature in Ukraine, was severely beaten. One week later, two newspapers were temporarily shut down and forced to pay $15,000 in fines by a district court in Kiev for publishing supposedly "negative and non-factual" news about MAUP.[29] Although a direct link to the

Orange regime cannot be established, these acts were perceived by the Union of Councils for Jews in the Former Soviet Union as government-backed moves to silence critics of anti-Semitism in Ukraine.[30] Yushchenko finally sealed his presidency by declaring the former OUN-leader, Stepan Bandera, a national hero. The act forced the Simon Wiesenthal Center, a leading Jewish human rights group named after the famous Nazi hunter, to respond in condemnation: "It's a terrible signal to send, giving that kind of recognition to someone whose group cooperated with the Nazis, and whose followers were linked to the massacres of Jews."[31]

Nevertheless, the propaganda efforts of Yushchenko failed to fundamentally take root. In 2012, the Ukrainian scholar Ivan Katchanovski commissioned a Kiev International Institute of Sociology (KIIS) survey and found that:

> the absolute majority of the residents of Ukraine, given a choice of the various forces active in Ukraine during World War II, support most the Soviet Army [which counted approximately 5 million Ukrainians] (75%). In addition, 4% favor the Soviet partisans. The UPA is a choice of 8% of the respondents. ... The relative majorities (41% each) of adult Ukrainians have negative views of both Stalin and Shukhevych [commander of the UPA] during the war. However, a much greater percentage (32%) hold very positive or mostly positive views of the wartime activities of Stalin, compared to Shukhevych (14%).[32]

Predictably, there were significant variations among regions, political parties, and ethnic, language and age groups. Nevertheless, support for the UPA or its leadership received majority support in only a very few categories. Even half of Svoboda's supporters preferred the Red Army over the OUN. Indeed, Yushchenko will be remembered for having given both the former and the current ultranationalist movement nothing but the veneer of acceptability, just enough to lay the groundwork for its definitive rise in 2014.

Endnotes

1. This is hardly a secret and footage is not hard to come by. Here is just one compilation. Die Wahrheit über die Demonstrationen in Kiew (Ukraine) 2013. (2013, December 31). Retrieved from https://www.youtube.com/watch?v=PwtmezqZltI
2. Факельное шествие Свободы в Киеве 01.01.2014. (2014, January 01). Retrieved from https://www.youtube.com/watch?v=AthFgiD1_pU
3. CEDOS. (2014, July 28). The real face of Maidan: Statistics from protests that changed the country. Retrieved from http://www.cedos.org.ua/uk/releases/36
4. Rudling, P. A. (2011). The OUN, the UPA and the Holocaust: A Study in the Manufacturing of Historical Myths. *The Carl Beck Papers in Russian and East European Studies,* (2107), p. 8.
5. Ibid, p.17
6. Ibid, p. 10
7. Katchanovski, I. (2015). Terrorists or national heroes? Politics and perceptions of the OUN and the UPA in *Ukraine. Communist and Post-Communist Studies,* 48(2), 217-228, p. 221.
8. Svoboda. (n.d.). History of "Svoboda" party. Retrieved February 09, 2016, from http://en.svoboda.org.ua/about/history/
9. Stern, D. (2012, December 26). Svoboda: The rise of Ukraine's ultranationalists - BBC News. Retrieved from http://www.bbc.com/news/magazine-20824693
10. Ibid.
11. Ukrainian MPs in mass brawl after Russian is spoken in Parliament. (2013, March 20). Retrieved from http://www.telegraph.co.uk/news/worldnews/europe/ukraine/9942004/Ukrainian-MPs-in-mass-brawl-after-Russian-is-spoken-in-Parliament.html
12. Stonov, L. (2013, August). The Extremism and Xenophobia of Ukraine's Svoboda (Freedom) Party - UCSJ. Retrieved from http://www.ucsj.org/2013/08/22/svoboda/
13. European Parliament resolution of 13 December 2012 on the situation in Ukraine. (2012, December 13). Retrieved from http://www.europarl.europa.eu/sides/getDoc.do?pubRef=-//EP//TEXT TA P7-TA-2012-0507 0 DOC XML V0//EN
14. Sussman, G., & Krader, S. (2008). Template revolutions: Marketing US regime change in Eastern Europe. *Westminster Papers in*

	Communication and Culture,5(3); Vasovic, A. (2015, January 03). Far-right group flexes during Ukraine "revolution". Retrieved from http://community.seattletimes.nwsource.com/archive/?date=20050103
15	Ukraine's Main Extremist Groups. (2008, November 26). Retrieved from https://www.wikileaks.org/plusd/cables/08KYIV2323_a.html
16	Contemporary Global Anti-Semitism: A Report Provided to the United States Congress. (2008, March 13). Retrieved from http://www.state.gov/j/drl/rls/102406.htm
17	Anders Rudling, P. (2006). Organized anti-semitism in contemporary Ukraine: Structure, influence and ideology. *Canadian Slavonic Papers,* 48(1-2), 81-118, pp. 81, 84; State Statistics Committee of Ukraine. (2003-2004). All-Ukrainian population census 2001. Retrieved from http://2001.ukrcensus.gov.ua/eng/results/general/nationality/
18	P. A. Rudling. *Organized anti-semitism in contemporary Ukraine: Structure, influence and ideology*, pp. 81, 88.
19	Ibid, p. 90.
20	Ibid, p. 91.
21	Ibid, p. 94.
22	Ukraine's Main Extremist Groups. (2008, November 26). Retrieved from https://www.wikileaks.org/plusd/cables/08KYIV2323_a.html
23	"The Return of the Ukrainian Far Right: The Case of VO Svoboda," in Ruth Wodak and John E. Richardson (eds.) *Analyzing Fascist Discourse: European Fascism in Talk and Text (*London and New York: Routledge, 2013), 228-255, p. 231.
24	Ibid, p. 231.
25	Ibid.
26	Ibid, p. 248.
27	Ibid, p. 231.
28	Ibid, p. 245; P. A. Rudling, *The OUN, the UPA and the Holocaust: A Study in the Manufacturing of Historical Myths*, p. 28.
29	P. A. Rudling. *Organized anti-semitism in contemporary Ukraine: Structure, influence and ideology*, p. 117.
30	Ibid, p. 118.
31	Ames, M. (2010, February 12). The Hero of the Orange Revolution Poisons Ukraine. Retrieved from http://www.thenation.com/article/hero-orange-revolution-poisons-ukraine/
32	Katchanovski, I. (2014). The politics of World War II in contemporary Ukraine.*The Journal of Slavic Military Studies*, 27(2), 210-233, p. 225.

| Chapter Three |

THE MILITARIZATION OF MAIDAN

The fourth day of the almost 100-day revolution saw the first violent escalation. *Business New Europe* reported that: "police used tear gas and batons to disperse a crowd around the government headquarters *after numerous protesters hurled rocks and tried to tear off officers' helmets*" (emphasis mine).[1] Associate-professor Gordon Hahn documented several other reports that confirm the violence was initiated by the protestors, accompanied by calls to storm government buildings, the presidential palace and parliament.[2] Svoboda figured prominently front and center in the pictures. By all accounts, the majority of the protestors were middle-class moderates, but Svoboda would have a strong influence on the dynamics of the protest. A giant portrait of the former OUN-leader Stepan Bandera hung to the left of the stage at Maidan.[3] Before and after nearly every speech, the speaker would shout: "Glory to Ukraine!," to which the crowd would respond: "Glory to the heroes!," the slogan of the former OUN. (The slogan became so mainstream during Maidan that many protestors did not necessarily associate it with the OUN).[4]

Svoboda, however, is just the most prominent political representative of the far right movement. Just five days after the first demonstration on Maidan, four organizations joined forces to found the openly militant ultranationalist Right Sector: UNA-UNSO, Stepan Bandera's Trident, White Hammer and the Social National Assembly. The latter's program openly proclaims all the classic fascist goals for Ukraine—from absolute single-leader rule to striving for global domination—and they openly speak about the existence of a race hierarchy. The Right Sector was estimated to have several hundred members in Kiev and their headquarters overlooked the Maidan square.

On November 30th, hundreds of riot cops attempted to clear the square. They resorted to disproportionate violence, brutally beating many defenseless protestors with batons and tear gas. Yanukovych condemned the excess and promised an investigation. Later on, the strongly pro-Maidan politician, Anatolii Hrytsenko, would admit that opposition leaders had foreknowledge of the dispersal due to intercepted radio-communications, but chose not to act on it.[5] As noted, the November 30th beating turned Maidan into a truly massive movement and also provoked the first occupations of government buildings. In addition, the far-right attempted to storm the presidential palace the day afterwards.[6]

Regardless, the movement's numbers were eventually dwindling again, prompting one activist to publish a piece titled "Why Did Ukraine's Eurolution Fail?"[7] This is when Yanukovych, unwilling to talk to the opposition, made the fatal mistake of passing a series of repressive anti-protest laws, which were dubbed "the dictator laws." The laws significantly limited freedom of peaceful assembly and freedom of speech, criminalizing many of the typical forms of protest used by Maidan activists, and they were passed in breach of parliament protocols. The laws breathed new life into the Maidan movement and provoked another wave of occupations of multiple government buildings in Kiev, including the Justice Ministry building. Dozens more buildings were occupied across Western and Central Ukraine. The new uprising also saw massive street violence in the center of Kiev—including the use of bricks, batons and Molotov cocktails—where the Right Sector first gained major media prominence in Ukraine. A few days later, amid intense street clashes, the first three protestors died in Kiev, two of them shot. Government snipers were assumed to be responsible, but the culprits have yet to be identified. Notably, a year after the incident, pro-Maidan Ministry of Internal Affairs deputy chief Vitaliy Sakal admitted that: "The investigation is also considering among other versions a killing in order to provoke an escalation of the conflict and justify the use of weapons by protesters. It is confirmed by numerous materials from public sources, where people with firearms were recorded."[8] In November that year, the Prosecutor General Office of Ukraine officially confirmed that the three Maidan protesters were not killed from Berkut positions, but rather from Maidan-controlled areas from a distance of a few meters.[9] Around the same time a Kiev journalist reported that the leader of White Hammer, one of the founders of the Right Sector, had told her that the first two Maidan protesters were killed in January 2014 by their own side, and that these false flag killings were one of the reasons that White Hammer eventually split from Right Sector.[10]

Two other events would be widely publicized, arguably the most damning indications of government violence, provoking rumours of "death squads" operating in Ukraine. One day after the annulment of the anti-protest laws, the leader of AutoMaidan, Dmitriy Bulatov, claimed to have been kidnapped and tortured, even crucified, by government sponsored thugs. Apart from some minor bruises, however, the only serious visible sign of torture was a seemingly clipped part of his left ear, prompting some doctors who examined him to claim the affair was fake. Confirmation came recently, when his former deputy and now leader of AutoMaidan, Sergey Poryakov, admitted in a radio interview that the kidnapping was a hoax.[11] At the time, Bulatov was visited by soon-to-be president Poroshenko in the hospital, and he would later be rewarded with the position of Minister of Sport and Youth in the interim-government. The hoax had been preceded by a similar case one month earlier: the supposed government-sponsored beating of the prominent anti-government journalist and activist, Tatyana Chornovol. This beating did actually take place, but was rather committed by an angry driver after Chornovol dangerously cut off his car. The a-political nature of the event has recently been confirmed by the verdict of a Maidan regime court.[12] In the interim-government, Chornovol would also be rewarded with a prominent position, head of the National Anti-Corruption Committee. Finally, it is worth mentioning that Chornovol used to work as the press secretary for the aforementioned UNA-UNSO, which is also a part of Right Sector.[13]

The major street clashes, as well simultaneous negotiations with the opposition parties, forced Yanukovych to annul the anti-protest laws two weeks after they were signed. But the Maidan movement had already taken on a quasi-military form with 42 self-defence units, referred to as sotnyas (squadrons, literally 'hundreds'), a historical Ukrainian name for a 'company' (as a military unit). Most of the squadrons fell under the orders of the self-defence committee, which was headed by the 'commandant,' Andriy Parubiy, one of the former founders of the Social-National Party of Ukraine, the predecessor of Svoboda, and the former leader of its para-military front, Patriot of Ukraine.[14] Athough he left those structures in 2004, he also admitted in a 2008 interview that his views had not changed since that time.[15] The official tasks of the squadrons ranged from escorting protestors safely from and to Maidan, to strictly controlling the entrance to the square in order to filter out 'titushki.' Kiev-based sociologist Volodymyr Ishchenko explains:

> [T]itushki are poor, often unemployed youths whom the government used to hire as provocateurs and street bullies—to harass or attack protesters, often in cooperation with the police. Among some of the middle-class Maidan protesters, there was a kind of social chauvinism towards these people. AutoMaidan was a part of the movement that carried out ... titushka hunts, driving round Kiev looking for them, capturing them and forcing them to make a public confession. But how did they define who was a titushka and who was not? Often it was based on what they looked like, whether they were wearing a tracksuit, these kinds of social markers.[16]

There were many different squadrons, including all-Jewish and all-women sotnyas. The most visible and active squadrons, however, came from the far-right. In fact, by examining surveys of

Maidan participants, Bryn Rosenfeld found that pro-EU liberals eventually became marginal even among the wider protest population, conluding that "the group which occupied the square during the protests' final phase was strikingly different than the earlier participatory core of nonviolent activists."[17] Another study found that the presence of women in Maidan tents dropped from 44 to 12 percent.[18] Queer people also participated in the protests, but decided to follow a "strategy of invisibility" due to persisting queerphopbia.[19] As the conflict became militarized, two members of the Antifascist Union Ukraine explain how, in some cases, the far-right even repressed competing protest activities at Maidan square:

> Early on a Stalinist tent [in reality a trade union agitation point] was attacked by Nazis. One was sent to the hospital. Another student spoke out against fascism and he was attacked. ... [Later on approximately 30] anarchists tried to arrange their own self-defense group, different Anarchist groups came together for a meeting on the Maidan. While they were meeting a group of Nazis came in a larger group, they had axes and baseball bats and sticks, helmets; they said it was their territory. They called the Anarchists things like Jews, blacks, Communists. There weren't even any Communists, that was just an insult. The Anarchists weren't expecting this and they left. (...) One of the worst things is that ... [the far-right] has this official structure. They are coordinated. You need passes to go certain places. They have the power to give or not give people permission to be active. We're trying to be active but we have to avoid Nazis, and I'm not going to ask a Nazi for permission![20]

Endnotes

1 Ukraine's president tries to calm tensions as clashes continue. (2013, November 26). Retrieved from http://www.intellinews.com/ukraine-s-president-tries-to-calm-tensions-as-clashes-continue-500018205/?source=russia&archive=bne

2 Hahn, G. M. (2015, May 08). Violence, Coercion and Escalation in the Ukraine Crisis, Parts 1-5: November 2013 - January 2014. Retrieved from http://gordonhahn.com/2015/04/08/violence-coercion-and-escalation-in-the-ukraine-crisis-parts-1-5-november-2013-january-2014/

3 Sakwa, R. (2014). Frontline Ukraine: crisis in the borderlands. IB Tauris, p. 36.

4 Luhn, A. (2014, January 21). The Ukrainian Nationalism at the Heart of 'Euromaidan'. Retrieved from http://www.thenation.com/article/ukrainian-nationalism-heart-euromaidan/

5 Katchanovski, I. (2015). The 'Snipers' Massacre' on the Maidan in Ukraine. Available at SSRN 2658245, p. 61.

6 Ibid, p. 61.

7 Maheshwari, V. (2014, January 05). Why Did Ukraine's Eurolution Fail? Retrieved from http://www.thedailybeast.com/articles/2014/01/05/why-did-ukraine-s-eurolution-fail.html

8 Maidan activists Nihoian and Zhiznevskiy 'not killed by police.' (2015, January 26). Retrieved from http://www.unian.info/society/1036260-maidan-activists-nihoian-and-zhiznevskiy-not-killed-by-police.html

9 Убийцы Нигояна, Жизневского и Сеника пока не установлены - ГПУ. (2015, November 18). Retrieved from http://zn.ua/UKRAINE/ubiycy-nigoyana-zhiznevskogo-i-senika-poka-ne-ustanovleny-gpu-195840_.html

10 Мельникова, Л. (2015, November 18). Facebook. Retrieved from https://www.facebook.com/mlnkv/posts/1002533856477859?fref=nf

11 Булатова никто не похищал - лидер Автомайдана. (2014, November 20). Retrieved from http://korrespondent.net/ukraine/politics/3446285-bulatova-nykto-ne-pokhyschal-lyder-avtomaidana

12 Суд освободил обвиняемых в избиении Чорновол. (2015, April 07). Retrieved from http://korrespondent.net/ukraine/3500556-sud-osvobodyl-obvyniaemykh-v-yzbyenyy-chornovol

13 Chornovol, T. (2010, September 16). Таня Чорновіл: "Фактично з усіма я маю погані стосунки!" Retrieved from http://mediananny.com/intervju/13312

14 Sakwa, R. (2014). Frontline Ukraine: crisis in the borderlands. IB Tauris, p. 93.

15 Чат з Андрієм Парубієм. (2008). Retrieved from http://vgolos.com.ua/chat/35
16 Ishchenko, V. (2014, June 16). Ukraine's Fractures. New Left Review 87. Retrieved from http://newleftreview.org/II/87/volodymyr-ishchenko-ukraine-s-fractures
17 Rosenfeld, B. (2016, November). A Case-Control Method for Studying Protest Participation and Other Rare Events: An Application to Ukraine's EuroMaidan. Paper presented at the 48th Annual Convention of the Association for Slavic, East European and Eurasian Studies, Washington, DC. Abstract retrieved from https://convention2.allacademic.com/one/aseees/aseees16/index.php?program_focus=view_paper&selected_paper_id=1215011&cmd=online_program_direct_link&sub_action=online_program
18 Martsenyuk, T. (2016). Sexuality and Revolution in Post-Soviet Ukraine: LGBT Rights and the Euromaidan Protests of 2013–2014. Journal of Soviet and Post-Soviet Politics and Society, 2(1), 49-74, p. 57.
19 Ibid.
20 Eastman, T. (2014, February 19). An Interview with Mira, Andrei, and Sascha of AntiFascist Action Ukraine. Retrieved from http://web.archive.org/web/20150108054536/http://www.timothyeastman.com/uncategorized/an-interview-with-mira-andrei-and-sascha-of-antifascist-action-ukraine/

| Chapter Four |

FAR RIGHT-BACKED REGIME CHANGE

The 14th of February saw the last attempt to salvage the situation. All of the 234 protesters arrested since December were released and amnesty was promised for criminal activities enacted during Maidan. In return, several occupied government buildings were vacated. Four days later, however, all hell would break lose. On the 18th of February, violence would escalate rapidly with the initiation of another attempt to storm parliament and the burning down of Yanukovych's Party of Regions headquarters, provoking violent counter-attacks and attempts to clear Right Sector's headquarters where, according to the riot police, there were major stashes of weaponry. Both sides suffered dozens of casualties, including deaths.[1] Across the country, government weapons depots were plundered by the Right Sector, Svoboda and unaffiliated masses of protestors.[2] Countless pictures and videos of armed protesters emerged from the 18th onwards. *The New York Times* reported on the psychological effect of the weapons captures:

> Andriy Tereschenko, a Berkut [police] commander from Donetsk who was holed up with his men in the Cabinet Ministry, the government headquarters in Kiev, said that 16 of his men had already been shot on Feb. 18 and that he was terrified by the rumors of an armory of automatic weapons on its way from Lviv. 'It was already an armed uprising, and it was going to get worse,' he said. 'We understood why the weapons were taken, to bring them to Kiev.'[3]

Buckling under the pressure, a truce was declared and Yanukovych finally entered into negotiations with the opposition. Nevertheless, on the 20th of February, the violence culminated into an unprecedented tragedy when dozens of protestors and police were shot dead. The slain protestors would become known as 'the heavenly hundred.' Yanukovych was immediately blamed for the tragedy, causing his downfall two days later. By now, however, the first and so far only 80-page academic research into the blood bath has been published by the Ukrainian scholar, Ivan Katchanovski of the University of Toronto, which was accepted for presentation at the Annual Meeting of the American Political Science Association, the largest academic conference of political scientists in the world that rejects the absolute majority of paper proposals in their peer-review process. A summary of the research was also included in a book published by the leading academic press Routledge.[4] Based on an enormous quantity of footage, intercepted radio-communications, eye witnesses, ballistic research, among other evidence, Katchanovski concludes that:

> Armed groups and the leadership of the far right organizations, such as the Right Sector and Svoboda, and oligarchic parties, such as Fatherland [the party of Tymoshenko and soon-to-be prime-minister Yatsenyuk], were directly or indirectly involved in various capacities in this massacre of the protesters and the police. This mass killing was a successful false flag operation, which was organized and conducted by elements of the Maidan leadership and concealed armed groups in order to win the asymmetric conflict during the "Euromaidan" and seize power in Ukraine.[5]

Soon after the publication, Katchanovski's house in Ukraine, which he used for his research, was seized by a dubious trial, while a flood of unsubstantiated slander attempted to discredit him. He was hospitalized several times in Canada, according to his doctors due to unhealthy levels of stress. Some of his key assertions, however, have been corroborated by several Western media investigations, including, among others, the German public news agency *ARD*, American documentary maker John-Beck Hoffman, *Reuters news agency*, *Foreign Policy Magazine*, associate professor Gordon Hahn and eventually even the official Ukrainian trial.[6] Furthermore, two Maidan protesters have publicly confessed to having shot policemen during the massacre.[7] And perhaps most shockingly, exactly three years after the massacre—even the Deputy head of the Ukrainian parliament suggested that current top government officials were involved and therefore obstructed proper investigation.[8] The behavior of some neo-Nazi groups, such as the Svoboda-affiliated C14, has also been highly suspicious: disrupting the massacre trial multiple times, threatening the judges and burning tires in front of the courtoom, all while the police stood idly by.[9]

More than a year after the incident, an extensive 120-page report by an International Advisory Panel—set up by the Council of Europe—confirmed that the investigation into the killings during Maidan is being grossly underfunded, lacks independence, and even faces 'obstruction' by the post-Maidan Ministry of the Interior.[10] In addition, a special UN representative proclaimed that the investigation contains "systemic failings" and that much of the evidence surrounding the killings had been destroyed.[11] It is impossible to do justice to all these research efforts, and I will not attempt to summarize them here. I will, however, mention that INTERPOL (the international police agency based in Lyon, France) would refuse to add any of the Maidan regime's suspects to its wanted list because they feared the case was politically motivated.[12] In contrast, they did put out a warrant requested by Russia for the leader of Right Sector, Dmitriy Yarosh, for "public incitement to terrorist [and] ... extremist activities."[13] Indeed, even the Estonian foreign minister, Urmas Paet, privately agreed with their conclusions. In a leaked call with the EU foreign affairs chief Catherine Ashton, he had reported on his findings from his visit to Kiev shortly after the change of government:

What was quite disturbing, this same Olga [Bogomolets, a pro-Maidan activist who claimed that Paet had misinterpreted her and was soon rewarded with the position of presidential adviser and number three on the president's electoral list][14] told that, well, all the evidence shows that people who were killed by snipers from both sides, among policemen and people from the streets, that they were the same snipers killing people from both sides ... So she also showed me some photos, she said that as medical doctor, she can say it is the same handwriting, the same type of bullets, and it's really disturbing that now the new coalition, that they don't want to investigate what exactly happened. ... So there is a stronger and stronger understanding that behind snipers it was not Yanukovych, it was somebody from the new coalition.[15]

After the sniper massacre, Yanukovych came to an agreement with the opposition leaders, signing, among other things, to pull back all police forces from the city center, hold early elections and return the country within 48 hours to the 2004 constitution, which would limit his presidential powers, and allow the parliament to form a new "government of national unity" within ten days.[16] The fiercely anti-Russian Polish foreign minister Sikorski admitted that it was Putin who managed to convince Yanukovych to sign the agreement.[17] However, when the opposition leaders came to Maidan to present the agreement, they were forced to apologize for even shaking Yanukovych's hand. One of the squadron leaders, Volodymyr Parasyuk, would whip up the crowd, saying that "We don't want to see Yanukovych in power. We don't want deals with them. On Saturday [22 February] at 10am he must step down. And unless this morning you come up with a statement demanding that he steps down, then we will take arms and go, I swear."[18] Parasyuk was reported to be the commander of some of the riflemen who participated in the 20th of February massacre.[19] In an interview, he said he had negotiated his leadership with Right Sector and had received paramilitary training by several ultranationalist organizations in the past.[20] After Parasyuk's speech, Right Sector leader Yarosh would repeat his threats, listing all the weapons they had at their disposal.[21]

In accordance with the agreement, the police had retreated from the center of Kiev, while the armed protestors kept storming government buildings. This occurred under the scope of a wider disintegration of the state apparatus. Many Berkut officers from Western Ukraine returned home by their own volition to repent publicly. On the other hand, dozens of MPs from Yanukovych's PoR turned sides and left his party. Finally, on the 22nd, while armed insurgents were strutting around the debating chamber, Yanukovych was impeached.[22] Many members of parliament had fled and were not present at the vote. Even ignoring the armed militant presence, the impeachment was in violation of the constitution which requires a three-fourths majority vote and a review of the case by Ukraine's constitutional court.[23]

The far right Svoboda party, one of the three former opposition parties and political representatives of the Maidan movement, was invited to join the new government. They were given four, mainly secondary, positions in the new government, including in the ministries of defense, environment and agriculture. Svoboda also gained the positions of prosecutor general and deputy prime-minister. Several more people in the interim government had participated in ultranationalist movements in the past, including Serhiy Kvit (the minister of education), the secretary of the National Anti-Corruption commission Tetyana Chornovil, and the secretary of the National Security and Defense Council Andriy Parubiy. And the new deputy prime minister, Svoboda member Oleksandr Sich, had earlier told the EU parliament on the 4th of February that "the fascist dictatorship is the best way to rule a country", thus reports the Italian Panorama.[24]

The atmosphere in Kiev that followed was described by Estonia's foreign minister in the aforementioned leaked call:

"There is enormous pressure against members of parliament, that there are uninvited visitors during the night to party members. Well, journalists, some journalists who were with me, they saw during the day that one member of parliament was just beaten in front of the parliament building by these guys with the guns on the streets."[25] Shortly after the change of regime, parliament voted overwhelmingly for the abolition of Russian as the second language of the eastern Ukrainian provinces. Countless Lenin statues across the country, including a war memorial for fallen soldiers against the Nazis, were toppled and covered with Nazi symbols.[26]

Endnotes

1   МОЗ: З початку сутичок померло 28 людей. (2014, February 20). Retrieved from https://web.archive.org/web/20140220223801/http://www.pravda.com.ua/news/2014/02/20/7015026/

2   Parry, R. (2014, August 10). NYT Discovers Ukraine's Neo-Nazis at War. Retrieved from https://consortiumnews.com/2014/08/10/nyt-discovers-ukraines-neo-nazis-at-war/; Франківці кидають коктейлі Молотова в приміщення обласного СБУ. (2014, February 19). Retrieved from http://styknews.info/novyny/ns/2014/02/19/frankivtsi-kydaiut-kokteili-molotova-v-prymishchennia-oblasnogo-sbu; У СБУ заявили про крадіжку трьох кулеметів, 268-ми пістолетів і 15-ти тисяч патронів. (2014, February 19). Retrieved from http://tsn.ua/politika/u-sbu-zayavili-pro-kradizhku-troh-kulemetiv-268-mi-pistoletiv-i-15-ti-tisyach-patroniv-335355.html; У Рівному штурмують базу «Беркуту» (2014, February 18). Retrieved from http://www.pravda.com.ua/news/2014/02/18/7014576/; Офіційно: З міліції Львова винесено майже 1200 одиниць вогнепальної зброї. (2014, February 19). Retrieved from http://zik.ua/news/2014/02/19/ofitsiyno_z_militsii_lvova_vyneseno_mayzhe_1200_odynyts_vognepalnoi_zbroi_462336

3   Higgins, A., & Kramer, A. E. (2015). Defeated Even Before He Was Ousted. New York Times, 1.

4   Black, J. L., & Johns, M. (Eds.). (2016). The Return of the Cold War: Ukraine, The West and Russia. Routledge.

5   Katchanovski, I. (2015). The 'Snipers' Massacre' on the Maidan in Ukraine. Available at SSRN 2658245, p. 63.

6   Gatehouse, G. (2015, February 12). The untold story of the Maidan massacre. Retrieved from http://www.bbc.com/news/

magazine-31359021; Gathmann, M., & Schepp, M. (2014, February 19). Jahrestag der Maidan-Todesschüsse: Das unaufgeklärte Massaker. Retrieved from http://www.spiegel.de/politik/ausland/maidan-jahrestag-in-kiew-das-unaufgeklaerte-massaker-a-1019044.html; Stuchlik, S., Sviridenko, O., & Jahn, P. (2014, April 04). Todesschüsse auf dem Maidan. Retrieved from http://operation-gladio.net/sniper-attack-in-kiev-who-is-responsible-for-the-massacre-on-maidan-wdr-monitor-4-apr-2014; Hoffman, J. B. (2015, February 14). Maidan Massacre. Retrieved from https://www.youtube.com/watch?v=Ary_l4vn5ZA; Stecklow, S., & Akymenko, O. (2014, October 10). Special Report: Flaws found in Ukraine's probe of Maidan massacre. Retrieved from http://www.reuters.com/article/us-ukraine-killings-probe-special-report-idUSKCN0HZ0UH20141010; Gorchinskaya, K. (2016, February 26). He Killed for the Maidan. Retrieved from http://foreignpolicy.com/2016/02/26/he-killed-for-the-maidan/; Hahn, G. (2015, May 08). Violence, Coercion, and Escalation in Ukraine's Maidan Revolution: Escalation Point 6 - The 'Snipers' of February. Retrieved from http://gordonhahn.com/2015/05/08/violence-coercion-and-escalation-in-ukraines-maidan-revolution-escalation-point-6-the-snipers-of-february/; Katchanovski, I. (2017, February 20). Interview with Telepolis magazine (Germany) Concerning New Revelations in the Maidan Massacre Investigation. Retrieved from https://www.academia.edu/31531210/Interview_with_Telepolis_magazine_Germany_Concerning_New_Revelations_in_the_Maidan_Massacre_Investigation_Full-text_English-Language_Version_

7   He Killed for the Maidan. Retrieved from http://foreignpolicy.com/2016/02/26/he-killed-for-the-maidan/; Analysis and links to the admissions provided by Katchanovski, I. (2016, April 7). Facebook. Retrieved from https://www.facebook.com/ivan.katchanovski/posts/1226384980724719

8   Сыроид допускает причастность представителей сегодняшней власти к событиям, происходившим на Евромайдане. (2017, February 18). Retrieved from http://112.ua/politika/syroid-dopuskaet-prichastnost-predstaviteley-segodnyashney-vlasti-k-sobytiyam-proishodivshim-na-evromaydane-372879.html

9   Analysis and links to the footage provided by Katchanovski, I. (2017, January 12). Facebook. Retrieved from https://www.facebook.com/ivan.katchanovski/posts/1476093402420541; Katchanovski, I. (2017, Januari 10). Retrieved from https://www.facebook.com/ivan.katchanovski/posts/1474419965921218.

10   REPORT of the International Advisory Panel on its review of the Maidan Investigations. (2015, March 31). Retrieved from https://

rm.coe.int/CoERMPublicCommonSearchServices/DisplayDCTMContent?documentId=09000016802f038b

11 End-of-visit statement of the Special Rapporteur on extrajudicial, summary or arbitrary executions, Christof Heyns Ukraine: Lives lost in an accountability vacuum. (2015, September 18). Retrieved from http://www.ohchr.org/EN/NewsEvents/Pages/DisplayNews.aspx?NewsID=16460; ООН: Большинство доказательств преступлений на Майдане уничтожено. (2015, September 18). Retrieved from http://korrespondent.net/world/worldabus/3565156-oon-bolshynstvo-dokazatelstv-prestuplenyi-na-maidane-unychtozheno

12 Interpol rejects Ukrainian murder charges against ex-officials. (2015, January 12). Retrieved from https://www.kyivpost.com/content/kyiv-post-plus/interpol-rejects-ukrainian-murder-charges-against-ex-officials-377233.html

13 Rachkevych, M. (2014, July 25). Interpol issues wanted notice for nationalist leader Yarosh at Russia's behest. Retrieved from https://www.kyivpost.com/content/ukraine/interpol-issues-wanted-notice-for-nationalist-leader-yarosh-at-russias-behest-357964.html?flavour=mobile

14 Mitchell, G. (2014, March 08). Key Source Denies Claim That Protesters Hired Snipers in Kiev. Retrieved from http://www.thenation.com/article/key-source-denies-claim-protesters-hired-snipers-kiev/

15 Bergman, M. (2014, March 5). Breaking: Estonian Foreign Minister Urmas Paet and Catherine Ashton discuss Ukraine over the phone. Retrieved from https://www.youtube.com/watch?v=ZEgJ0oo3OA8

16 Sakwa, R. (2014). Frontline Ukraine: crisis in the borderlands. IB Tauris, pp. 97-98.

17 Krever, M. (2014, February 26). Putin phone call convinced Yanukovych to change attitude, says Polish foreign minister. Retrieved from http://amanpour.blogs.cnn.com/2014/02/26/vladimir-putin-viktor-yanukovych-radoslaw-sikorski-ukraine-poland-russia/

18 Sakwa, R. (2014). Frontline Ukraine: crisis in the borderlands. IB Tauris, p. 98

19 Violence, Coercion, and Escalation in Ukraine's Maidan Revolution: Escalation Point 6 - The 'Snipers' of February. Retrieved from http://gordonhahn.com/2015/05/08/violence-coercion-and-escalation-in-ukraines-maidan-revolution-escalation-point-6-the-snipers-of-february/

20 Коваленко, О. (2014, February 24). Сотник, який переломив хід історії: Треба було дотискати. Retrieved from http://www.pravda.com.ua/articles/2014/02/24/7016048/

21 Violence, Coercion, and Escalation in Ukraine's Maidan Revolution:

	Escalation Point 6 - The 'Snipers' of February. Retrieved from http://gordonhahn.com/2015/05/08/violence-coercion-and-escalation-in-ukraines-maidan-revolution-escalation-point-6-the-snipers-of-february/
22	Sakwa, R. (2014). Frontline Ukraine: crisis in the borderlands. IB Tauris, p. 103.
23	Sindelar, D. (2014, February 23). Was Yanukovych's Ouster Constitutional? Retrieved from http://www.rferl.org/content/was-yanukovychs-ouster-constitutional/25274346.html
24	Mazzone, A. (2014, March 10). Ucraina, e se Usa e Ue stessero appoggiando i neonazisti? Retrieved from http://www.panorama.it/news/marco-ventura-profeta-di-ventura/ucraina-putin-crimea-neonazisti-svoboda/
25	Bergman, M. (2014, March 5). Breaking: Estonian Foreign Minister Urmas Paet and Catherine Ashton discuss Ukraine over the phone. Retrieved from https://www.youtube.com/watch?v=ZEgJ0oo3OA8
26	Monument to soldiers who died liberating Ukraine from Nazis toppled (PHOTOS, VIDEO). (2014, February 23). Retrieved from https://www.rt.com/news/war-monument-toppled-ukraine-351/

| Chapter Five |

OLIGARCH-BACKED REGIME CHANGE

At this point, it might be useful to asses some of the forces that operate behind the scenes in Ukraine. The roots of the Ukrainian political system traces back to its founding in 1991. Dozens of Ukrainians with connections were able to amass vast riches, while the economy as a whole shrank by 60 percent. By comparison, the US economy shrank by just 30 percent during the great depression. Most former Soviet states would suffer the same fate, but (in addition to Kyrgyzstan) only Ukraine has still not recovered to its 1991 GDP level.[1] This is especially damning if one considers that Ukraine was a major industrial base of the Soviet Union, and still leads in many high-technology sectors such as aircraft, rocket and shipbuilding industries, while boasting a well-educated workforce coming fourth in the world in terms of IT professionals.[2] Ukraine also has significant energy resources and huge agricultural potential with 30 percent of the world's black earth soil.[3] Regardless, as of 2010, a quarter of its population struggled below the poverty line, while the wealth of fifty oligarchs equaled nearly half of the country's GDP, and they owned most of the major media channels.[4] One in five Ukrainians told a 2010 survey they were willing to sell their vote.[5] A 120-page report by the aforementioned Polish think tank OSW concludes that "big business at present does not have such a strong influence on politics in any other Eastern European country as it does in Ukraine."[6] In fact, "one may risk stating that it is the interplay of the interests of the oligarchs that is the real mechanism which shapes Ukrainian politics."[7]

One of the major political parties behind Maidan was the oligarchic Fatherland party. The founder and leader of this party is the co-leader of the 2004 western-backed revolution, Yulia Tymoshenko, who was serving a seven-year prison sentence at the time of the Maidan uprising. In 1999, she had briefly served as deputy-prime minister for the fuel and energy sector, but was soon dismissed and prosecuted for gas-smuggling and tax evasion. Her closest business partner, Pavlo Lazarenko, fled to the US where he was sentenced to eight years imprisonment for extortion and money laundering. In that court case, Tymoshenko was continuously mentioned as 'co-conspirator,' but was inexplicably not prosecuted. FBI investigator Bryan Earl explained the arrangement:

> When he [Pavlo Lazarenko] was the chairman of Dnepropetrovsk Oblast, he visited all the successful businessmen and said: 'give me 50% of your profits […] if you give me the money, I'll guarantee that you'll stay in business and that your business will be successful.' Later Lazarenko moved higher up the political ladder, becoming deputy prime minister and then prime minister. […] When he emerged on to the national stage, he began to extensively manipulate the structure of natural gas imports. Whereupon, virtually overnight, Yulia Tymoshenko and her company became Ukraine's largest gas importer.[8]

After the western-backed Orange revolution, Tymoshenko would serve as prime minister under Yushchenko, where she was involved in several gas scandals. After his victory, Viktor Yanukovych would imprison her for embezzlement and abuse of power, which was considered by many as selective prosecution. She was freed the same day parliament was stormed, and her Fatherland party was rewarded with most of the remaining positions in the interim-government, including the ministries of justice, social policy, internal affairs and infrastructure. Most importantly, however, her party delivered the acting president Oleksandr Turchynov, the prime-minister Arseniy Yatseniuk, the first vice-prime-minister, the minister of the cabinet of ministers, and the parliament's speaker.

The second richest man in Ukraine (according to *Forbes'* Ukraine rating 2015) is Viktor Pinchuk, the son-in-law of Leonid Kuchma, president of Ukraine between 1994 and 2005. Devoutly pro-European, he set up the Yalta European Strategy which, among other things, hosts a yearly conference in favor of aligning Ukraine more closely to Europe. The conference always includes a number of prominent European, American and NATO officials. Pinchuk has also been funding foundations owned by Tony Blair and the Clintons, as well as those of post-Maidan prime minister Yatsenyuk.[9] Indeed, in a 2008 Wikileaks cable from the US embassy in Ukraine, the assertion was made that Pinchuk was at the helm of launching the early career of Yatsenyuk, harboring close relations with the politician.[10] Similarily, reporting on an interview with Pinchuk, the *Financial Times* wrote that the oligarch had been busy "hand-picking ... future Ukrainian leaders, educating them in western universities and seconding them to London banks and law firms."[11]

Another noteworthy oligarch is the multi-billionaire, Ihor Kolomyskyi, with $6 billion the third richest man in Ukraine. A particularly corrupt figure, he is famous for having built his imperium through literally hostile takeovers, "hiring an army of thugs to descend upon ... [a company] with baseball bats, gas and rubber pistols, iron bars and chainsaws ... and then a mix of phony court orders (often involving corrupt judges and/or registrars)."[12] After Maidan, Kolomoyskyi profiled himself as the most "patriotic" businessperson in Ukraine. Inter alia, he offered $10,000 for every caught Russian "saboteur", pumped tens of millions of dollars into the creation of several volunteer battalions, and proposed to build a 2000 km wall that would separate Ukraine from Russia.[13]

In the interim government, two of his close associates were

granted the ministries of finance and energy.[14] In terms of energy, he gained exclusive contracts to provide the military with fuel, including a possible extension for exclusively supplying the agricultural industry.[15] In terms of finance, Kolomoyskyi's Privatbank has been the biggest recipient of what the IMF called "emergency liquidity assistance" to Ukrainian banks. Shortly after the IMF granted its first $3.2-billion tranche to Ukraine, it reported that "the banking system faced large foreign currency outflows ($3.1 billion). Investigative journalist John Helmer asserted that, in other words, most of the IMF money had now disappeared offshore.[16] Kolomoyskyi's influence, however, became even more blatant when he was named head of the regional Dnepropetrovsk government, where important corporations of his Privat Group, Including PrivatBank, are stationed. There he set up a committee for investment and strategic development of the region, widely considered to be used for his own enrichment.[17] At the same time, he deployed his volunteer battalions to violently take over corporations of competitors.[18]

Although Kolomoyskyi's raiding practices are extraordinarily widespread, the strategy is not shunned by other oligarchs either, and has continually been used after the regime change.[19] Furthermore, Kolomoyskyi's appointment as regional governor wasn't unique either. The steel magnate, Serhiy Taruta, with a net worth of $3 billion, was appointed as the governor of the Donetsk region, where his Industrial Union of Donbass is stationed (he is also a funder of a foundation owned by Prime Minister Yatsenyuk). Furthermore, the billionaires Yaroslavsky and Novinsky were both offered key positions in the east.[20]

The 25th of May 2014 presidential elections would show that the oligarchs still had a strong grip on the country. They were won with 55% of the votes by "chocolate king" Poroshenko. A true chameleon, he was one of the founders of Yanukovych's Party of Regions and minister under the presidency of both Yanukovych and his predecessor, Yuschchenko. Owning $1.3 billion and one of the four biggest TV stations in Ukraine, he can squarely count himself as part of the oligarchic class. A Wikileaks cable from the

American embassy described him as a "disgraced oligarch" who "was tainted by credible corruption allegations."[21] The runner up was 'gas princess' Tymoshenko, whose corrupt record I've explained above at some length.

The Ukrainian coverage of both the Maidan revolution and the post-Maidan government was almost invariably positive, often in severely propagandistic fashion. The popular news-site *Ukrainska Pravda*, for example, managed to make the extraordinary claim that Russia used tactical nuclear weapons in the Donbass.[22] More crucially, even among former pro-Yanukovych channels, voices were remarkably similar. In particular, multibillionaires Akhmetov and Firtash used to be Yanukovych's most important allies, but behind the scenes they started funding the opposition months before Maidan.[23] When the protests started and their television channels voiced critical opinions of the government, it was clear that they were letting Yanukovych fall.

According to Serhiy Leshchenko—one of Ukraine's most respected investigative journalists—the US state department had threatened Akhmetov with far-reaching sanctions to get him this far.[24] Leshchenko also reported that the oligarch controlled some 50 deputies in Yanukovych's Party of Regions. The Ukrainian political analyst Taras Berezovets concurred there were at least 40 such MPs.[25] The German *Spiegel* estimated the number to be 60, with another 30 following the orders of Firtash.[26] The influence of the oligarchs was undoubtedly important for the ease with which the anti-Russian parties were able to dominate the interim-government and pass controversial laws. At a rally in Donetsk, Akhmetov would later accuse the eastern Ukrainian rebels of leading the country towards a "genocide."[27] Firtash, on his part, would be visited by President Poroshenko in Vienna, where Firtash was facing extradition to the United States on corruption charges at the request of the FBI (the trial was politically motivated, according to the oligarch, an accusation that was later confirmed in court).[28]

It must be emphasized, however, that the oligarchs are deadly competitors—even when they share political positions. A good example is a major public conflict that occurred in spring 2015 between the pro-Western oligarchs Petro Poroshenko andIhor Kolomoyskyi, the latter of whom was slowly threatening to disturb the balance of powers among the oligarchs. In a dispute over the control of the state company Ukrnafta—the largest oil and gas producer of Ukraine—Kolomoyskyi send one of his volunteer battalions (Dnipro-1) to the headquarters of Ukrnafta in Kiev. President Poroshenko ordered law enforcement officers to clean the corporate offices and Kolomoyskyi was forced to resign from his post as regional governor.[29] (Under the radar, some important concessions were made. Among other things, he received retrospective dividend payments from Ukrnafta, a lack of audits into his past business activities there, and he was actually succeeded as governor by one of his allies. Nevertheless, a major corporation had been wrested from his control.)[30]

The Polish think tank OSW published another extensive report on the oligarchic class one year after the fall of Yanukovych, a few months after the parliamentary elections of October 2014. With the exception of the Self-Reliance party—which contains seven percent of the seats in parliament—the report documented the major role of oligarchs in all of the elected parties. It concluded that "The Maidan revolution has left the Ukrainian oligarchic system unshaken, and the parliamentary elections have shown that the most powerful oligarchs have gained serious opportunities to influence Ukrainian politics."[31]

Endnotes

1   Sakwa, R. (2014). Frontline Ukraine: crisis in the borderlands. IB Tauris, p. 83.
2   Ibid, p. 84.
3   Ibid, p. 84.
4   Central Intelligence Agency (Ed.). (2015). The World Factbook 2014-15. Government Printing Office; Wilson, A. (2013, June 18). Pathways to Freedom: Chapter Preview. Retrieved from http://www.cfr.org/democratization/ukraine/p30818
5   Every Fifth Ukrainian 'Ready To Sell Vote' (2010, October 22).

	Retrieved from http://www.rferl.org/content/Survey_Shows_Every_Fifth_Ukrainian_Ready_To_Sell_Vote/2197889.html
6	Matuszak, S. (2012). The oligarchic democracy: The influence of business groups on Ukrainian politics. *OSW Studies*, 42, 1-112, p. 9.
7	Ibid, p.5.
8	Cited in Sakwa, R. (2014). Frontline Ukraine: crisis in the borderlands. IB Tauris, p. 73.
9	Mendick, R., & Malnick, E. (2013, February 10). Revealed: Tony Blair and the oligarch bankrolling his charity. Retrieved from http://www.telegraph.co.uk/news/politics/tony-blair/9859780/Revealed-Tony-Blair-and-the-oligarch-bankrolling-his-charity.html; Ukraine: Yatensyuk, Rising Politician. (2008, July 03). Retrieved from https://wikileaks.org/plusd/cables/08KYIV1300_a.html
10	Ukraine: Yatensyuk, Rising Politician. (2008, July 03). Retrieved from https://wikileaks.org/plusd/cables/08KYIV1300_a.html
11	Bender, Y. (2014, March 27). In the wake of turmoil, the role of Ukraine's oligarchs is under scrutiny. Retrieved from https://www.ft.com/content/1a06857a-ae60-11e3-aaa6-00144feab7de
12	Nadeau, J. (2014, January 15). Ukraine's real problem: Crony capitalism. Retrieved from http://thehill.com/blogs/congress-blog/foreign-policy/195549-ukraines-real-problem-crony-capitalism For a detailed examination of corporate raiding in Ukraine, consult Rojansky, M. (2014). Corporate raiding in Ukraine: Causes, methods and consequences. Demokratizatsiya, 22(3), 411-444.
13	Luhn, A. (2014, April 17). Ukrainian oligarch offers bounty for capture of Russian 'saboteurs' Retrieved from http://www.theguardian.com/world/2014/apr/17/ukrainian-oligarch-offers-financial-rewards-russians-igor-kolomoisky; Cullison, A. (2014, June 27). Ukraine's Secret Weapon: Feisty Oligarch Ihor Kolomoisky. Retrieved from http://www.wsj.com/articles/ukraines-secret-weapon-feisty-oligarch-ihor-kolomoisky-1403886665; Kolomoisky suggests Ukraine build 2,000-kilometers wall against Russia. (2014, June 13). Retrieved from http://www.kyivpost.com/content/ukraine/kolomoisky-suggests-ukraine-build-2000-kilometers-wall-against-russia-351751.html
14	Steinberg, S. (2014, February 28). US, Europe step up threats against Russia over Ukraine. Retrieved from https://www.wsws.org/en/articles/2014/02/28/ukra-f28.html
15	Sakwa, R. (2014). Frontline Ukraine: crisis in the borderlands. IB Tauris, p. 77.
16	Helmer, J. (2014, June 24). Stress test for IMF in Ukraine -Ihor Kolomisky's PrivatBank is the biggest beneficiary of the IMF's emergency liquidity assistance (ELA). Retrieved from http://

	johnhelmer.net/?p=11035
17	Sakwa, R. (2014). Frontline Ukraine: crisis in the borderlands. IB Tauris, p. 133.
18	The best and most prominent example was undoubtedly the standoff between the Dnipro battalion and the state's security forces, concerning ownership of the country's largest oil and gas producer. See the end of this chapter.
19	Rachkevych, M., Gordiienko, O., & Degeler, A. (2014, October 23). An overview of alleged recent raider attacks. Retrieved from http://www.kyivpost.com/content/business/an-overview-of-alleged-recent-raider-attacks-369191.html For a detailed examination of corporate raiding in Ukraine, consult Rojansky, M. (2014). Corporate raiding in Ukraine: Causes, methods and consequences. Demokratizatsiya, 22(3), 411-444.
20	Kramer, A. E. (2014, March 02). Ukraine Turns to Its Oligarchs for Political Help. Retrieved from http://www.nytimes.com/2014/03/03/world/europe/ukraine-turns-to-its-oligarchs-for-political-help.html
21	Taylor, A. (2014, May 29). The not-very-nice things U.S. officials used to say about Ukraine's new president. Retrieved from https://www.washingtonpost.com/news/worldviews/wp/2014/05/29/the-not-very-nice-things-u-s-officials-used-to-say-about-ukraines-new-president/
22	Гелетей: РФ могла використати ядерну зброю в зоні АТО. (2014, September 20). Retrieved from http://www.pravda.com.ua/news/2014/09/20/7038392/
23	Neef, C. (2014, February 25). Yanukovych's Fall: The Power of Ukraine's Billionaires. Retrieved from http://www.spiegel.de/international/europe/how-oligarchs-in-ukraine-prepared-for-the-fall-of-yanukovych-a-955328-2.html
24	Leshchenko, S. (2013, December 13). Akhmetov broke silence - after meeting with Nuland. Retrieved from http://blogs.pravda.com.ua/authors/leschenko/52aad6189a2bc/
25	Williams, S. (2014, January 29). Behind the scenes, football tycoon pulls strings in Ukraine crisis. Retrieved from https://sg.news.yahoo.com/behind-scenes-football-tycoon-pulls-strings-ukraine-crisis-183016202.html
26	Neef, C. (2014, February 25). Yanukovych's Fall: The Power of Ukraine's Billionaires. Retrieved from http://www.spiegel.de/international/europe/how-oligarchs-in-ukraine-prepared-for-the-fall-of-yanukovych-a-955328-2.html
27	Ukrainian tycoon Rinat Akhmetov confronts rebellion. (2014, May 20). Retrieved from http://www.bbc.com/news/world-europe-27483719
28	This trial will be examined further in the chapter: The Imperial Desire for War.

29	Pinkham, S. (2015, April 02). Watching the Ukrainian Oligarchs. Retrieved from http://www.newyorker.com/news/news-desk/watching-the-ukrainian-oligarchs
30	Mefford, B. (2015, April 9). Poroshenko Goes Hunting for Oligarchs. Retrieved from http://www.atlanticcouncil.org/blogs/new-atlanticist/poroshenko-goes-hunting-for-oligarchs
31	Konończuk, W. (2015, February 16). Oligarchs after the Maidan: The old system in a 'new' Ukraine. Retrieved from http://www.osw.waw.pl/en/publikacje/osw-commentary/2015-02-16/oligarchs-after-maidan-old-system-a-new-ukraine

| Chapter Six |

WESTERN-BACKED REGIME CHANGE

The Maidan uprising, however, was not only backed by ultranationalists and oligarchs. Western states too played a role in the uprising (and the backstage politics of the oligarchs, as I've noted above). In a speech sponsored by the US Ukraine Foundation and held at the National Press Club in Washington on December 13, 2013, Victoria Nuland, Assistant Secretary of State for European and Eurasian Affairs, expressed her support to the opposition. She proudly stated that the United States had invested over $5 billion in "Ukrainian democracy".[1] Today there is ample documentation of the role Western-funded NGOs had played in the Orange revolution of 2004.[2] In many ways, this was a precedent to the Maidan revolution. After Viktor Yanukovych falsified his election in 2004, mass protests arose in the streets of Western and Central Ukraine. These proved successful: new elections were scheduled and won by the pro-Western candidate, Viktor Yushchenko. This change of power was characterized by most Southern and Eastern-Ukrainians as a 'coup d'état supported by the west,' or a 'coup d'état supported by the political opposition' (mostly the former).[3] The Yushchenko presidency would be characterized by internal power struggles within the Orange coalition, a lack of fundamental changes in national policy, a persistence of major corruption scandals and the acceleration and normalization of nationalism. By the end of his presidency, only 6.7 percent of Ukrainians still trusted his cabinet, 5.3 percent trusted the courts, 4.7 percent trusted the president and 4.2 percent trusted parliament.[4] It was this damning track record that allowed Yanukovych to win free and fair elections in 2010.

In fact, the Yushchenko presidency had even undermined Ukraine's very faith in democracy and capitalism. A 2009 Pew Research survey found that two-thirds of Ukrainian believed life was better under communism (12 percent said it was worse), while only 30 percent still approved of the change to a multiparty system.[5] The skepticism towards the Ukrainian political system became nearly universal. Indeed, as time progressed, even many former supporters of the Orange Revolution changed their minds on the former movement, and more and more Ukrainians considered themselves to be losing due to the changes.[6] Mass mobilization, it seemed, had been abused by sections of the Ukrainian elite to seize power. Indeed, the Orange president Viktor Yushchenko and prime-minister Yulia Tymoshenko had been familiar faces in Ukrainian politics. Among other prominent positions, they had served respectively as prime minister and deputy prime minister in the cabinet of Leonid Kuchma. Cambridge political scientist David Lane concluded that the Orange Revolution was a 'revolutionary coup,' emphasizing the fundamental ambiguity between mass popular participation and elite power struggles.[7]

Regardless, the pro-European elites would try again, and they had major funds to back them. In an interview with the *Financial Post* in 2012 Oleh Rybachuk, former deputy prime minister for European integration under Yushchenko, stated that: "We now have 150 NGOs in all the major cities ... The Orange Revolution was a miracle ... We want to do that again and we think we will."[8] Rybachuk is, amongst other things, the founder and head of Center UA, an umbrella organization linked to various activist projects and NGOs.[9] One of them is the New Citizen campaign which, according to the *Financial Times*, "played a big role in getting the protest up and running".[10] Another example is the Stronger Together Campaign, which aims to " popularize the ideas of European integration and encourage authorities to implement them effectively."[11] Yanukovych felt so threatened that he implemented a series of draconian laws shortly before his fall, which included obligatory registration of NGOs with foreign funding as foreign agents who would need to pay more taxes and endure extra monitoring. The Kyivpost reports that "Center UA received more than $500,000 in 2012, ... 54 percent of which came from Pact Inc., a project funded by the U.S. Agency for International Development. Nearly 36 percent came from Omidyar Network, a foundation established by eBay founder Pierre Omidyar and his wife. Other donors include the International Renaissance Foundation, whose key funder is billionaire George Soros, and the National Endowment for Democracy, funded largely by the U.S. Congress."[12]

In addition, as in other recent uprisings, social media sowed the seeds of the spring. The EuroMaidan Facebook page garnered over a 100,000 followers while #EuroMaidan was tweeted between 1500 and 3000 times an hour on average.[13] In this context, it is useful to recall that USAID, responsible for investing American development aid, was caught using social media to undermine the Cuban government.[14] In addition, a leaked document from Snowden shows that Western secret services make use of social media to move the masses to their likings.[15] Indeed, while much has been made of the fact that Russia spends $1 million on 'an army of internet trolls,' three years earlier it was already documented that a similar yet more sophisticated US program, Operation Earnest Voice, was running on a budget of $200 million.[16]

Another good example of Western propaganda was the slick and heart-breaking "I am a Ukrainian" video that went viral with 8 million views on Youtube.[17] In the "behind the scenes" section Larry Diamond is visible in the picture, described as "executive director" and "inspiration".[18] Diamond is a senior advisor for the National Endowment for Democracy (NED), which was established under the Reagan administration to stimulate regime changes. Indeed, one of its founders, Allen Weinstein, admitted in 1991 that "A lot of what we do today was done covertly 25 years ago by the CIA."[19] Unsurprisingly then, the organization receives nearly all of its funding from the US government, which is also the source for most of its senior staff.[20] As to be expected, the NED has already been active for years in Ukraine. Its long list of 65 projects range from stimulating "activism" to supporting "civic journalism", to organizing seminars and spreading leaflets.[21]

But the European Commission has been investing substantial sums as well. According to its Financial Transparency System, just between 2007 and 2014, it poured 1.3 billion Euros into Ukraine.[22] Although this sum lumps together all types of funding (including, for example, R&D funding), a substantial part of the recipient list contains civil and activist front groups such as the Center for European Co-operation and the Center for European Initiatives. Furthermore, well-connected Western oligarchs— such as George Soros, who is worth some $25 billion—have also been investing substantial sums to amplify pro-Western movements in Ukraine. According to its annual financial reports, Soros' International Rennaissance Foundation (IRF) invested nearly $110 million in Ukraine between 2004 and 2014.[23] Internal minutes released by DC leaks show a former board member, Victoria Siumar, going as far as to argue that "partners of the IRF were the main driving force and the foundation of the Maidan movement" and that without Soros' efforts "the revolution might not have succeeded."[24] Her remarks echo an internal document on the IRF's strategy in March 2014, which claims that "based on NGOs traditionally supported by IRF and other Western donors, new forms of self-organization of citizens have emerged ... Like during the Maidan protests, IRF representatives are in the midst of Ukraine's transition process."[25] In public, Soros was more humble, but did argue that the IRF "played an important part in events now."[26]

Of course, these might be exaggerated self-congratulatory statements, but the IRF minutes do demonstrate a significant degree of interference and leverage. After Maidan, for example, the documents show that Soros and the IRF had direct access to high-level officials in both the Ukrainian and US governments, who actively sought their advice. Furthermore, as the post-Maidan regime was scraping for financial support, the American oligarch planned to use his network for "effectively helping to design and to influence the actions of international donors in order to guide them on how to best direct their funding."[27] Indeed, at one point, Soros publicly offered to invest $1 billion in Ukraine himself, in order to persuade Western governments to increase their backing of the post-Maidan regime.[28]

Soros' agenda was characterized by a myriad of issues, including anti-corruption efforts and technocratic reforms. In the immediate aftermath of Maidan, however, Soros worried that an impending federalization of Ukraine was "the number one problem today for Ukraine" because it would, among other things, "mean a victory for Putin."[29] "Soros suggested activating the Maidan to come out against any proposed federal system," the leaked document reads.[30] The oligarchs' anti-Russian outlook becomes especially obvious in a number of loaded statements recorded in the minutes, such as the exaggeration of the dangers of federalization, the idea that Russia controlled the Donbass uprising as early as March 2014, and most ridiculous of all, the notion that Right Sector was a Russian conspiracy.[31] Indeed, this was no different for the NED, which also saw the struggles of Ukraine through a distinctly anti-Russian lens. A few months before the Maidan uprising Carl Gershman, president of the NED, wrote a piece in the *Washington Post* on the waning Russian influence in Eastern Europe, where the NED, Soros and the European commission have been highly active as well. He proclaimed that "Ukraine is the biggest prize," and added that "Russians, too, face a choice, and Putin may find himself on the losing end not just in the near abroad but within Russia itself."[32] Indeed, the NED had over a 100 projects running in Russia too, but was banned by the Russian state in the summer of 2015.[33]

Not only did Western states fund the Maidan uprising, many officials also participated in the rallies at Maidan. US Deputy Secretary of State Victoria Nuland and US Ambassador to Kiev Geoffrey Pyatt went to Maidan to pledge their support and hand out cookies. German Foreign Minister Guido Westerwelle followed suit asserting that "Ukraine should be on board with Europe."[34] The Polish Foreign Ministry reportedly even set up a tent on Maidan Square.[35] Other visits to rallies on Maidan included Dutch Foreign Minister Frans Timmermans, European Parliament Vice President Jacek Protasiewicz, former European Parliament President Jerzy Buzek, the former head of the Polish government, and Jaroslaw Kaczynski, the leader of the Law and Justice party, among others.[36] In addition, US State Department spokesperson Jen Psaki suggested the US might impose sanctions on Ukraine; a threat that was repeated by the head of the US Helsinki Commission, the US-funded think tank Freedom House, and a bill introduced by eleven US senators, which was passed without amendments and by a unanimous vote.[37] The knowledge that the most powerful states in the world backed the Maidan uprising surely emboldened the demonstrators to continue their efforts.

That being said, no actual sanctions commenced until the final bloody episode of the uprising. This lead to mocking jokes among Maidan protestors that Western support was 'mere talk.' Besides, the European Parliament had condemned the violent actions of ultranationalists in a joint resolution on the situation in Ukraine.[38] These reservations on the protest activities, however, were de-emphasized and easily drowned out by the countless pledges of unreserved support by prominent EU and US officials. Indeed, the abovementioned foreign interference is damning enough. One can only imagine the outrage if Russia was openly funding pro-Russian front-groups in Ukraine with billions of dollars, and subsequently sent multiple high-ranking officials to whip up the crowd when their efforts bore fruit, accompanied with threats of sanctions. Indeed, outrage was exactly the tone when Russia used its own carrots and sticks—in the form of sanctions, a loan and a cut in gas prices—to persuade the Yanukovych regime against the EU agreement.

We must also consider the relation of Western states with the most violent and ultranationalist elements of the Maidan uprising. It would certainly not be the first time since WW2 that Europe and the United States sided with fascism. The US State Department had always seen fascism as compatible with US economic interests. Many government officials had praised it as an effective answer to liberalism, socialism, anarchism and communism, which were simply all labelled as "Bolshevism". Mussolini, for example, was considered "a sound and useful leader" for putting his "own house in order..." not least because "... A class war was put down".[39] A 1937 State Department report stated that "if Fascism cannot succeed by persuasion [in Germany], it must succeed by force."[40] While American investments plummeted throughout Europe during the great depression, they increased in Nazi Germany by almost 50%. "A half-dozen key U.S. companies—International Harvester, Ford, General Motors, Standard Oil of New Jersey, and du Pont—had become deeply involved in German weapons production."[41]

Even though the fascist axis had become the enemy during the Second World War, a renunciation of fascism itself had never occurred. Operation PAPERCLIP smuggled Nazi scientists to the US to work for the American government.[42] Indeed, in order to prevent "chaos, bolshevization or civil war" in Greece, Italy, Germany, France, Japan and South Korea, anti-fascist movements were violently repressed and fascist collaborators kept in power and supported by the United States.[43] It is not surprising then, that recently declassified files show that the CIA got along well with the former OUN in Ukraine.[44] The fascists were smuggled to America and trained to fight a guerrilla war against the Soviet Union. But once they returned to Ukraine, the KGB was able to eliminate them one by one. Their leader, Stepan Bandera, was killed in 1959 by the KGB.

But a large part of the former OUN fascists stayed in America where they organized themselves in the Ukrainian Congress Committee of America (UCCA), which was able to accumulate significant influence. The former Nazi-collaborators were able to secure top positions in Republican campaign teams. "We have spent years quietly penetrating positions of influence", one member told Russ Bellant, who documented their rise in what was, according to the *Harvard Educational Review*, a "well-documented and reliable" book.[45] Russ Bellant explains how the UCCA could count on personal visits from presidents Reagan and

Bush themselves throughout the eighties. Reagan, for example, told UCCA member Stetsko, who personally oversaw a slaughter of 7000 Jews in Lviv, "your struggle is our struggle, your dream is our dream."[46] Indeed, UCCA members piled into the Reagan administration. Paula Dobriansky, daughter of the chair, was even placed on the National Security Council of America.

In a recent interview Russ Bellant tells how, with the fall of the Soviet Union, many UCCA members returned to Ukraine where they started the ultranationalist organizations from which Svoboda and the Right Sector would later emerge.[47] Others stayed in the US to lobby for the UCCA in Washington—with success; the UCCA even to this day receives funding from the aforementioned NED, i.e. the US government.[48] But the ultranationalists remained quite marginal in Ukraine itself until the western-backed Orange revolution of 2004. As mentioned, the new pro-Western Yushchenko had much sympathy for the Ukrainian ultranationalists. His wife had served in the Reagan administration and the far-right had provided his supporters protection during the Orange revolution.[49]

In the process, other European and North American countries have themselves gotten involved in efforts to rewrite history by, among other things, legitimizing the double genocide thesis that claims exact equality between Soviet and Nazi crimes.[50] Several Baltic states also started to glorify former Waffen-SS battalions, such as the Latvian Legion. In 2012 a UN resolution against the "glorification of the Nazi movement and former members of the Waffen-SS organization" was adopted with 133 votes in favor. The United States, Canada and Palau were the only ones voting against the resolution (most European countries abstained).[51] The vote was repeated with similar results after the fall of Yanukovych: Ukraine, Canada and the US voted against the resolution.[52]

Aside from the ideological support, there were also multiple meetings between Western officials and the ultranationalist movement. Both John McCain and Victoria Nuland met with Svoboda leader Tyahnybok and the post-Maidan prime minister

Yatsenyuk in the run up to the fall of Yanukovych.[53] *The New York Times* also reports that "European [and American] envoys met at the German Embassy with Andriy Parubiy," the aforementioned commandant of the Maidan self-defense forces.[54] Most damning of all, the leader of the Neo-Nazi C14 sotnya confessed that his battalion had used the Canadian embassy in Kiev as a fallout base, at the very height and culmination of the Maidan uprising.[55] Of course, Waschuk, the Canadian ambassador in Kiev, assured CBC news that no harm came from opening the doors to the insurgents. It was simply "a gesture designed to react and to reach out to the people suffering in the turmoil."[56] The level of foreign interference in Ukrainian affairs is perhaps best illustrated by a leaked call between Deputy Secretary of State Victoria Nuland and US ambassador Geoffrey Pyatt, days before the formation of the post-Maidan regime, where they more or less hand-picked the interim government of Ukraine.

> [Pyatt:] I think we're in play. ... The Klitschko [Vitaly Klitschko, one of the three major opposition leaders] piece is obviously the complicated electron here. Especially the announcement of him as deputy prime minister. ... I think your argument to him, which you'll need to make, I think that's the next phone call you want to set up, is exactly the one you made to Yats [Arseniy Yatseniuk]. And I'm glad you sort of put him on the spot on where he fits in this scenario.
>
> [Nuland:] Good. I don't think Klitsch should go into the government. I don't think it's necessary, I don't think it's a good idea.
>
> [Pyatt] Yeah, I guess... in terms of him not going into the government, just let him stay out and do his political homework and stuff.

[Nuland affirms:] I think Yats is the guy who's got the economic experience, the governing experience. He's the... what he needs is Klitsch and Tyahnybok [leader of Svoboda] on the outside. He needs to be talking to them four times a week, you know. I just think Klitsch going in... he's going to be at that level working for Yatseniuk, it's just not going to work.

[Pyatt:] Yeah, no, I think that's right. OK. Good. Do you want us to set up a call with him as the next step?[57]

Indeed, Klitschko and his party did not become part of the interim government, while Nuland's favoured candidate, Arseniy Yatsenyuk, became the prime minister—and his party received nearly every major office in the cabinet. This hardly represented the popular will. In the most recent survey, taken three weeks before the fall of Yanukovych, Klitschko was by far the most popular opposition leader, garnering 28.7% in the polls, while Yatsenyuk did not even register 3% (the pro-Russian president Yanukovych was actually leading with 29.5%).[58] Klitschko would also pull out of the subsequent presidential race, and use his party apparatus to support the aforementioned oligarch Petro Poroshenko.

We can conclude that there is overwhelming evidence of systematic foreign interference in Ukraine. It is especially revealing, however, to consider these indications in their historical context. William Blum, historian and former US state department official, documented that the United States has successfully overthrown over 40 foreign governments since WW2—most of which were democratically elected.[59] Many of these regime changes involved military coup d'états, without any movement or popular participation whatsoever. Indeed, regime change has been a fundamental pillar of Western foreign policy for decades. It is with this history in mind that George Friedman—the founder, former chief intelligence officer, financial overseer, and CEO of what is perhaps the single most prominent (US) private intelligence corporation, Stratfor—said provocatively that Maidan "truly was the most blatant coup in history."[60]

Endnotes

1. Victoria Nuland's Admits Washington Has Spent $5 Billion to "Subvert Ukraine" (2014, February 09). Retrieved from https://www.youtube.com/watch?v=U2fYcHLouXY
2. Traynor, I. (2004, November 25). US campaign behind the turmoil in Kiev. Retrieved from http://www.theguardian.com/world/2004/nov/26/ukraine.usa; Sussman, G., & Krader, S. (2008). Template revolutions: Marketing US regime change in Eastern Europe. Westminster Papers in Communication and Culture,5(3
3. Lane, D. (2008). The Orange Revolution:'People's Revolution'or Revolutionary Coup?. The British Journal of Politics & International Relations, 10(4), 525-549.
4. Kuzio, T., & Hamilton, D. S. (Eds.). (2011). Open Ukraine: Changing Course Towards a European Future. Center for Transatlantic Relations, Paul H. Nitze School of Advanced International Studies, Johns Hopkins University, p. 2.
5. End of Communism Cheered but Now with More Reservations. (2009, November 02). Retrieved from http://www.pewglobal.org/2009/11/02/end-of-communism-cheered-but-now-with-more-reservations/
6. Surveys taken over time after the Orange Revolution by Lane, D. (2008). The Orange Revolution:'People's Revolution'or Revolutionary Coup?. The British Journal of Politics & International Relations, 10(4), 525-549.
7. Ibid.
8. Francis, D. (2012, March 10). In Ukraine, 'how little has changed' even after Orange Revolution. Retrieved from http://opinion.financialpost.com/2012/03/10/in-ukraine-how-little-has-changed-even-after-orange-revolution/
9. Team. (n.d.). Retrieved February 10, 2016, from http://centreua.org/en/team/445/
10. Olearchyk, R. (2013, December 14). Ukraine: Inside the pro-EU protest camp. Retrieved from http://blogs.ft.com/beyond-brics/2013/12/14/ukraine-inside-the-pro-eu-protest-camp/?Authorised=false
11. Initiatives. (n.d.). Retrieved February 10, 2016, from http://centreua.org/en/
12. Rachkevych, M. (2014, February 10). Rybachuk: Democracy-promoting nongovernmental organization faces 'ridiculous'

investigation. Retrieved from http://www.kyivpost.com/content/ukraine-abroad/rybachuk-democracy-promoting-nongovernmental-organization-faces-ridiculous-investigation-336583.html

13   Kapliuk, K. (2013, December 01). Role of social media in EuroMaidan movement essential. Retrieved from http://www.kyivpost.com/content/ukraine/role-of-social-media-in-euromaidan-movement-essential-332749.html

14   Chiacu, D. (2014, April 03). U.S. built secret 'Cuban Twitter' to stir unrest. Retrieved from http://www.reuters.com/article/us-usa-cuba-twitter-idUSBREA321F920140403

15   Full-Spectrum Cyber Effects. (2014, April 5). Retrieved from https://theintercept.com/document/2014/04/04/full-spectrum-cyber-effects/

16   Johnson, A. (2015, April 14). Reporting on Russia's Troll Army, Western Media Forget West's Much Bigger, Sophisticated Troll Army. Retrieved from http://fair.org/home/reporting-on-russias-troll-army-western-media-forget-wests-much-bigger-sophisticated-troll-army/

17   Whisper Roar. (2014, February 10). I Am a Ukrainian. Retrieved from https://www.youtube.com/watch?v=Hvds2AIiWLA

18   Behind the Scenes. (n.d.). Retrieved from http://awhispertoaroar.com/about-the-film/behind-the-scenes/

19   Blum, W. (2006). Rogue state: a guide to the world's only superpower. Zed Books, p. 149

20   Report of the Independent Auditors. (2014, January 24). Retrieved from http://www.ned.org/docs/2013annual/2013 NED Annual Report - audit.pdf

21   Ukraine | National Endowment for Democracy. (n.d.). Retrieved February 10, 2016, from http://www.ned.org/region/central-and-eastern-europe/ukraine-2014/

22   Financial Transparency System (FTS) - European Commission. (n.d.). Retrieved from http://ec.europa.eu/budget/fts/index_en.htm

23   Approximately $109,342,000 in current US dollars (author's calculation). Annual reports available at International Renaissance Foundation. (n.d.). Retrieved from http://www.irf.ua/en/about/irf/

24   GS Ukraine Visit. (2014, March), p. 27. Retrieved from http://soros.dcleaks.com/view?div=europe. The content of the leaks has so far remained undisputed, and the authenticity of a number of other DC leaks has been confirmed by the targeted parties, such as Phillip Karber and Colin Powell.

25   International Renaissance Foundation - Emergency Response and Strategy Update in early 2014. (2014, March), p. 1. Retrieved from https://docs.google.com/viewerng/viewer?url=http://soros.dcleaks.com/fview/Europe/Ukraine+Working+Group+2014/_irf_emergency-response-strategy-feb-28-2.docx

26   Fareed Zakaria GPS Transcript. (2014, May 25). Retrieved from http://transcripts.cnn.com/TRANSCRIPTS/1405/25/fzgps.01.html
27   GS Ukraine Visit. (2014, March), p. 35. Retrieved from http://soros.dcleaks.com/view?div=europe
28   Nasralla, S., & Ablan, J. (2015, March 30). Soros says ready to invest $1 billion in Ukraine if West helps. Retrieved from http://www.reuters.com/article/us-ukraine-crisis-soros-idUSKBN0MQ0FP20150330
29   GS Ukraine Visit. (2014, March), p. 42. Retrieved from http://soros.dcleaks.com/view?div=europe
30   Ibid, p. 42.
31   "GS [George Soros]: Belief that the Pravy Sector is an FSB plot and has been funded to destabilize Ukraine." Ibid, p. 3.
32   Gershman, C. (2013, September 26). Former Soviet states stand up to Russia. Will the U.S.? Retrieved from https://www.washingtonpost.com/opinions/former-soviet-states-stand-up-to-russia-will-the-us/2013/09/26/b5ad2be4-246a-11e3-b75d-5b7f66349852_story.html
33   Russia | National Endowment for Democracy. (n.d.). Retrieved February 10, 2016, from http://www.ned.org/region/eurasia/russia-2014/
34   Weir, F. (2013, December 13). Russia cries foul over Western embrace of Ukraine's demonstrators. Retrieved from http://www.csmonitor.com/World/Europe/2013/1213/Russia-cries-foul-over-Western-embrace-of-Ukraine-s-demonstrators
35   Yanukovych backed into corner as EU suspends talks. (2013, December 16). Retrieved from http://www.intellinews.com/kyiv-blog-yanukovych-backed-into-corner-as-eu-suspends-talks-500018263/?source=russia&archive=bne
36   Timmermans bij betogers Kiev. (2013, December 4). Retrieved from http://nos.nl/artikel/582671-timmermans-bij-betogers-kiev.html; European diplomats, officials join rally in Kyiv. (2013, December 1). Retrieved from http://www.kyivpost.com/content/politics/european-diplomats-officials-join-opposition-rally-in-kyiv-332734.html
37   Hahn, G. M. (2016, February 26). Working Paper—Revised/Updated Edition: Escalation Points 1-5 in the Ukrainian Revolutionary Crisis, November 2013—January 2014. Retrieved from https://gordonhahn.com/2016/02/26/working-paper-revisedupdated-edition-escalation-points-1-5-in-the-ukrainian-revolutionary-crisis-november-2013-january-2014; Murphy, C. (2014, January 07). Text - S.Res.319 - 113th Congress (2013-2014): A resolution expressing support for the Ukrainian people in light of President Yanukovych's decision not to sign an Association Agreement with the European Union. Retrieved from https://www.congress.gov/bill/113th-congress/senate-resolution/319/text

38	Joint motion for a resolution on the situation in Ukraine. (2014, February 5). Retrieved from http://www.europarl.europa.eu/sides/getDoc.do?type=MOTION
39	Chomsky, N. (1991). Deterring democracy. London: Verso, p. 91
40	Chomsky, N. (2013). The Footnotes For: Understanding Power: The Indispensible Chomsky. Chapter 5, p. 13 The New Press. Retrieved from http://www.understandingpower.com/files/AllChaps.pdf
41	Ibid, p. 14.
42	Jacobsen, A. (2014). Operation Paperclip: The secret intelligence program that brought Nazi scientists to America. Little, Brown.
43	Chomsky, N. (2013). The Footnotes For: Understanding Power: The Indispensible Chomsky. Chapter 5, pp. 12-16 The New Press. Retrieved from http://www.understandingpower.com/files/AllChaps.pdf
44	Ruffrer, K. C. (2004-2006). Cold War Allies: The Origins of CIA's Relationship with Ukrainian Nationalists (S). Retrieved from http://www.foia.cia.gov/sites/default/files/document_conversions/1705143/STUDIES IN INTELLIGENCE NAZI - RELATED ARTICLES_0015.pdf
45	Bellant, R. (1991). Old Nazis, the New Right, and the Republican Party: Domestic fascist networks and their effect on US Cold War politics. Boston: South End; Harvard Educational Review. (n.d.). Retrieved from http://hepg.org/her-home/issues/harvard-educational-review-volume-65-issue-1/herbooknote/old-nazis,-the-new-right,-and-the-republican-party. Many of Bellant's assertions were later corroborated in an extensive study published by the US national archives, based on an immense amount of recently declassified intelligence reports: Breitman, R., & Goda, N. J. (2010). Hitler's shadow: Nazi war criminals, U.S. intelligence, and the Cold War. Washington, D.C.: National Archives and Records Administration.
46	Ibid.
47	Rosenberg, P. H. (2014, March 18). Seven Decades of Nazi Collaboration: America's Dirty Little Ukraine Secret. Retrieved from http://fpif.org/seven-decades-nazi-collaboration-americas-dirty-little-ukraine-secret/
48	Ukraine | National Endowment for Democracy. (n.d.). Retrieved February 10, 2016, from http://www.ned.org/region/central-and-eastern-europe/ukraine-2014/
49	Far-right group flexes during Ukraine "revolution". Retrieved from http://community.seattletimes.nwsource.com/archive/?date=20050103
50	Lazare, D. (2014). Timothy Snyder's Lies. Retrieved from https://www.jacobinmag.com/2014/09/timothy-snyders-lies/; Parry, R. (2014,

	August 16). The Hushed-Up Hitler Factor in Ukraine. Retrieved from https://consortiumnews.com/2014/08/16/the-hushed-up-hitler-factor-in-ukraine/
51	United Nations. (2012, December 20). Retrieved from http://www.un.org/News/Press/docs/2012/ga11331.doc.htm
52	United Nations. (2014, November 21). Retrieved from http://www.un.org/en/ga/third/69/docs/voting_sheets/L56.Rev1.pdf
53	Taylor, A. (2013, December 16). John McCain Went To Ukraine And Stood On Stage With A Man Accused Of Being An Anti-Semitic Neo-Nazi. Retrieved from http://www.businessinsider.com/john-mccain-meets-oleh-tyahnybok-in-ukraine-2013-12?IR=T
54	Higgins, A., & Kramer, A. E. (2015). Defeated Even Before He Was Ousted. *New York Times*, 1.
55	A link to the confession, as well as several other relevant materials regarding the C14 battalion are provided by Katchanovski, I. (2015, December 20). Facebook. Retrieved from https://www.facebook.com/ivan.katchanovski/posts/1141705079192710
56	Brewster, M. (2015, July 12). Canadian embassy used as safe haven during Ukraine uprising, investigation finds. Retrieved from http://www.cbc.ca/news/politics/canadian-embassy-used-as-safe-haven-during-ukraine-uprising-investigation-finds-1.3148719
57	Marcus, J. (2014, February 7). Ukraine crisis: Transcript of leaked Nuland-Pyatt call, BBC News. Retrieved from http://www.bbc.com/news/world-europe-26079957
58	Дані спільного загальноукраїнського соціологічного дослідження Центру соціальних та маркетингових досліджень «СОЦИС» та Київського міжнародного інституту соціології. (2014, February 7). Retrieved from http://www.socis.kiev.ua/ua/press/dani-spilnoho-zahalnoukrajinskoho-sotsiolohichnoho-doslidzhennja-tsentru-sotsialnykh-ta-marketyn.html
59	Blum, W. (2003). *Killing hope: US military and CIA interventions since World War II*. Zed Books. He updates the list every year on his website. William Blum. (2013, February). Retrieved from http://williamblum.org/essays/read/overthrowing-other-peoples-governments-the-master-list. The list is, however, not complete. Missing, for example, was the attempted coup against Hamas in 2006 (successful in the West Bank). Abunimah, A. (2014). *The Battle for Justice in Palestine*. Haymarket Books. As well as the successful coup in Azerbaijan: Ahmed, N. M. (2009). Our terrorists. New Internationalist, 426.
60	Chernenko, E., & Gabuev, A. (2014, September 12). "Russian and US interests in relation to Ukraine are incompatible with each other". Retrieved from http://www.kommersant.ru/doc/2636177

| Chapter Seven |

IMPOSING AUSTERITY

It didn't take long for Yatsenyuk to reveal the reasons behind Nuland's preference. The first question in an interview with Bloomberg on the 27th of February was "Your first job as the prime minister of Ukraine is what"? After some vague promises like stability and peace he clearly responds "to have the deal with the IMF and the European Union". Like a real technocrat he proudly stated that "I will be the most unpopular prime minister in the history of my country... We will do everything not to default ... if we get the financial support from the United States, from the European Union, from the IMF, we will do it."[1] Yatsenyuk was a man of his word: He signed the EU agreement, secured the IMF loan, and discarded the necessity to negotiate on any of its conditions—before any elections had even taken place.[2]

To understand what this would entail for a country like Ukraine, let us start with some words about the nature of the IMF. Voting power is determined by a one-dollar-one-vote system. Japan and seven NATO countries have a majority vote, while the United States, with 23.6% of the vote, is the only country with veto power. (Changes to the mandate require an 85% majority).[3] By comparison, all the BRICS countries combined—Brazil, Russia, India, China and South Africa, who constitute approximately 42 percent of the global population—together have less than 8 percent of the IMF vote.[4] Though the IMF and World Bank purport to be international organizations, every managing director of the IMF has come from a NATO country. Even more striking, every single president in the history of its sister institution, the World Bank, has come from the United States, including a former Secretary of Defense. Zbigniew Brzezinski, the foremost political strategist of the democratic establishment in Washington, put it bluntly: "One must consider as part of the American system the global web of specialized organizations, especially the 'international' financial institutions. The International Monetary Fund (IMF) and the World Bank can be said to represent "global" interests, and their constituency may be construed as the world. In reality, however, they are heavily American dominated and their origins are traceable to American initiative, particularly the Bretton Woods Conference of 1944."[5]

George Kennan, commonly referred to as a moderate dove within the US political spectrum, wrote the following in 1948 when he worked for the US State Department:

> We have about 50% of the world's wealth but only 6.3 of its population. ... Our real task in the coming period is to devise a pattern of relationships, which will permit us to maintain this position of disparity without positive detriment to our national security. To do so we will have to dispense with all sentimentality and daydreaming; and our attention will have to be concentrated everywhere on our immediate national objectives. ... We should cease to talk about vague—and for the Far East—unreal objectives such as human rights, the raising of the living standards, and democratization. The day is not far off when we are going to have to deal in straight power concepts. The less we are hampered by idealistic slogans, the better.[6]

A similar mentality could be seen in the World Bank when, in an internal memo, its Chief economist Larry Summers wrote the following:

Just between you and me should, shouldn't the World Bank be encouraging more migration of the dirty industries to the LDC's [Less-developed countries]?... I think the economic logic behind dumping a load of toxic waste in the lowest wage country is impeccable and we should face up to that... I've always thought that underpopulated countries in Africa are vastly under-polluted, their air quality is probably vastly inefficiently low compared to Los Angeles or Mexico City. The concern over an agent that causes a one in a million change in the odds of prostate cancer is obviously going to be much higher in a country where people survive to get prostate cancer than in a country where under 5 mortality is 200 per thousand... the problem with the arguments against all of these proposals for more pollution in LDC's (intrinsic rights to certain goods, moral reasons, social concerns, lack of adequate markets etc.) could be turned around and used more or less effectively against every Bank proposal for liberalization.[7]

Two-thirds of the world's economies are controlled or have been controlled by the World Bank and the IMF.[8] These institutions became especially intrusive from the 80's onwards when their loans became conditional upon extensive 'structural adjustment programs,' serving as the main vehicles for the globalization of neoliberal capitalism. The standard package involved radical cuts in government spending—including welfare and health care—accompanied by extensive trade and market liberalization, which opened up the country for foreign capital. In the year 1950, profits from the rest of the world amounted to only a tenth of domestic profits in the US. From the 80s onwards, this income from the rest of the world sky-rocketed to a steady 80 percent of domestic profits on average, having doubled in just a few years in the early 1980s.[9] The last decades of IMF and World Bank rule have been characterized by lower growth rates, stagnating quality of life indicators, rising inequality and accelerating deforestation nearly across the board.[10] For example, between 1994 and 2003—at the pinnacle of IMF and World Bank influence—the World Bank admitted to a shocking 75 percent rise in the number of Africans living under poverty.[11] Overall GDP declined as well.

Cambridge economist Ha-Joon Chang convincingly documented how trade and market liberalization have historically been the result of economic development, rather than the cause.[12] The reason is simple: only advanced industries are able to compete without state intervention. He also demonstrates that the Structural Adjustment Programs closely resemble so-called "unequal trade agreements," which were forced on many countries of the global south in the 19th century by the barrel of a gun. In fact, neoliberal theory quite explicitly preserves the post-colonial system. The inability of countries to export anything else than raw materials is taken as a given, and efficiency is subsequently maximized within that given context. In other words, such countries should not attempt to produce high-technology products in the medium or long-term future, but should produce and export unprocessed oil and food as efficiently as possible in the here and now.

Admittedly, even food production has been wiped out in many of these countries, as they were flooded by subsidized foodstuffs from the United States and Europe, which, hypocritically, remain protected. Perhaps the failure of these Structural Adjustment Programs (SAPs) is best captured by a 3-year multi-country study released in 2002 by the Structural Adjustment Participatory Review International Network, in collaboration with none other than the World Bank itself. The report concluded that:

> [SAP's have been] expanding poverty, inequality and insecurity around the world...[They have]

Imposing Austerity 73

torn at the heart of economies and the social fabric. Increasing tensions among different social strata, fueling extremist movements and de-legitimizing democratic principles. Their effects particularly on the poor are so profound and pervasive that no amount of targeted social investment can begin to address the social crisis they have engendered.[13]

Regardless, these countries are expected to pay exorbitant interest rates. Between 1980 and 1996, Sub-Saharan Africa paid twice the sum of its total debt in the form of interest, yet still ended up owing three times more in 1996 than it did in 1980.[14] The result is that a lot of government revenue has to be allocated to interest repayments. The Sri Lankan government, for example, spent 67 percent of its 2013 budget on debt servicing, while a total of 15 percent went to health, education and social protection.[15] Increasing debt invites new loans from the IMF and World Bank —all tied to structural adjustment programs. This vicious cycle has led third world debt to boom more than ten-fold, from $400 billion as of 1980 to a whopping $5.5 trillion as of 2013.[16] Entire nations are trapped in economic deadlocks—and many entered these agreements unwillingly in the first place. Indeed, 41 countries are still paying for debts incurred under the rule of dictatorships, most of which received loans from the IMF.[17]

The overall impact of the structural adjustment programs has been damning, even on narrow economic terms. During 1960-1980, per capita income in the developing countries grew by 3.0% annually, the best they have ever achieved. During 1980-2005, this nearly halved to an annual growth rate of 1.7%. The countries to buck the global trend of economic stagnation were, almost exclusively, those who managed to avoid the IMF and World Bank, such as China. Indeed, income per capita in Latin America grew by more than 80 percent from 1960-1979, but only about 11 percent from 1980-2000, and 3 percent for 2000-2005. In Sub-Saharan Africa, per capita income grew by 36 percent from 1960-1980. But from 1980-2000, income per capita actually declined—a rare event in modern economic history over a 20-year period—by about 15 percent.[18] Indeed, the "hegemony" of the 'American system,' in Brzezinski's words, is arguably more unequal and exploitative than formal colonialism. For every dollar of aid given to the global south, $15 flow back to the north through tax avoidance, unequal trade agreements and debt payments.[19] During the period of formal administrative colonialism, the gap between the richest countries and the poorest countries widened from 3:1 to 30:1. The "American system" was able to widen that gap to 74:1 by 1997, in mere decades.[20]

Within this context, it was easy for anyone to predict what would happen in Ukraine, when Yatsenyuk promised he'd become "the most unpopular prime minister in the history of my country." Indeed, the IMF had harsh demands. In 2014, the two biggest expenditure items—social payments and spending on education—were cut by 5 percent, and spending on health care by seven percent. Accompanied with a 12 percent inflation rate this put these cuts at around 17 percent.[21] But it didn't stop there. Inflation hit another 49 percent in 2015—the highest Ukraine had seen in 19 years—while nominal budgets for health, social payments and education stayed close to 2013 levels, leading to cuts in real terms between 27 and 33 percent.[22] In addition, funding for environmental protection was cut by approximately 41 percent in real terms compared to 2013.

The austerity effects were quickly felt: ten percent of civil servants were laid off, pensions decreased and child support abolished. Minimum wages were frozen for two years until September 2015, when they were just slightly increased despite the major currency devaluation. The result was shocking: even after the long delayed pay raise, the minimum wage had still plummeted by 32 percent in real terms since December 2013.[23] Dmitry Chistyakov, a reporter for the Ukrainian TV show "Utro" ("Morning"), lived on the minimum salary for a month, concluding that "You cannot live like this, you can barely survive." He was forced to cut back on food and lost 10 kilograms within 30 days, yet still regarded himself as lucky due to the good weather:

"To buy warmer clothing, one would have to save for months." Notably, he didn't even have to pay any rent, because he owned his apartment. The average monthly rent for a studio apartment in Kiev is nearly five times the minimum monthly wage.[24] Ukraine's first president, Leonid Kravchuk, stated that living standards in Ukraine had fallen by half since Maidan.[25] According to KIIS surveys, the percentage of Ukrainians unable to afford food rose from 9 percent before Maidan to 19 percent by May 2015.[26] All of this was hardly in the popular interest. A KIIS poll from the spring of 2015 showed that only a quarter of Ukrainians was prepared to suffer from economic reforms, *under the condition that this would lead to increased prosperity for the country.* Half of those polled did not expect any positive changes from the reforms.[27]

In point of fact, Ukraine is among the poorer countries in the world. In 2014, its per capita GDP was about half that of worn-torn Iraq and Libya—and well under the world's average.[28] And this is only worsening. In 2015, Ukraine's economy shrank by another 10 percent.[29] The projected one percent GDP growth for 2016 would be but a drop in the bucket. Ukraine's public debt hit 79 percent by the end of 2015, doubled from just 40 percent in 2013.[30] Indeed, money spent on interest payments on public debt increased by almost 50 percent in real terms since 2013, now taking a vastly larger share of the state budget than payments for health care.[31] The dedication not to default no doubt pleased European banks, which had more than 23 billion euros of outstanding loans when Yanukovych was ousted.[32] Indeed, making sure that western banks are paid in full has always been the highest priority of the IMF, according to Joseph Stiglitz, former chief economist of the World Bank.[33]

To counterbalance this, in November 2015, foreign corporations agreed to a haircut of 20 percent—as happened in a number of developing countries since the late 90s—saving Ukraine $3 billion. But this hardly created a sustainable situation. Much of the savings on the health, education and welfare budgets were offset by the tripling of nominal interest payments. Combined with a huge increase in military spending—which more than doubled since 2013 in real terms—total government expenditure was barely reduced.[34] Furthermore, the haircuts came with strings attached. If the Ukrainian economy were to grow by three to four percent in real terms, 15 percent of that growth will be paid out to private foreign creditors as a bonus. If real GDP increases by more than 4 percent within a given year, a whopping 40 percent will have to be paid out as a bonus, shattering any dreams of servicing the debts.[35]

Much of the aforementioned inflation was due to the fact that, under pressure of the IMF, the Hryvnia, the national currency of Ukraine, was allowed to fluctuate freely.[36] Its value to the US dollar plummeted by 75 percent within a year, triggering major inflation due to Ukraine's dependency on imported goods.[37] On top of this, the currency devaluation was solely responsible for raising the level of public debt by 20 percent of GDP, simply because most of the loans were denominated in foreign currencies.[38] As of 2013, this was also the case for a third of private sector loans, leading to many defaults among households and businesses.[39] Indeed, over 50 percent of the banks' portfolios are now estimated to consist of toxic assets.[40] As a result, much of the IMF money is spent on "emergency liquidity assistance" to keep Ukrainian banks afloat.

This all sounds awfully familiar. In an extensive study on the Ukrainian economy, Oleksandr Kravchuk and a number of other economists documented how foreign currency loans had been essential for triggering the 2008-9 crisis, when Ukraine saw the worst economic recession in the world, on par with Lithuania.[41] By the end of 2006, the real estate bubble had reached some 400% of Ukrainian GDP, at a time when even the "bloated" US market was set at 160%.[42] This was largely caused by the entry of foreign banks and speculative capital, which doubled the amount of foreign currency loans in Ukraine between 2005 and September 2008.[43] Unfortunately, such loans only continued to increase after the financial crisis, despite some governmental attempts to lower its dependency on foreign currency lending. When Kiev then released the Hryvnia under IMF pressure, between 2014-15, Ukraine's public debt in foreign currencies exploded by nearly threefold. As Kravchuk et al. rightly conclude: "fulfilling debt obligations has become practically impossible in the long term."[44]

The logical result is that Ukraine's credit raitings have significantly decreased, giving the IMF tremendous leverage over the administration.[45] The situation has also made the country more vulnerable to speculative capital, with foreign hedge funds cashing in on the free-floating Hryvnia. As a 100-page report by The Vienna Institute for International Economic Studies (wiiw), funded by the Central Bank of Austria and a myriad of major international banks and corporations, pointed out: "The foreign exchange market continues to be rather 'thin', with only a few currency speculators able to generate substantial exchange rate fluctuations—a task made nowadays particularly easy because of the military conflict and the related 'bearish' market sentiments."[46]

Gas prices were also raised, in a combined speed and magnitude that has arguably been unprecedented in history. The aim was to arrive at 'cost-recovery' levels—meaning equal to import prices—before April 2017.[47] This would eliminate the massive implicit subsidies paid annually by the Ukrainian state, estimated at $8.5 billion in 2013, representing a whopping 4.6 percent of GDP and more than the entire social welfare budget of that year.[48] Due to a marked decline in European gas prices the target was achieved in 2016, one year ahead of time; albeit with a still enormous tariff hike of approximately 540 percent in real terms.[49] Electricity prices were also increased substantially.[50] Even though significant subsidies were made available for lower income households—to the tune of $2 billion—over 80 percent of Ukrainians now say they are unable to pay their utility bills, and only six percent understand the necessity for the tariff hikes.[51] In a February 2017 wiiw report, Vasily Astrov and Leon Podkaminer concur that the price increases have been far higher than necessary. While the cost-recovery tarriffs are measured at import-price levels, by 2015 Ukraine's total residential gas consumption had actually become lower than domestic production.[52] Indeed, that same year, the state gas company Naftogaz already earned a major profit of $1 billion; and the wiiw study estimates this to rise to the tune of $2 billion annually after the 2016 tariff hikes.[53]

The steep prices prompted a government minister to urge rural Ukrainian residents to stop heating their homes with gas at all, their primary source of heating.[54] Indeed, to some extent, this is already happening, as residential gas consumption dropped by approximately one-third.[55] As the wiiw-linked economist Vasily Astrov points out:

> At face value, the observed reduction in residential gas consumption over the past two years in response to the price shock could be interpreted as evidence of success of the government strategy. However, this reduction has been essentially achieved at the expense of lower heating standards: a smaller number of rooms being heated, a lower temperature in rooms which are heated, and a shorter heating season. All of this essentially meant some degree of sacrifice on the part of consumers: to save on their energy bills, they had to accept lower living standards.[56]

Admittedly, the reason the IMF wants the energy subsidies phased out eventually is reasonable. Ukraine's economy is amongst the most energy-intensive in the world, its costs weighing heavily on its economy and the state budget. In addition, Ukraine is primarily dependent on Russian energy which jeopardizes its independence. Nevertheless, as the wiiw report points out:

> As long as households continue using old Soviet-style heating infrastructure which does not allow to regulate the temperature, any hopes for a [meaningful] reduction in energy consumption in response to tariff hikes may be elusive. [Rather, the hikes should accompany investments in insulation, the installation of heating metres etc.] Government subsidies along these lines would be crucial in solving the long-term structural

problem of excessive energy consumption, and should enjoy priority over the short-term task of fiscal consolidation (which is probably the real motivation for the implemented tariff hikes).[57] [round brackets in the original]

Notably, the reform agenda also had a profound impact on the revenue side of governance. In order to improve the "ease of doing business," corporate social contributions were cut in half, import taxes abolished and taxes on extractive industries lowered.[58] In their extensive study of the post-Maidan economy, Oleksandr Kravchuk et al. documented a significant "tendency to transfer the tax burden from companies to individuals."[59] In January-February 2015, for example, collected personal income taxes more than tripled compared to the same months in 2014, while the collected corporate profit taxes decreased by 37 percent.[60] Furthermore, regressive indirect taxes—such as VAT and excise, which simply raise the prices of goods and as such disproportionally hit the poor—are responsible for increasingly large parts of Ukraine's state revenue.[61]

It is important to emphasize that when under the 2004 constitution of Ukraine, which was re-enforced after the ouster of Yanukovych, the prime minister wields the most influence over economic and financial policy. As Nuland asserted, 'Yats is the guy who's got the economic experience,' which is why he got the post. But American interference would become even more blatant. Echoing several earlier Ukrainian media reports, including pro-government sources, Bloomberg View wrote that "Americans are highly visible in the Ukrainian political process. The U.S. embassy in Kiev is a center of power, and Ukrainian politicians openly talk of appointments and dismissals being vetted by U.S. Ambassador Geoffrey Pyatt and even U.S. Vice President Joe Biden."[62]

Indeed, the former US official Natalie Jaresko was appointed as Ukraine's finance minister. Other foreign appointments in the Kiev administartion included top Slovak and Polish politicians, respectively Ivan Mikloš and Leszek

Balcerowicz.[63] The latter was chiefly responsible for implementing economic shock therapy in Poland during the 90s, whose devastating impact on the Polish economy and social fabric is often misconstrued.[64] According to several Ukrainian media reports, the foreign appointments were encouraged by US vice-president Joe Biden.[65]

A Poroshenko Bloc MP affirmed that, compared to normal lobbyists, US ambassador "Pyatt is a different story. You cannot say no to him." In fact, it seems that Ukraine has turned into a US client state. A deputy minister serving for the Poroshenko Bloc told RBC-Ukraine: "Geoffrey Pyatt meets with the boss [Poroshenko] approximately once every two weeks. I was present during one of such meetings. It lasted 15 minutes. The ambassador immediately took out his notes and in a firm manner pointed out the actions to be taken. After this, the boss shortly elaborated upon what has already been done."[66] The kind of 'actions to be taken' were elaborated upon by Joe Biden, during a speech to the Ukrainian parliament on December 2015:

> For Ukraine to continue to make progress and to keep the support of the international community you have to do more, as well. The big part is moving forward with your IMF program—it requires difficult reforms. And they are difficult.
> Let me say parenthetically here, all the experts from our State Department and all the think tanks, they come and tell you, that you know what you should do is you should deal with pensions. You should deal with—as if it's easy to do. Hell, we're having trouble in America dealing with it. We're having trouble. To vote to raise the pension age is to write your political obituary in many places.
> Don't misunderstand that those of us who serve in other democratic institutions don't understand how hard the conditions are, how difficult it is to cast some of the votes to meet

the obligations committed to under the IMF. It requires sacrifices that might not be politically expedient or popular. But they're critical to putting Ukraine on the path to a future that is economically secure. And I urge you to stay the course as hard as it is. Ukraine needs a budget that's consistent with your IMF commitments.[67]

Endnotes

1 Yatsenyuk: I'll Be Ukraine's Least Popular PM. (2014, February 27). Retrieved from http://www.bloomberg.com/news/videos/b/0ec700b1-6b37-4cc2-b030-d23f8c5a7967
2 The conditions of the IMF loans can be read in a series of memoranda of understanding, available on the IMF website. Ukraine and the IMF. (2016, February 11). Retrieved February 13, 2016, from https://www.imf.org/external/country/ukr/index.htm?type=23
3 IMF Members' Quotas and Voting Power, and IMF Board of Governors. (2016, February 13). Retrieved February 13, 2016, from https://www.imf.org/external/np/sec/memdir/members.aspx
4 Ibid.
5 Brzezinski, Z. (1998). The Grand Chessboard: American Primacy and Its Geostrategic Imperatives. Basic Books, p. 27.
6 Memo PPS23 by George Kennan. (2013, September 28). Retrieved from https://en.wikisource.org/wiki/Memo_PPS23_by_George_Kennan#cite_note-1
7 Summers, L. (2001). Our Words: The Lawrence Summers Memo. Retrieved from http://www.whirledbank.org/ourwords/summers.html
8 Pieper, U., & Taylor, L. (1998). The revival of the liberal creed: the IMF, the World Bank, and inequality in a globalized economy. Globalization and progressive economic policy, 37-63, p. 37.
9 Harvey, D. (2005). A brief history of neoliberalism. OUP Oxford, p. 30.
10 Vreeland, J. R. (2002). The effect of IMF programs on labor. World Development, 30(1), 121-139; Easterly, W. (2000). The effect of IMF and World Bank programs on poverty. Available at SSRN 256883; Vreeland, J. R., Sturm, R. K., Raymond, J., Robynn, V., Sturm, K., & Durbin, S. W. (2001). The Effect of IMF Programs on Deforestation; Przeworski, A., & Vreeland, J. R. (2000). The effect of IMF programs on economic growth. Journal of development Economics, 62(2), 385-

	421; Weisbrot, M., Baker, D., & Rosnick, D. (2006). The scorecard on development: 25 years of diminished progress. International Journal of Health Services,36(2), 211-234.
11	Ismi, A. (2004). Impoverishing a continent: The World Bank and the IMF in Africa. Canadian Centre for Policy Alternatives, p. 11.
12	Chang, H. J. (2002). Kicking away the ladder: development strategy in historical perspective. Anthem Press; Chang, H. J. (2007). Bad Samaritans: The myth of free trade and the secret history of capitalism. Bloomsbury Publishing USA.
13	Ismi, A. (2004). Impoverishing a continent: The World Bank and the IMF in Africa. Canadian Centre for Policy Alternatives, pp. 5-6.
14	Monbiot, G. (2004). The Age of Consent. Harper Perennial, p. 157.
15	IMF figures are compiled by http://www.governmentspendingwatch.org/ For the debt servicing only planned spending figures were available.
16	International DEBT Statistics (Rep.). (2015). Retrieved from World Bank website: http://data.worldbank.org/sites/default/files/ids2015.pdf
17	Gottiniaux, P., Toussaint, E., Sanabria, A., & Munevar, D. (2015, March 31). World Debt Figures 2015 (Rep.), pp. 39-41. Retrieved from Committee for the Abolition of Third World Debt website: http://cadtm.org/World-Debt-Figures-2015; Use of IMF credit (DOD, current US$). (n.d.). Retrieved February 13, 2016, from http://data.worldbank.org/indicator/DT.DOD.DIMF.CD
18	Figures can be found in Bad Samaritans: The Myth of Free Trade and the Secret History of Capitalism. Bloomsbury Publishing USA. They are also documented in Weisbrot, M., Baker, D., & Rosnick, D. (2006). The scorecard on development: 25 years of diminished progress. International Journal of Health Services,36(2), 211-234.
19	Calculation done by The Rules based on data from World Bank, OECD, Global Financial Integrity, Robert Pollin. Inequality Video Fact Sheet. (2013). Retrieved from http://therules.org/inequality-video-fact-sheet/
20	Jolly, R. (1999). Humand Development Report 1999 (Rep.), p. 3. Retrieved from United Nations website: http://web.archive.org/web/20120304122637/http://hdr.undp.org/en/media/HDR_1999_EN.pdf
21	Adarov, A., Astrov, V., Havlik, P., Hunya, G., Landesmann, M., & Podkaminer, L. (2015). How to Stabilise the Economy of Ukraine. wiiw and United Europe, April, p. 19.
22	For inflation figures consult State Statistics Service of Ukraine. Індекси споживчих цін у 1993 - 2010рр. (до відповідного періоду попереднього року). (2016). Retrieved from http://www.ukrstat.

gov.ua/operativ/operativ2006/ct/cn_rik/isc/isc_u/isc_per_u_.htm; For government expenditure consult Ukraine's Ministry of Finance. Execution of the budget of Ukraine 2014/2015. (2015, December 30). Retrieved from http://www.minfin.gov.ua/en/news/view/pokazniki-vikonannja-bjudzhetu-ukraini-20142015-rik?category=bjudzhet

23 Minimum Wages in Ukraine with effect from 01-01-2016 to 30-07-2016. (2016, January 28). Retrieved from http://www.wageindicator.org/main/salary/minimum-wage/ukraine

24 Salaries and Costs of Living in Ukraine. (2015, September 20). Retrieved from http://blogs.elenasmodels.com/en/salaries-and-costs-of-living-in-ukraine/

25 Украина готова к неповиновению и взрыву. (2016, January 18). Retrieved from http://112.ua/interview/ukraina-gotova-k-nepovinoveniyu-i-vzryvu-285795.html

26 Kharchenko, N., & Paniotto, V. (2015, May 17). Ukrainian Society (May 2015). Retrieved from http://www.kiis.com.ua/?lang=eng

27 Kharchenko, N., & Paniotto, V. (2015, May). Ukrainian Society May 2015, slide 11. Retrieved from http://www.kiis.com.ua/?lang=eng&cat=reports&id=529&page=1&t=7

28 World Bank Data.

29 Ukraine: Reforms Helped to Stabilize Economy, but Continued and Faster Reforms are Key. (2015, October 5), slide 7. Retrieved from http://www.worldbank.org/en/news/press-release/2015/10/05/ukraine-macroeconomic-update-october-2015

30 Popina, E., & Doff, N. (2015, June 25). Goldman Sees Ukraine Default in July as Debt Standoff Holds. Retrieved from http://www.bloomberg.com/news/articles/2015-06-25/goldman-sees-ukraine-in-solvency-crisis-likely-default-in-july-ibbnk177

31 For government expenditure consult Ukraine's Ministry of Finance. Execution of the budget of Ukraine 2014/2015. (2015, December 30). Retrieved from http://www.minfin.gov.ua/en/news/view/pokazniki-vikonannja-bjudzhetu-ukraini-20142015-rik?category=bjudzhet

32 Luhn, A. (2014, April 07). Will the IMF Bailout Turn Ukraine Into Another Greece? Retrieved from http://www.thenation.com/article/will-imf-bailout-turn-ukraine-another-greece/

33 Hari, J. (2003, November 10). Joseph Stiglitz—An Interview. Retrieved from http://johannhari.com/2003/11/10/joseph-stiglitz-an-interview/

34 For government expenditure consult Ukraine's Ministry of Finance. Execution of the budget of Ukraine 2014/2015. (2015, December 30). Retrieved from http://www.minfin.gov.ua/en/news/view/pokazniki-vikonannja-bjudzhetu-ukraini-20142015-rik?category=bjudzhet

35	Україна та Спеціальний комітет кредиторів погодили попередні умови для реструктуризації державних та гарантованих державою єврооблігацій. (2015, August 27). Retrieved from http://www.minfin.gov.ua/news/view/ukraina-ta-specialnij-komitet-kreditoriv-pogodili-poperedni-umovi-dlja-restrukturizacii-derzhavnih-ta-garantovanih-derzhavoju-evroobligacij?category=borg
36	IMF Survey : Ukraine Unveils Reform Program with IMF Support. (2014, April 30). Retrieved from https://www.imf.org/external/pubs/ft/survey/so/2014/new043014a.htm
37	Adarov, A., Astrov, V., Havlik, P., Hunya, G., Landesmann, M., & Podkaminer, L. (2015). How to Stabilise the Economy of Ukraine. wiiw and United Europe, April, p. 15.
38	Ibid, p. 16. Exact breakdown of the creditors is available at the Ukrainian Ministry of Finance website. Статистичні матеріали щодо державного та гарантованого державою боргу України станом на 31.12.2015. (2016, January 31). Retrieved from http://www.minfin.gov.ua/news/view/statystychni-materialy-shchodo-derzhavnoho-ta-harantovanoho-derzhavoiu-borhu-ukrainy-u--rotsi?category=borg
39	Adarov, A., Astrov, V., Havlik, P., Hunya, G., Landesmann, M., & Podkaminer, L. (2015). How to Stabilise the Economy of Ukraine. wiiw and United Europe, April, p. 16.
40	Petro, N. N. (2016). Why Ukraine and Russia Need Each Other. Russian Politics, 1(2), 184-202.
41	Kravchuk, O., Hladun, A., Dudin, V., Dutchak, O., Neboha, M., Odosiy, O., & Popovych, Z. (2016). Alternative mechanisms for the socio-economic development of Ukraine. Kiev: Center for Social and Labor Research, 2016.
42	Ibid, p. 16.
43	Ibid, p. 16.
44	Ibid, p. 27.
45	Ibid, pp. 20-21.
46	Adarov, A., Astrov, V., Havlik, P., Hunya, G., Landesmann, M., & Podkaminer, L. (2015). How to Stabilise the Economy of Ukraine. wiiw and United Europe, April, p. 17.
47	Ibid. p. 21.
48	Rozwałka, P., & Tordengren, H. (2016, July). The Ukrainian residential gas sector: A market untapped (Rep.), p. 19. Retrieved from Oxford Institute for Energy Studies website: https://www.oxfordenergy.org/wpcms/wp-content/uploads/2016/07/The-Ukrainian-residential-gas-sector-a-market-untapped-NG-109.pdf
49	Astrov, V., & Podkaminer, L. (2017, February). Energy Tariff Reform in Ukraine: Estimated Effects and Policy Options (Rep.). Retrieved

	http://wiiw.ac.at/energy-tariff-reform-in-ukraine-estimated-effects-and-policy-options-p-4124.html
50	Wesolowsky, O., & Komarova, T. (2016, March 1). Electric Shock: Ukraine Dramatically Raises Utility Rates. Retrieved from http://www.rferl.org/a/ukraine-raises-electricty-rates-household/27583618.html
51	Отношение украинцев к повышению тарифов. (2016, July 1). Retrieved from http://rb.com.ua/rus/projects/omnibus/9118/; Astrov, V. (2016, August 11). Energy tariff reform in Ukraine: going too far? Retrieved from http://www.financialobserver.eu/cse-and-cis/energy-tariff-reform-in-ukraine-going-too-far/
52	Astrov, V., & Podkaminer, L. (2017, February). Energy Tariff Reform in Ukraine: Estimated Effects and Policy Options (Rep.). Retrieved http://wiiw.ac.at/energy-tariff-reform-in-ukraine-estimated-effects-and-policy-options-p-4124.html
53	Ibid.
54	For the statement of the government minister consult Сельским жителям посоветовали отказаться от газа. (2016, May 6). Retrieved from http://korrespondent.net/ukraine/3679023-selskym-zhyteliam-posovetovaly-otkazatsia-ot-haza
55	Approximately one-third of this decrease can be explained by the de-facto secession of Crimea and parts of Donbass. Rozwałka, P., & Tordengren, H. (2016, July). The Ukrainian residential gas sector: A market untapped (Rep.), p. 2. Retrieved from Oxford Institute for Energy Studies website: https://www.oxfordenergy.org/wpcms/wp-content/uploads/2016/07/The-Ukrainian-residential-gas-sector-a-market-untapped-NG-109.pdf Furthermore, Astrov and Podkaminer (2017) estimate another 9 percent drop due to the 2016 tarriff hikes; they also show that non-energy consumption has decreased due to the higher utility bills.
56	Astrov, V. (2016, August 11). Energy tariff reform in Ukraine: going too far? Retrieved from http://www.financialobserver.eu/cse-and-cis/energy-tariff-reform-in-ukraine-going-too-far/
57	Adarov, A., Astrov, V., Havlik, P., Hunya, G., Landesmann, M., & Podkaminer, L. (2015). How to Stabilise the Economy of Ukraine. wiiw and United Europe, April, p. 23.
58	Mast, J., Beek, B., Van, Ploeg, C., De, & Beunders, S. (2016, March 22). 'Het beleid van het IMF doet meer kwaad dan goed in Oekraïne' Retrieved from https://www.ftm.nl/artikelen/imf-oekraine
59	Kravchuk, O., Hladun, A., Dudin, V., Dutchak, O., Neboha, M., Odosiy, O., & Popovych, Z. (2016), p. 26. Alternative mechanisms for the socio-economic development of Ukraine. Kiev: Center for Social

and Labor Research, 2016.
60　Ibid, p. 26.
61　Ibid.
62　Bershidsky, L. (2015, November 6). Ukraine Is in Danger of Becoming a Failed State. Retrieved from http://www.bloombergview.com/articles/2015-11-06/unreformed-ukraine-is-self-destructing
63　Порошенко ввел в Кабмин польского реформатора. (2016, April 22). Retrieved from http://korrespondent.net/ukraine/politics/3673317-poroshenko-vvel-v-kabmyn-polskoho-reformatora
64　For a discussion of the impact of the Polish economic shock therapy see Adarov, A., Astrov, V., Havlik, P., Hunya, G., Landesmann, M., & Podkaminer, L. (2015). How to Stabilise the Economy of Ukraine. wiiw and United Europe, April, pp. 24-31.
65　Analysis and links provided by Katchanovski, I. (2016, April 22). Facebook. Retrieved from https://www.facebook.com/ivan.katchanovski/posts/883905151639372
66　Kamenev, M., & Speicher, T. (2015, August 13). Ротация Кабмина: роль США и торги за Конституцию. Retrieved from https://www.rbc.ua/rus/analytics/rotatsiya-kabmina-rol-ssha-torgi-konstitutsiyu-1439464418.html
67　Biden, J. (2015, December 9). Remarks by Vice President Joe Biden to The Ukrainian Rada. Retrieved from https://www.whitehouse.gov/the-press-office/2015/12/09/remarks-vice-president-joe-biden-ukrainian-rada

| Chapter Eight |

CONDONING CORRUPTION

Further elaborating on the US governmental vetting process, a representative of the Ukrainian presidential administration told RBC-Ukraine: "The crucial positions in government the president discusses with Pyatt. For example, the resignation of Nalivaichenko [head of Security Service of Ukraine] was fully agreed with the [US] ambassador."[1] Notably, in an interview just days after his dismissal, Nalivaichenko indicated what might have been the reasons for same:

> Officials on the highest level have not stepped back from business ties, but it's not just business, not just accountants, who are using these [offshore] schemes, but also the 'enforcers' [informal parliamentary party whips] who run $500,000 through offshores each week. A simple question—where is this money going to? The answer: to pay off MPs, government officials, law enforcement.
>
> People who for many years have not run the most transparent businesses (...) have taken power together with their corrupt offshore schemes and set up a cynical system. They take a cut in the sale of [government] posts, and at night send the profits to offshores.[2]

He also accused the financial inspectors of malpractice, affirming that "I have not yet seen a single offshore closed." He continued. "As soon as I and my colleagues have documented and caught the trail of this particular offshore corruption scheme—in fact, the explicit use of power by people from the business circle—we immediately became a target. They began to call for interrogation of other cases, insisted to give in documents, another obstacle appeared as well. As a consequence, I said to myself, 'Enough being a part of such a regime!'. I decided it was time to fight it. Since I was not given this investigation and was removed from the position of head of the SBU (Security Service of Ukraine), I will find alternative methods."[3]

A similar story was told by the Czech investor, Tomas Fiala, founder of Kiev's largest brokerage, Dragon Capital, and head of the European Business Association. In an interview, he claimed that the ruling parties had only a few competent professionals among their ranks—to write the laws and face the cameras—while most of the backbenchers (the Ukrainian parliament has 450 seats) had paid for their entrance, motivated by business interests.

> They [the pro-Western parties] were selling seats on the party lists (...) they filled up the back of the list for $3mn-$10mn contributions [per seat] to finance the campaign.
> Having these people with very questionable reputations, who were very much tied to the old Ukraine, being re-elected is now haunting them and hurting their political capital.[4]

In fact, these kinds of schemes have long become institutionalized in Ukraine, driving Ukraine's massive shadow economy to nearly half of GDP.[5] A well-constructed study by Graham Stacks, published in the peer-reviewed *Journal of Money Laundering Control*, gives a good insight into this 'black money' market. The conversion of black money has been outsourced to so-called 'conversion centers,' which are specialized in the practise of disappearing currency—useful for tax evasion or the embezzlement of state funds. According to the head of Ukraine's tax service, through 2014, Ukraine's conversion centers had a turnover of approximately 28 billion Euros, roughly one-seventh of GDP.[6] Over half arose from "the sale of fraudulently created tax credits", and 30-40 percent derived from the embezzlement of state funds. This does not represent the total amount of embezzled money, as the conversion centers normally take a 5-15 percent cut for their services—implying an absolutely huge amount of embezzlement.[7] These figures might however be inflated. A leaked report by Ukraine's security service put the total annual turnover of conversion centers at roughly $7.5 billion in 2011.[8] Nevertheless, even taking the lowest figures, this implies that $15 billion of state funds were embezzled in 2014—more than three times the amount of IMF assistance. Stacks draws the inevitable conclusion: "state officials tolerate institutionalised tax evasion because they use the same institutional arrangements to embezzle state funds. As a result, an equilibrium is reached whereby conversion centers help deplete state expenditure as well as state revenue."[9]

In theory, this conversion center industry could serve as an internal tax haven, but due to its enormous size illicit international flows become necessary. There's a simple reason: international banks can more easily 'break the chain' so that the illicit funds cannot be traced by the authorities. As Ukraine's state financial monitoring service asserts: "Moving funds offshore and moving them onshore with subsequent conversion to cash for the purpose of breaking the chain [is] one of the biggest current problems in the economy."[10] Here is where the incredible irony comes in: international banks situated in the hawkish Baltic States (EU members) facilitate the money laundering. Stacks analyzed three case studies of conversion centers, which were eventually shut down by the Ukrainian authorities. Between 2005 and 2014, they collectively laundered over $3 billion of black cash—viewed by Stacks as a very conservative estimate, as no data was available for most years. The catch: "the [post-Maidan] chairman of the Ukrainian parliamentary sub-committee on questions of anti-money laundering and financial monitoring is co-owner of a Latvian bank linked to all thee case studies."[11] As Stacks concludes: "While the market in "conversion" services is divvied up anew after changes in government, the constellation of banks centered in the Baltics, providing the nexus between Ukraine's shadow economy and the global financial system, has remained constant, as different administrations in Kiev have come and gone. This underscores the extent to which Ukraine's underground "black cash" system is anchored internationally, generating billions of dollars of illicit international flows."[12]

Notably, legalized forms of tax evasion are also facilitated by the Netherlands and Cyprus, both EU member states; by Switzerland, a member of the common European market; by Belize and the British Virgin Islands.[13] These countries either have substantially lower tax rates than Ukraine, or (in the case of the Netherlands) facilitate the tax-free in- and out-flow of income to other countries that do not have tax agreements with Ukraine. As a result, Ukrainian oligarchs set up shell companies in these states— and invest in their own countries from there, in order to make use of these favourable tax regimes. This is how the curious development arises that, as of 2014, about half of Ukraine's Foreign Direct Investment (comprising 50 percent of Ukrainian GDP) came from the tiny Netherlands, Cyprus, Switzerland, Belize and the Virgin Islands.[14] The Ukrainian economist Alexander Liakhovich calculated that, accounting only for trade in grains and oilseeds between 2012 and September 2015, approximately $1.5-1.7 billion of state revenue were lost due to tax schemes like these.[15] Ironically, while the Dutch minister of foreign affairs visited the encampments at Maidan, the Dutch embassy was sending around invitations for a free "event [that] brings together Ukrainian businesses ... and provides a practical update on their (tax) efficient structuring using the Dutch companies."[16] As of 2012, over 95 percent of Dutch FDI flows to Ukraine concerned 'Special Financial Institutions.' In other words: shell companies avoiding taxation.[17] As Cambridge economist Ha-Joon Chang demonstrated, corruption normally does not severely harm economies as long as the bribes are re-invested into the local economy. It is exactly these kinds of off-shore schemes that truly devastate the Ukrainian economy.[18]

Returning to US influence, Nikolay Tomenko, an MP elected on Proshenko's party ticket, affirmed that: "The USA has provided evaluation of ministers with whose progress they are satisfied. This list includes Natalia Jaresko (Minister of Finance), Aivaras Abromavichus (Economy Ministry), Aleksei Pavelko (Minister of Agrarian Policy and Food) who promised to privatize land, Andrei Pivovarskiy (Minister of Transportation). Both American and European businesses have their own interests, a fact that neither of them hides."[19]

According to the US energy information administration, Ukraine has Europe's third largest shale gas reserves, amounting to 42 trillion cubic feet.[20] The extraction of shale gas, better known as fracking, is avoided in most European countries due to severe environmental implications like earthquakes and ground water contamination.[21] But already in 2013, the American ambassador Geoffrey Pyatt was "determined to cooperate with the Ukrainian government in strengthening Ukraine's energy independence."[22] The International Business Times reports that "One of the ways the U.S. is ... helping the country develop its shale gas [is] by bringing in companies like Chevron ... and Exxon Mobil."[23] At the time, these corporations had also shown interest in the offshore gas fields of Crimea, which will now probably be developed by the Russian state company Gazprom (the profits from the gas fields do not actually compensate for the costs of yearly subsidies and pensions that the relatively poor region of Crimea will receive).[24]

Notably, within three months of Yanukovych's ouster, a son of US vice-president Joe Biden joined the board of directors of Burisma Holdings, Ukraine's largest gas producer. He was accompanied by David Leiter, the former Senate Chief of staff of John Kerry, the US secretary of state. As *Time* magazine reported, "Leiter's involvement in the firm rounds out a power-packed team of politically-connected Americans that also includes a second new board member, Devon Archer, a Democratic bundler and former adviser to John Kerry's 2004 presidential campaign. Both Archer and Hunter Biden [a son of the vice-president] have worked as business partners with Kerry's son-in-law, Christopher Heinz, the founding partner of Rosemont Capital, a private-equity company."[25] A month before his son joined Burisma Holdings, Joe Biden had travelled to Kiev where—in an echo of Geoffrey Pyatt—he urged the Ukrainian government "to reduce its dependence on Russia for supplies of natural gas." Notably, Burisma Holdings has recently announced its participation in the 4-year-long USAID Municipal Energy Reform Project, which aims to increase Ukraine's energy security, involving a good amount of green-washing.[26] According to the Ukrainian Anticorruption Centre, Burisma Holdings is owned by the 'patriotic' oligarch, Ihor Kolomoyskyi.[27]

Ukrainian government officials have announced their desire to privatize parts of the enormous state oil and gas company, as a part of the biggest privatization round since Ukrainian independence, comprising over 2000 state-run enterprises.[28] From harbors to mines and farms, 342 companies have already been put up for sale. Indeed, the Oakland Institute points to another relevant sector. Ukraine, also known as the "breadbasket of Europe," is the world's third largest exporter of corn and the world's fifth largest exporter of grain, which makes it one of the "most promising growth markets for farm-equipment giant [John] Deere, as well as seed producers Monsanto and DuPont".[29] Notably, China had reached a historic agreement on 3 million acres of land under Yanukovych, which is now being disputed.[30]

The minister of finance, Natalie Jaresko, actually received Ukrainian citizenship a day before she gained her ministerial position. Previously, she had functioned as a US diplomat in charge of a $150 million USAID program—the Western NIS Enterprise Fund (WNISEF)—to help jump-start an investment economy in Ukraine and Moldova. Summarizing his extensive research on Jaresko's dealings there, the seasoned investigative journalist, Robert Parry, writes:

> Jaresko's compensation was capped at $150,000 a year, a salary that many Americans would envy, but it was not enough for her. So, she engaged in a

variety of manoeuvres to evade the cap and enrich herself by claiming millions of dollars in bonuses and fees.

Ultimately, Jaresko was collecting more than $2 million a year after she shifted management of the Western NIS Enterprise Fund (WNISEF) to her own private company, Horizon Capital, and arranged to get lucrative bonuses when selling off investments, even as the overall WNISEF fund was losing money, according to official records.

For instance, Jaresko collected $1.77 million in bonuses in 2013, according to WNISEF's latest available filing with the Internal Revenue Service. In her financial disclosure forms with the Ukrainian government, she reported earning $2.66 million in 2013 and $2.05 million in 2014, thus amassing a sizeable personal fortune while investing U.S. taxpayers' money supposedly to benefit the Ukrainian people.

It didn't matter that WNISEF continued to haemorrhage money, shrinking from its original $150 million to $89.8 million in the 2013 tax year, according to the IRS filing. WNISEF reported that the bonuses to Jaresko and other corporate officers were based on "successful" exits from some investments even if the overall fund was losing money. ... (It also turns out that Jaresko did not comply with Ukrainian law that permits only single citizenship; she has kept her U.S. passport exploiting a loophole that gives her two years to show that she has renounced her U.S. citizenship.)[31]

Western disregard for matters of corruption was again demonstrated by their handling of the Kiev cabinet crisis in February 2016. The year before, several high-profile corruption scandals emerged in Yatsenyuk's party, most notably a Swiss probe into a $40 million bribe accepted by Mykola Martynenko, the deputy head of People's Front.[32] By October 2015, the party's rating had become abysmally low, so much so that they decided to pull out of the local elections. A petition calling for Yatsenyuk's resignation as prime minister was able to garner over 25.000 signatures within mere days.[33] But if a new coalition wasn't formed within 30 days of Yatsenyuk's resignation, this could have led to snap elections for parliament. In October 2015, a picture was taken of hand-written notes by Serhiy Leshchenko, Ukraine's most famous investigative journalist, who was elected to parliament in 2014 under Poroshenko's party list. It explained: 'It is not that the US is protecting Yatsenyuk, but it is more the case that they fear the new elections. In a conversation between Nuland and Saakashvili, she told him that if one were to remove Yatsenyuk without elections, it is OK, but as determined by history—Ukraine has two clans.'"[34]

On December 11th, the prime minister's year-long immunity from dismissal finally expired, and a vote of no confidence in the cabinet of ministers was scheduled for the 16th of February 2016. The minister of economic development and trade resigned two weeks before the vote, citing unfathomable corruption. He also specifically named Ihor Kononenko, leader of the Poroshenko Bloc parliamentary group, as a corrupt figure. He gave examples of the practices he encountered,

> ranging from a sudden removal of my security detail to the pressure to appoint questionable individuals to my team or to key positions in state-owned enterprises. I can only interpret these actions as a persistent attempt to exert control over the flow of money generated by the state-owned enterprises, especially NAK Naftogaz [the huge state oil and gas corporation] and the defence industry. ... We learned how to overcome the resistance of the old system. Turned out, some of the "well-meaning newcomers" are much worse.[35]

In December 2015, a Gallup poll had already found that only 8 percent of the population still had confidence in their government, down from 19 percent under Yanukovych.[36] And of all the major parties, Yatsenyuk's People's Front was distrusted the most. Poroshenko publicly supported the vote of no confidence, making Yatsenyuk's dismissal on February 16th seemingly inevitable.[37] Nevertheless, somehow the vote of no confidence failed to pass. There was a notable lack of votes among parliamentarians in the Poroshenko Bloc and the Opposition Bloc. Two parliamentarians of the Poroshenko Bloc, including investigative journalist Serhiy Leschenko, told the Ukrainian press that this was the result of a backroom deal between Petro Poroshenko, Arseniy Yatsenyuk and the oligarchs Ihor Kolomoyskyi and Rinat Akhmetov.[38] Several Opposition Bloc deputies confirmed the same story the next day, adding that 20 deputies within the party had planned to vote for the no-confidence vote, which subsequently dropped to 8 in accordance with the agreement.[39]

The motivation from the side of the oligarchs Kolomoyskyi and Akhmetov—who maintain good relations with Yatsenyuk—was obvious. Indeed, according to the same Opposition Bloc sources, the Akhmetov-controlled deputies weren't planning on voting for the no-confidence vote in any event. The Poroshenko Bloc, however, seems to have voted against its own interests, continuing to rule with an extremely unpopular party that caters to opposing oligarchs. Sources from the very respected liberal and pro-Maidan newspaper, *Mirror Weekly*, said the turnaround could only be explained by input from Washington.[40] For one, the American ambassador, Geoffrey Pyatt, apparently approached several parliament deputies, warning them hysterically that they would "jump of a cliff without a parachute!" More importantly, even Vice President Joe Biden—who said he had spent a thousand hours on the phone with Poroshenko for 'longer periods ... than with my wife'—weighed in on the matter.[41] On the 12th of February, he told the Ukrainian president that Yatsenyuk ought to stay. And indeed, four days later and against all odds, the prime minister kept his position. The *Mirror Weekly* concluded that Poroshenko was in fact a US "puppet."

A similar story was later published by the pro-Maidan news site *Ukrainska Pravda*, based on interviews with three officials from the ruling coalition and several European diplomats.[42] They proclaimed that European and US officials feared early elections, something the US ambassador Geoffrey Pyatt would later state publicly.[43] *Ukrainska Pravda* also reported that negotiations were being held about a voluntary resignation of Prime Minster Yatsenyuk—rather than including the entire cabinet of ministers, as would have happened in case of a successful no-confidence vote on February 16th—making early elections much less likely. These negotiations were tightly controlled by the United States. After Poroshenko, Biden and Nuland held a meeting at the start of April, another well-connected pro-government newspaper reported that the US had set the 12th of April as the deadline for Yatsenyuk's resignation.[44] And indeed, as predicted, on April 12th, 2016 Yatsenyuk resigned without triggering new elections. Victoria Nuland reportedly told Ukrainian officials that the US had feared gains for pro-Russian parties.[45] Indeed, the Opposition Bloc now rivalled Poroshenko's party in nearly all the polls, although the majority of seats would surely remain with pro-western parties. Importantly, it was unpredictable what kind of coalition would come out of new elections, and it seems the US was adamant to preserve the current subservient administration.

Clearly, the United States has tremendous leverage in Ukraine. Yet matters of corruption are of secondary interest, and the proposed reforms are largely cosmetic. Joe Biden, for example, bragged about succesfully pressuring Poroshenko to fire Viktor Shokin, a notoriously corrupt figure, from the prosecutor general's office.[46] Yet Biden then cheered on the subsequent appointment to that office of Yuriy Lutsenko, another of Poroshenko's close allies, who doesn't even have a legal education.[47] Consequently, under Lutsenko's watch, the Prosecutor General's Office raided the offices of the National Anti-Corruption Bureau of Ukraine (NABU); later detained two NABU officials, who were beaten while in custody, and blocked NABU's access to the national database of criminal investigations.[48]

Other cases of supposed anti-corruption progress proved equally disappointing. The European Court of Auditors, for example, commended a range of anti-corruption laws that were passed under EU pressure, as well as the establishment of the NABU offices. Nevertheless, they also noted that "impact will depend on genuine law enforcement" and that "the results of anti-corruption measures remain to be seen."[49] Indeed, as an extensive review of high-level corruption by Kudelia demonstrated, cosmetic anti-corruption reforms have a long history in Ukraine: "More than thirty presidential decrees and government resolutions combined with a dozen legislative acts adopted over the last two decades have targeted all types of corrupt practices."[50] Yet as Kudelia documented, and as the discovery of Yanukovych's obscene wealth had demonstrated, these measures have proven to be extremely ineffective. Surely then, formal legal criteria cannot be the benchmark for measuring anti-corruption progress in Ukraine. Indeed, as of December 2016, nearly 90 percent of the population considered these efforts to be a failure.[51]

The persistence of widespread corruption means that average Ukrainians barely benefit from the enormous amount of Western debts incurred, even though the average tax-payer will foot the bill for decades to come. I have already noted John Helmer's assertion that the first IMF loan tranche disappeared offshore and that, using the most conservative figures from Graham Stacks' research, the total amount of state embezzlement is likely to be much larger. Furthermore, the European Court of Auditors admitted that there was no mechanism in place to account for how European financial assistance, primarily loans, were spent.[52] They also noted that "Ukraine's state finances have deteriorated over the years, mainly due to mismanagement of public funds."[53] Again, there is a historical pattern at work here, aptly summarized by Dean Muraya:

> Transparency International listed the top 3 most

corrupt politicians [in history]:
1. Mohamed Suharto President of Indonesia from 1967-1998 (31 years)
2. Ferdinand Marcos President of the Philippines from 1972-1986 (14 years)
3. Mobutu Sese Seko President of Zaire (Now the DRC) from 1965-1997 (32 years)

The World Bank and The I.M.F have had special relationships with all 3.

Let's start with number 1.
Suharto was named president in 1967 and stayed until 1998. Walt Rostow, special advisor to Lyndon Johnson, told the World Bank president Robert McNamara that "The World Bank's support is essential if Suharto is to stay afloat." The Bank complied and gave him 30 billion between 1966-1998. 10 billion was stolen with the banks full knowledge. In an internal memo dated 1997, it stated: "We estimate that at least 20-30% of development budget funds are diverted through informal payments to Indonesian Government officials and staff." This did not seem to deter the Bank in the slightest. The bank also sent 1 billion to Suharto to finance the transmigration program that resulted in the massacre of 200,000 East Timorese.

Number 2.
Ferdinand Marcos was president of the Philippines from 1965-1986. He stole 5-10 billion dollars. During his reign the Philippines incurred the largest single debt derived from a bogus infrastructure scheme approved by the World Bank. The project was to build a nuclear power plant called the Baatan Nuclear power station to

the tune of 2 billion dollars. The plant was built but was never used, because it was built on an earthquake fault at the foot of a volcano. Not a single Watt of electricity has been produced by the plant, but the Filipino people still have to pay 170,000 dollars a day until the year 2018. The bank has the largest budget for research with top economists, experts and academics at their disposal; this was not a mistake but a calculated scheme to make a profit off of the Filipino people.

Number 3
Mobuto Sese Seko, was president of Zaire, now the DRC, from 1965-1997. When Mobutu came into power the I.M.F put their own man, Ian Blumenthal, in a key position in the Central bank of Zaire. He resigned within a year citing unfathomable corruption. After his resignation the I.M.F granted Mobutu the largest loan it had ever given to an African country which was 700 million.[54]

Endnotes

1. Kamenev, M., & Speicher, T. (2015, August 13). Ротация Кабмина: роль США и торги за Конституцию. Retrieved from https://www.rbc.ua/rus/analytics/rotatsiya-kabmina-rol-ssha-torgi-konstitutsiyu-1439464418.html
2. Интервью с Валентином Наливайченко: «Смотрящий» за фракцией в ВР еженедельно прогоняет через офшоры по 500 000 долларов» (2015, July 9). Retrieved from http://www.segodnya.ua/life/interview/intervyu-s-valentinom-nalivaychenko-prishel-sluzhit-lyudyam-tak-pust-tvoy-biznes-im-sluzhit-630104.html
3. Ibid.
4. Bonner, B. (2015, July 9). Fiala, EBA president and Dragon Capital CEO, says 'patience is thin' Retrieved from http://www.kyivpost.com/content/ukraine/fiala-eba-president-and-dragon-capital-ceo-says-patience-is-thin-393118.html

5	Graham Stack, (2015) "Money laundering in Ukraine: Tax evasion, embezzlement, illicit international flows and state capture", *Journal of Money Laundering Control*, Vol. 18 Iss: 3, p. 383.
6	Ibid, p. 383.
7	Ibid, 384.
8	Ibid, p. 383.
9	Ibid, p. 390.
10	Ibid, p. 386.
11	Ibid, p. 391.
12	Ibid, p. 390.
13	Kravchuk, A. (2015, December 08). Україна офшорна. Історія формування вітчизняної моделі економіки. Retrieved from http://commons.com.ua/ukrayina-ofshorna-istoriya-formuvannya-vitchiznyanoyi-modeli-ekonomiki/; Niece, M. (2015, December 18). Економічні наслідки офшорної торгівлі україни. Retrieved from http://commons.com.ua/ekonomichni-naslidki-ofshornoyi-torgivli-ukrayini/; Also see the following endnotes.
14	Kirchner, R., Kravchuk, V., & Ries, J. (2015, June). Foreign Direct Investment in Ukraine: Past, Present, and Future (Rep.). Retrieved http://www.beratergruppe-ukraine.de/wordpress/wp-content/uploads/2014/06/PP_02_2015_en.pdf
15	Alexander, L. (2016, January 04). Торгівля через офшорні зони: раціональна необхідність чи перепона для розвитку України? Retrieved from http://commons.com.ua/torgivlya-cherez-ofshorni-zoni-ratsionalna-neobhidnist-chi-perepona-dlya-rozvitku-ukrayini/
16	Dutch Holding Companies: New Opportunities for Structuring of Ukrainian Business. (2013, November 27). Retrieved from http://ukraine.nlembassy.org/news/2013/11/dutch-holding-companies-new-opportunities-for-structuring-of-ukrainian-business.html
17	Calculated from OESO and IMF data by Blok, A. (2014, March 05). Hoe rijk Oekraïne de belasting ontwijkt in paradijselijk Nederland. Retrieved from https://decorrespondent.nl/819/Hoe-rijk-Oekraine-de-belasting-ontwijkt-in-paradijselijk-Nederland/95882552766-a52472a3
18	Chang, H. J. (2002). Kicking away the ladder: development strategy in historical perspective. Anthem Press; Chang, H. J. (2007). Bad Samaritans: The myth of free trade and the secret history of capitalism. Bloomsbury Publishing USA.
19	Kamenev, M., & Speicher, T. (2015, August 13). Ротация Кабмина: роль США и торги за Конституцию. Retrieved from https://www.rbc.ua/rus/analytics/rotatsiya-kabmina-rol-ssha-torgi-konstitutsiyu-1439464418.html

20	Ukraine crisis sharpens focus on European shale gas. (2014, March 14). Retrieved from http://www.reuters.com/article/europe-shale-ukraine-idUSL6N0MB1WI20140314
21	Hromadko, J., & Torry, H. (2014, July 4). Germany Shelves Shale-Gas Drilling For Next Seven Years. Retrieved from http://www.wsj.com/articles/germany-shelves-shale-gas-drilling-for-next-seven-years-1404481174
22	Kashi, D. (2013, September 18). Shale Gas Development By the US In The Ukraine Can Help Promote Energy Security. Retrieved from http://www.ibtimes.com/shale-gas-development-us-ukraine-can-help-promote-energy-security-1407944
23	Ibid.
24	Bush, J. (2014, April 08). Factbox - Costs and benefits from Russia's annexation of Crimea. Retrieved from http://uk.reuters.com/article/2014/04/08/uk-ukraine-crisis-crimea-costs-factbox-idUKBREA370NY20140408
25	Scherer, M. (2014, July 7). Ukrainian Employer of Joe Biden's Son Hires a D.C. Lobbyist. Retrieved from http://time.com/2964493/ukraine-joe-biden-son-hunter-burisma/
26	Burisma Holdings teams up with USAID Municipal Energy Reform Project (MERP). (2014, October 23). Retrieved from http://burisma.com/en/news/burisma-holdings-teams-up-with-usaid-municipal-energy-reform-project-merp/
27	Kings of Ukrainian Gas. (2012, August 26). Retrieved from http://antac.org.ua/en/2012/08/kings-of-ukrainian-gas/
28	Stern, D. (2015, August 26). Horses for sale in Ukraine's privatisation drive - BBC News. Retrieved from http://www.bbc.com/news/business-34055256
29	Mousseau, F., & Mittal, A. (2014, July 28). Walking on the West Side: The World Bank and the IMF in the Ukraine Conflict (Rep.), p. 4. Retrieved from Oakland Institute website: http://www.oaklandinstitute.org/press-release-world-bank-and-imf-open-ukraine-western-interests
30	Ibid, p. 4.
31	Parry, R. (2016, January 6). Consortiumnews. Retrieved from https://consortiumnews.com/2016/01/06/reality-peeks-through-in-ukraine/
32	Is Ukraine blocking Swiss investigation of Yatsenyuk ally? (2015, September 19). Retrieved from http://www.kyivpost.com/article/content/ukraine/is-ukraine-blocking-swiss-investigation-of-yatsenyuk-ally-398159.html
33	Petition to appoint Saakashvili as Ukrainian PM gains over 25,000 signatures. (2015, September 8). Retrieved from http://uatoday.tv/news/petition-to-appoint-saakashvili-as-ukrainian-pm-gains-over-25-

	000-signatures-489799.html
34	США согласны на отставку Яценюка: запись депутата в Раде. (2015, October 7). Retrieved from http://korrespondent.net/ukraine/3573242-ssha-sohlasny-na-otstavku-yatsenuika-zapys-deputata-v-rade
35	Abromavicius, A. (2016, February 3). Statement by the Minister of Economic Development and Trade. Retrieved from http://www.me.gov.ua/News/Detail?lang=en-GB&id=f13fa574-3e1b-4eca-b294-f9e508910e01&title=StatementByTheMinisterOfEconomicDevelopmentAndTradeOfUkraineAivarasAbromavicius
36	Ukrainians Disillusioned With Leadership. (2015, December 23). Retrieved from http://www.gallup.com/poll/187931/ukrainians-disillusioned-leadership.aspx
37	Квартальный мониторинговый отчет. (2016, February 16). Retrieved from http://www.pravda.com.ua/news/2016/02/16/7099204/
38	Отставка не прошла из-за сговора Порошенко, Яценюка и олигархов - нардеп. (2016, February 16). Retrieved from http://korrespondent.net/ukraine/politics/3630449-otstavka-ne-proshla-yz-za-shovora-poroshenko-yatsenuika-y-olyharkhov-nardep; Leshchenko, S. (2016, February 16). Сергій Лещенко: ‹›Карточный домик›› Петра Порошенко. Retrieved from http://blogs.pravda.com.ua/authors/leschenko/56c390f55beae/
39	АП просила «Опоблок» не голосувати за відставку Яценюка— джерело. (2016, February 19). Retrieved from http://www.pravda.com.ua/news/2016/02/19/7099653/
40	Bridge, J. (2016, February 19). Мы делили апельсин… Retrieved from http://gazeta.zn.ua/internal/my-delili-apelsin-_.html
41	Biden says he spends longer periods on phone with Poroshenko than with own wife. (2015, December 7). Retrieved from http://www.unian.info/politics/1205503-biden-says-he-spends-longer-periods-on-phone-with-poroshenko-than-with-own-wife.html
42	Zhartovskaya, M. (2016, March 4). Якщо йдеш—іди. Як в АП вмовляють Яценюка подати у відставку, і хто стане наступним прем'єром. Retrieved from http://www.pravda.com.ua/articles/2016/03/4/7101127/
43	Pyatt warns against early Rada elections. (2016, April 1). Retrieved from https://web.archive.org/web/20160402170838/http://www.kyivpost.com/article/content/ukraine-politics/pyatt-warns-against-early-rada-elections-411173.html
44	АП и руководство ВР разработали пакет документов для выхода из политического кризиса. (2016, April 08). Retrieved from http://zn.ua/POLITICS/ap-i-rukovodstvo-vr-razrabotali-paket-dokumentov-

	dlya-vyhoda-iz-politicheskogo-krizisa-209940_.html
45	Кредиты в обмен на Минск. Апрельские тезисы Виктории Нуланд. (2016, April 26). Retrieved from http://strana.ua/articles/analysis/10496-kredity-v-obmen-na-minsk-aprelskie-tezisy-viktorii-nuland.html
46	Clemons, S. (2016, August 22). The Biden Doctrine. Retrieved from https://www.theatlantic.com/international/archive/2016/08/biden-doctrine/496841/
47	Krasnolutska, D. (2016, May 12). Ukrainian President's Ally Takes Top Prosecutor's Job. Retrieved October 01, 2016, from http://www.bloomberg.com/news/articles/2016-05-12/ukraine-eases-path-to-prosecutor-s-job-for-presidential-ally; Biden welcomes Lutsenko's appointment as Ukraine's prosecutor general. (2016, May 14). Retrieved from http://en.interfax.com.ua/news/general/343311.html
48	Prentice, A. (2016, August 17). Ukraine anti-graft activists protest 'gangster-style' state attacks. Retrieved from http://www.reuters.com/article/uk-ukraine-crisis-corruption-prosecutor-idUKKCN10S1JF; Луценко закрыл доступ НАБУ к базе уголовных дел. (2016, December 17). Retrieved from http://nv.ua/ukraine/politics/lutsenko-zakryl-dostup-nabu-v-bazu-ugolovnyh-del-sytnik-332807.html
49	Fazakas S., Milasiute A., Baranyi M., Kaszap B., Lesiewicz B., Joret F., & Geoffroy C. (2016, December 6). Special Report: EU assistance to Ukraine (Rep.), p. 32. Retrieved http://www.eca.europa.eu/Lists/ECADocuments/SR16_32/SR_UKRAINE_EN.pdf; EU assistance to Ukraine: results so far are "fragile", say Auditors. (2016, December 7). Retrieved from http://www.eca.europa.eu/Lists/ECADocuments/INSR16_32/INSR_UKRAINE_EN.pdf
50	Kudelia, S. (2016). 4 Corruption in ukraine: Perpetuum mobile or the endplay of Post-Soviet elites?. Beyond the Euromaidan: Comparative Perspectives on Advancing Reform in Ukraine, p. 62.
51	Leshchenko, S. (2016, December 30). Ukraine's corrupt counter-revolution. Retrieved from https://www.opendemocracy.net/od-russia/sergii-leshchenko/ukraine-s-corrupt-counter-revolution
52	Gotev, G. (2016, December 07). Court of Auditors unable to say how EU money was spent in Ukraine. Retrieved from https://www.euractiv.com/section/europe-s-east/news/court-of-auditors-unable-to-say-how-eu-money-was-spent-in-ukraine/
53	EU assistance to Ukraine: results so far are "fragile", say Auditors. (2016, December 7). Retrieved from http://www.eca.europa.eu/Lists/ECADocuments/INSR16_32/INSR_UKRAINE_EN.pdf
54	Muraya, D. (2015, January 16). The I.M.F and The World Bank: Tools of Neoliberal Imperialism. Retrieved from http://theoutrospect.blogspot.nl/2015/01/the-imf-and-world-bank-tools-of.html

| Chapter Nine |

DISMANTLING RUSSOPHONE UKRAINE

Figures like Natalie Jaresko and Hunter Biden suggest a profiteering motive on the side of Ukraine's financial backers, but there is certainly more to this story. Even though Ukraine has huge potential, its current economy amounts to less than two percent of EU GDP, and many of the most profitable state-run enterprises had been sold off years ago to the national oligarchy.[1] Although a certain level of neoliberal fundamentalism can surely explain a lot, it also seems that Ukraine's financial backers have political motivations. I already mentioned how the Eastern and Southern regions are heavily dependent on exports to the Russian market. These provinces are also, with the exception of the capital city of Kiev, the main exporting regions of Ukraine in general. This is no small feat: exports and imports each accounted for some 45-50% of Ukraine's GDP in 2013. Between 2003 and 2013, 28% of Ukraine's exports and 34% of imports were traded with the EU. For just three countries of the Eurasian Economic Union (EEU)—Russia, Belarus and Kazakhstan—these figures came down to 30% of exports and 38% of imports. This export ratio was very steady until 2014.[2]

Nevertheless, these figures still understate the importance of the EEU markets, crucially ignoring the composition of traded goods.[3] Two-thirds of Russian imports in 2013 were energy commodities, essential for the functioning of the entire Ukrainian economy. Equally important, nearly all of Ukraine's advanced industries—machinery, equipment, aircraft, vessels, nuclear reac-

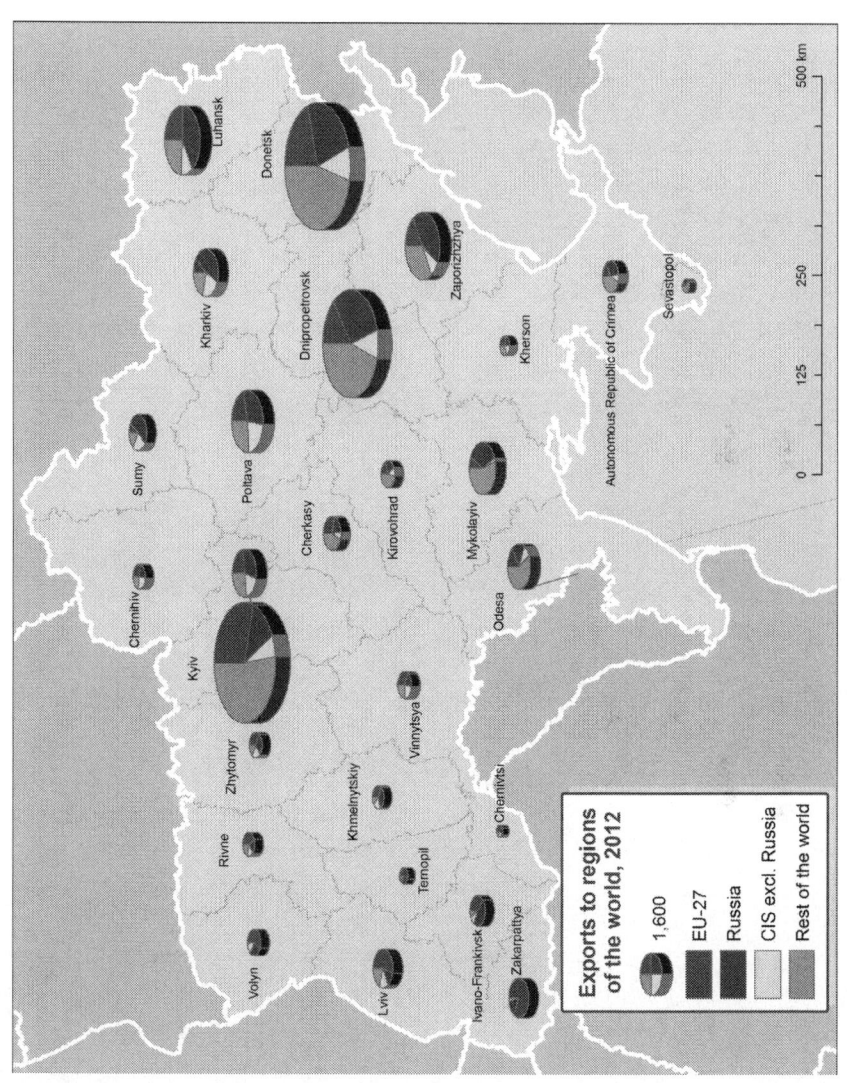

Note: Size of the pie corresponds to the value of regions' exports in USD million. Source: Adarov, A., Astrov, V., Havlik, P., Hunya, G., Landesmann, M., & Podkaminer, L. (2015). *How to Stabilize the Economy of Ukraine*.

tors and boilers, railway/tramway rolling stocks, inorganic chemicals, among others—depend heavily on exports to the post-Soviet market. As the wiiw report points out: "estimates show that just 15% of Ukraine's major export positions traded with the Russian-led EEU could be potentially relocated to other markets and the annual revenue loss may reach some USD 15 billion."[4]

Indeed, the machinery industry alone has an annual revenue of nearly $20 billion, and is responsible for employing some 600 thousand people in Southern and Eastern Ukraine.[5] Not only would trade disruptions with the EEU countries devastate the Southern and Eastern economies, they would also lead to a de-industrialization of Ukraine—and this process has already started.[6] By December 2015, Ukraine's exports had dropped by over 40 percent since 2013, and Russia now only constituted 12.7 percent of the total.[7] The result: total industrial production had shrunk by 22 percent.[8] The export of machinery, equipment and minerals lowered by approximately 58 percent, and chemicals and metals by respectively 50 and 45 percent.[9] Although all export commodities suffered, easily the least hit was the agricultural sector, whose exports declined by 12 percent.[10] In 2014, Ukraine's most important export goods were semi-finished steel products. By August 2015, Ukraine's largest export commodities became corn and sunflower oil.[11] In fact, as Kravchuk *et al.* calculated, the agricultural sector is effectively being subsidized, as its share of tax payments is 20 (!) times lower than its share of GDP.[12] This is partially "because of fictitious official data about profitability of production and a large fraction of shadow market for its products."[13]

Southern and Eastern Ukrainians might bitterly remember that, under pressure from Maidan, Russia had offered a $15 billion loan to Yanukovych, accompanied by a 35% cut in gas prices.[14] Indeed, quite early on, Russia had urged for trilateral negotiations with the EU and Ukraine, which could have perhaps made the Eurasian customs union and the association agreement compatible. Commissioner Manuel Barosso, however, simply quipped that "Russia's inclusion in the talks on setting up an Association Agreement between the EU and Ukraine is wholly unacceptable."[15] Štefan Füle, the commissioner for enlargement and European neighbourhood policy, admitted:

> It is true that the Customs Union membership is not compatible with the DCFTAs which we have negotiated with Ukraine, the Republic of Moldova, Georgia, and Armenia. This is not because of ideological differences; this is not about a clash of economic blocs, or a zero-sum game. This is due to legal impossibilities: for instance, you cannot at the same time lower your customs tariffs as per the DCFTA and increase them as a result of the Customs Union membership.
> ... The development of the Eurasian Economic Union project must respect our partners' sovereign decisions. Any threats from Russia linked to the possible signing of agreements with the European Union are unacceptable. [...] The European Union will support and stand by those who are subject to undue pressures.[16]

Russia should indeed not meddle in sovereign affairs, but who were EU officials to talk, when the association agreement was to be signed by means of back-room politics and would—like the Eurasian Customs Union—almost certainly not have passed a popular referendum in November 2013?[17] Furthermore, Russia had additional concerns over the compatibility of the EU agreement with already existing free-trade agreements with Ukraine, namely the CISFTA, a free-trade agreement among former Soviet states. The Russian government argued that the association agreement would allow EU exports to reach Russia tariff-free through Ukraine. Although these concerns seem exaggerated—multiple free-trade regimes have proved compatible in many instances, mainly by tracking the origin of goods—the complete refusal to talk to Russia at all did seem unreasonable. After Russia threatened to unilaterally terminate its CISFTA obligations towards Ukraine, trilateral negotiations were finally initiated, and the Ukrainian tariff removals for the EU as stipulated by the association agreement were postponed until the 1st of January 2016. According to a leaked report obtained by Ukrainian media, Russia had demanded some 2000 tariff removals to be scrapped during the negotiations.[18] In the end, however, the association agreement was not amended at all, and fully entered into force in January 2016.

Since, Russia revoked its CISFTA obligations towards Ukraine and—combined with countermeasures from Ukraine—trade relations are sure to hit rock bottom. Indeed, until 2016 most of the declining exports had rather been due to the devastating war in the Donbass region, which accounted for 25 percent of Ukrainian exports in 2013.[19] Although most of the aforementioned statistics exclude the 'anti-terrorist operation zone,' many of these industries were interlinked with those outside of the war-zone, therefore causing a ripple effect. In addition, there have been some back-and-forth ad hoc trade restrictions between Russia and Ukraine, as well as a complete seizure of co-operation in military industries. The latter has cost the Ukrainian defence and aviation industries an estimated 80 percent of their revenue.[20] As the wiiw notes: "Interrupted Russian-Ukrainian cooperation in space and defense sectors hurts not only the affected production facilities in Ukraine …, but also Russia and other countries which used Ukraine-supplied rockets and electronic components in space launching programs. … The cancellation of the Russian order for 60 AN-70 military cargo planes produced at the Kiev Region-based Antonov plant will result in a loss of more than USD 4 billion."[21]

As former Fulbright research scholar in Ukraine, Nicolai Petro, asserts, some of Kiev's policies concern overly blatant political posturing in favor of anti-Russian rhetoric. A great deal was made, for example, about the import of European gas and South African coal in order to replace their respectively Russian and Donbass counterparts. In both cases, however, Ukraine was simply buying the same goods from Donbass and Russia, but resold at a significantly higher price by South Africa and Europe acting as middlemen, at a huge cost to the Ukrainian tax-payer.[22]

Another pertinent example involves the construction of a 517 million dollar wall between Russia and Ukraine, unsupported by a single military expert due to its uselessness against an actual Russian attack, which then prime minister Yatsenyuk dubbed "the eastern border of Europe" and "the great wall of Ukraine."[23] The project was stalled after 10 percent was built, mostly in areas outside of the fighting, yet construction is reported to resume eventually.[24] The project bears some similarities with Donald Trump's proposed wall between Mexico and the United States, which too is unfeasible to build and useless for its intended purposes, even if it could actually be constructed.[25] In fact, the similarity did not go unnoticed by Yatsenyuk, who offered Trump a helping hand with a blueprint of his building plans.[26] In both cases, however, the sole purpose is to make an ideological point—with disastrous consequences.

While Ukraine is severing its ties with Russia, it doesn't have sufficient access to other markets to make up for the losses. Not by a long shot. Notably, Ukraine had already been benefiting from unilateral tariff removals by the EU since spring 2014. Even under these favourable conditions, Ukrainian exports to the EU declined by 23 percent in 2015,[27] partially because quotas for goods where Ukraine is competitive—such as chicken and honey—are largely maintained in the association agreement.[28] This meant that the January 2016 enforcement of the trade agreement mainly entailed the opening of the Ukrainian market for EU goods, as well as huge expenditure costs for adopting the so-called 'EU acquis'—the EU body of law. The total costs are estimated by the Ukrainian Industrialist Union to be 170-180 billion euros over the next ten years, similar to previous EU commission assessments on other enlargement programs.[29] That's substantially more than Ukraine's entire annual GDP.

Thus, Ukraine is expected to adopt the entire body of EU law on most economic and financial matters. In case of any disputes, the interpretation will be decided by a ruling of the Court of Justice of the European Union.[30] The association agreement in large part mirrors EU membership, although Ukraine gave away its sovereignty without any of the benefits, most notably representation in the legislative process to which it is now bound. Indeed, a similar arrangement with Russia would certainly have been dubbed colonial, underpinning the ideological privilege with which the EU is endowed for being perceived as the 'civilized' party.

While European legislation and standards are supposed to be superior to Ukraine's, an extensive review of Ukrainian and EU labor legislation by the Ukrainian lawyer, Vitaliy Dudin, suggests otherwise: "Ukrainian labor legislation is still soaked with the greater spirit of workers' protection, caused by the Soviet origin of the Ukrainian Labor Code. It is full of limits, restrictions and regulations that put employers in very strict margins, concerning the work arrangements implementation and give very little freedom in their settlement with the consent of workers."[31] Vitaliy Dudin does recognize many flaws in the legislation—especially its datedness to the changing economic environment, as well as the fact that many of these laws are selectively enforced—and acknowledges that EU law might be superior in some respects. Nevertheless, he finally concludes that: "the Ukrainian labor legislation's adaptation to the European one in general may have negative consequences for workers. They may lose their high standards of working conditions, stated by the current labor legislation ... On their own terms, these changes won't lead to better payouts, but rather the contrary, the indignity of domestic workers will make them more exploited."[32]

In 2014, Ukraine received over $9 billion from foreign lenders, half from the IMF and the rest from the World Bank, the EBRD, the EU, the United States and Japan. Another 25 billion is expected to be lent from 2015 to 2019.[33] Regardless, the wiiw study asserts that "still, these funds will be almost certainly not enough to meet Ukraine's external financing requirement, which in 2015 alone is projected by wiiw at approximately USD 15 billion."[34] Rather than austerity, the wiiw asserts that Ukraine will need a huge 'Marshall plan' to reconfigure Ukraine's economic composition, requiring massive investments if it is to replace its post-Soviet industry—which seems especially necessary now that the industrial heartlands of the Donbass have been severed from Ukraine. Currently, however, it seems such financing would only come in the form of loans with conditions attached, which ensure a lack of investment in advanced industries and rather optimize the continued export of unprocessed Ukrainian resources. Indeed, allocation of state resources to the 'national economy' was cut by 34 percent in real terms since 2013, mainly due to a huge reduction from 2014 onwards of capital spending, i.e. long-term investments in the Ukrainian economy.[35]

In other words, the current finance packages do not solve Ukraine's problems, but rather keeps the regime afloat for some time—allowing it to continue its costly military operations in the Donbass. Therefore, these institutions are essentially financing a proxy war with Russia, as well as severing Ukraine economically from its neighbour. Indeed, the contracts signed by the unelected interim government did not limit themselves to economic policies. When Yatsenyuk signed the EU association agreement on the 21st of March, this also entailed the "gradual convergence on foreign and security matters with the aim of Ukraine's ever-deeper involvement in the European security area. ... Ukraine and the European Defence Agency (EDA) [a defense agency of the European Union] will establish close contacts to discuss military capability improvement, including technological issues."[36] The relevance of the association agreement was emphasized during the Maidan protests by NATO Secretary General Anders Fogh Rasmussen, one month before the fall of Yanukovych. "An association pact with Ukraine would have been a major boost to Euro-Atlantic security," the general proclaimed. "I truly regret that it could not be done. The reason is well-known: pressure that Russia exerts on Kiev. ... We have real differences and real issues. It's obvious that Russia's attitude is clearly hostile to the (NATO) alliance opening to the east."[37]

Endnotes

1   World Bank data.
2   Export and Import figures Adarov, A., Astrov, V., Havlik, P., Hunya,

G., Landesmann, M., & Podkaminer, L. (2015). How to Stabilise the Economy of Ukraine. wiiw and United Europe, April, p. 33.

3 Composition of traded goods are explored extensively in ibid, pp. 32-38.

4 Ibid, p. 44.

5 Ibid, p. 44.

6 Kravchuk, A., Popovych, Z., Knottnerus, R., & Heijningen, D., Van. (2016, March). The expected impact of the EU-Ukraine Association Agreement (Rep.). Retrieved https://www.tni.org/files/publication-downloads/online_tni_issue_brief_oekraine.pdf

7 Commodity Pattern of Foreign Trade of Ukraine, January-November 2015. (2016, January 19). Retrieved from http://www.ukrstat.gov.ua/operativ/operativ2015/zd/tsztt/tsztt_e/tsztt1115_e.htm; Commodity Pattern of Foreign Trade of Ukraine, January-November 2013. (2014, January 20). Retrieved February 12, 2016, from http://www.ukrstat.gov.ua/operativ/operativ2013/zd/tsztt/tsztt_e/tsztt1113_e.htm; State Statistics Service of Ukraine. (2016, January 19). Retrieved February 12, 2016, from http://www.ukrstat.gov.ua/operativ/operativ2015/zd/ztt/ztt_u/arh_ztt2015.html

8 Index of Industrial Production in Ukraine for 2010-2015. (2016, January 27). Retrieved February 12, 2016, from http://www.ukrstat.gov.ua/operativ/operativ2014/pr/ipp/ipp_e/ipp_e14.htm

9 National Bank of Ukraine. (2016). Retrieved February 12, 2016, from http://www.bank.gov.ua/doccatalog/document?id=24491409

10 Ibid.

11 Арбузов, С. (2015, August 20). Collapse of Ukrainian exports to Russia and Europe in first six months of 2015. Retrieved from https://newcoldwar.org/collapse-of-ukrainian-exports-to-russia-and-europe-in-first-six-months-of-2015/

12 Kravchuk, O., Hladun, A., Dudin, V., Dutchak, O., Neboha, M., Odosiy, O., & Popovych, Z. (2016), p. 157. Alternative mechanisms for the socio-economic development of Ukraine. Kiev: Center for Social and Labor Research, 2016.

13 Ibid, p. 157.

14 Walker, S. (2013, December 18). Vladimir Putin offers Ukraine financial incentives to stick with Russia. Retrieved from http://www.theguardian.com/world/2013/dec/17/ukraine-russia-leaders-talks-kremlin-loan-deal

15 Sakwa, R. (2014). *Frontline Ukraine: crisis in the borderlands.* IB Tauris, p. 87.

16 Ibid, p. 88.

17 Polls cited in Chapter One: A Divided Country.

18	ZN,UA. (2015). Retrieved from http://zn.ua/static/file/russian_proposal.pdf
19	The differences and interlinkages between the export industries of the different regional economies are extensively explored in Adarov, A., Astrov, V., Havlik, P., Hunya, G., Landesmann, M., & Podkaminer, L. (2015). How to Stabilise the Economy of Ukraine. wiiw and United Europe, April, pp. 64-73.
20	Потери Украины от разрыва контрактов с РФ в космической и военных отраслях составят 2 млрд грн. (2016, February 9). Retrieved from http://vybor.ua/news/poteri_ukrainy_ot_razryva_kontraktov_s_rf_v_kosmicheskoy_i_voennyh_otraslyah_sostavyat_2_mlrd_grn.html
21	Adarov, A., Astrov, V., Havlik, P., Hunya, G., Landesmann, M., & Podkaminer, L. (2015). How to Stabilise the Economy of Ukraine. wiiw and United Europe, April, p. 36.
22	Petro, N. N. (2016). Why Ukraine and Russia Need Each Other. *Russian Politics*, 1(2), 184-202.
23	Ibid.
24	Ibid.
25	Oliver, J. (2016, March 20). Border Wall: Last Week Tonight with John Oliver (HBO). Retrieved from https://www.youtube.com/watch?v=vU8dCYocuyI
26	Яценюк готовий повчити Трампа будувати стіну на кордоні. (2017, February 9). Retrieved from http://www.pravda.com.ua/news/2017/02/9/7134931/
27	Petro, N. N. (2016). Why Ukraine and Russia Need Each Other. *Russian Politics*, 1(2), 184-202.
28	Beunder, S., Mast, J., Beek, B., Van, & Ploeg, C., De. (2016, April 01). Wie profiteert er eigenlijk van het associatieakkoord met Oekraïne? Retrieved from https://www.ftm.nl/artikelen/wie-profiteert-associatieakkoord
29	Adarov, A., Astrov, V., Havlik, P., Hunya, G., Landesmann, M., & Podkaminer, L. (2015). How to Stabilise the Economy of Ukraine. wiiw and United Europe, April, p. 44.
30	Article 322 of the Association agreement between the European Union and its Member States, of the one part, and Ukraine, of the other part (2014, September 25). Retrieved from http://eeas.europa.eu/ukraine/docs/association_agreement_ukraine_2014_en.pdf
31	Vitalii Dudin. (2015). The European integration's consequences for the Ukrainian labor market and social system changes, p. 21.
32	Ibid, p. 21.
33	Adarov, A., Astrov, V., Havlik, P., Hunya, G., Landesmann, M., &

Podkaminer, L. (2015). How to Stabilise the Economy of Ukraine. wiiw and United Europe, April, p. 18.
34 Ibid, p. 17.
35 Ibid, p. 20; for inflation and more government expenditure figures, consult endnotes 21 and 22.
36 Article 4 and 10 of the Association agreement between the European Union and its Member States, of the one part, and Ukraine, of the other part (2014, September 25). Retrieved from http://eeas.europa.eu/ukraine/docs/association_agreement_ukraine_2014_en.pdf
37 NATO's Rasmussen criticizes Russian pressure on Ukraine. (2014, January 29). Retrieved from http://www.reuters.com/article/us-ukraine-nato-idUSBREA0S0HW20140129

| Chapter Ten |

THE EAST RESPONDS

The question on the lips of NATO officers was perhaps whether Putin would keep his reported promise, to annex Crimea, from 2008.[1] This answer would arrive shortly. The first steps of the brand new interim government threw Crimea right into the hands of Putin. The Parliament in Kiev voted overwhelmingly for the abolition of Russian as the second language of the eastern Ukrainian provinces.[2] No steps were taken to rein in the ultranationalists. In fact, as mentioned earlier, they were granted high-level positions in the interim-government. Although the Ukrainian interim president vetoed the attack on the Russian language a week after the vote, in response to protest activities, it proved to be too little, too late.[3]

In a dozen cities the relatively passive eastern Ukrainians took to the streets in thousands. The biggest, a 30,000 strong demonstration, took place in Sevastopol, Crimea.[4] This was in fact a continuation of the anti-Maidan demonstrations that had been taking place since the very start in November 2013, although these were top-down organized by the Party of Regions until Yanukovych's fall. Things escalated in Crimea when sketchy "self-defense squads" emerged all over the peninsula. According to assessments of a private Swedish arms expert, their equipment indicated with "a very high probability" that these were Russian forces.[5] Shortly after Crimea's secession, Putin himself would admit that, at the very least, "Crimean self-defense forces were ... backed by Russian servicemen."[6] Indeed, one year later, the retired Russian Admiral Ihor Kasatonov bragged about a Russian special operation involving Crimea, which blocked several Ukrainian military bases.[7] Whatever the exact amount of support, then, it is obvious that a Russian military intervention was crucial for facilitating the post-Maidan developments in Crimea.

On February 27, 2014 the Crimean parliament sacked the regional government, voted in favor of a referendum on greater autonomy, and appointed Sergey Aksyonov as prime minster, whose Russian Unity party had only gained four percent of the vote during the previous elections in 2010. Indeed, the conditions under which the votes were taken resembled those of Yanukovych's impeachment and, in fact, they were worse. The building had been seized by armed pro-Russian insurgents; the legislative website and telephone connections had been disconnected; attending parliamentarians had their phones seized while others, including the incumbent prime minister, claimed they were denied entry; the votes were unanimous and no one from the parliament secretariat had been present.[8] As a result, it was impossible to verify whether the necessary amount of parliamentarians had actually voted—and under which circumstances—or if other people had been pushing their voting buttons; indeed, one lawmaker registered as present denied having been anywhere near the building.[9] Something similar happened with another crucial resolution—to modify the referendum to be about accession to Russia—which was passed on March 6, 2014. The Norwegian newspaper *Aftenposten* contacted dozens of Crimean parliamentarians—including many who had supposedly voted in favor—to conclude that only 36 members had been present for the vote; as opposed to 51 members, as legally required, and 61 members, as was officially reported.[10]

The referendum went ahead anyway. Representatives of the Organization for Security and Co-operation in Europe—a pan-European co-operation body that often observes elections—were invited but refused to show, because they found the referendum to be illegal.[11] The results were overwhelming: 97% of the voters wanted to join Russia with a turnout of 83 percent. Crimea's accession to Russia was subsequently formalized on the 28th of

March. The referendum lacked international standards and was conducted in a militarized environment. Nevertheless, every single survey since the annexation of Crimea has indicated that it had majority support.[12] An extensive poll done by Pew Research, a reputable American polling organization, stated that 88% of Crimean citizens think Kiev should recognize the results.[13] Another poll from the American Gallup registered 83% support and a Canadian-sponsored survey registered 93%.[14]

This was not actually that surprising. Sixty-five percent of the population is ethnic Russian, nearly everyone speaks the language and many Crimeans undoubtedly desired the higher Russian pensions.[15] In fact, the accession of Crimea into the Ukrainian state itself had been quite arbitrary, stemming from a top-down administrative change of the Soviet bureaucracy in 1954 when it became part of the former Ukrainian province within the USSR. Indeed, Crimea has been a part of Russia for 170 years, much longer than its history as a Ukrainian province. It is for these reasons that, in several polls conducted by the United Nations Development Program—long before the regime change in Kiev—the vast majority of Crimeans had already indicated a desire to join Russia.[16] Admittedly, different results have been found in different surveys at differing times, the findings being largely dependent on political circumstances, such as the presence of a pro-Russian or pro-European cabinet in Ukraine. Indeed, under Yanukovych in 2013, less than half of Crimeans indicated a desire to separate from Ukraine. The Ukrainian political scientist Ivan Katchanovski argues, however, that the political context in 2008—when a Razumkov Center survey was taken—most closely resembles that of post-Maidan Ukraine.[17] In addition to the presence of a pro-Western cabinet, the survey was taken soon after the Russian-Georgian war, which saw an attempt by the Georgian state to seize the de-facto independent secessionist and pro-Russian region of South Ossetia, leading to a Russian military intervention. The Russo-Georgian war was undoubtedly closely monitored by most Crimeans—and 73 percent of them favoured an accession of Crimea to Russia at that time.

The small discrepancy between the 2014 referendum results and the post-Maidan surveys in Crimea probably stem from a boycott by the Crimean Tatar minority (12%). It is important to emphasize that- when Crimea became part of the Russian empire by force in 1783, Crimean Tatars represented some 80 percent of the population. They were deported in several waves over two centuries—most tragically under Stalin's regime after WW2, which deported all the remaining 230,000 Crimean Tatars to Uzbekistan. Perestroika in the 80s enabled them to return to their homeland. Russia still seems to distrust them. There is now a five year prison sentence on the expression of separatist views, and the Crimean Tatar political leader, Mustafa Dzhemilev, was refused entry to Crimea for five years.[18] After the annexation, some 20,000 people fled Crimea, including non-Tatar Crimeans who feared repression, such as local Maidan activists.[19]

Nevertheless, the Russian state has also attempted to persuade the Crimean Tatar population with carrots. On the 21st of April 2014, the Crimean Tatars were formally rehabilitated by presidential decree, in effect granting an old demand of Crimean Tatar protest in the former Soviet Union.[20] This meant that Crimean Tatar, alongside Russian and Ukrainian, was accorded the status of an official language, and several initiatives were undertaken to resolve issues of land ownership. On the other hand, Kiev's efforts to woo the Crimean Tatar population have not proven entirely convincing. Admittedly, after the annexation, the Ukrainian parliament recognized the Crimean Tatar population as the indigenous people of Crimea, yet not a single piece of legislation was passed to aid the 20,000 Crimeans who left their homes to go to Ukraine. The Poroshenko administration even condoned a blockade of Crimea, supported by the aforementioned Crimean Tatar leader, Mustafa Dzhemilev and Right Sector, severing transportation from Ukraine proper on which the Crimean peninsula was heavily reliant.[21] Kiev then followed this up with an official trade ban.

Further emboldened by Kiev's position, the Crimean Tatar activists and Right Sector prevented the repair of two electricity pylons supplying the peninsula after they were bombed, leading to major power shortages in Crimea, which received 70 percent of its energy from Ukraine.[22] All things considered, some Crimean Tatar organizations have now voiced their support for Crimea's reunification with Russia. One such organization is Milli Firka, whose chair argued that: 'In less than two months Russia has done far more for the Crimean Tatars than Ukraine ever did. Only after Crimea became part of Russia did Kiev even remember that we exist.'[23]

One year after Crimea was reunified with Russia, an extensive scientific survey sponsored by the US National Science Foundation indicated that the Russian state retained much legitimacy in the formerly Ukrainian peninsula.[24] Eighty-four percent of ethnic Ukrainians and Russians in Crimea said that annexation was an 'absolutely right decision,' while a slight majority of Crimean Tatars found it either 'mostly' or 'absolutely' a right decision. In addition, 85 percent of Crimeans indicated that the peninsula was 'heading in the right direction' (a slight majority of Tatars disagreed), compared to only 22 percent when Crimea was part of Ukraine in 2013. The aforementioned Canadian sponsored survey had also found that—a year after annexation—most people's financial status had either 'significantly improved' (21 percent) or 'improved' (30 percent). Only thirteen percent of Crimeans saw their financial status deteriorate.

Endnotes

1   NEWSru. (2008, April 07). Путин пригрозил аннексировать Крым и Восточную Украину в случае принятия Украины в НАТО. Retrieved from http://www.newsru.com/russia/07apr2008/annex.html

2   На Украине отменили закон о региональном статусе русского языка. (2014, February 23). Retrieved from http://lenta.ru/news/2014/02/23/language/

3   Kramer, A. E. (2014, March 02). Ukraine Turns to Its Oligarchs for Political Help. Retrieved from http://www.nytimes.com/2014/03/03/world/europe/ukraine-turns-to-its-oligarchs-for-political-help.html

4   Митинг народной воли в Севастополе 23 февраля 2014. Фото.

	(2014, February 24). Retrieved from http://sevastopolnews.info/2014/02/lenta/sobytiya/069214706/
5	Pulkki, A. (2014, March 3). Crimea Invaded By High Readiness Forces Of The Russian Federation. Retrieved from https://web.archive.org/web/20150330124704/http://www.suomensotilas.fi/en/artikkelit/crimea-invaded-high-readiness-forces-russian-federation
6	Putin acknowledges Russian military serviceman were in Crimea. (2014, April 17). Retrieved December 04, 2016, from https://www.rt.com/news/crimea-defense-russian-soldiers-108/
7	NATO Recon Missed Everything: Admiral Reveals Details of Crimea Operation. (2015, March 13). Retrieved from https://sputniknews.com/russia/201503131019448901/
8	Number of Crimean deputies present at referendum resolution vote unclear. (2014, February 27). Retrieved from http://en.interfax.com.ua/news/general/193292.html
9	Carbonnel, A., De. (2014, March 13). RPT-INSIGHT-How the separatists delivered Crimea to Moscow. Retrieved December 07, 2016, from http://in.reuters.com/article/ukraine-crisis-russia-aksyonov-idINL6N0M93AH20140313
10	Aale, P. K. (2014, March 03). Voting fraud secured pro-Russian majority in Crimean parliament. Retrieved from http://www.aftenposten.no/verden/Voting-fraud-secured-pro-Russian-majority-in-Crimean-parliament-94104b.html
11	Golubkova, A., Vasovic, A., Heritage, T., & Popeski, R. (2014, March 10). Crimea invites OSCE observers for referendum on joining Russia. Retrieved from http://www.reuters.com/article/us-ukraine-crisis-referendum-osce-idUSBREA2910C20140310
12	There had been news circulating—first published by Forbes magazine—that the Russian Presidential Human Rights Council accidentally posted the 'real' referendum results online for a brief period, and that only fifteen percent of Crimeans had voted in favor of secession. The report that was referred to, however, remained online, and certainly proved no such thing. Reporting on a four-day visit to Crimea, three present and former member of the Presidential Human Rights Council presented some critical notes, one of the members was even against the secession. Based on a minor survey—with a sample of only twenty people—the group had estimated that 50-60 percent voted in favor with a turnout of 30-50 percent, excluding Sevastopol which they say voted 'overwhelmingly' in favor. In other words, the fifteen percent figure was a misleading calculation that included turnout and was based on the lowest estimates, excluding Sevastopol—based on a minor unscientific survey with an extremely small sample—and

reported on by a working-group divided over Crimea's secession and with no official status. Forbes' claim that the fifteen percent figure represented the 'real' results was a complete distortion. See Fitzpatrick, C. (2014, May 9). Russia This Week: Surge of Nationalism on Victory Day (5-9 May). Retrieved from http://www.interpretermag.com/russia-this-week-poll-indicates-most-russians-dont-favor-annexation-but-many-yearn-for-soviet-re-union/#1719; The Crimea referendum "15% for" myth. (2014, May 6). Retrieved from https://humanrightsinvestigations.org/2014/05/06/the-crimea-referendum-15-percent-for-myth/

13   Despite Concerns about Governance, Ukrainians Want to Remain One Country. (2014, May 07). Retrieved from http://www.pewglobal.org/2014/05/08/despite-concerns-about-governance-ukrainians-want-to-remain-one-country/

14   Newsgathering and Policy Perceptions in Ukraine (Rep.). (2014). Retrieved http://www.bbg.gov/wp-content/media/2014/06/Ukraine-slide-deck.pdf; Survey on attitudes of the Crimea people to the events of 2014. (2015, March 1). Retrieved February 13, 2016, from https://newcoldwar.org/survey-on-attitudes-of-the-crimea-people-to-the-events-of-2014/

15   Russian Census of Crimea: Nationality Results. (2015, March 19). Retrieved from https://eurasianstudies.wordpress.com/2015/03/19/russian-census-of-crimea-nationality-results/

16   Квартальный мониторинговый отчет (Rep.). (2010). Retrieved http://web.archive.org/web/20140415042714/http://www.undp.crimea.ua/img/content/file/monitoring_ru_2010_10-12.pdf; Отчет о мониторинге (Rep.). (2011). Retrieved from http://web.archive.org/web/20140502005021/http://www.undp.crimea.ua/img/content/Strategy Implementation Monitoring Report (October to December 2011)(5).pdf

17   Katchanovski, I. (2014, August 28). East or West? Regional Political Divisions in Ukraine since the "Orange Revolution" and the "Euromaidan". Retrieved from https://www.academia.edu/8351374/East_or_West_Regional_Political_Divisions_in_Ukraine_since_the_Orange_Revolution_and_the_Euromaidan_

18   Anteleva, N. (2014). The Crimean Tatars' Bitter Anniversary. Retrieved from http://www.newyorker.com/news/news-desk/the-crimean-tatars-bitter-anniversary

19   Количество переселенцев из Крыма и зоны АТО превысило 630 тысяч человек. (2015, January 7). Retrieved from http://www.unian.net/society/1029504-kolichestvo-pereselentsev-iz-kryima-i-zonyi-ato-prevyisilo-630-tyisyach-chelovek.html

20. Sakwa, R. (2014). *Frontline Ukraine: crisis in the borderlands.* IB Tauris, p. 118.
21. Bugriy, M. (2015, October 16). Ukraine's uneasy blockade of Russian-occupied Crimea. Retrieved from http://europe.newsweek.com/ukraines-uneasy-blockade-russian-occupied-crimea-334936?rm=eu
22. Crimea hit by power blackout and Ukraine trade boycott. (2015, November 23). Retrieved October 01, 2016, from http://www.bbc.com/news/world-europe-34899491
23. Sakwa, R. (2014). *Frontline Ukraine: crisis in the borderlands.* IB Tauris, p. 119.
24. O'Loughlin, J., & Toal, G. (2015, March 3). The Crimean conundrum. Retrieved from https://www.opendemocracy.net/od-russia/john-o'loughlin-gerard-toal/crimean-conundrum

| Chapter Eleven |

CIVIL WAR DARKENS THE UKRAINIAN LANDSCAPE

Thus, by and large, the annexation of Crimea seems to be acceptable to the local population. That being said, the consequences would reach far beyond the formerly Ukrainian autonomous republic. Inspired by the seizure of government buildings in Crimea and the announcement of a referendum on February 27th, 2014, protestors in other Ukrainian regions would follow suit. Nevertheless, the most common justification for the seizure of state property remained its widespread occurrence during EuroMaidan. Indeed, in an echo of the Yanukovych regime, the post-Maidan security apparatus reacted with mass arrests and threats of lengthy prison sentences.[1] March also saw multiple clashes between Ukrainian and pro-Russian protestors, including fatalities on both sides of the conflict.

After Crimea was annexed on the 28th of March the situation would further escalate. In an echo of Maidan, from the 6th of April onwards, protestors would raid weapon armories, especially in the Donbass. Arguably the most important escalation happened on April 12th, when a volunteer militia led by the ultranationalist Russian military veteran Ihor Strelkov seized the police department and Security Service of Ukraine offices in Sloviansk. Strelkov admitted to having served as an FSB colonel until 2012, and Kiev even accused him of still working for the Russian security services in Ukraine. The latter seems to be a stretch, however, considering that

Strelkov later turned against Putin for failing to mount a full-scale invasion in Ukraine, and even predicted a revolt against the Russian president in his published manifesto.[2] Nevertheless, it's obvious that Russia at least tolerated the movement of this militia into Ukrainian territory, which it cannot have missed. In fact, the Russo-Ukrainian border remained wide open for volunteers throughout the conflict. In addition, Russian citizens fighting in Eastern Ukraine didn't face any legal consequences—and could even be openly recruited, funded and equipped by private networks in Russia, in sharp contrast to fighters heading for Syria who could be jailed for five to ten years.[3] The post-Maidan regime announced an 'anti-terrorist operation' the day after the Strelkov battalion entered Sloviansk: a full-scale military operation to retake the government buildings. The military operation, however, became a disaster. When Ukrainian soldiers were confronted with blockades of unarmed demonstrators one after the other gave up their weapons and left. Some would even join the rebellion.[4] Many local police officers joined the rebels too. The 24th of May, the Ukrainian interior ministry published a "list of shame" with the names of 17,000 law enforcement officers who had joined the armed uprising.[5]

This statement ironically contradicts the official position of the Kiev regime: that the armed uprising in the Donbass was a Russian invasion. Clearly, there has been Russian military support for the rebels and Russian ultranationalists played a pivotal role in major escalations, but that doesn't mean that local elements were irrelevant. In fact, foreign backing is an almost universal aspect of civil wars. (The exact role of Russia in Ukraine will be examined in a later chapter). A KIIS poll in early May 2014 found that the majority of Donbass citizens characterized the insurgency as a "people's revolt."[6] A recent KIIS survey—taken two years down the line—showed that only 6 percent of Donbass citizens thought there were Russian troops in Ukraine, just 8 percent thought there was a war between Russia and Ukraine.[7] On the 11th of May 2014, a referendum on independence was held in rebel-controlled territory in the Donbass, in which supposedly 89% voted in favor. The poll obviously did not adhere to international standards—some voters were even shot at by the Ukrainian national guard, which attempted to disrupt the voting process.[8] Polls were also taken on the day of the Referendum by the German AFZ, the *Washington Post* and five other international media. This poll indicated that a 65.6% majority was in favor of independence, and that voters against independence were mostly planning to stay home.[9] Nevertheless, the poll reflected a very small sample of the population concerned, nor is it clear how random its selection was. According to the Interior Ministry of Ukraine, the turnout was 32 percent.[10] The rebels claimed a turnout of 75 percent.[11]

During his field research on the Donbass insurgency, Ukrainian scholar Serhiy Kudelia found that local officials helped to lay the ground for the independence referenda, among other things, long before militants arrived on the scene—in a very chaotic process which he dubs a "quiet secessionism:' "there was clearly no hierarchical subordination to any elite actor at the very top. And a lot of the decisions that were taken by local officials were taken on their own."[12] Kudelia is unconvinced by the tapes, recently leaked by the Ukrainian prosecutor general's office, which purportedly demonstrate that the Russian state orchestrated the Donbass insurgency. In the taped conversations between Russian presidential adviser Sergey Glazyev, Russian official Konstantin Zatulin and several separatist leaders, we hear Glazyev and Zatulin urging the separatists to occupy buildings and to subsequently plea for a Russian military intervention, among other things. Nevertheless, not only were the tapes clearly edited and did they exclude any references to protests within Donbass, but the actual conversations largely confirmed Kudelia's findings: the protestors seemed without a clear strategy or guidance on the ground, and were in a seemingly drunken state asking Glazyev and Zatulin for money over the phone, something Zatulin actually complains about.[13] In fact, both Russian officials didn't seem to fully trust these separatists. Rather than showing a Russian state in control of the process, we see someone from his safe offices in Moscow making a chaotic attempt to influence some of the local protesters in three cities in Southern and Eastern Ukraine. Furthermore, as

Katchanovski notes, it isn't even clear whether the men were acting for the Russian government or in their own capacities—both have private connections to Ukraine, and Zatulin's complaints about having to pay a few thousand dollars seem to suggest a complete lack of funding from the Russian state.[14]

Returning to the armed insurgents, even some devoutly nationalist Ukrainian commanders—in addition to the post-Maidan interim-deputy head of Ukraine's presidential administration—in 2014 publicly admitted that the majority of rebels were 'local idiots.'[15] Two years later, the International Crisis Group (ICG) interviewed many Ukrainian officers, who unanimously confirmed that they were primarily fighting against locals.[16] Katchanovski also demonstrated the presence of a Ukrainian majority among the insurgents, through statistical analysis of publicly available data. He writes that "the list of separatists sanctioned by the Ukrainian government shows that out of 188 separatist leaders, commanders, officials, and fighters on this list, 64% were identified as Ukrainian citizens, 8% Russian citizens, 4% citizens of other countries, and 24% had no citizenship information. Similarly, a leaked and Myrotvorest-published list of 1,572 people, who joined armed formations of the Donetsk Peoples Republic (DNR) in the summer of 2014, were 78% Ukrainian citizens, 19% Russian citizens, 2% citizens of other countries, and 1% persons with unknown citizenship."[17] Writing on the ground for the *The New York Times*, Chivers and Sneider report that most of the insurgents were indeed Ukrainians.[18] Admittedly, their identities were often entangled with Russia: some had migrated from there, others had family just across the border, and many were veterans of the former Soviet army. Such history, however, is not uncommon for citizens of the Donbass and rather explains some of their motivations for revolt. Indeed, as Kudelia notes, citing Ukrainian surveys," in contrast to all other regions, the majority has traditionally supported the unification of Ukraine with Russia (66 percent) and regretted the collapse of the Soviet Union (61 percent)."[19] Indeed, Chivers and Sneider report that the fighters were supported by local civilians who brought supplies and cooked for them.[20]

The *NYT* journalists also correctly emphasized that the soldiers were hardly homogenous, and had many disagreements regarding the future of their oblast (region).[21] Three options were commonly considered: independence, accession to Russia and remaining part of Ukraine within a federalized structure. In regards to federalism, its difference from decentralization or devolution of powers must be emphasized. Whereas decentralization can easily be reversed by the central authorities, federalism involves constitutional guarantees for the local administration. In addition, federalism can in some cases accompany the ability for local administrations to influence or veto national policies that affect them—such as the decision to sign the EU association agreement, which is why the Kremlin had supported this solution since March 2014. Whereas Kiev paid lip-service to decentralization, it was unwilling to even discuss the notion of federalization until the regime was forced to by the specter of military defeat in August 2014. Although federalism is a very common form of rule across the world—including in the United States and Canada—Kiev argued that Crimea too had been an autonomous republic within Ukraine and that this federal structure had led to secession just as the Donbass insurgents—Russian soldiers according to Kiev—made their demands.

Taken together, these three options—federalization, independence and accession to Russia—all indicate a desire for a change in the status quo, and are supported by a majority of Donbass residents according to a KIIS survey from July 2014.[22] An earlier Ukrainian poll found 59 percent for federalization and a third for secession (just 10 percent said they would actively resist a Russian military presence).[23] Another Ukrainian survey in September 2014 found that—even in the Donbass territories controlled by the Ukrainian government—40 percent wanted independence or accession to Russia, while 25 percent wanted greater autonomy (the latter was not clearly defined).[24] One of the more recent surveys came from the University of Maryland and KIIS in March 2015, which questioned both rebel-held and government-controlled territory within the Donbass.[25] Forty-one percent of the former supported independence or accession to Russia (federalization was not provided as an option), 58 percent approved of Putin and 67 percent had a positive view of Russia. Perhaps most telling—concerning the local roots of the rebellion—is that these figures were much lower in government-controlled Donbass. Indeed, one of the most forceful arguments in favor of the notion that the roots of the Donbass rebellion are local, is that its success has been bound to a very specific territory. In fact, anti-Maidan protests were very significant in Kharkov and Odessa oblasts as well, but only in the Donbass, where separatist/federalist views are by far the most prevalent, did war ensue.

Serhiy Kudelia demonstrated a correlation between the percentage of Russian speakers within Donbass towns, and the subsequent ability of the rebels to hold that territory.[26] Most towns with over eighty percent native Ukrainian speakers were never under insurgent control. By contrast, in the majority of towns where native Ukrainians speakers represented a minority of less than 20 percent, the rebellion was able to maintain control for at least six months. Indeed, separatist views were more prevalent among ethnic or linguistic Russians than ethnic/linguistic Ukrainians. Even the Kiev-appointed governor of state-controlled territories in Lugansk, Gennadiy Maskal, corroborated this: "Speaking of pro-Russian sentiment, [I can attest] that it is very high—in some residential areas—reaching 95%, in others—80%. The lowest level of support—30% was recorded on the Ukrainian side of the region, where historically more Ukrainians resided."[27] Elise Guiliano collected the prevalent protest themes in Donetsk during the first two months after the ouster of Yanukovych and found that Russian language rights and culture were present in the (slight) majority of protest activities.[28]

She calls for caution however, because several polls indicated that the issue of language was not the most important to the wider Donbass population, which could indicate that (ultra)nationalist pro-Russian Ukrainians had a disproportionate representation within the Donbass uprising.[29] Indeed, data from the aforementioned Center for Social and Labour Research suggests that, from March 2014 onwards, over half of anti-Maidan protests had a presence of Russian nationalists.[30] Therefore, Guiliano argues that the relevance of ethnicity and linguistic factors for rebel success is better explained as a reaction to the ethnic nationalism propagated under Yushchenko. For the first time, on the highest political level, Ukrainian identity was built around one language, culture and very divisive ultranationalist figures such as Stepan Bandera. This also involved an identity of victimhood by the Soviet Union, to which Russia is considered the successor nation, making ethnic and linguistic Russians easy scapegoats for ultranationalists. Indeed, as Kudelia notes: "In early April, 46 percent in the Donetsk region and 33 percent in the Luhansk region viewed disarming illegal radical groups [alluding to Ukrainian ultranationalists] as the main step in maintaining the country's unity. Instead, the government authorized transforming them into semi-private militia battalions tasked with fighting separatists in the east"[31] (More on this in the next chapter.) Indeed, 'anti-fascism' was a theme present in nearly half of the protests in Donetsk during the two months after Maidan. Notably, the anti-fascist stance was mainly directed against the Ukrainian far right. Russian ultranationalists—and even neo-Nazis —were almost universally tolerated.[32]

Two subsequent events in early May greatly increased this perception of threat from Ukrainian ultranationalists: the Odessa and Mariupol tragedies. In Odessa, there had been peaceful encampments in front of the trade union building. On May 2nd, an ultranationalist march was attacked by a small armed pro-Russian group, killing one Right Sector member. Strangely, the armed group was able to shoot from behind police lines. The event took place a few blocks away from the trade-union building—and the ultranationalist mob subsequently marched on toward the peaceful anti-Maidan encampments. Dozens of pro-Russian activists there, none of them armed, were forced into the trade union building, which was subsequently burned with Molotov cocktails. An ultranationalist shot at the windows when people tried to escape, others were beaten. Most of them burned alive. Both the police and the fire department did not get involved for hours. The official dead count is set at 40 people. Everything was visible the same day on video.[33] Regardless, the pro-Russian survivors were blamed themselves for the massacre and imprisoned.

Two German and French documentaries, as well as a research paper by Ivan Katchanovski, documented most of the pertinent facts surrounding the tragedy, which I will not summarize here.[34] Indeed, the impunity enjoyed by the ultranationalists is perhaps best illustrated by the blatant admission of Right Sector on their website that the massacre constituted a "bright page in our national history." They go on to say that "[A]bout a hundred members of 'Right Sector' and patriotic-minded Odessa residents countered the rebels (…) Dmitro Yarosh, ignored the expedience of the election campaign to counter the Russian aggression."[35] Unsurprisingly, a report by the special commission of the Council of Europe found that the official investigation of the Odessa massacre has been ineffective, politically selective and involved falsification of evidence: "As to the fire in the Trade Union Building, no-one has been notified of suspicion of causing the fire, including the throwing of Molotov cocktails towards or into the building. Although the faces of some of those who prepared and threw Molotov cocktails are visible on video footage, the authorities claim not to have established their identities."[36]

In the case of Mariupol, soldiers had opened fire on a crowd of mostly unarmed Anti-Maidan protesters after violent clashes with rebel fighters at a police station.[37] Later research from Bellingcat shows that individual armed protesters were among the crowd, and opened fire first.[38] Nevertheless, the incident was widely perceived in South-East Ukraine as unprovoked—or at least excessive—use of force. No doubt, the Mariupol and Odessa tragedies were important escalations that served to pull the country further into a civil war.

Nevertheless, Elise Guiliano argues that a fear of ultranationalists was not the only factor explaining the insurgency. In fact, economic needs were just as important. Mid-way April 2014, a KIIS survey found that approximately 70 percent of Donbass residents still favored joining the Russian-led customs union over joining the EU, a much higher percentage than its neighboring regions.[39] There are good reasons for this. The Donbass is especially dominated by Soviet-era industries such as mining, metallurgy and machine building, which primarily export to Russia. Some individual militants have made this quite explicit in interviews, such as a fighter of the Vostok Batallion: "Many mines started to close. I lost my job. Then, with what happened during the spring, I decided to go out and defend my city".[40]

Going one step further, based on statistical research, political scientist Yuri Zhukov argues that ethno-linguistic divisions are much less important than economic factors.[41] Whereas the latter were very strong predictors of the level of insurgent activity, the former only had a significant effect when economic incentives were lacking. Indeed, Sean Guillory documented some of the rebel support from the mining sector, including demonstrations, strikes and even the formation of a miner-battalion.[42] Support for the rebels was definitely not universal among miners, but it was significant nevertheless. There had been important historical precedent for this: a general strike in the Donbass in 1993, which involved 230 of the region's 250 mines and 400 other enterprises, demanding regional autonomy for Donbass, closer ties to Russia, and a referendum on the resignation of the political leadership in Kiev.[43]

After 1996, the mining industry became less profitable and by 2013, having become heavily reliant on subsidies, its deficits equaled roughly $410 million.[44] In fact, many of the subsidies likely ended up propping up the black market, including hundreds of illegal mines—and it's unclear how much of the subsidies actually benefited the local population.[45] The subsidies were cut as a condition of the IMF loans after Maidan, eventually by $230 million.[46] Combined with deteriorating trade relations with Russia, the future of the mining industry looked bleak. In May 2014, three months after the fall of Yanukovych, Kiev announced that the majority of operational mines would be shut down by 2020.[47] This industry employed some 500.000 Ukrainians.[48]

Endnotes

1 Kharkiv settles down, while pro-Russian separatists still hold buildings in Luhansk, Donetsk. (2014, April 8). Retrieved from http://www.kyivpost.com/article/content/ukraine/kharkiv-settles-down-while-pro-

2   russian-separatists-still-hold-buildings-in-luhansk-donetsk-342517.html Walker, S. (2016, June 05). Russia's 'valiant hero' in Ukraine turns his fire on Vladimir Putin. Retrieved from https://www.theguardian.com/world/2016/jun/05/russias-valiant-hero-in-ukraine-turns-his-fire-on-vladimir-putin

3   Shuster, S. (2014, May 12). Meet the Cossack 'Wolves' Doing Russia's Dirty Work in Ukraine. Retrieved from http://time.com/95898/wolves-hundred-ukraine-russia-cossack/

4   Coghlan, T. (2014, April 16). Ukranian troops defect and fly the Russian flag. Retrieved from http://www.thetimes.co.uk/tto/news/world/europe/article4064836.ece; MARQUARDT, A. (2014, April 16). Ukraine's Offensive Falters as Elite Units Defect to Pro-Russia Side. Retrieved from http://abcnews.go.com/blogs/headlines/2014/04/ukraines-offensive-falters-as-elite-units-defect-to-pro-russia-side/; Russian Roulette: The Invasion of Ukraine (Dispatch 28). (2014, April 21). Retrieved from https://news.vice.com/video/russian-roulette-the-invasion-of-ukraine-dispatch-twenty-eight; Kramer, A. E. (2014, April 16). Ukraine Push Against Rebels Grinds to Halt. Retrieved from http://www.nytimes.com/2014/04/17/world/europe/ukraine-crisis.html?_r=0; Karmanau, Y. (2014, April 17). Pro-Russian gunmen make inroads in eastern Ukraine. Retrieved from http://bigstory.ap.org/article/combat-vehicles-east-ukraine-raise-russian-flag; New head of Ukraine's navy defects in Crimea. (2014, March 2). Retrieved from http://www.bbc.com/news/world-europe-26410431; Civilians Blocking Tanks East Ukraine. (2014, May 15). Retrieved from http://www.dailymotion.com/video/x1ubdz7_civilians-blocking-tanks-east-ukraine_news?start=7

5   MSW Ukrainy: 17 tys. milicjantów w Donbass ie zdradziło. (2014, May 24). Retrieved from http://wiadomosci.wp.pl/kat,1356,opage,3,title,MSW-Ukrainy-17-tys-milicjantow-w-Donbasie-zdradzilo,wid,16628860,wiadomosc.html?ticaid=1167af; MSW Ukrainy: W Donbass ie zdradziło 17 tys. milicjantów. (2014, May 24). Retrieved from http://www.tvn24.pl/msw-ukrainy-w-donbasie-zdradzilo-17-tys-milicjantow,431902,s.html

6   Results of the join study of KIIS, SOCIS and "RATING" (2014, May 21). Retrieved from http://www.kiis.com.ua/?lang=eng&cat=news&id=317&page=1

7   Shpiker, M. (2016, March 15). Is there a war going on between Russia and Ukraine? Retrieved from http://www.kiis.com.ua/?lang=eng

8   Ukraine guardsmen open fire on crowd in east after referendum. (2014, May 11). Retrieved from http://www.cbsnews.com/news/ukraine-guardsmen-open-fire-on-crowd-in-east-after-referendum/

9   Referendum im Gebiet Donezk: Separatisten verkünden große Mehrheit

	für Abspaltung. (2014, May 11). Retrieved from http://www.faz.net/aktuell/politik/ausland/separatisten-verkuenden-grosse-mehrheit-fuer-abspaltung-von-ukraine-12934681.html
10	Турчинов спростував описані сепаратистами чудеса явки на «референдум» (2014, May 12). Retrieved from http://www.pravda.com.ua/news/2014/05/12/7025064/
11	Referendum results in Donetsk and Lugansk Regions show landslide support for self-rule. (2014, May 11). Retrieved from https://www.rt.com/news/158276-referendum-results-east-ukraine/
12	Kudelia, S. (2016, September 12). The Origins of the Donbass War From Below. Retrieved from http://seansrussiablog.org/2016/09/12/the-origins-of-the-donbas-war-from-below/
13	Ibid.
14	Katchanovski, I. (2016, August 22). Retrieved from https://www.facebook.com/ivan.katchanovski/posts/1317871884909361
15	Семен Семенченко: Мы победим, но не через месяц. (2014, August 6). Retrieved from http://m.liga.net/news/politics/196781-semen_semenchenko_my_pobedim_no_ne_cherez_mesyats.htm; Karpenko, K. (2014). «Вы не представляете, как тяжело было заставить армию воевать» / Журнал «Вести.Репортер». Retrieved from http://reporter.vesti-ukr.com/art/y2014/n25/9093-vy-ne-predstavljaete-kak-tjazhelo-bylo-zastavit-armiju-voevat.html; Айдаровец о войне на востоке Украины. (2014, July 13). Retrieved from https://www.youtube.com/watch?v=IBlDpmgf9k8
16	Ukraine: The Line (Rep.). (2016, July 18). Retrieved from International Crisis Group website: https://d2071andvip0wj.cloudfront.net/ukraine-the-line.pdf
17	Katchanovski, I. (2016). The "Euromaidan," Democracy, and Political Values in Ukraine. *Democracy, and Political Values in Ukraine* (September 3, 2016), p. 25.
18	Chivers, C. J., & Sneider, N. (2014, May 03). Behind the Masks in Ukraine, Many Faces of Rebellion. Retrieved from http://www.nytimes.com/2014/05/04/world/europe/behind-the-masks-in-ukraine-many-faces-of-rebellion.html?_r=1
19	Kudelia, S. (2016). The Donbass Rift. *Russian Politics & Law*, 54(1), 5-27, p. 11.
20	Chivers, C. J., & Sneider, N. (2014, May 03). Behind the Masks in Ukraine, Many Faces of Rebellion. Retrieved from http://www.nytimes.com/2014/05/04/world/europe/behind-the-masks-in-ukraine-many-faces-of-rebellion.html?_r=1
21	Ibid.
22	Katchanovski, I. (2014, July 20). What do citizens of Ukraine actually

	think about secession? Retrieved from https://www.washingtonpost.com/news/monkey-cage/wp/2014/07/20/what-do-citizens-of-ukraine-actually-think-about-secession/
23	Ставлення українців до територіального устрою країни та статусу Криму. (2014, March 14). Retrieved from http://ratinggroup.ua/research/ukraine/otnoshenie_ukraincev_k_territorialnomu_ustroystvu_strany_i_statusu_kryma.html
24	Лишь 8% жителей Донбасса высказались за создание «ДНР» и «ЛНР» (ИСЛЕДОВАНИЕ). (2014, September 26). Retrieved from http://glavcom.ua/news/236502.html
25	Kull, S., & Ramsey, C. (2015, March 9). The Ukrainian People on the Current Crisis (Rep.). Retrieved http://www.public-consultation.org/studies/Ukraine_0315.pdf
26	Kudelia, S. (2014). The Donbass Insurgency: Origins, Organization and Dynamics of Violence. Retrieved from http://www.danyliwseminar.com/#!serhiy-kudelia/cfss; Kudelia, S. (2014, September). Domestic Sources of the Donbass Insurgency. Retrieved from http://www.ponarseurasia.org/memo/domestic-sources-donbas-insurgency; Kudelia, S. (2014, November 6). Getting to the Bottom on the Sources of the Donbass Insurgency. Retrieved from http://www.ponarseurasia.org/node/7349
27	Cited in Black, J. L., & Johns, M. (Eds.). (2016), pp. 212-213. *The Return of the Cold War: Ukraine, The West and Russia.* Routledge.
28	Giuliano, E. (2015, October). The Origins of Separatism: Popular Grievances in Donetsk and Luhansk. Retrieved from http://www.ponarseurasia.org/memo/origins-separatism-popular-grievances-donetsk-and-luhansk; Giuliano, E. (2015). The Social Bases of Support for Self-determination in East Ukraine. *Ethnopolitics,* 14(5), 513-522.
29	Ibid..
30	Ishchenko, V. (2016, January 22). The Ukrainian Left during and after the Maidan Protests, p. 55. Retrieved from https://www.academia.edu/20445056/The_Ukrainian_Left_during_and_after_the_Maidan_Protests
31	Kudelia, S. (2014, September). Domestic Sources of the Donbass Insurgency, p. 5. Retrieved from http://www.ponarseurasia.org/memo/domestic-sources-donbas-insurgency
32	Volodymyr Ishchenko, The Ukrainian Left During and After the Maidan Protests.
33	An early video reconstruction of the Odessa Massacre is available here: The Odessa Massacre - What REALLY Happened. (2014, May 12). Retrieved from http://stormcloudsgathering.com/the-odessa-massacre-what-really-happened.

34	A summary of a research paper by Ivan Katchanovski on the Odessa massacre prepared for presentation at the upcoming Canadian Association of Slavists conference in Ottawa is available on Facebook. (2015, May 3). Retrieved from https://www.facebook.com/ivan.katchanovski/posts/1017994261563793; Moreira, P. (2016, February 7). LiveLeak. com - Documentary: Ukraine - Masks of revolution. Eng. Subs. Retrieved from http://www.liveleak.com/view?i=30e_1454796647; Heyden, U., & Benson, M. (2015, March 13). The atrocities of Odessa on May 2, 2014. Retrieved from https://www.youtube.com/watch?v=OErKKcuBTlY
35	Hahn, G. (2014, September 23). The Ukrainian Revolution's Neo-Fascist Problem. Retrieved from http://www.fairobserver.com/region/europe/the-ukrainian-revolutions-neo-fascist-problem-14785/
36	Special Commission of the Council of Europe. (2015). Retrieved from https://rm.coe.int/CoERMPublicCommonSearchServices/DisplayDCTMContent?documentId=0900001680488551b
37	Walker, S. (2014, May 11). East Ukraine goes to the polls for independence referendum. Retrieved from http://www.theguardian.com/world/2014/may/10/donetsk-referendum-ukraine-civil-war; Dispatches: Truth a Casualty in Ukraine Conflict. (2014, May 10). Retrieved from https://www.hrw.org/news/2014/05/10/dispatches-truth-casualty-ukraine-conflict
38	Huis, P. V. (2015, January 28). A Reconstruction of Clashes in Mariupol, Ukraine, 9 May 2014. Retrieved from https://www.bellingcat.com/news/uk-and-europe/2015/01/28/a-reconstruction-of-clashes-in-mariupol-ukraine-9-may-2014/
39	Giuliano, E. (2015). The Social Bases of Support for Self-determination in East Ukraine. Ethnopolitics, 14(5), 513-522, p. 518.
40	Zhukov, Y. M. (2015, May 11). Why the Ukraine rebellion is unlikely to spread. Retrieved from http://europe.newsweek.com/why-ukraine-rebellion-unlikely-spread-397530?rm=eu
41	Zhukov, Y. M. (2015, November 10). The Economics of Rebellion in Eastern Ukraine. Retrieved from http://voxukraine.org/2015/11/10/the-economics-of-rebellion-in-eastern-ukraine/; Zhukov, Y. M. (2015). Trading hard hats for combat helmets: The economics of rebellion in eastern Ukraine. Journal of Comparative Economics.
42	Guillory, S. (2014, July 15). Donbass Miners and the People's Republics. Retrieved from http://www.warscapes.com/opinion/Donbas-miners-and-peoples-republics
43	Ibid.
44	Ibid.
45	Ibid.
46	Ibid.

47   Ibid.
48   Ibid.

| Chapter Twelve |

THE RAVAGES OF WAR

Due to the disintegration of the country's armed forces, the Kiev regime had issued a mandatory military draft on the 1st of May, 2014.[1] However, few Ukrainians were willing to die for its war—even in the supposedly 'patriotic' provinces. As of September 2014, the Ukrainian military asserted that over 85,000 residents in 13 Western and Central Ukrainian provinces had failed to report to their draft offices.[2] A good example is the supposedly nationalist region of Volyn in Western Ukraine. Official data revealed that, as of April 2015, some 8,000 people appeared for their draft, while 12,000 Volynians chose evasion.[3] Only 532 people volunteered. What's more, the majority of those who obeyed their draft notice never entered the army for medical reasons—a significant proportion of which were made up. Stories even appeared of 'patriotic' Western-Ukrainians fleeing to Russia, the supposed aggressor nation, in order to get out of the draft.[4] In fact, the army became so desperate that it started drafting adopted Ukrainians from as far away as Spain.[5] In addition, as of January 2015, approximately 1100 of the Volynians who finally entered the army eventually deserted during their military service. One month later, the Ukrainian parliament passed a law which allowed the military to shoot deserters.[6] Yet such measures did little to improve the army's morale. In 2016, for example, 55 percent of Ukraine's casualties occured outside of combat, with soldiers dying from suicide, alcohol abuse and murder, among other causes.[7]

As a result of the disintegrating military and the failure of the draft, the Ukrainian regime became reliant on volunteer battalions, some of which were dominated by ultranationalists.

Probably the most extreme example is the commander of the Azov battalion, who wrote that "The historic mission of our nation in this critical moment is to lead the White Races of the world in a final crusade for their survival ... A crusade against the Semite-led Untermenschen."[8] A *New York Times* report also showed that several Islamist battalions from Chechnya were fighting alongside the Ukrainian armed forces, some of which were devout fundamentalists. French security forces had detained two battalion members for being linked to the Islamic State in Syria and Iraq.[9] Hidden in the last three paragraphs of another *New York Times* report is a surprisingly honest description of Kiev's 'Anti-terrorist operation':

> The fighting for Donetsk has taken on a lethal pattern: The regular army bombards separatist positions from afar, followed by chaotic, violent assaults by some of the half-dozen or so paramilitary groups surrounding Donetsk who are willing to plunge into urban combat.
>
> Officials in Kiev say the militias and the army coordinate their actions, but the militias, which count about 7,000 fighters, are angry and, at times, uncontrollable. One known as Azov, which took over the village of Marinka, flies a neo-Nazi symbol resembling a Swastika as its flag.
>
> In pressing their advance, the fighters took their orders from a local army commander, rather than from Kiev. In the video of the attack, no restraint was evident. Gesturing toward a suspected pro-Russian position, one soldier screamed, 'The bastards are right there!' Then he opened fire.[10]

Der Spiegel later reported on the volunteer-battalion Tornado who "had prisoners' tortured by means of an object similar to a power generator. The prisoners were held in the basement, stripped naked, placed on a concrete wall and doused with water. Then they were touched with live wires to various body parts, such as at the temple, the genitals and the testicles. (…) According to a statement of a former prisoner, prisoners 'were forced under threat of death to rape another prisoner.'[11] A few months earlier an Amnesty International report had already documented dozens of cases of torture and summary executions on both sides of the conflict, though there were no indications that this practice was 'systemic.'[12]

The report of Der Spiegel sheds some light on the mentality of some of the worse elements in Kiev: "Tornado commander Ruslan Onischenko had several prior convictions, but for his political supporters that was no reason for caution. On the contrary, the nationalist Radical Party's boss Oleh Lyashko wants to send even more criminal offenders to the front; offenders would simply 'fight better'." The commander of another militia, the Aidar battalion, tells an Amnesty International researcher: "The law has changed, procedures have been simplified… If I choose to, I can have you arrested right now, put a bag over your head and lock you up in a cellar for 30 days on suspicion of aiding separatists."[13] In fact, even direct co-operation between volunteer battalions and the regular security forces in regard to torture has been documented by Human Rights Watch.[14] In addition, a UN report indicated that secret prisons have been established in Ukraine, whose practices happen completely in the dark.[15] Supporting evidence for these secret detentions were later provided in a report by Amnesty International and Human Rights Watch.[16]

It would be a grave mistake, however, to focus solely on the collaboration of the Kiev regime with ultranationalist forces. Many of the bombardments by the regular army constitute war crimes as well—and these are often more deadly than those committed by the ultranationalist battalions. Lots of footage has emerged of fighter jets, and especially artillery, shelling residential areas. Official documentation of the war crimes has come from the UN, OSCE, Amnesty International and Human Rights Watch, among others.[17] Even hospitals and schools are not spared. Furthermore,

The New York Times, Human Rights Watch, Armament Research Services and the OSCE all separately documented the use of cluster munitions by the Ukrainian military.[18] These weapons are banned by 118 countries due their inability to discriminate between civilian and military targets. Cluster munitions also leave behind unexploded ordinances that can remain a threat for years, even decades, after the armed hostilities have ended. Indeed, UN special rapporteur Christof Heyns was "concerned by allegations that the conflict is being waged in part using inherently indiscriminate weapons such as cluster munitions and landmines. … I also note with concern that Ukraine failed to fulfil its commitment to destruct all its stockpiled anti-personnel mines before 1 June 2010. According to its official reports, Ukraine still retains over 5 million anti-personnel mines."[19] The International Crisis Group later found rampant use of land-mines on both sides of the conflict, which demining experts say will take five to twenty years to remove, depending on the level of funding.[20] It didn't stop there. Human Rights Watch also documented the use of incendiary weapons by the Ukrainian army, asserting that "There was no clear military objective (to the attack in Ilovaisk), we saw civilian houses burned. Any military advantage perceived as being gained by using these weapons is outweighed by the humanitarian consequences."[21]

Indeed, the widespread use of banned weapons only underscores a more general point: civilians in the Donbass are indiscriminately bombed. As war-correspondent Keith Gessen wrote from Donetsk for the *London Review of Books*: "I never once saw an actual military target—the SBU, for example—get hit, only civilian locations."[22] Alexander Lukyanchenko, who was the state-recognized mayor of Donetsk during the war, assessed the damage to his city in September 2014: 'Over 900 buildings in Donetsk have been damaged or destroyed, including 35 schools, 17 kindergartens, and very many enterprises, especially mining […] and a number of energy facilities—electrical power sub-stations—for good.'[23] As of February 2015, officially reported damages included some 10 thousand apartment buildings, 1,080 objects of energy infrastructure, 1,514 railway infrastructure facilities, 1,561 km of public roads, 33 bridges, and 28 air traffic control facilities—and it's unclear how much of the damage in rebel-controlled territories the government was able to assess.[24]

The widespread destruction of civilian infrastructure was combined with a siege by the Ukrainian military—a brutal war tactic that intends to deprive the entire civilian population of a region. Dozens of trucks carrying humanitarian aid have been intercepted by the military.[25] In addition, Kiev stopped all government transactions to the Donbass, including pensions and welfare benefits, as well as educative and medical facilities.[26] The regime ordered all its 252 state-owned enterprises in the Donbass to halt their operations and evacuate their holdings—including employees and assets—to government controlled territory.[27] Kiev also froze the entire banking system in the Donbass, so that no-one could access their savings. The siege was intensified before the onset of winter in 2014-15, when the UN warned that five million Donbass citizens were facing 'mounting hardships' with many 'struggling to survive.'[28] A KIIS survey had just estimated that a third of the remaining Donbass residents said living there was simply "no longer possible;" 60 percent stated they had an urgent need for food.[29] The Ukrainian Independent Information Agency had already documented 22 cases of starvation in the city of Donetsk.[30] In December, a local pastor told *USA Today* that 100 pensioners in his neighborhood had starved within one month's time.[31] According to UNICEF, 750,000 people lacked access to clean drinking water in February, a figured that nearly doubled to 1.3 million by July 2015.[32] In April 2016, the United Nations World Food Program reported that 1.5 million people in Donbass were hungry, with 300,000 severely food insecure and in need of immediate food assistance.[33] Medical shortages had become so severe that many medical centers were abandoned. As one doctor explained: "we're often treating people with words, not medicines."[34]

To make matters worse, on January 15th 2015, Kiev issued an order to control people's movement, forcing refugees to register through a complicated system of military checkpoints before leaving the conflict-zone. An extensive report by the OSCE monitoring mission found that "the permit system has severely limited the capacity of individuals to leave conflict-affected areas or to access safe areas and life-saving assistance, including humanitarian aid."[35] All the application locations were "situated within areas of active hostilities."[36] People were forced to wait for hours in long lines, some of which were subsequently bombed. Some queues, residing in the middle of an active war-zone, actually took multiple days to sit through. The processing subsequently took an average of 17 days—forcing people to travel back and forth through highly dangerous territory, not even knowing whether their permits would be approved.

As of November 2016, over 1,150,000 people had fled to Russia and an estimated 150.000 to Belarus; by March 2016, approximately 1.6 million were internally displaced in Ukraine, between 800.000 and one million of which had fled to government-controlled territory.[37] The official UN dead count has been put near 10.000, with another 22,500 wounded, though the report warns that "the actual number of casualties is likely to be far higher since military and civilian casualties remain under-reported."[38] Indeed, many bodies never made it to the morgue as people trapped by the fighting had to hastily bury their relatives in fields and backyards.[39] Some unmarked graves with multiple bodies have already been uncovered from both sides.[40] Citing a German intelligence official, the *Frankfurter Allgemeine Sonntagszeitung* (FAZ) reported in February 2015 that "Germany's special services estimate the probable number of deceased Ukrainian servicemen and civilians at up to 50,000 people. This figure is about 10 times higher than official data. Official figures are clearly too low and not credible."[41]

Of course, the rebels also bear culpability for the state of Donbass. Concerning the humanitarian crisis, for example, in September and October 2015 the rebel authorities kicked out all Western aid agencies, with the sole exception of People in Need and the International Committee of the Red Cross (ICRC), for allegedly spying for Western governments, among other things.[42] Notably, this is not the first time that the ICRC is among the only Western aid agencies allowed to remain in a conflict zone. As David Chandler documented in his authoritative treatise *From Kosovo to Kabul and Beyond*, aid agencies have become increasingly politicized since the 90's, including indicating widespread support for Western 'humanitarian interventions,' explicitly abandoning the code of neutrality that is still followed by the ICRC.[43] Accordingly, these agencies also bear a level of responsibility for the distrust they engender among groups hostile to Western interests. Nevertheless, it is obvious that such expulsions are very grave decisions in the context of a humanitarian crisis, and the blanket decision to expel nearly all but the ICRC within two months surely seems arbitrary and disproportional. Clearly, the plethora of remaining local agencies could not fill the gap. This role was seemingly reserved for the Russian government, which sent 59 large convoys of 40+ aid trucks by the end of 2016.[44] Yet the former rebel commander Ihor Strelkov admitted in an interview that "the Russian state aid, first, is not enough, and secondly, for the most part, it hits the markets and does not reach the population." Asked whether some of it is stolen, Girkin Strelkov affirmed that "some of the recipients of the aid ... are largely dishonest."[45]

Especially at the start of the conflict, the rebels lacked a central chain of command, nor have they been an internationally recognized state, signatory to a wide range of international human rights conventions. But let it be clear that human rights violations have also been rife among some rebel formations. An attempt to make a systemic estimate of non-military threats to Donbass civilians was done by the Center for Social and Labour Research for August and September 2014. The top 3 threats were robbery (93 cases), detention or arrest by the Ukrainian authorities (52 cases) and kidnapping or hostage taking (46 cases). A third of the former and over half of the latter were reportedly perpetrated by separatist militants, the rest by unknown armed people (who could just be criminal gangs).[46] The report, based on a systemic coding of regional Ukrainian media reports, makes an important caveat that the data is "inevitably incomplete" and that "it is also important to keep in mind the situation of information warfare and the Ukrainian media's tendency to ignore the violence of the Ukrainian forces and to exaggerate the violence from the other side."[47] Furthermore, an obvious limitation concerns the topic of sexual violence, which is not coded in the CSLR dataset. An extensive investigation by Nina Potarska, based on a wide range of interviews with women in Donbass, found that sexual assault is a looming threat on both sides of the contact line:

> We have often heard stories about the way soldiers behave and things that happen to women in captivity, stories about why it is dangerous for women to go outside in the dark; still nobody from the people who told us these stories would testify in court; moreover, the victims of sexual violence usually do not contact the police. On Ukrainian-controlled territory this is considered undesirable information which taints the "hero" image of soldiers, whereas on the territory of Donetsk People's Republic the courts haven't been working for quite a long time. Sexual violence in the military conflict is often silenced and perceived as something obvious and normalized—it is thought that a woman just performs the function of sexual service to a sex starved "warrior".[48]

In the final analysis, the vast majority of civilians have been killed by the active hostilities between government and rebel forces, which is also the main cause for the destruction of civilian infrastructure and hence the humanitarian crisis. Furthermore, it is obvious that the war provides the context for the perpetration of the other human rights violations just mentioned and, as such, should be central to any analysis of culpability.

Of course, it is not always easy to pinpoint responsibility for bombardments in a war zone, and in a significant number of cases—including one inquiry into the use of cluster munitions—investigations of war crimes led back to the insurgents.[49] Nevertheless, in most cases where responsibility could be established—including the use of cluster munitions and incendiary weapons—the Ukrainian military was responsible. Indeed, a scant look at the regular monitoring reports of the OSCE indicates that the majority of bombardments have fallen on rebel-held territory.[50] Through regular monitoring of OSCE, UN and other reports, Katchanovski came to similar observations, although he argues that the rebels were responsible for most civilian casualties during the major hostilities of January and February 2015.[51]

Importantly, then, the Ukrainian Armed Forces were the first to escalate the conflict with the massive use of artillery bombardments in the summer of 2014.[52] Indeed, this observation is corroborated by the chronology of the refugee flows. It was only after the 2015 rebel offensive—and Kiev's illegal decision to tie social welfare and pension payments to people's location of residence[53]—that proportionally significant numbers of refugees fled to government-controlled areas, rising from approximately one in six to one in three.[54] (Incidentally, most of these refugees were then barred from voting in the local elections of October 2015.)[55] These proportional changes were not due to a low number of refugees at the start of the conflict. On the contrary, there were over 1.5 million people displaced by the end of 2014, fleeing serious levels of violence. The city of Pervomais'k serves as a pertinent example. When OSCE monitors spoke with a group of refugees on the 11th of August, they testified that the city had been under heavy shelling since July: only 1 out of 8 residents was still living there, nearly all flats were damaged and only 30% of detached houses remained standing.[56] These reports were subsequently confirmed by the mayor of Pervomais'k. Indeed, the OSCE gathered similar stories from Luhansk, where all electricity, water and mobile connections had been cut off as government forces encircled the city, shelling from 04:00 to 02:00, everyday.[57]

Endnotes

1   В. о. Президента України Олександр Турчинов підписав указ про заходи щодо підвищення обороноздатності держави. (2014, May 01). Retrieved from http://web.archive.org/web/20150117044730/http:/president.gov.ua/news/30329.html

2   Luhn, A. (2015, February 18). The Draft Dodgers of Ukraine. Retrieved from http://foreignpolicy.com/2015/02/18/the-draft-dodgers-of-ukraine-russia-putin/

3   Волинські бійці на східному фронті. Інфографіка. (2015, May 13). Retrieved from http://www.volynnews.com/news/vidsichagresoruukrayinayedina/volynski-biytsi-na-skhidnomu-fronti-infohrafika/

4   Will the Ceasefire Hold in Ukraine? (2015, February 15). Retrieved from http://therealnews.com/t2/index.php?option=com_content&task=view&id=31&Itemid=74&jumival=13225

5   Intxausti, A. (2015, February 20). Why Ukrainians adopted by Spanish families may have to go to war. Retrieved from http://elpais.com/elpais/2015/02/20/inenglish/1424430816_082650.html

6   Sharkov, D. (2014, April 16). Ukraine Passes Law Allowing Military to Shoot Deserters. Retrieved from http://web.archive.org/web/20150222080850/http:/www.newsweek.com/ukraine-passes-law-shoot-deserters-304911

7   Kiev reports over 460 Ukrainian servicemen killed in Donbass in 2016, 256 of them not in combat. (2017, January 11). Retrieved from https://www.kyivpost.com/ukraine-politics/kyiv-reports-460-ukrainian-servicemen-killed-donbas-2016-256-not-combat.html

8   Parfitt, T. (2014, August 11). Ukraine crisis: The neo-Nazi brigade fighting pro-Russian separatists. Retrieved from http://www.telegraph.co.uk/news/worldnews/europe/ukraine/11025137/Ukraine-crisis-the-neo-Nazi-brigade-fighting-pro-Russian-separatists.html

9   Kramer, A. E. (2015, July 07). Islamic Battalions, Stocked With Chechens, Aid Ukraine in War With Rebels. Retrieved from http://www.nytimes.com/2015/07/08/world/europe/islamic-battalions-stocked-with-chechens-aid-ukraine-in-war-with-rebels.html?_r=0

10   Parry, R. (2014, August 10). NYT Discovers Ukraine's Neo-Nazis at War. Retrieved from https://consortiumnews.com/2014/08/10/nyt-discovers-ukraines-neo-nazis-at-war/

11   Hahn, G. M. (2015, October 05). America's Ukraine Policy and Maidan Ukraine's War Crimes. Retrieved from http://gordonhahn.com/2015/08/05/americas-ukraine-policy-and-maidan-ukraines-war-crimes/#_ftnref3

The Ravages of War 147

12 Ukraine: Overwhelming new evidence of prisoners being tortured and killed amid conflict. (2015, May 22). Retrieved from https://www.amnesty.org/en/latest/news/2015/05/ukraine-new-evidence-prisoners-tortured-and-killed-amid-conflict/
13 Ukraine: Overwhelming new evidence of prisoners being tortured and killed amid conflict. (2015, May 22). Retrieved from https://www.amnesty.org/en/latest/news/2015/05/ukraine-new-evidence-prisoners-tortured-and-killed-amid-conflict/
14 Dispatches: A Damning Silence From Kiev. (2014, May 07). Retrieved from https://www.hrw.org/news/2014/05/07/dispatches-damning-silence-kiev
15 Heyns, C. (2015, September 21). UN special rapporteur on torture issues sharply critical report on Ukraine. Retrieved from https://newcoldwar.org/un-special-rapporteur-on-torture-issues-sharply-critical-report-on-ukraine/
16 Ukraine: Authorities must commit to a thorough investigation after 13 people released from secret detention. (2016, August 29). Retrieved from https://www.amnesty.org/en/latest/news/2016/08/ukraine-authorities-must-commit-to-a-thorough-investigation-after-13-people-released-from-secret-detention/
17 What follows is a limited selection of reports that have documented war-crimes committed by the Ukrainian armed forces. Also see endnotes 18-22, 49-52. Ukraine: Unguided Rockets Killing Civilians. (2014, July 24). Retrieved from https://www.hrw.org/news/2014/07/24/ukraine-unguided-rockets-killing-civilians; Ukraine: Forces must stop firing on civilians after nine killed in Donetsk. (2014, October 1). Retrieved from https://www.amnesty.org/en/latest/news/2014/10/ukraine-forces-must-stop-firing-civilians-after-nine-killed-donetsk/; Latest from OSCE Special Monitoring Mission (SMM) to Ukraine based on information received as of 19:30 (Kiev time), 7 July 2015. (2015, July 8). Retrieved from http://www.osce.org/ukraine-smm/171186; Latest from OSCE Special Monitoring Mission (SMM) to Ukraine based on information received as of 18:00 (Kiev time), 12 August 2014. (2014, August 13). Retrieved from http://www.osce.org/ukraine-smm/122607; Latest from OSCE Special Monitoring Mission (SMM) to Ukraine based on information received as of 18:00 (Kyiv time), 5 September 2014. (2014, September 6). Retrieved from http://www.osce.org/ukraine-smm/123256; Latest from Special Monitoring Mission (SMM) to Ukraine based on information received as of 18:00 (Kyiv time), 23 September 2014. (2014, September 24). Retrieved from http://www.osce.org/ukraine-smm/124216; Ukraine: Shelling endangers civilians in Lugansk. (2014, September 3). Retrieved from https://www.icrc.org/eng/resources/documents/interview/2014/09-

03-ukraine-lugansk-civilians-shelling.htm; Muižnieks, E. N. (2015, November 16). Humanitarian situation in eastern Ukraine: Report by Council of Europe commissioner. Retrieved from https://newcoldwar. org/humanitarian-situation-in-eastern-ukraine-report-by-council-of-europe-commissioner/; Shelling in east Ukraine's Donetsk kills four civilians. (2014, October 19). Retrieved from http://www.reuters.com/article/us-ukraine-crisis-donetsk-idUSKCN0I80G820141019; Two civilians killed in shelling in east Ukraine rebel city. (2014, November 27). Retrieved from http://www.reuters.com/article/us-ukraine-crisis-idUSKCN0JB22S20141127; Russian journalist killed in Ukraine as gunmen fire on media bus. (2014, June 30). Retrieved from http://www.theguardian.com/world/2014/jun/30/russian-journalist-dead-cameraman-ukraine-avidiivka; Weavner, C. (2015, February 13). School lessons and shelling forge new identity in east Ukraine. Retrieved from http://www.ft.com/intl/cms/s/0/e53188e8-b392-11e4-9449-00144feab7de.html#axzz3RleNPxf2; Reed, J. (2014, June 10). Kiev anti-terror operation takes toll on Slavyansk residents. Retrieved from http://www.ft.com/intl/cms/s/d8aa9386-f0b9-11e3-9e26-00144feabdc0,Authorised=false.html?siteedition=intl; Tartakovsky, J. (2015, May 18). Retrieved from http://www.truth-out.org/speakout/item/30740-donetsk-a-defiant-and-besieged-city; Final two paragraphs in Tavernise, S., & Ponomarev, S. (2014, June 04). Border Guards in Ukraine Abandon Posts. Retrieved from http://www.nytimes.com/2014/06/05/world/europe/rebels-in-eastern-ukraine-capture-government-posts.html; ОБСЕ установила направление обстрела автобуса под Донецком. (2015, January 18). Retrieved from https://tvrain.ru/news/obse_ustanovila_napravlenie_obstrela_avtobusa_pod_donetskom-380728/; Cohen, S. (2014, July 15). Kiev's Atrocities and the Silence of the Hawks. Retrieved from http://www.thenation.com/article/kievs-atrocities-and-silence-hawks/; Russian Roulette (Dispatch 49). (2014, June 19). Retrieved from https://news.vice.com/video/russian-roulette-dispatch-49; German TV broadcasts rare look at the victims of Kiev's shelling in eastern Ukraine. (2015, January 17). Retrieved from https://newcoldwar.org/german-tv-broadcasts-rare-look-victims-kievs-shelling-eastern-ukraine/; "Свобода" предлагает за 48 часов эвакуировать Славянск и разбомбить террористов Джерело: Fakty.ictv.ua. (May 18). Retrieved from http://fakty.ictv.ua/ru/index/read-news/id/1515161; Malkina, Y. (2015, February 11). Crimethinks and doublethinks in the civil war regime of Ukraine. Retrieved from https://newcoldwar.org/crimethinks-doublethinks-civil-war-regime-ukraine/; Lugansk war crime. (2014, June 05). Retrieved from http://humanrightsinvestigations.org/2014/06/05/lugansk-war-crime/; Including for pro-Russian sources would bump up the number of reported war-crimes significantly. Of course, the reliability of such reports is hard to determine, but to just give an impression I added two links. Grim toll of rising Ukrainian shelling in Donbass, eastern Ukraine. (2015, August 18). Retrieved from https://newcoldwar.org/grim-toll-of-rising-ukrainian-shelling-in-donbas-eastern-ukraine/; Ukraine includes report on human rights violations on its list of banned Russian publications. (2015, August 12). Retrieved from https://newcoldwar.org/ukraine-includes-report-on-human-rights-violations-on-its-list-of-banned-russian-publications/

18 Roth, A. (2014, October 20). Ukraine Used Cluster Bombs, Evidence Indicates. Retrieved from http://www.nytimes.com/2014/10/21/world/ukraine-used-cluster-bombs-report-charges.html?emc=edit_th_20141021; Ukraine: Widespread Use of Cluster Munitions. (2014, October 20). Retrieved from https://www.hrw.org/news/2014/10/20/ukraine-widespread-use-cluster-munitions; Spot report by the OSCE Special Monitoring Mission to Ukraine (SMM), 3 February 2015: Civilians killed and wounded in strike with cluster munitions in Izvestkova Street in Luhansk city. (2015, February 3). Retrieved from http://www.osce.org/ukraine-smm/138906; Salem, H. (2014, October 22). 'I Couldn't Move for Five Minutes from Fear': An Investigation Into Cluster Bombs in Eastern Ukraine. Retrieved from https://news.vice.com/article/i-couldnt-move-for-five-minutes-from-fear-an-investigation-into-cluster-bombs-in-eastern-ukraine

19 Heyns, C. (2015, September 21). UN special rapporteur on torture issues sharply critical report on Ukraine. Retrieved from https://newcoldwar.org/un-special-rapporteur-on-torture-issues-sharply-critical-report-on-ukraine/

20 Ukraine: The Line (Rep.). (2016, July 18), p. 6. Retrieved from International Crisis Group website: https://d2071andvip0wj.cloudfront.net/ukraine-the-line.pdf

21 Salem, H. (2014, November 13). 'A Rain of Fire': Ukrainian Forces Used Little-Known Soviet-Era Incendiary Weapons to Attack Ilovaisk. Retrieved from https://news.vice.com/article/a-rain-of-fire-ukrainian-forces-used-little-known-soviet-era-incendiary-weapons-to-attack-iloviask

22 Gessen, K. (2014, September 11). Why not kill them all? Retrieved from http://www.lrb.co.uk/v36/n17/keith-gessen/why-not-kill-them-all

23 Sakwa, R. (2014). *Frontline Ukraine: crisis in the borderlands.* IB Tauris, p. 242.

24 Adarov, A., Astrov, V., Havlik, P., Hunya, G., Landesmann, M., & Podkaminer, L. (2015). How to Stabilise the Economy of Ukraine. wiiw and United Europe, April, p. 13.

25 Dimitrovisiy, A. (2014, December 18). Warning of humanitarian

catastrophe comes as trucks with humanitarian aid turned back on way to Donbass. Retrieved from http://www.kyivpost.com/article/content/ukraine/warning-of-humanitarian-catastrophe-comes-as-trucks-with-humanitarian-aid-turned-back-on-way-to-donbas-375485.html; Eastern Ukraine: Humanitarian disaster looms as food aid blocked. (2014, December 24). Retrieved from https://www.amnesty.org/en/latest/news/2014/12/eastern-ukraine-humanitarian-disaster-looms-food-aid-blocked/

26 Kramer, A. E. (2014, November 05). Ukraine to Freeze Payments in Separatist Areas. Retrieved from http://www.nytimes.com/2014/11/06/world/europe/ukraine-to-freeze-payments-in-separatist-areas.html?_r=0

27 Bartalmai, M. (2014, November 29). Kiev's blockade - Stranglehold of Donbass. Retrieved from http://kaceo.info/2014/11/29/kievs-blockade-stranglehold-of-Donbas/

28 UN report details dire plight of people in eastern Ukraine amid ongoing rights violations. (2014, December 15). Retrieved from http://web.archive.org/web/20150108224450/http:/www.un.org.ua/en/information-centre/news/1936

29 Третина жителів Донбасу вважають, що жити на окупованих територіях вже неможливо - опитування. (2014, November 24). Retrieved from http://www.unian.ua/society/1013022-tretina-jiteliv-donbasu-vvajayut-scho-jiti-na-okupovanih-teritoriyah-vje-nemojlivo-opituvannya.html; 60% населення Донбасу не вистачає їжі - дослідження. (2014, November 24). Retrieved from http://www.unian.ua/society/1013013-60-naselennya-donbasu-ne-vistachae-jiji-doslidjennya.html

30 Goryachova, T., & Foster, H. (2014, December 25). Retirees starve in rebel-held eastern Ukraine. Retrieved from http://www.usatoday.com/story/news/world/2014/12/25/ukraine-donetsk-starvation-separatists-russia/20824485/?siteID=je6NUbpObpQ-hvXi8Av5DdSg.Nq4xKNDwQ

31 Ibid.

32 OSCE. (2015, September 18). Access to water in conflict-affected areas of Donetsk and Luhansk regions (Rep.), p. 3. Retrieved from http://www.osce.org/ukraine-smm/183151?download=true

33 Two years of conflict leaves 1.5 million people hungry in eastern Ukraine. (2016, April 04). Retrieved from http://www.un.org/apps/news/story.asp?NewsID=53602#.V-60WPmF69J

34 Cited in Black, J. L., & Johns, M. (Eds.). (2016), p. 218. *The Return of the Cold War: Ukraine, The West and Russia.* Routledge.

35 OSCE. (2015, May 6). Protection of Civilians and their Freedom of Movement in the Donetsk and Luhansk Regions (Rep.), p. 3. Retrieved

	from http://www.osce.org/ukraine-smm/156791?download=true
36	Ibid, p. 3.
37	Russian figures cited in Weir, F. (2015, December 1). Ukrainian refugees in Russia: Did Moscow fumble a valuable resource? Retrieved from http://www.csmonitor.com/World/Europe/2015/1201/Ukrainian-refugees-in-Russia-Did-Moscow-fumble-a-valuable-resource; Earlier Russian figures were considered credible by the UNHCR. See UNHCR: 730,000 have Left Ukraine for Russia Due to Conflict. (2014, August 5). Retrieved from https://www.youtube.com/watch?v=lfCdoaiPeCY; EU gives €300,000 in humanitarian assistance to Belarus for helping Ukrainian refugees. (2015, November 11). Retrieved from http://www.enpi-info.eu/eastportal/news/latest/43072/EU-gives-€300,000-in-humanitarian-assistance-to-Belarus-for-helping-Ukrainian-refugees; ECHO Factsheet. (2016, February). Retrieved from http://ec.europa.eu/echo/files/aid/countries/factsheets/ukraine_en.pdf
38	Cumming-bruce, N. (2015, December 09). At Least 9,115 Killed in Ukraine Conflict, U.N. Says. Retrieved from http://www.nytimes.com/2015/12/10/world/europe/ukraine-conflict-toll.html
39	Salem, H. (2014, August 23). 'Nowhere Is Definitely Safe Anymore': Inside the Besieged Ukrainian City of Luhansk. Retrieved from https://news.vice.com/article/nowhere-is-definitely-safe-anymore-inside-the-besieged-ukrainian-city-of-luhansk
40	Gorbunova, Y. (2014, July 24). Dispatches: Mass Grave Found in Eastern Ukraine. Retrieved from https://www.hrw.org/news/2014/07/24/dispatches-mass-grave-found-eastern-ukraine; Rebels Find Another Mass Graves in Donetsk. (2014, September 28). Retrieved from http://www.telesurtv.net/english/news/Rebel-Find-Another-Mass-Graves-in-Donetsk-20140928-0018.html
41	Ukraine: Sicherheitskreise: Bis zu 50.000 Tote. (2014, February 8). Retrieved from http://www.faz.net/aktuell/politik/ausland/ukraine-sicherheitskreise-bis-zu-50-000-tote-13416132.html
42	Ukraine's Donetsk rebels ban MSF, UN agencies. (2015, October 24). Retrieved from https://www.yahoo.com/news/ukraines-donetsk-rebels-ban-msf-un-agencies-035942955.html
43	Chandler, D. C. (2005). From Kosovo to Kabul and Beyond: human rights and international intervention. Pluto Press.
44	59th Russian humanitarian convoy on the way to Ukraine. (2016, December 22). Retrieved from http://112.international/ukraine-top-news/59th-russian-humanitarian-convoy-on-the-way-to-ukraine-12328.html
45	Стрелков: гуманитарную помощь из России разворовывают. (2014, November 17). Retrieved from https://www.gazeta.ru/politics/

news/2014/11/17/n_6656949.shtml
46 Ishchenko, V. (2014, October 23). Robbery, arrests, kidnapping were the main threats to the residents of Donbass after shelling. Retrieved from http://cslr.org.ua/en/robbery-arrests-kidnapping-were-the-main-threats-to-the-residents-of-Donbas-after-shelling2/
47 Ibid.
48 Potarska, N. (2015, October 25). The Voice of Non-Militants: the Experience of Women from Eastern Ukraine. Retrieved from http://cslr.org.ua/en/the-voice-of-non-militants-the-experience-of-women-from-eastern-ukraine/
49 Ukraine: More Civilians Killed in Cluster Munition Attacks. (2015, March 19). Retrieved from https://www.hrw.org/news/2015/03/19/ukraine-more-civilians-killed-cluster-munition-attacks
50 These were also the findings of a systemic review of all the OSCE reported cease-fire violations between April 15 and May 15, 2015—although the rebels and the Ukrainian Armed Forces were violating on a similar scale. Charts of Minsk 2 ceasefire violations. (2015, August 18). Retrieved from https://www.armedpolitics.com/560/charts-of-minsk-2-ceasefire-violations/
51 Katchanovski, I. (2016). The Separatist War in Donbass: A Violent Break-up of Ukraine?. *European Politics and Society*, 1-17.
52 Ibid.
53 The fact that war-crimes and other human rights abuses by the rebels have contributed to the refugee flow is fairly obvious and well-documented. In a report on refugees residing in government-controlled areas, however, the OSCE also notes that "in many instances, the removal of government benefits from non-government-controlled areas contributed to the initial displacement from Donbass." See Conflict-related Displacement in Ukraine: Increased Vulnerabilities of Affected Populations and Triggers of Tension within Communities (Rep.). (2016, July), p. 16. Retrieved http://www.osce.org/ukraine-smm/261176?download=true. The Kiev Appeal Administrative Court ruled that the cabinet decision to suspend social payments is invalid under Ukrainian law. Kiev: Ukraine to resume social payments in occupied territories of Donbass only after their liberation. (2015, April 03). Retrieved from http://www.unian.info/politics/1063465-kyiv-ukraine-to-resume-social-payments-in-occupied-territories-of-donbas-only-after-their-liberation.html
54 As of the 2nd of September 2014, the UN reported that there were approximately 260,000 internally displaced people (IDP's), and how many of the IDP's fled to government-controlled territory is unclear. There is no reason to believe that this proportion would be larger

than that reported in March 2016 (50 - 62.5 percent). In fact, because the 260,000 figure preceded both the major rebel offensive of early 2015 and the seizure of social payments and government services to residents of rebel-held teritories, the proportion of IDP's residing in government-held territories would likely be smaller. By comparison, as of the 2nd of September 2014, the UN reported that 814.000 refugees had fled to Russia. As such, it is clear that initially, the vast majority of refugees did not flee to government-controlled areas. For these refugee figures, consult Ukraine conflict: UN says million people have fled. (2014, September 02). Retrieved from http://www.bbc.com/news/world-europe-29029060. Even taking the 467,000 total IDP figure of 19 November 2014—shortly after Kiev had announced its decision to cut government-benefits, but still before implementation on December 1st—the overall picture remains largely the same, with refugees in government-held territory comprising less than one-sixth of the total (excluding Belarus). For the 467,000 figure, consult Serious human rights violations persist in eastern Ukraine despite tenuous ceasefire. (2014, November 20). Retrieved from http://www.ohchr.org/EN/NewsEvents/Pages/DisplayNews.aspx?NewsID=15316 By the end of November, over one million refugees had fled to Russia, as reported by Weir, F. (2015, December 1). Ukrainian refugees in Russia: Did Moscow fumble a valuable resource? Retrieved from http://www.csmonitor.com/World/Europe/2015/1201/Ukrainian-refugees-in-Russia-Did-Moscow-fumble-a-valuable-resource. (Less than) one-sixth is the author's calculation, assuming that half of the IDP's resided in government-held territory. Using the aforementioned 2016 figures would make refugees in government-held territory comprise approximately one-third of the total (excluding Belarus).

55   Conflict-related Displacement in Ukraine: Increased Vulnerabilities of Affected Populations and Triggers of Tension within Communities (Rep.). (2016, July), pp. 18-19. Retrieved http://www.osce.org/ukraine-smm/261176?download=true

56   Latest from OSCE Special Monitoring Mission (SMM) to Ukraine based on information received as of 18:00 (Kyiv time), 11 August 2014. (2014, August 12). Retrieved from http://www.osce.org/ukraine-smm/122578

57   Latest from OSCE Special Monitoring Mission (SMM) to Ukraine based on information received by 18:00 (Kyiv time), 7 August 2014. (2014, August 8). Retrieved from http://www.osce.org/ukraine-smm/122495

| Chapter Thirteen |

DEHUMANIZING THE DONBASS, EMBRACING THE FAR RIGHT

Most of the rebels are fighting, in one form or another, for their local region, the destruction of which would directly jeopardize their own future. A random survey of fifty-five rebels, conducted by Kudelia, showed that the most frequent reason for taking up arms was "the desire to protect family, friends, and civilians (85.5 percent)."[1] Indeed, nearly all of the volunteers were said to have been loyal to the Ukrainian state before Maidan. For two-thirds of them, either the burning of the Odessa trade union building or the shelling of Donbass civilians had made the crucial difference.[2] By contrast, Donbass civilians have frequently been referred to by the other side as 'filth,' 'pests' or a 'plague.' The head of the propaganda and analysis division of the Ukrainian secret service—a devout neo-Nazi—had earlier advocated extensive shelling of the rebel city of Slovyansk, with the goal of turning it into 'a lunar landscape.'[3] And he is not alone in his contempt for the people of Donbass. The International Crisis Group conducted a wide range of interviews with Ukrainian officers, most of whom aren't ultranationalists, only to find that local civilians were widely considered traitors who were getting what they deserved. That includes civilians living in government-controlled territory. As one senior officer put it: "50 per cent of my civilians are separatists."[4]

Indeed, the ultranationalist and dehumanizing discourses have become deeply entrenched in the wider Ukrainian society.[5]

After the Odessa tragedy, the popular official EuroMaidan PR page uploaded a walk-through of the burned corpses on Youtube, under the heading "Russian terrorists burned alive."[6] Dehumanization has also seeped into everyday language. 'Koloradi', which is short for Colorado beetle bug, has become a common way of referring to pro-Russian protesters, who often wear St. George ribbons,[7] symbolic of the 'great patriotic war' against the Nazis, whose colors resemble those of the bug. There was even an openly Russophobe art exhibition in Kiev titled "Do not Pass By: Kill Colorado!"[8] Another shocking example: a fundraiser in a Ukrainian high school for the 'anti-terrorist' operation, where the teachers and kids were selling 'tanks on Moscow' cookies and stewed fruit drink called 'the blood of Russian babies.'[9]

Indeed, even politicians as senior as the minister of interior, Arsen Avakov, have called the rebels 'Koloradi.'[10] President Poroshenko's TV station has been airing a commercial that promises to kill the bugs "on the spot".[11] The use of language in the highest corridors of power in Kiev is indeed disturbing. Speaking about the Donbass, the president proudly proclaimed that "Our children will go to schools and kindergartens. Theirs will hole up in basements. Because they are not able to do anything."[12] When a fighter jet was downed by rebels, Prime Minister Yatsenyuk stated that: "they lost their lives ... in a situation facing a threat to be killed by invaders and sponsored by them subhumans. First, we will commemorate the heroes by wiping out those who killed them and then by cleaning our land from the evil."[13] Ilya Kiva, the vice-head of the Interior Ministry police in Donetsk, justified the brutal siege of rebel-controlled territory in Donbass by referring to 'these lovers of referenda' as 'plague and filth.' He assures us: "There are no more nuances! There's only 'ours' and the enemy! That's the only way we'll defeat this plague."[14]

Bearing in mind, these are not the ultranationalists. These are supposedly moderate center-right/right-wing politicians. Indeed, Keith Gessen wrote for the *London Review of Books* that even moderate "liberals" were anxious to get rid of the Donbass residents, who had thwarted their European aspirations for decades with their voting behavior:

> All the enemies of progress in one place, all the losers and has-beens: wouldn't it be better just to solve the problem once and for all? Wouldn't it be a better long-term solution just to kill as many as you could and scare the shit out of the rest of them, forever? This is what I heard from respectable people in Kiev. Not from the nationalists, but from liberals, from professionals and journalists. All the bad people were in one place—why not kill them all?[15]

The way government-controlled areas are governed does not bode well for the future either. The current head of the military-civilian administration for Donbass, Pavel Zhebrivsky, expanded martial law because, in his words, "an insignificant number" of civil servants remained loyal.[16] It's not difficult to see why. Zhebrivsky calls for "an open, serious war between Russia and Ukraine" and even insists on an invasion of Southern Russia, to liberate the "authentic Ukrainian regions" of Voronezh, Kursk and Krasnodar.[17] Even after peace returns in Donbass, Zhebrivsky assures us that Ukraine will need to "impose . . . a normal democratic agenda on those people," with garrisons of troops stationed in every major city.[18] It seems such military occupation wouldn't be short-lived because, says Zhebrivsky, it will take "a very long time" to awaken the Donbass citizens from their 'hibernation.'[19] Another 'moderate' politician.

The recaptured city of Slovyansk, under government control since two years, remains in a state of disrepair. Its newly elected mayor, Opposition Bloc member Vadim Lyakh, told *Der Spiegel* that "none of the close to 500 destroyed or damaged buildings have been rebuilt—nor the major building complex of the psychiatric hospital, which has lay in ruin since the battles."[20] The one exception is a new-build radio tower which Kiev uses to disseminate propaganda—in the Ukrainian language, even though most in the region speak better Russian.[21] The regime's virulent nationalism seems to trump any genuine effort to win the hearts and minds of Donbass. President Poroshenko has now adopted OUN slogans like "Glory to Ukraine! Glory to the Heroes" and "Ukraine above all" that have become mainstream throughout Ukraine.[22] He has stepped into Yushchenko's shoes, calling OUN and UPA members "heroes" who deserve to be officially recognized as such by the state.[23] In fact, in April 2015, the Ukrainian parliament passed a law which made it illegal to "publicly exhibit a disrespectful attitude" toward the OUN and UPA.[24] What's more, the day of the supposed founding of the UPA has been made a public holiday.[25] To be entirely clear: at least 63% of top UPA and OUN-B leaders, including at least 74% of top UPA commanders, collaborated with Nazi-Germany.[26] In addition, the bill criminalized denial of the "criminal character of the communist totalitarian regime of 1917-1991 in Ukraine," thus including the Perestroika reforms in the 1980s.[27] Soviet symbols have become illegal—from tiny USSR souvenirs to singing the Internationale. Millions of dollars will likely be spent to rename a huge number of cities and streets and to replace statues and monuments which are connected to the Soviet past. When surveys in two major cities showed that the vast majorities did not want the name-changes—and if necessary, preferred czarist era names—their opinions were discarded out of hand, the speaker of parliament even implying that descendants of "Muscovite occupiers" did not deserve a voice.[28] Finally, Poroshenko gave new life to the aforementioned Ukrainian Institute of National Memory and the ultranationalist historian Volodymyr Viatrovych, crucial to Yushchenko's ultranationalist campaign after the 2004 revolution, by signing into law a bill that would allow them access to enormous quantities of state archives in order to re-write the history of Ukraine.[29]

In this context, the complete acceptance of ultranationalists within mainstream political institutions is not surprising—and perhaps not the worse aspect of Ukrainian politics. The aforementioned Azov commandor, Andriy Biletskiy—who spoke of "a crusade against the Semite-led Untermenschen"—was made lieutenant-colonel of the police.[30] His former vice-commander, Vadim Troyan, was named head of Kiev's regional police.[31] In March 2016, he was even promoted to the position of first deputy head of the national police.[32] Other positions given to the far right were two vice-chairs of the parliamentary committee on national security and defense and the first vice-chair of the parliamentary committee on law enforcement.[33] Furthermore, the founder of the Joseph Goebbels political research center was appointed head of the propaganda and analysis division of the Ukrainian secret service.[34]

Neither Right Sector nor Svoboda passed the five percent voting threshold to enter parliament. Nevertheless, all pro-Western parties have now tolerated and supported ultranationalists. The party of Prime Minister Yatsenyuk, for example, appointed several leaders of far-right battalions in its military council, including the aforementioned Neo-Nazi leader of the Azov Battallion, Andriy Biletskiy. Biletskiy was also supported by Yatsenyuk's People's Front in his successful bid for a seat in the national parliament, where he was accompanied by twelve more far-right colleagues who frequently gained their positions through the electoral lists of supposedly 'moderate' parties.[35] In fact, ultranationalists had become political assets due to their hero status as anti-Russian soldiers, though this has little to do with their ultranationalist ideology. Indeed, ordinary criminals had become venerated as well. Even the aforementioned commander of the Tornado battalion, now suspected of widespread torture and rape, had gone "from the criminal to hero and back again." *Der Spiegel* reported that he was "a publicly celebrated hero. Filaret, head of the Ukrainian Orthodox Church, had awarded him with a medal."[36]

Endnotes

1 Kudelia, S. (2016). The Donbass Rift. Russian Politics & Law, 54(1), 5-27, p. 20.

2 Ibid.
3 "Свобода" предлагает за 48 часов эвакуировать Славянск и разбомбить террористов Джерело: Fakty.ictv.ua. (May 18). Retrieved from http://fakty.ictv.ua/ru/index/read-news/id/1515161
4 Ukraine: The Line (Rep.). (2016, July 18), p. 5. Retrieved from International Crisis Group website: https://d2071andvip0wj.cloudfront.net/ukraine-the-line.pdf
5 An impressive range of examples are documented in Molchanov, Mikhail A., Russia as Ukraine's 'Other': Identity and Geopolitics (March 5, 2015). in Ukraine and Russia: People, Politics, Propaganda and Perspectives, edited by Agnieszka Pikulicka-Wilczewska & Richard Sakwa, 2015.
6 Russian Terrorists Burnt Alive In Trade Union Building Fire In Odessa Ukraine, May 2 2014. (2014, May 3). Retrieved from http://web.archive.org/web/20140514231941/http://www.youtube.com/watch?v=ycfOCxR5mxM
7 Sindelar, D. (2014, April 28). What's Orange And Black And Bugging Ukraine? Retrieved from http://www.rferl.org/content/ukraine-colorado-beetle-separatists/25365793.html
8 Pogrebinskiy, M., Alshaer, A., Bahceci, S., Eiran, E., Tabachnik, A., Kedem, N., ... & Onuch, O. (2015). Russians in Ukraine: Before and After Euromaidan. Ukraine and Russia: People, Politics, Propaganda and Perspectives, 90, p. 97.
9 Ibid, p. 97.
10 Ishchenko, V. (2014, November 13). Ukraine has ignored the far right for too long—it must wake up to the danger. Retrieved from http://www.theguardian.com/commentisfree/2014/nov/13/ukraine-far-right-fascism-mps
11 Sindelar, D. (2014, April 28). What's Orange And Black And Bugging Ukraine? Retrieved from http://www.rferl.org/content/ukraine-colorado-beetle-separatists/25365793.html
12 Poroshenko: "Their children will hole up in the basements - this is how we win the war!" [ENG SUBS]. (2014, November 14). Retrieved from https://www.youtube.com/watch?v=aHWHqi8g7Bk
13 Day of mourning declared after Ukrainian military plane shot down. (2014, June 18). Retrieved from http://web.archive.org/web/20140615062948/http://usa.mfa.gov.ua/en/press-center/news/24185-mi-uvichnimo-pamjaty-gerojiv-ochistivshi-nashu-zemlyu-vid-nechistiarsenij-jacenyuk-u-spivchutti-ridnim-i-blizykim-zagiblih-vojiniv-u-lugansyku
14 Спикер донецкой милиции хочет расстреливать автобусы, едущие в ДНР. (2015, May 29). Retrieved from http://korrespondent.net/

ukraine/3521103-spyker-donetskoi-mylytsyy-khochet-rasstrelyvat-avtobusy-eduschye-v-dnr

15 Gessen, K. (2014, September 11). Why not kill them all? Retrieved from http://www.lrb.co.uk/v36/n17/keith-gessen/why-not-kill-them-all

16 Cited in Petro, N. N. (2016, September 7). Ukraine's Perpetual War for Perpetual Peace. Retrieved from http://nationalinterest.org/feature/ukraines-perpetual-war-perpetual-peace-17614

17 Cited in ibid.

18 Cited in ibid.

19 Cited in ibid.

20 Neef, C. (2017, February 17). Battling for Hearts and Minds: Kiev Fights for Loyalty in Eastern Ukraine. Retrieved from http://www.spiegel.de/international/europe/kiev-fights-for-loyalty-in-eastern-ukraine-a-1134900.html

21 Ibid.

22 Eyewitness report by Katchanovski, I. (2014, September 18). Facebook. Retrieved from https://www.facebook.com/ivan.katchanovski/posts/883905151639372

23 Babiak, M. (2014, September 26). Poroshenko: 'UPA are heroes,' will consider giving veterans legal status -. Retrieved from http://euromaidanpress.com/2014/09/26/poroshenko-to-consider-giving-upa-veterans-legal-status/

24 Shavel, O. (2015, May 07). "De-Communization Laws" Need to Be Amended to Conform to European Standards. Retrieved from http://voxukraine.org/2015/05/07/de-communization-laws-need-to-be-amended-to-conform-to-european-standards/

25 Shandra, A. (2014, October 15). New October 14 'Day of Defender of Ukraine' holiday marks break with Soviet past. Retrieved from http://euromaidanpress.com/2014/10/15/changing-the-date-of-defenders-day-breaks-ukraine-free-from-the-soviet-embrace/

26 Katchanovski, I. (2013, December 5). The Organization of Ukrainian Nationalists, the Ukrainian Insurgent Army, and the Nazi Genocide in Ukraine, pp. 13, 16. Retrieved from https://www.academia.edu/6414323/The_Organization_of_Ukrainian_Nationalists_the_Ukrainian_Insurgent_Army_and_the_Nazi_Genocide_in_Ukraine

27 Luhn, A. (2015, May 21). Ukraine bans Soviet symbols and criminalises sympathy for communism. Retrieved from http://www.theguardian.com/world/2015/may/21/ukraine-bans-soviet-symbols-criminalises-sympathy-for-communism

28 Petro, N. N. (2016, September 7). Ukraine's Perpetual War for Perpetual Peace. Retrieved from http://nationalinterest.org/feature/

ukraines-perpetual-war-perpetual-peace-17614

29 Cohen, J. (2016, May 2). The Historian Whitewashing Ukraine's Past. Retrieved from http://foreignpolicy.com/2016/05/02/the-historian-whitewashing-ukraines-past-volodymyr-viatrovych/

30 Ishchenko, V. (2014, November 13). Ukraine has ignored the far right for too long – it must wake up to the danger. Retrieved from http://www.theguardian.com/commentisfree/2014/nov/13/ukraine-far-right-fascism-mps

31 Ibid.

32 ЗМІ: Троян погодився стати першим заступником Деканоідзе. (2016, Maart 2). Opgehaald van http://www.pravda.com.ua/news/2016/03/2/7100934/

33 Комітет з питань національної безпеки і оборони. (2014, December 4). Retrieved from http://w1.c1.rada.gov.ua/pls/site2/p_komity?pidid=2633; Депутати перетрусили комітети під Ляшка. Син Порошенка теж перейшов. (2014, December 11). Retrieved from http://www.pravda.com.ua/news/2014/12/11/7051672/

34 Kolesnik, D. (2014, October 24). Svoboda nazi apologist quits party to become head of Security Service propaganda. Retrieved from https://ukraineantifascistsolidarity.wordpress.com/2014/10/25/svoboda-nazi-apologist-quits-party-to-become-head-of-security-service-propaganda/

35 Coynash, H. (2014, October 10). Dangerous war heroes on Ukraine's political scene. Retrieved from http://khpg.org/en/index.php?id=1414100027; Nemtsova, A. (2014, September 9). Ukraine's President Wowed Congress, But His Party Has a Dark Side. Retrieved from http://www.thedailybeast.com/articles/2014/09/19/ukraine-s-president-wowed-congress-but-his-party-has-a-dark-side.html; Ishchenko, V. (2014, November 13). Ukraine has ignored the far right for too long—it must wake up to the danger. Retrieved from http://www.theguardian.com/commentisfree/2014/nov/13/ukraine-far-right-fascism-mps; The far right in the new Ukrainian Parliament. (2014, December 14). Retrieved from https://ukraineantifascistsolidarity.wordpress.com/2014/12/14/the-far-right-in-the-new-ukrainian-parliament/; И вот имена. (2014, October 29). Retrieved from http://corneliu.livejournal.com/227792.html

36 Hahn, G. M. (2015, October 05). America's Ukraine Policy and Maidan Ukraine's War Crimes. Retrieved from http://gordonhahn.com/2015/08/05/americas-ukraine-policy-and-maidan-ukraines-war-crimes/#_ftnref3

| Chapter Fourteen |

BEYOND POPULISM: ASSESSING THE INFLUENCE OF THE FAR RIGHT

Acceptance of the far-right and other dubious figures has not been universal. The commander of the Tornado Battalion, for example, was eventually arrested and is now facing prosecution. But these cases remain rare and highly selective. In fact, it is not clear whether the state can even control the ultranationalist battalions at this point. Multiple cases against far-right activists were dismissed after their organizations threatened the concerned judges in court. Ulrich Heyden addresses a pertinent example:

> On November 30, 100 members of the Right Sector stormed the Malinowski Court in Odessa. Security officers were simply pushed aside. Masked men and muscular women stood threateningly before the three judges. The judges had approved a ruling to release on bail five people detained since the violent events of May 2, 2014 in the city.
>
> The judges were threatened by masked vigilantes if they didn't sign letters of resignation. A video report captures the confrontation. It shows the anxious looks on the judges' faces.

They signed the resignation letters and exited the courtroom.

A short time later, the ruling to release the five anti-Maidan protesters was reversed, due, it was said, to "the failure to take account of certain facts". Their detentions were extended for two months.

… The five detainees in Odessa have been imprisoned for one and a half years without any concrete evidence presented against them. … The reversal of the three judges' decision was a shock. One of the detainees, 32-year-old Evgeny Medvedov (Eugene Mefĕdo), slashed his arms in court on December 4 in protest over the decision as it was announced.[1]

In another case, in a local parliament, a Right Sector member pulled out an AK-47 to make clear that they will never disarm.[2] Indeed, there have been multiple clashes between the far-right and police forces. In July 2015, for example, a shoot-out between Right Sector and law enforcement officers in Western Ukraine left seven wounded.[3]

Right Sector and other far-right battalions have almost routinely threatened to turn on Kiev in case of 'treason' and to overthrow them 'like Yanukovych.' The war in the Donbass, where any concession to the rebels are considered to be 'capitulation to Russia,' is especially sensitive. When the national parliament tried to pass a decentralization bill, which did not even ensure genuine federalism, several far-right groups, including Right Sector and Svoboda, demonstrated in front of parliament. The event turned bloody when a member of a Svoboda-affiliated battalion threw a hand grenade at security officers, provoking further clashes.[4] Three national guard soldiers—all of them young draftees—were killed, and over 130 law enforcement officials were injured.[5] The bill passed its first reading, though it was unclear whether the necessary two-thirds majority would be reached for a final vote in January 2016. Indeed, parliament procedures were changed shortly before the date, and the vote has been further postponed.[6] As Associate professor Gordon Hahn notes, the far right has successfully influenced policy in the past. He gives the example of Poroshenko's decision not to extend a ceasefire that was first proclaimed on the 20th of June, 2014:

> On the eve of President Poroshenko's pivotal June 30 [2014] meeting with Parubiy, Avakov and the powerful Defense and Security Council, Semenchenko and members of his battalion led a several thousand-strong demonstration backed by two other "volunteer"—Dnepr and Aidar—battalions. The demonstrators demanded that Poroshenko end the truce, declare martial law and destroy the eastern rebels, or they would remove the president from power "like Yanukovych." (…) At the demonstration, a journalist was beaten up and stun grenades were thrown, seriously injuring several demonstrators.
>
> (…) Before the June 30 council meeting, Poroshenko had said he intended to extend the truce after its June 30 deadline, in accordance with the wishes of Brussels and Moscow. However, after the four-hour long meeting, he emerged to announce an end to the truce and ordered a new offensive to wipe out rebels. The Donbass Battalion and its ilk had prevailed over the great powers of Europe and Russia.[7]

Although significant, the 'muscle' of the far-right should not be overestimated either. The volunteer battalions were especially important in the early phases of the war in 2014. The regime in Kiev cynically exploited the far-right when they were necessary, but now seems determined to neutralize their threat by assimilating them into the army and national guard. This has been achieved with a decent level of success—and despite the frequent threats of coups d'état—the aforementioned clashes remain the most significant to date. This weakness has led to splits in Right Sector, partially over its militant course. Its leader resigned in November 2015 to form a new political party, aiming to unite ultranationalists with the center-right. In a statement, he proclaimed: "We do not abandon the revolutionary road, but we forsake pseudo-revolutionary activity that threatens the existence of the state of Ukraine and stains the reputation of patriots. We are opposed to the current government, but do not believe it appropriate (and doomed to failure) to revolt against it."[8] In a later interview, Yarosh admitted to have "overestimated the organizational capacity of Right Sector"—seeing they were unable to organize a popular referendum on a vote of no-confidence in the Kiev administration.[9] In terms of Right Sector fighters on the frontline—they are estimated at 2000, and remain one of the few battalions that refused Kiev's request for assimilation.[10]

The far-right is thus definitely not dominant in Ukraine. Nevertheless, the issue is not as black and white as many propagandists frame the debate. Indeed, the fact that Kiev cannot simply disarm the ultranationalists, but rather aims to assimilate them into the state—therefore giving the far right significant resources and legitimacy—is anything but reassuring. Now, the infamous Azov fighters are, for example, patrolling the streets of Kharkov alongside the police, on the pay-roll of the Ukrainian state as part of the national guard.[11] The Ukrainian authorities even sent 300 Azov troops to police Odessa during the 2016 anniversary of the May 2th massacre, sending a clear message to anyone who wished to commemorate the bloodbath.[12] A few months later, the same regional government gave their tacit approval to a pogrom against dozens of Roma in an Odessan village, who fled their homes before their property was vandalized. One house burned to the ground, and anyone wishing to collect their belongings was met with threats of lynching.[13] Azov troops arrived at the scene soon afterwards, voicing their support and coming to act as 'self-defense' forces.[14]

Being part of the Ukrainian National Guard has not prevented the Azov regiment from threatening the state either.

During a torch-lit rally in front of parliament in May 2016, Andriy Biletsky threatened to overthrow the president if he agreed to hold elections in the rebel-controlled territories, an obligation under the peace accords which has still not been met.[15] Notably, when the International Crisis Group interviewed a range of military officers in April-May 2016—most of whom are not from the far-right—they also encountered a striking hostility towards Poroshenko. None went as far as to threaten a military coup, but when every officer is critical of the president, on quite nationalist terms, it does prompt the question where the military would stand if a power struggle ensues. Indeed, all of the interviewees considered the Minsk peace accords to be "dead," wanted to solve the crisis by military means and were frustrated by the ceasefire orders.[16]

Nor are the electoral failures of Svoboda and Right Sector that comforting—given the fact that many of its leaders entered parliament on the ticket of the center right, which itself has adopted language such as 'Koloradi' and Sub-humans.' Apologists often make a comparison with the European Union—where far-right parties have taken up to 25 percent of the votes—failing to recognize the extraordinary extent to which ultranationalist rhetoric and policies have become the norm among the political center in Ukraine.

This is, of course, not to say that the far-right threat in Europe is insignificant. On the contrary, as an extensive Tell Mama-commissioned report by Nafeez Ahmed demonstrates, European far-right parties harbor significant relations with neo-Nazi groups, constituting a growing international network with serious claims to power in the near to medium-term future.[17] Notably, some of these parties also maintain ties (although often exaggerated) with elements of the Kremlin establishment and are laudatory about Putin.[18] Yet the European far-right glorification of Russian 'anti-fascist' resistance rings hollow, not least because of Svoboda's observer member status in the European Alliance of Nationalist Movements until 2013. Then-Front National leader, Jean-Marie le Pen, even visited a Svoboda party convention as an honored guest in 2000, when the organization was still called the Social-National Party of Ukraine.

Rather than cheering on either camp, it seems obvious that these movements ought to be resisted on all fronts. Pointing to the hypocrisy of the European far-right—or the Russian ultranationalists in Donbass, for that matter—in their support for 'anti-fascism' in Ukraine, does not make the latter any less real. In fact, such diversion tactics bear a striking resemblance to the 'Russian propaganda' that is so often decried.

Importantly, there are also some dangers that are particular to the Ukrainian context. EU member states are not facing severe instability, nor are their far-right movements armed and trained in military combat. As recently as the spring of 2017, the far-right showed its ability to challenge the state's monopoly on violence by initiating a blockade against coal supplied from rebel-held territories in Donbass. The ultranationalists continued even after the Ukrainian prime-minister was forced to declare a state of emergency in the country's energy market, and both the United States and Europe backed Kiev's calls to end the blockade.[19] In fact, just as the UN's Office for the Coordination of Humanitarian Affairs announced harsh humanitarian consequences—with some vulnerable households seeing their coal supply drop by two-thirds—Kiev made a U-turn and formally supported the blockade.[20] As such, it only took the far right two months to change the government's policy, dealing yet another blow to the Minsk peace process which requires "'a full restoration of social and economic connections."[21] As I have documented, within the current security environment in Ukraine, the far right has extra-legal means of exerting influence over national policy.

This ties into another crucial point: it does not really matter how much support the far right has among the population, if they already control significant state resources while they're fighting a war against 'Semite-led Untermenschen.' The most important lesson of the Second World War seems to be missed by many people. MIT Professor Chomsky writes that:

despite Hitler's personal appeal, direct support for his genocidal projects was never high. ... Norman Cohn observes that even among Nazi party members, in 1938 over 60% 'expressed downright indignation at the outrages' carried out against Jews, while 5 percent considered that "physical violence against Jews was justified because 'terror must be met with terror'." In the Fall of 1942, when the genocide was fully under way, some 5% of Nazi Party members approved the shipment of Jews to "labor camps," while 70% registered indifference and the rest "showed signs of concern for the Jews." Among the general population, support for the Holocaust would have surely been still less. The Nazi leaders required no popular enthusiasm in order to carry out what the Nazi press described as the 'defensive action against the Jewish world-criminals', ...and to purify the society, and the world, by eliminating the 'bacteria, vermin and pests [that] cannot be tolerated.' For these tasks, the leadership needed little more than 'a mood of passive compliance,' apathy, the willingness to look the other way.[22]

Endnotes

1 Heyden, U. (2015, December 18). Ukraine: When the Right Sector Runs the Courtroom. Retrieved from http://www.counterpunch.org/2015/12/18/ukraine-when-the-right-sector-runs-the-courtroom/

2 Shynkarenko, O. (2014, March 1). Can Ukraine Control Its Far Right Ultranationalists? Retrieved February 14, 2016, from http://www.thedailybeast.com/articles/2014/03/01/can-ukraine-control-its-far-right-ultranationalists.html

3 Kramer, A. E. (2015, July 12). Police in Western Ukraine Clash With Paramilitary Group; 7 Are Hurt. Retrieved from http://www.nytimes.com/2015/07/13/world/europe/police-in-western-ukraine-clash-with-paramilitary-group-7-are-hurt.html?_r=0

4	Ishchenko, V. (2015, September 04). Ukraine's government bears more responsibility for ongoing conflict than the far-right. Retrieved from http://www.theguardian.com/world/2015/sep/04/ukraine-government-svoboda-clashes-conflict
5	Ibid.
6	Poroshenko approves extension of amendments to Constitution consideration term by parliament. (2016, January 21). Retrieved from http://en.censor.net.ua/news/371482/poroshenko_approves_extension_of_amendments_to_constitution_consideration_term_by_parliament
7	Hahn, G. (2014, September 23). The Ukrainian Revolution's Neo-Fascist Problem. Retrieved from http://www.fairobserver.com/region/europe/the-ukrainian-revolutions-neo-fascist-problem-14785/
8	Yarosh, D. (2015, December 28). Ярош оголошує про заснування нового руху та виходить з НВР ПС. Retrieved from http://ps-zahid.info/news/yarosh-oholoshuje-pro-zasnuvannya-novoho-ruhu-ta-vyhodyt-z-nvr-ps/
9	Chernyshev, R. (2016, February 01). Ярош: Я переоценил организационные возможности Правого сектора. Retrieved from http://news.liga.net/interview/politics/8764969-yarosh_ya_pereotsenil_organizatsionnye_vozmozhnosti_pravogo_sektora.htm
10	Ibid.
11	Азов выпустил на улицы Харькова десять патрулей. (2016, February 4). Retrieved from http://korrespondent.net/city/kharkov/3624818-azov-nachal-patrulyrovat-kharkov
12	Walker, S. (2016, May 02). Tensions run high in Odessa on anniversary of deadly clashes. Retrieved from https://www.theguardian.com/world/2016/may/02/Odessa-ukraine-second-anniversary-clashes
13	Pigman, L. (2016, August 30). Mob in Ukraine Drives Dozens of Roma From Their Homes. Retrieved from http://www.nytimes.com/2016/08/31/world/europe/ukraine-roma.html?_r=0
14	Одесский центр Гражданского Корпуса «АЗОВ» взял под свой контроль ситуацию в Лощиновке. (2016, August 30). Retrieved from http://azov.press/ru/odes-kiy-oseredok-civil-nogo-korpusu-azov-uzyav-pid-sviy-kontrol-situaciyu-u-loschinivci
15	Азовцы пригрозили физической расправой нардепам. (2016, May 20). Retrieved from http://korrespondent.net/ukraine/3685301-azovtsy-pryhrozyly-fyzycheskoi-raspravoi-nardepam
16	Ukraine: The Line (Rep.). (2016, July 18), p. 9. Retrieved from International Crisis Group website: https://d2071andvip0wj.cloudfront.net/ukraine-the-line.pdf
17	Ahmed, N. (2016, June 20). Return of the Reich: Mapping the Global

	Resurgence of Far Right Power. Retrieved from https://medium.com/return-of-the-reich
18	Consult the final chapter for a discussion of these ties.
19	Zinets, N. (2017, February 16). Ukraine faces energy crisis after blockade cuts off coal supply. Retrieved from http://www.reuters.com/article/ukraine-crisis-blockade-idUSL8N1G15LA Furthermore, when the Ukrainian President and Prime-minister warned that these actions only "served Russian interests," causing the Ukrainian economy an estimated $2 billion and forcing it to turn to Russia for coal exports, the far-right activists simply responded by extending the blockade to Russia. Штаб блокады выдвинул ультиматум Укразализныце. (2017, March 5). Retrieved from http://korrespondent.net/ukraine/3823049-shtab-blokady-vydvynul-ultymatum-ukrazalyznytse
20	Ukraine: Humanitarian Snapshot (as of 14 March 2017). (2017, March 14). Retrieved from http://reliefweb.int/report/ukraine/ukraine-humanitarian-snapshot-14-march-2017; Штаб блокады приветствовал решение СНБО. (2017, March 15). Retrieved from http://korrespondent.net/ukraine/3827106-shtab-blokady-pryvetstvoval-reshenye-snbo
21	Article 8 of Minsk agreement on Ukraine crisis: Text in full. (2015, February 12). Retrieved from http://www.telegraph.co.uk/news/worldnews/europe/ukraine/11408266/Minsk-agreement-on-Ukraine-crisis-text-in-full.html
22	Cited in Kelly, K. R. (2012). The context of the Iraq genocide (Unpublished master's thesis). University, Palmerston North, New Zealand, p. 44. Retrieved from https://ongenocide.files.wordpress.com/2012/02/context-of-iraq-genocide.pdf

| Chapter Fifteen |

REPRESSION AND DIVERSION IN DIVIDED UKRAINE

Having established the relevance of the ultranationalists, it is now time to more deeply assess their relation to the right-wing, nationalist and oligarchic establishment in Kiev. Indeed, it would be a mistake to argue that the Kiev regime is simply capitulating to ultranationalists. The anti-communist hysteria, the virulent nationalism and the pro-war rhetoric also converges with their own interests. This political course has, in fact, justified a great deal of repression from the central government. In connection to the anti-Soviet law, for example, the communist party of Ukraine—which garnered 13 percent of the vote in the parliamentary elections of 2012—was banned for using Soviet symbolism and having the word 'communist' in its name, among other things.[1] In addition, Russian news channels were taken off the air, while dozens of Russian books were banned.[2] Repressive war legislation has been passed: people can be wiretapped and imprisoned without court warrants.[3] Ukraine has passed legislation banning officials from criticizing government.[4] An anti-terrorist law was even drafted that would allow the administrative authorities to restrict or ban information appearing on television, radio, print, internet and telecommunication—indefinitely and without a court order.[5] Luckily, the most extreme provisions were dropped after a wave of protest from journalist unions, international media watchdogs and the OSCE.[6] Two years later, however, a Western-sponsored media-watchdog reported that Ukrainian TV-channels have had "content supervisors" ever since Maidan, citing an anonymous source within law enforcement.[7] Finally, by February 2017, Poroshenko issued a decree to formally institute government censorship and surveillance of the internet and mass media within Ukraine.[8]

A Kiev-based NGO, the Institute of Mass Information (IMI), recorded 113 criminal offenses against reporters in the first half of 2016 alone, 50 of which were committed by identified government officials and six by law enforcement.[9] These are no exceptions. Kiev is condoning extra-legal means of repressing dissent by giving the far-right cart-blanche to intimidate pro-Russian politicians, citizens and journalists. In April 2015, Amnesty International called attention to a recent 'spate of suspicious deaths' among pro-Russian journalists and politicians.[10] Two of these killings, one journalist and an opposition politician, occurred just days after their identities and contact information were published on Myrotvorest, a website founded by a Ukrainian deputy minister, created with the purpose of publishing the identities of supposed "enemies of Ukraine."[11] Rather than changing its policy after the killings of April 2015, a year later Myrotvorest published the personal data of 4,508 journalists and other media staff, mostly citizens of Ukraine and other western countries, who had received accreditation from a separatist agency to report in rebel-controlled territories in Donbass.[12] Since this accreditation is quite crucial for the safety of journalists—and far from a guarantee as multiple cases of torture and detention have demonstrated—it seems that the simple act of reporting from enemy territory is already considered "co-operation with terrorists."[13]

The International Federation of Journalists suspects Myrotvorest of having "close links" to the Ukrainian security services.[14] In any case, the website was defended by the minister of interior affairs, Arsen Avakov, as a valuable "ally" and no legal action has been taken to close it down.[15] Emboldened by the lack of response, the leaks have continued, with many reporters on the list receiving death threats.[16] And even these threats, clearly criminal offences, do not engage the interest of the Ukrainian government. So much became clear when the deputy minister of Information Policy, Tetiana Popova, resigned in August 2016 because the government systemically failed to properly investigate the now rampant threats against journalists.[17]

Yet even actual cases of murder aren't properly investigated. In July 2016, award-winning journalist Pavel Sheremet was assassinated with a car-bomb on the busy streets of Kiev—a high-profile and visible killing intended to send a message. One more journalist was killed and another beaten during the same week. Months later, no suspects have been identified, even though the prosecutor-general publicly stated that the first deputy head of the national police had Sheremet under surveillance before the killing. In fact, the officer curiously decided to go on a vacation.[18]

Let's take just one more high-profile case. On September 5th, 2016, the headquarters of Ukraine's most popular TV station was set on fire by two dozen nationalists—seriously injuring one journalist—after other offices of the TV station had already been attacked in January and February of that same year.[19] As occurred with the Odessa massacre, one ultranationalist publicly boasted about the arson during a radio-interview and even threatened to assault another TV station.[20] Again, the police claim to be unable to identify any suspects, which gives some credibility to a recent Ukrainian news report, which cites anonymous sources among the far-right, parliament and Inter TV, claiming that the attack was ordered and paid for by the Ministry of Internal Affairs, with the goal of seizing control over the TV channel.[21]

The Ukrainian state has also used semi-legal means to repress dissent. Ruslan Kotsaba, for example—a formerly pro-Maidan journalist who named the Donbass conflict a 'fratricidal civil war,' and subsequently called on Ukrainians to resist the draft—was arrested and charged with treason, which carries a 12 to 15 years prison sentence.[22] Although he was eventually acquitted, Kotsaba ended up spending one and a half years in prison for his statements. Multiple opposition politicians and journalists faced similar charges, and many of these cases pass with little notice.[23] The prominent human rights activist Volodymyr Chemerys, who campaigned for Ukrainian independence under the Soviet Union, is busy compiling a list of prisoners of conscience, which already includes 110 names.[24]

Horrified by the course of his country, in October 2016, Chemerys proceeded to publish a piece detailing how Ukraine is suffering from "totalitarian tendencies."[25] He was especially troubled by the rise of "totalitarian movements," consisting of both pro-Maidan 'liberals' and ultranationalists, who aligned themselves around "a single way of thinking" for the sake of "victory over the objective enemy."[26] Rather than acting as a civil counterbalance to the state, Chemerys argues that these movements are increasingly justifying, propagating and acting as informants for state repression.

We have seen such practices even by the highly respected pro-Western and liberal Kharkiv Human Rights Protection Group (KHPG), which echoed Kiev's call on Canal Plus not to air a French documentary on the Ukrainian far right.[27] They also cried foul about critical statements from the Committee to Protect Journalists and the US-funded Freedom House, who condemned Kiev for banning an independent and anti-Putin Russian media channel, Dozhd TV.[28] The KHPG argued that Dozhd TV had portrayed maps of Russia that included Crimea, even though they admit that doing otherwise would violate Russian legislation and potentially land the employees in jail. Yet despite Dozhd TV's otherwise critical coverage, the supposed human rights advocate shockingly concluded that: "International NGOs might well consider whether the country's [Ukraine's] attempt to protect its population from the aggressor's distortion of that situation really constitutes *censorship*".[29]

In this context, it is worth citing the Ukrainian scholar Ivan Katchanovski at length, who already summarized the deteriorating political environment in August 2014:

The leaders and many leading members of the

main opposition parties, such as the Party of Regions and the Communist Party, were targets of politically motivated selective prosecutions. ... The scale of such prosecutions far exceeded similar politically motivated selective prosecutions of the opposition leaders and activists, such as Yulia Tymoshenko, on various criminal charges during the Yanukovych government. In addition, many Party of Regions and Communist leaders and activists and their parties' Offices and houses were subjected to violent attacks and assaults by the far right organizations and groups, such as the Right Sector, Svoboda, its C14 neo-Nazi affiliate, and the Maidan Self-Defense. Such violence and threat of violence was also directed at many members of the parliament from these opposition parties. For the first time since Perestroika in Soviet Ukraine in the end of 1980s, the absolute majority of parliamentary votes involved no votes cast against approved legislation [a statistic that was re-confirmed in Katchanovski's September 2016 paper].[30] The first round of the 2014 presidential elections was the least free and fair in post-Soviet Ukraine in terms of the opposition participation. For instance, all three pro-Russian and Communist Party candidates were publicly assaulted by the far right and other Maidan activists during the election campaign, and two of them dropped from the race. All major television channels, including those controlled by formerly pro-Yanukovych oligarchs, presented pro-government positions after the "Euromaidan" and during the civil war in Donbass. Russian Television channels were officially prohibited in Ukraine, and formerly pro-Yanukovych TV channels and pro-Russian, pro-communist or pro-separatist media were often targeted by the far right or the central authorities to force them to change or stop their coverage.[31]

The repression of dissent was combined with an active propaganda campaign. In December 2014, the Orwellian ministry of 'Information Policy' was founded, which intends to manage public opinion in the 'information war' with Russia.[32] The ministry started openly recruiting internet trolls that aim to influence discussions with fake and anonymous accounts.[33] These trolls seem to be used, among other things, for organized attacks against critical Ukrainian journalists, spreading slanderous lies initiated by the government.[34] On the 18th of February 2016, a presidential adviser told the Ukrainian press that Poroshenko had asked him to "lie, lie, lie" about the battle of Debaltseve—which continued for days after the Minsk II peace accords—in a concerted disinformation campaign involving Ukrainian bloggers.[35] Indeed, an extensive journalistic investigation showed that trolls, bloggers, journalists and even political scientists were being paid to toe the government line, or to serve other oligarchic factions willing to pay the price.[36] There were also multiple reports about President Poroshenko attempting to consolidate his control over the media by, among other things, pressuring Kolomoyskyi to sell his channel 1+1 with threats of nationalizing his PrivatBank.[37] Indeed, a content analysis of the four most popular TV stations in the country demonstrated a shocking level of conformity: of all the references to President Poroshenko, a mere 1-2 percent were negative.[38]

The extraordinary level of repression in post-Maidan Ukraine was justified, at every step, by a supposedly uphill propaganda struggle against the Russian state. Yet, a KIIS survey from October 2014 showed that Ukraine was clearly winning the information war.[39] As their top 3 news sources, 84 percent of the population watched Ukrainian television, contrasted with 21 percent who also watched Russian television. For newspapers and magazines, this number was 29 percent to 2 percent, and for the radio it was 16 to one. Furthermore, 22 percent of the population fully trusted Ukrainian television, while 60 percent trusted it partially. For its Russian counterpart, these percentages were respectively five and 26 percent. The Donbass was included in this poll. Even at the heart of the armed resistance, only 24 percent regularly watched Russian television while only 21 percent of the population fully trusted it (seven percent fully trusted Ukrainian television). In a different survey, KIIS found that the balance of trust-distrust—the percentage of Ukrainians that trust a certain medium minus the percentage that distrust it—was two percent in favor of the 'Ukrainian mass-media,' while this balance was struck at minus 70 percent for the 'Russian mass-media.'[40] A KIIS poll from February 2015 found that the majority of Ukrainians either fully or somewhat trusted Ukrainian mass media, while 60 percent of the population 'fully distrusted' Russian mass media and only 9 percent maintained full or partial trust.[41] The most recent KIIS survey of June 2016 is hardly different: nearly 90 percent watched Ukrainian television daily or a few times a week, with just 9 percent for its Russian counterpart.[42] The balance of trust-distrust was set at 9 percent for Ukrainian TV, while struck at minus 60 for Russian TV. As for Donbass, the survey showed that nearly all media was distrusted there, with only internet and social media having a slightly positive balance. Whatever the exact figures then, the general trend is clear: the Ukrainian media maintains decent levels of trust among the population, while the Russian media has been ostracized to the margins of society. It is no wonder that in August 2015, only 13.6 percent of Ukrainians characterized the conflict in the Donbass as a civil war.[43]

In this context, it is especially striking that the political divisions in Ukrainian society have largely persisted. Admittedly, the predominance of separatist/federalist views are unique to the Donbass and Crimea, but other issues remain polarizing. In May 2016, for example, roughly half of Ukrainians still wanted friendly relations with Russia, including open borders without customs and visas.[44] Admittedly, support for joining the Eurasian Economic Union (EEU)—led by Russia—has more than halved, but this has not lead to an embrace of the European Union. About half of the population now favors joining the EU, while a third wants accession neither to the European Union nor the Eurasian Customs Union.[45] On the question of joining NATO, support and opposition are almost evenly split.[46] In fact, a February 2017 Gallup poll found that more Ukrainians considered NATO a threat than a protection.[47] Some recent polls have suggested that NATO-membership would pass a referendum—largely because opponents would not show up for the vote. All of these statistics reveal stark regional variations, and many do not even take rebel-controlled territories into account.

Indeed, a February 2017 KIIS survey, sponsored by the Swedish embassy and excluding separatist regions, showed that majorities in the South and East still perceive the Maidan as an illegal armed coup.[48] Even the concept of Novorossiya—which is very much tied to rebel sympathies—has gained traction in Southern and Eastern Ukraine, according to an extensive survey funded by the US National Science Foundation.[49] This concept was practically unknown until the rebel leadership proclaimed a desire to restore 'greater Novorossiya.' Even Putin recognized the concept when he stated on public television that: "in the tsarist days Kharkov, Lugansk, Donetsk, Kherson, Nikolayev and Odessa were not part of Ukraine." The US-funded survey found that, excluding the Donbass, only half of 'greater Novorossiya' people's considered the concept a myth designed for Russian expansion, which is the standard Western position. Notably, the majority in Kharkiv and Odessa oblasts found it either 'hard to say'—a common reply for politically incorrect stances, the scientists emphasize—or considered Novorossiya to be an 'expression of residents of South-East Ukraine's desire for independence.'

The election results have shown similar regional variations. The nationalist parties, who also opposed the peace accords—People's Front, Self-Reliance, the Radical Party and Fatherland—gained 46 percent of the votes, almost exclusively in Western and Central Ukraine. On the other hand, the more moderate Poroshenko Bloc gained 22 percent of the votes, mostly from

Central and Southern Ukraine. The Opposition Bloc, successor to the Party of Regions and the only pro-Russian party to pass the five percent threshold, won in five of the eight participating Southern and Eastern Ukrainian provinces. Regardless, they did not even garner ten percent of the vote. Indeed, the starkest regional division can be observed in the election turnouts—including presidential, parliamentary and local—which have been the lowest in the history of Ukraine. Turnout in all of the Eastern and Southern provinces consistently fell under the national average, in some cases dropping as low as thirty percent. Even excluding Donetsk and Lugansk, at the extremes the inter-regional turnout differences were 32 percent for the presidential elections, over 30 percent for the parliamentary elections, less than 19 percent for the first round of the local elections and 35 percent for the second.[50] Of course, all of these preceding figures do not include rebel-controlled territory, where no elections were held at all. As Mikhail Pogrebinskiy notes:

> there is limited representation of regions with [a] high percentage of Russian-speaking population in that [Ukrainian] parliament, with 55 deputies from the South-East—Donetsk, Lugansk, Odessa, and Kharkov regions, 24 of whom represent 'Petro Poroshenko Block' and 'The Popular Front' party of Arseny Yatsenyuk—both openly anti-Russian. In contrast, Kiev and Western regions—Lviv, Ivano-Frankivsk, Ternopil, and Chernivtsi—have 257 deputies [despite having less than half the population size of the aforementioned South-East oblasts]. The [relatively] large number of anti-Russian deputies [among the 55 that were elected] from the South-East regions, is due to two factors: the fact that they were included into nation-wide lists of pro-Maidan parties and the low attendance of voters in the South-East in general—and the voters of opposition parties in particular.[51]

In a KIIS poll, over two-thirds of abstainers said they would not vote for at least one of three reasons: unfairness of the election process, inability of parliament to change actual policy and a lack of favorable parties.[52] The latter reason was picked by over one third of abstainers, a percentage that was probably higher among Eastern and Southern Ukrainians. This presents a damning indictment of the Opposition Bloc and the Communist Party of Ukraine, who claim to represent the Southern and Eastern provinces of Ukraine. Indeed, before it was officially banned in 2015, the Communist Party of Ukraine had failed to even pass the five percent threshold to enter parliament. Unsurprisingly then, neoliberal reforms seem to have bipartisan support in Ukrainian politics. A good example is a new labour code, introduced in the framework of implementing the EU association agreement. Although the bill was universally opposed by independent trade unions in Ukraine, it received bipartisan support in parliament. Ukrainian lawyer Vitaliy Dudin summed up some of the problems in the bill:

> the new code will remove the ban on employing women with children under the age of three for night shifts. The maximum probation period will be extended from three to six months. Moreover, the employer can now give 'additional duties' to an employee when it appears that their 'full employment' is not guaranteed (Article 37). If they now carry out work of a lower qualification, then additional payment is not provided. Thus it cannot be excluded that a programmer will have to work as a cleaner without additional pay. (..)
> Article 30 of the draft code will permit employers to control the actions of their employees with the aid of technology. This could include video surveillance or inspections of emails. This kind of constant oversight could lead to unreasonable psychological pressure, as noted

by the Rada's scientific committee. At the same time, people may now find it difficult to leave their jobs of their own accord, even if working conditions decline, in cases where the employer attempts to prove that their employee has improved their qualifications at the company's expense. Here, the employee is deprived of the right to leave until they work off their 'debt'. Otherwise, they will have to pay compensation.[53]

Thus, the current pro-Russian parties hardly represent a true alternative, but rather fit the long Ukrainian tradition of abusing either pro-Western or pro-Russian rhetoric in order to mask unpopular policies and corruption. Nevertheless, the existence of a decent opposition can sometimes help to prevent or diminish overly blatant abuses of power. Therefore, the unprecedented consolidation of power in the hands of the pro-Western factions is a worrying development. Notably, it is also a self-reinforcing one. For a start, the pro-Western government adopted a new lustration law which could potentially fire up to one million government officials who had served under the presidency of Yanukovych.[54] Ironically, president Poroshenko had served as a minister in the Yanukovych administration himself, and was one of the founding members of the Party of Regions. According to a Wikileaks Cable from the American embassy, he was also a 'disgraced oligarch' and 'tainted by credible corruption allegations.'[55] Poroshenko also betrayed his election promise to sell parts of his assets to avoid conflicts of interest. In fact, he's the only oligarch whose net worth has increased since Maidan, despite the free fall of the Ukrainian economy.[56] In 2014, his income increased seven-fold, on which he only paid five percent taxes.[57]

Since Poroshenko assumed the presidency, numerous controversies were sparked over investigations of his corporate dealings. Being implicated in the Panama Papers, an extensive investigation by the award-winning OCCRP strongly suggested that Poroshenko set up an off-shore holding company to avoid paying taxes, right in the middle of the war effort, breaking two Ukrainian laws in the process.[58] Just a few months later, another investigation by the US-funded RFE/RL showed that Poroshenko and other high-level officials owned lavish multi-million-dollar villas in the most luxurious neighborhoods of Spain—hidden from public view, possibly in violation of new transparency laws.[59] Furthermore, the former parliamentarian and Poroshenko ally, Alexander Onishchenko, accused the President of a whole range of corrupt practices, including systemic bribing of MPs for votes. Although Onishchenko fled to Germany in the midst of corruption charges against him, which he claims are fabricated, Leshchenko documented how some elements of Onishchenko's story are corroborated by subsequent events, not least the complete silence over his testimony on Ukrainian television.[60] Finally, to make matters even worse, research by Business New Europe found strong indications that—at the height of the Maidan sniper massacre—Yanukovych and his cronies fled Kiev with private jet services from Ukrprominvest VIP. This corporation was founded by three senior pro-Maidan politicians: leader of the Poroshenko Bloc parliamentary groupIhor Kononenko, the first deputy secretary of the National Security and Defence Council Oleh Gladkovsky—and none other than president Poroshenko himself. Top Yanukovych associates had been using the services already since 2010 and normally paid in cash.[61] Needless to say, large-scale abuse of the lustration law in the form of selective prosecutions is very likely; a matter that was also flagged by the prominent Kharkiv Human Rights Protection Group.[62]

But not only the administrative powers are being cleansed of politicians that had served under Yanukovych. Judges can now be fired by a commission, the majority of whose members are appointed by the government, directly infringing on the separation of powers between the judiciary and the administration.[63] Indeed, it became apparent that the Poroshenko administration was willing to use its leverage over the judiciary, when the constitutional court of Ukraine reversed its leaked decision to render the aforementioned lustration law unconstitutional after threats of new dismissals.[64]

As previously noted, Poroshenko also made a number of political appointments to the Prosecutor General's Office.

But not only formal institutions are facing repression, so are ordinary citizens who protest—often directly from the state. Even excluding the 'Anti-terrorist Operation' in the Donbass, data from the aforementioned Center for Social and Labour research found that the number of state-sanctioned repressive actions (including arrests, beatings, imprisonment etc.) were 97 per 100 separatist/federalist protests in 2014.[65] In the most recent data from April-August 2015, this number increased to a whopping 568 per 100 protests, meaning that nearly all pro-separatist/federalist protests faced multiple forms of state repression.[66] Admittedly, a slight majority of these protests were coded as violent (containing threats, assaults or vandalism). Nevertheless, a comparison with anti-communist protest activities—in practice mostly Ukrainian nationalists—are revealing here. In 2014, over two-thirds were coded as violent, while the repression rate was only 15 per 100 protests. In April-August 2015, this slightly changed to respectively 59 percent coded as violent and 25 repressive actions per 100 events. Thus, a clear trend of selective repression is visible here. Nevertheless, this pro-Russian vs. anti-Russian framework masks a truth that is perhaps even more disturbing: state-sanctioned repression against protest activity has been raised nearly across the board. Protests with socio-economic or civil rights demands, for example, now face a significantly higher rate of repression than under Yanukovych. In fact, civil rights protests saw the same rate of repression as anti-communist ones, even though only 8 percent of the civil rights protests were coded as violent. Thus, we can see how the Kiev regime caters to the war-rhetoric of the ultranationalists, subsequently creates an extensively repressive state machinery, which it then uses to attack its political opponents and oppress wider protest activity. Ukrainian sociologist Volodymyr Ishchenko adds that:

> The mobilization [of the army] has acquired a clear class character because it is easier to locate

and draft villagers or workers than for example a freelance, middle class person, who is not so easy for the military commission to locate. They are more able to defend their rights, they have money to pay bribes, and it is easier for these people to go abroad and escape the draft. So the burden of this war falls more on the shoulders of the poor than on the middle class and especially the rich.[67]

In another interview, he adds that:

they recruit ... very often using the support of the local administration in the villages, or in the case of the cities they also sometimes use the support of [the] factory station management. ... the [factory] management in one of [the] industrial Ukrainian cities, Kryvyi Rih, actually sent this draft card to all the union members in the factory. So, like in [the] good old times, the recruitment of the army can be used for political repression as well, against union activists in this case.[68]

By December 2016, a UN-sponsored survey found that since Maidan, only four percent of Ukrainians saw improvements in the human rights situation.[69] Even a professor, Maidan supporter and former volunteer for Right Sector, Yevheniia Bilchenko, admitted that there is genuine fear of speaking out against the rise of neo-Nazis, government repression and the war in Donbass—because of potential retaliation from the far-right and the state.[70]

Apart from legitimizing repression, however, the nationalist rhetoric of 'moderate' politicians also serves another purpose: it helps to divert attention from Kiev's devastating economic policies. As previously noted, protest data from the aforementioned Center for Social and Labour research found that for four consecutive years before Maidan, the most frequent protest demands had been of a socio-economic nature. Indeed, 2013 saw a record number of socio-economic protest activities. However, with the onset of the war in 2014, the primary protest issues had become ideological and political.[71] In a change of direction, under the crippling conditions of the IMF reforms, in April-August 2015 socio-economic demands returned to nearly half of the protests. Nevertheless, these all came in small numbers. Mass mobilization remains exclusive to ideological and political protest.[72]

Endnotes

1 Ukraine bans Communist party for 'promoting separatism' (2015, December 17). Retrieved from http://www.theguardian.com/world/2015/dec/17/ukraine-bans-communist-party-separatism
2 OSCE. (2014, March 11). Retrieved February 14, 2016, from http://www.osce.org/fom/116312
3 President signs repressive 'anti-terrorist' laws. (2014, August 22). Retrieved from http://khpg.org.ua/en/index.php?id=1408631275
4 Prentice, A. (2016, Maart 01). Ukraine bans officials from criticizing government. Opgehaald van http://www.reuters.com/article/us-ukraine-crisis-censorship-idUSKCN0W351A
5 Repressive media restrictions dropped in law on sanctions. (2014, August 14). Retrieved from http://khpg.org/en/index.php?id=1408019890
6 OSCE representative calls on Ukrainian authorities to drop legislative provisions endangering media freedom and free flow of information. (2014, August 12). Retrieved from http://www.osce.org/fom/122579
7 «1 1», «Ера», «112 Україна», NewsOne: чи купують їх люди Порошенка? (2016, August 29). Retrieved from http://detector.media/medialife/article/118246/2016-08-29-11-era-112-ukraina-newsone-chi-kupuyut-ikh-lyudi-poroshenka/
8 Інтернет і ЗМІ будуть моніторити щодо загроз інформаційній безпеці. (2017, February 25). Retrieved from http://www.pravda.com.ua/news/2017/02/25/7136486/
9 Miller, C. (2016, August 16). In Ukraine, Attacks On Journalists Chill Media Landscape. Retrieved from http://www.rferl.org/a/ukraine-attacks-on-journalists-media-landscape-press-freedom/27923284.html
10 Dalhuisen, J. (2015, April 17). Ukraine's spate of suspicious deaths must be followed by credible investigations. Retrieved from https://www.amnesty.org/en/latest/news/2015/04/ukraine-suspicious-deaths-

need-credible-investigations/
11. Katchanovski, I. (2016). The "Euromaidan," Democracy, and Political Values in Ukraine. Democracy, and Political Values in Ukraine (September 3, 2016), pp. 21-22.
12. Bateson, I. (2016, September 6). Live by the Pen, Die by the Sword. Retrieved from http://foreignpolicy.com/2016/09/06/live-by-the-pen-die-by-the-sword-ukraine-russia-media-war-on-journalism/
13. Ibid.
14. Ibid.
15. Ibid.
16. Ibid.
17. Ibid.
18. Ibid.
19. Pro-Russia TV station in Kiev evacuated after fire. (2016, September 05). Retrieved from https://www.theguardian.com/world/2016/sep/05/pro-russia-tv-inter-kiev-evacuated-fire-ukraine
20. Novinsky, V. (2016, September 23). The west looks on as corruption and bigotry rule in the 'new Ukraine'. Retrieved from https://www.theguardian.com/world/2016/sep/23/ukraine-corruption-bigotry-western-support-russia?CMP=twt_gu
21. Katchanovski, I. (2016, September 6). Interview with Jyllands-Posten (Denmark) Concerning Attacks on Journalists and Decline in Media Freedom in Ukraine (Full-Text English Version). Retrieved from https://www.academia.edu/28482296/Interview_with_Jyllands-Posten_Denmark_Concerning_Attacks_on_Journalists_and_Decline_in_Media_Freedom_in_Ukraine_Full-Text_English_Version_
22. Dalhuisen, J. (2015, April 17). Ukraine's spate of suspicious deaths must be followed by credible investigations. Retrieved from https://www.amnesty.org/en/latest/news/2015/04/ukraine-suspicious-deaths-need-credible-investigations/
23. Katchanovski, I. (2016, September 3). The "Euromaidan," Democracy, and Political Values in Ukraine.), p. 20. Also see the next endnote
24. Beek, B., Van, Ploeg, C., De, Mast, J., & Beunder, S. (2016, April 02). Hoe staat het met de mensenrechten in Oekraïne? Retrieved from https://www.ftm.nl/artikelen/mensenrechten-oekraine
25. Chemerys, V. (2016, October 26). Totalitarian tendencies in post-Maidan Ukraine. Retrieved from https://www.opendemocracy.net/od-russia/volodymyr-chemerys/totalitarian-tendencies-in-post-maidan-ukraine
26. Ibid.
27. Coynash, H. (2016, January 29). French filmmaker adopts Putin's 'Ukrainian fascist hordes' line for Canal Plus. Retrieved from http://

khpg.org/en/index.php?id=1453944128

28 Coynash, H. (2017, January 16). International NGOs should get the facts right re Ukraine's 'Ban' on Russian TV Dozhd. Retrieved from http://khpg.org/en/index.php?id=1484437621

29 Ibid. Emphasis in the original. 'Censorship' is put between quotation marks throughout the article.

30 Katchanovski, I. (2016). The "Euromaidan," Democracy, and Political Values in Ukraine. *Democracy, and Political Values in Ukraine* (September 3, 2016), p. 20.

31 Katchanovski, I. (2014, August 28). East or West? Regional Political Divisions in Ukraine since the "Orange Revolution" and the "Euromaidan", pp. 9-10. Retrieved from https://www.academia.edu/8351374/East_or_West_Regional_Political_Divisions_in_Ukraine_since_the_Orange_Revolution_and_the_Euromaidan_

32 Dangerous 'Truth' Ministry to defend nebulous 'national information security'. (2014, December 3). Retrieved from http://khpg.org/en/index.php?id=1417619985

33 Kottasova, I. (2015, February 25). Ukraine recruits Internet army to fight Russian trolls. Retrieved from http://money.cnn.com/2015/02/25/technology/ukraine-russia-internet-army/

34 Gorchinskaya, K. (2016, July 27). The rise of Kremlin-style trolling in Ukraine must end. Retrieved from https://www.theguardian.com/world/2016/jul/27/kremlin-style-troll-attacks-are-on-the-rise-in-ukraine-hromadske

35 Порошенко просив брехати про ситуацію в Дебальцевому,— Бірюков. (2016, February 18). Retrieved from http://www.volynnews.com/news/vidsichagresoruukrayinayedina/poroshenko-prosyv-brekhaty-pro-sytuatsiiu-v-debaltsevomu-biriukov/

36 Pasyutina, S., & Kryukov, A. (2016, June 2). Территория ботов. Retrieved from http://longread.strana.ua/territoriya_botov

37 Voskalo, M. (2016, August 28). Коломойский продает часть акций телеканала 1 1 "людям Порошенко", - источник ПЛ. Retrieved from http://pl.com.ua/ihor-kolomojskij-prodaet-chast-aktsij-telekanala-1-1-istochnik-pl/; «1 1», «Ера», «112 Україна», NewsOne: чи купують їх люди Порошенка? (2016, August 29). Retrieved from http://detector.media/medialife/article/118246/2016-08-29-11-era-112-ukraina-newsone-chi-kupuyut-ikh-lyudi-poroshenka/

38 Kuznetsov, E. (2016, September 7). Как рейтинговые телеканалы Украины освещают деятельность Петра Порошенко. Retrieved from http://www.pravda.com.ua/rus/articles/2016/09/7/7119879/

39 Novikova, L. (2014, October 29). The media and trust to Ukrainian and Russian media. Retrieved from http://www.kiis.com.ua/?lang=eng&cat=reports&id=425&page=1

40   Kharchenko, N., & Paniotto, V. (2015, May). Ukrainian Society May 2015. Retrieved from http://www.kiis.com.ua/?lang=eng&cat=reports&id=529&page=1&t=7
41   Index of Russian Efficiency Propaganda. (2015, March 3). Retrieved from http://www.kiis.com.ua/?lang=eng&cat=reports&id=510&page=6
42   Socio-political attitudes of the residents of Ukraine and support rating for parties and political leaders: May- June, 2016. (2016, December 9). Retrieved from http://www.kiis.com.ua/?lang=eng
43   Over 50% of Ukrainians see Donbass conflict as Russia's aggressive war. (2015, August 28). Retrieved from http://www.unian.info/society/1116514-over-50-of-ukrainians-see-donbas-conflict-as-russias-aggressive-war-poll.html
44   The dynamics of the positive attitude of the population of Ukraine to Russia and the Russian population to Ukraine. (2015, October 5). Retrieved from http://www.kiis.com.ua/?lang=eng&cat=reports&id=550&page=3
45   Petrenko, T. (2016, November 7). Which direction of integration ukraine should choose: the european union, the customs union or not joining any of the unions. Retrieved from http://www.kiis.com.ua/?lang=eng&cat=reports&id=655&page=3
46   What integration direction should Ukraine Choose: Referendum concerning joining the customs union, the European Union or NATO. (2015, May 19). Retrieved from http://www.kiis.com.ua/?lang=eng&cat=reports&id=530&page=5
47   Gallup, I. (2017, February 10). Most NATO Members in Eastern Europe See It as Protection. Retrieved from http://www.gallup.com/poll/203819/nato-members-eastern-europe-protection.aspx
48   Як російська пропаганда впливає на суспільну думку в Україні (дослідження). (2017, February 13). Retrieved from http://osvita.mediasapiens.ua/mediaprosvita/research/yak_rosiyska_propaganda_vplivae_na_suspilnu_dumku_v_ukraini_doslidzhennya/
49   Toal, G., & O'Loughlin, J. (2015, May 25). What people in southeast Ukraine really think of Novorossiya. Retrieved from https://www.washingtonpost.com/blogs/monkey-cage/wp/2015/05/25/what-people-in-southeast-ukraine-really-think-of-novorossiya/
50   Burn-Murdoch, J. (2014, May 25). Interactive: Ukrainian Presidential election results mapped. Retrieved from http://blogs.ft.com/ftdata/2014/05/25/ukrainian-presidential-election-live-results-and-regional-breakdown/?Authorised=false; Central Election Commission. (2014, October 26). Retrieved from http://www.cvk.gov.ua/pls/vnd2014/wp063e?PT001F01=910; CEC: Voter turnout at local elections in Ukraine exceeds 46%. (2015, October 26). Retrieved from http://en.interfax.com.ua/news/general/299011.html; Новини |

	Українська правда. (2015, November 16). Retrieved from http://pda.pravda.com.ua/news/id_7088897/
51	Pogrebinskiy, M., Alshaer, A., Bahceci, S., Eiran, E., Tabachnik, A., Kedem, N., ... & Onuch, O. (2015). Russians in Ukraine: Before and After Euromaidan. Ukraine and Russia: People, Politics, Propaganda and Perspectives, 90, p. 95.
52	Public opinion of the population of Ukraine: Parliamentary elections 2014 September. (2014, September 26). Retrieved from http://kiis.com.ua/?lang=eng&cat=reports&id=428&t=1&page=3
53	Dudin, V. (2015, June 4). Ukraine's labour reforms threaten workers' rights. Retrieved from http://cslr.org.ua/en/ukraine-s-labour-reforms-threaten-workers-rights-2/
54	http://www.bbc.com/news/world-europe-29239447
55	Taylor, A. (2014, May 29). The not-very-nice things U.S. officials used to say about Ukraine's new president. Retrieved from https://www.washingtonpost.com/news/worldviews/wp/2014/05/29/the-not-very-nice-things-u-s-officials-used-to-say-about-ukraines-new-president/
56	Stacks, G. (2016, August 29). Poroshenko's empire—the business of being Ukraine's president. Retrieved from http://www.intellinews.com/long-read-poroshenko-s-empire-the-business-of-being-ukraine-s-president-103790/
57	ВВС: Порошенко за последний год стал богаче в 7 раз. (2015, May 28). Retrieved September 29, 2016, from https://uainfo.org/blognews/1432790593-vvs-poroshenko-za-posledniy-god-stal-bogache-v-7-raz.html
58	Babinets, A., & Lavrov, V. (2016, April 3). Ukraine: The President's Offshore Tax Plan - The Panama Papers. Retrieved from https://www.occrp.org/en/panamapapers/ukraine-poroshenko-offshore/; Babinets, A., & Lavrov, V. (2016, May 20). Ukraine's president offshores revisited: Swiss trust and millions moved out of Ukraine - The Panama Papers. Retrieved from https://www.occrp.org/en/panamapapers/ukraines-president-offshores-revisited-swiss-trust-and-millions-moved-out-of-ukraine/; King, T. (2016, June 04). Our Panama Papers reporting on Petro Poroshenko was accurate and fair. Retrieved from http://www.politico.eu/article/our-panama-papers-reporting-on-petro-poroshenko-was-accurate-and-fair/
59	Miller, C., & Sedletska, N. (2016, November 16). Investigation Uncovers Ukrainian President's Spanish Villa. Retrieved from http://www.rferl.org/a/ukraine-poroshenko-rferl-investigation-spanish-villa/28116608.html
60	Leshchenko, S. (2016, December 30). Ukraine's corrupt counter-revolution. Retrieved from https://www.opendemocracy.net/od-russia/sergii-leshchenko/ukraine-s-corrupt-counter-revolution

61	Stack, G. (2015, October 20). Poroshenko's VIP jets flew Yanukovych cronies into exile after Ukraine massacre. Retrieved from http://www.intellinews.com/poroshenko-s-vip-jets-flew-yanukovych-cronies-into-exile-after-ukraine-massacre-500447470/?source=ukraine&archive=bne
62	Serious failings seen in new 'lustration' bill. (2014, August 14). Retrieved from http://khpg.org.ua/en/index.php?id=1407941071; Coynash, H. (2014, October 22); A Lustration Law for the Record—and the Elections. Retrieved from http://khpg.org.ua/en/index.php?id=1413758938
63	Ukraine: New Law Violates Judicial Independence. (2014, April 09). Retrieved from https://www.hrw.org/news/2014/04/09/ukraine-new-law-violates-judicial-independence
64	Katchanovski, I. (2016). The "Euromaidan," Democracy, and Political Values in Ukraine. Democracy, and Political Values in Ukraine (September 3, 2016), p. 26.
65	Center for Social and Labour Research. (2015, December). Repressions against protests April-August 2015. Retrieved from http://cslr.org.ua/wp-content/uploads/2015/12/ProtestRepressionsApril-August2015-ecj-edits.pdf
66	Ibid.
67	Ishchenko, V. (2015, March). A socialist case for Ukraine. Retrieved from http://socialistreview.org.uk/400/socialist-case-ukraine
68	Ishchenko, V. (2014, August 12). Ukrainian Government Criminalizing Support For Rebellions in the East. Retrieved from http://therealnews.com/t2/index.php?option=com_content&task=view&id=31&Itemid=74&jumival=12239 Another example is the town of Novovolynsk, where 800 protesting miners were drafted into the army. Tyszkiewicz, O. (2015, February 26). 800 protesting coal miners in Western region of Ukraine conscripted into army. Retrieved from https://newcoldwar.org/ukraine-conscripts-800-protesting-coal-miners-from-western-region/
69	*Оцінка ситуації з дотриманням прав людини* (Rep.). (2016, December 9). Retrieved http://dif.org.ua/uploads/pdf/1742578034584932a82edc82.24794361.pdf
70	Bilchenko, E. (2017, February 7). Страх. Retrieved from http://blog.liga.net/user/ebilchenko/article/25968.aspx
71	Center for Social and Labour Research. (2015, December). Repressions against protests April-August 2015. Retrieved from http://cslr.org.ua/wp-content/uploads/2015/12/ProtestRepressionsApril-August2015-ecj-edits.pdf
72	Ibid.

| Chapter Sixteen |

OBSTRUCTING PEACE

The 'moderates' in Kiev have arguably been a greater obstacle to peace than the ultranationalists. Of course, the ceasefire has been violated by both sides of the conflict, and some of the blame is certainly on the far-right. Most notably, the Minsk accords were immediately and publicly rejected by Right Sector leader Dmytro Yarosh, who vowed to fight on.[1] In addition, research by the Ukrainian scholar Ivan Katchanovski suggests that Right Sector also broke the Easter ceasefire in April 2014, when the conflict had not yet escalated to full-scale war.[2] Two years later former Right Sector leader Dmytro Yarosh would finally admit—to a pro-Ukrainian news site—that he indeed mounted the attack. The same publication, however, also mentions that the operation was authorized by the then-acting president Turchynov, thus potentially implicating the 'moderate' central government.[3]

In any case, the Minsk accords stipulate a path to peace, including a good number of measures that could be taken before the full observance of the ceasefire: constitutional guarantees for decentralization, passing a law on local elections in rebel territories, amnesty for everyone involved in the Donbass conflict, lifting the humanitarian blockade, re-starting social payments, re-opening Ukrainian banks, prisoner swaps and regular talks with the rebel leadership about these measures.[4] So far, only the prisoner swaps have been partially successful, mostly at the start of Minsk II.[5] Amnesty has been proposed—only for those not guilty of capital crimes—therefore necessarily excluding many rebel soldiers. The improvement of the humanitarian situation has not occurred at all. In fact, the Donbass banking system remains frozen and so do all government transactions. The Ukrainian military has also persisted in their interception of aid trucks, though some have finally been let through. An analysis by political scientist Gordon Hahn found Kiev to be in clear violation of seven articles and nine obligations under Minsk II, concluding that "Kiev is significantly more in violation of the agreement than the Donbass rebels and/or Moscow."[6]

Poroshenko, however, has consistently argued the opposite, claiming that the rebels first need to follow through on "security issues," such as disarmament and giving Kiev control over the Russian border. Yet these articles do not have clear timelines. In fact, the latter is made explicitly conditional upon the passing of constitutional amendments and local elections, as stipulated in article 9 of the accords. Furthermore, these political reforms (elaborated on in note one of the agreement) also include the possibility for local councils to create people's militias for maintaining order, meaning that some of the rebels would, in all likelihood, not have to disarm at all. Indeed, giving control over the border and disarmament would amount to surrender, and can therefore only be reasonably implemented after Kiev holds up its side of the bargain, especially the proposed political settlement through local elections and federalization. Such a settlement would also establish Kiev's sovereignty over Donbass and, as such, make the aforementioned security measures enforceable in the first place. In other words, the ball is largely in Kiev's court.

It is therefore quite damning that Kiev has done next to nothing to address these issues. Let us start with the local elections. In October 2015, eight months after the signing of Minsk II—and three months before the initial deadline—it had already become clear that Kiev was not following through on its obligations. Kiev had not even started talks with the rebel leadership about the elections, let alone implemented a special law, in accordance with these negotiations and note one of the accords, that would define the authority of the to-be-elected officials (article 4 and 12). On the contrary, Poroshenko simply insisted that rebel-territories should participate in the nation-wide local elections in October without any of these provisions met and, in fact, without even having passed the across-the-board amnesty law that would allow all the rebels to participate (necessitated by article 12 and note 1). The rebel authorities threatened to organize their own elections that month, which would mean another step towards full independence and a violation of the Minsk accords. A new summit with the Normandy four—Russia, France, Germany and Ukraine—was held, where an agreement was reached that Russia would pressure the rebels to postpone their elections, on the condition that Kiev would finally follow through on its Minsk obligations.[7] Although it was acknowledged that the December 31, 2015 deadline had become unrealistic, Kiev would need to start talks with the rebels straight away to ensure only a limited delay. The rebel leadership indeed postponed their elections—yet one year later Kiev is still refusing to talk to them.

That only leaves the federalization issue. The strong and violent opposition by ultranationalists against the decentralization bill, which involved constitutional amendments to ensure a special status for Donetsk and Luhansk, has already been noted. This bill has been postponed, far beyond the December 31, 2015 deadline that was agreed upon at Minsk II. At closer inspection, however, it becomes clear that, even if passed by parliament, these amendments would hardly ensure true autonomy for the Donbass.[8] On September 16, 2014, a law was passed "on a special local government order in certain districts of Donetsk and Luhansk regions," in order to accommodate the first Minsk Accords.[9] This 'special order,' however, was temporary and would need to be prolonged by a majority vote in the national parliament after three years. So-called 'constitutional guarantees' were given in a later draft of the constitution, after the Minsk II accords in September 2015. The draft constitution, however, only mentioned the issue of special status in the 'transitional provisions,' stating that this would be determined in a separate law. Poroshenko confirmed the reality of this provision in a parliamentary debate, stating that the draft constitution would "only admit the possibility of a specific order of the realization of the local government in certain administrative and territorial units of Lugansk and Donetsk regions, which is determined by a separate law."[10] In other words, there were no actual constitutional guarantees. The special status of the rebel territories are as of yet only recognized by a temporary law and the new constitution will do little to change this.

In addition, in violation of the Minsk accords, the rebel leadership was not consulted in the draft of this constitution. The rebel leadership stated that their proposals had been ignored. Kiev subsequently denied having received any 'official' proposals, the phrasing of which could suggest that the regime still does not recognize the People's Republics as 'official' actors worthy of dialogue.[11] Furthermore, the draft constitution does not guarantee federalization; it in fact yet again serves the agenda of the 'moderate' nationalists in Kiev, helping to concentrate power in the hands of the central administration. As sociologist Halyna Mokrushyna explains:

> in cases where a local government or its head adopts an "act" which does not respect the Constitution of Ukraine or threatens state sovereignty, territorial integrity or the national security of Ukraine, the president of the country is empowered to veto this act, suspend the offending local government (councils) and appoint an interim "state representative" who will "direct and organize" the work of the local executive organs of power.[12]

A constitutional court would subsequently examine the suspension of local governance. Regardless, many Ukrainian parliamentarians fear that the law can be abused to suspend regional governance by arbitrarily renewing charges of constitutional violations. Yet it doesn't stop there. In fact, even the decentralization clauses are underpinned by an austerity agenda. As the Ukrainian lawyer Vitaliy Dudin writes:

the base unit of self-governance is due to become the 'community' (obshchina), rather than town or village. In practice, this amendment will lead to the creation of enlarged neighborhood districts, and is designed to save financial resources. For instance, several neighborhoods could be amalgamated into a single 'community', and then served by a single hospital or school (the numbers of which are due to be cut by 5% in 2016), whereas in the past each neighborhood might have had its own polyclinic. Fundamental social provisions such as education, healthcare, transport and road repair could also be transferred to local council budgets. These measures are in complete accordance with the austerity policies thrust upon Ukraine by the IMF.[13]

It is clear that Kiev bears substantial responsibility for the failure of the Minsk accords, as it has continually privileged its own agenda over peace considerations, cynically exploiting and exacerbating the nationalist tide that swept Ukraine. In fact, as has been demonstrated, Kiev repeatedly found its own agenda to be compatible with that of the far right. This was no different for Minsk. Indeed, to finish this chapter, it would be fruitful to return one last time to the extensive report of the International Crisis Group (ICG), which offers another motivating factor for the failure of the peace accords.

During their field research, the ICG found that a number of officials consider the current stalemate—including the siege against a war-torn population—to be a useful strategy in their military struggle against Russia and the rebels.[14] Removal of western sanctions against Russia have been made conditional upon completion of the Minsk accords. In addition, with the Russian economy already in trouble, the current constellation pushes all the costs for humanitarian assistance and reconstruction onto the Russian state. During their interviews, the ICG found this strategy to have unanimous support among Ukrainian military officers. In fact, even politicians as senior as the Secretary of National Security and Defense, Aleksandr Turchynov, and the Speaker of Parliament, Andriy Parubiy, are on board. Proponents say President Poroshenko privately agrees as well, though he can't publicly say so for obvious reasons. Senior western ambassadors have apparently been briefed about this idea at the start of 2016, although the ICG emphasizes that the strategy has never been turned into official policy. Make no mistake, however, the Minsk II accords are backed by the full weight of the United Nations Security Council.[15] Ukraine was actually a rotating member of the Security Council when the resolution was passed. But they did not introduce the bill. That honor was reserved for the Russian Federation.[16]

Endnotes

1. Yatsyshyn, Y. (2015, February 14). Dmytro Yarosh: 'Right Sector' to fight until complete liberation of Ukraine from Russian occupants. Retrieved from http://euromaidanpress.com/2015/02/14/dmytro-yarosh-right-sector-fight-complete-liberation-ukraine-russian-occupants/#arvlbdata
2. Katchanovski, I. (2016). The Separatist War in Donbass: A Violent Break-up of Ukraine?. European Politics and Society, 1-17
3. Yuri, B. (2016, April 22). Дмитро ярош: "перший наступальний бій війни відбувся 20 квітня 2014-го - добровольці атакували блокпост під слов". Retrieved from http://censor.net.ua/resonance/385673/dmitro_yarosh_pershiyi_nastupalniyi_byi_vyini_vdbuvsya_20_kvtnya_2014go_dobrovolts_atakuvali_blokpost
4. Minsk agreement on Ukraine crisis: Text in full. (2015, February 12). Retrieved from http://www.telegraph.co.uk/news/worldnews/europe/ukraine/11408266/Minsk-agreement-on-Ukraine-crisis-text-in-full.html
5. Pro-Russia rebels release 1,200 prisoners, Poroshenko says. (2014, September 08). Retrieved from http://www.france24.com/en/20140908-pro-russian-rebels-release-1200-prisoners-poroshenko-ukraine/
6. Hahn, G. (2016, February 19). Who's More in Violation of Minsk-2—

	Kiev or Donbass ? Retrieved from https://gordonhahn.com/2016/02/19/whos-more-in-violation-of-minsk-2-kiev-or-Donbas/
7	Robinson, P. (2015, October 06). Holding Kiev to account. Retrieved October 01, 2016, from https://irrussianality.wordpress.com/2015/10/06/holding-kiev-to-account/
8	Mokrushyna, H. (2015, August 28). Decentralization Reform in Ukraine. Retrieved from http://www.counterpunch.org/2015/08/28/decentralization-reform-in-ukraine/
9	Ibid.
10	Ibid.
11	Ibid.
12	Ibid.
13	Dudin, V. (2015, September 16). The dark side of Ukraine's constitutional reform. Retrieved from https://www.opendemocracy.net/od-russia/vitaly-dudin/dark-side-of-ukraine's-constitutional-reform
14	Ukraine: The Line (Rep.). (2016, July 18), pp. 9-11. Retrieved from International Crisis Group website: https://d2071andvip0wj.cloudfront.net/ukraine-the-line.pdf
15	Unanimously Adopting Resolution 2202 (2015), Security Council Calls on Parties to Implement Accords Aimed at Peaceful Settlement in Eastern Ukraine. (2015, February 17). Retrieved from https://www.un.org/press/en/2015/sc11785.doc.htm
16	Ibid.

| Chapter Seventeen |

THE IMPERIAL DESIRE FOR WAR

Both sides of the conflict have seen foreign volunteers enter their battalions—albeit numerically more on the side of the rebels. Indeed, the first prime ministers of the rebel states—Donetsk and Luhansk People's Republics—were both Russian citizens.[1] The rebel ranks also included Russian ultranationalists. A good example is the Wolves' Hundred, who supported the Russian military in Crimea and subsequently swore to fight the "fascists" in Kiev.[2] Ironically, Shkuro, the founding father of the Wolves' hundred, was himself a Nazi-Collaborator. But this does not prevent them from proclaiming anti-fascist credentials, nor from whipping civilians.[3] On the rebel side too, there were Chechen battalions, linked to the Kremlin-backed regime of Ramzan Kadyrov.[4] Nevertheless, as several on the ground reports confirmed—published in, among others, *The New York Times*, the *London Review of Books*, the *New York Review of Books* and the *Sunday Times*—nearly all the rebels were locals.[5] In April 2014, EU intelligence chief Georgij Alafuzoff confirmed that no regular Russian troops were engaged in Ukraine, only some Russian citizens who came of their own volition, constituting but a minor part of the rebellion.[6] Indeed, Russia seemed to have little control over the rebels. When Putin asked them to postpone a referendum on independence on the 11th of May, the rebel leadership went through with it anyway.[7] By contrast, Putin did recognize the presidential and parliamentary elections in Ukraine proper as legitimate, directly challenging the rebel narrative that the government in Kiev is a fascist junta.[8]

Regardless, countless Western media kept reporting a Russian 'stealth invasion,' uncritically copying statements from NATO, US and Ukrainian officials. A good example was a *New York Times* front page article in early May, which claimed to show conclusive evidence of Russian military involvement in eastern Ukraine.[9] This was based on pictures forwarded by officials in Kiev and Washington to *The New York Times*, which allegedly showed the same group of armed men in two pictures: one of them taken in Russia, the other in Ukraine. But this evidence was very shaky. The men could well have been veterans and the pictures were very blurry. Indeed, higher quality versions were actually circulating on the internet, which clearly showed they were not the same men.[10] This was bad enough, but the problem turned out to be even worse: the actual photographer of the supposedly Russian picture publicly stated that the picture was actually taken in Ukraine.[11] The entire story fell apart. In fact, it seems Washington officials had just lazily picked two pictures from the internet, lowered the resolution and sold a fabricated story to 'prominent' Western journalists. The false information was subsequently uncritically reported throughout the Western world. This obviously showed a complete lack of professionalism in Western media, as well as a severe anti-Russian bias. Perhaps most damning, the affair showed that Western government officials were counting on this. As Oliver Boyd-Barrett demonstrated in his book *Western Mainstream Media and the Ukraine Crisis: A Study in Conflict Propaganda,* mainstream Western media were effectively serving as state propaganda outlets throughout the Ukraine crisis, similar to their conduct in previous conflicts.[12] It is perhaps unsurprising that a Gallup survey taken throughout the former Soviet Union showed that, among people following both Western and Russian media, a comfortable-to-vast majority in all countries—with the sole exception of Georgia—considered Russian media to be more reliable.[13]

All of this is not to say that the Russian state never backed the rebels. That would happen months later, in substantial volumes. The Ukrainian army was making steady headway into rebel-held territory, and halfway through August 2014 the situation changed decisively. Writing on the ground for the *New York Review of Books*, Tim Judah described the August offensive as "a catastrophic defeat ... [that] will long be remembered by embittered Ukrainians as among the darkest days of their history."[14] By the end of that month, the rebel leadership freely admitted that an estimated 3000 to 4000 Russian soldiers were fighting among their ranks (they were supposedly on a holiday), which were estimated to number between 10,000 and 20,000 fighters in July.[15] Indeed, it seems that Russian military support turned the tide of war in August, forcing Poroshenko to sign the Minsk peace accords on the 5th of September. According to official military records, at least a hundred regular Russian troops died that month during their service, all of them supposedly during training exercises.[16] Paul Robinson documented numerous other indications of direct Russian participation in August, such as social media posts by Russian soldiers, pictures of uniquely Russian military equipment in Donbass, Russian soldiers captured by the Ukrainian army and several admissions from rebel sources.[17] After almost two years of denial, Putin finally admitted that Russian 'military intelligence officers' have been active in the Donbass.[18]

This Russian incursion was thus a definite and important reality, but it's easy to overstretch its meaning. Paul Robinson, a military expert and British intelligence veteran, argues, in an extensive paper about the offensive, that Russian support was not the sole—or even the most important—reason for the August defeat.[19] Although the Ukrainian military had suffered years of neglect in the run-up to the civil war, Robinson shows that the rebels remained clearly outnumbered and under-equipped—even when accounting for Russian support. In other words, the reason for the August defeat must also be sought elsewhere. Robinson cites in particular the relevance of a range of strategic mistakes made by Ukrainian political and military leaders, such as an exclusive focus on gaining territory rather than neutralizing the opposing army; underestimating the forces required for specific battles by failing to predict local opposition; increasing this local opposition by indiscriminate shelling of residential areas; and refusing to withdraw from specific battles when defeat was very predictable. Matters beyond the control of the Ukrainian leadership, such as differences in army morale and the successful use of interior lines (a military strategy) by the rebels, are also documented.[20] Lastly, addressing the relevance of Russian military supplies during these initial phases of the war, an extensive report by the Armament Research Services in Australia in November 2014 concluded the following:

> ARES has assessed that it is very likely that pro-Russian separatist forces have received some level of support from one or more external parties, however the level of state complicity in such activity remains unclear. Despite the presence of arms, munitions, and armoured vehicles designed, produced, and allegedly even sourced from Russia, there remains no direct evidence of Russian government complicity in the trafficking of arms into the area. [It is clear, however, that from the very start of the insurgency, the Russian state tolerated the formation of quite extensive private Russian networks which openly gathered supplies and volunteer fighters for the Donbass rebels.] *The majority of arms and munitions documented in service with separatist forces have evidently been appropriated from the Ukrainian security forces and their installations within Ukraine.* ... The Ukrainian regime has access to more powerful weapon systems, in greater numbers, and with a more robust logistical chain than separatist forces could hope to muster without overt support from a foreign power. As it stands, the limited but noteworthy external support pro-Russian separatist forces have received has not proven significant enough to turn the tide in their favour.[21] [emphasis mine]

Notably, right after the August offensive most regular Russian troops left Ukraine again.[22] During the second major intensification of the conflict in January 2015, the Commander in chief of the Ukrainian armed forces made the following admission: "We have some evidence about individual members of the Russian Armed Forces and citizens of the Russian Federation being a part of the illegal armed groups in combat activities. Currently, [however,] we are not engaged in combat operations against the units of the regular Russian army."[23] A reappearance of regular Russian forces did happen shortly in February 2015, preceding the Minsk II accords. But they left again, straight afterwards. The OSCE recently confirmed that there is no evidence of regular Russian troops currently stationed in Ukraine.[24] The aforementioned April-May 2016 ICG interviews with Ukrainian officers unanimously confirmed the same.[25] Notably, even concerning the supply of military resources, the main conclusion of the 2014 ARES report was echoed in the 2015 Yearbook of the Stockholm International Peace Research Institute—possibly the world's most authoritative source on the international arms trade—which found that "most of the weapons used by both sides were in the Ukrainian inventory before the crisis started."[26]

Nevertheless, the Russian interventions preceding both of the Minsk accords does demonstrate the importance of the Russian state in tipping the balance when needed, pressuring Kiev to accept a negotiated settlement.[27] From 2015 onwards, the rebels also started talking quite openly about funds, training and military equipment supplied by the Russian state. An estimated $1 billion a year is paid to bankroll pensions, social benefits and salaries to local officials and the separatist military forces.[28] This support became increasingly important as the Ukrainian military revitalized from the initial chaos that followed Maidan.[29] In October 2015, the rebel leader Alexander Khodakovsky explained the ramifications during an interview: "Russia is behind us and there is the unambiguous hint that if you continue military aggression against us, then Russia will not refrain from supporting us in absolutely every way it can, and they [Kiev] understand that."[30]

During the ICG interviews, Ukrainian officers agreed, stating that Russia's support was the primary reason for Kiev's hesitance to embark on a new major offensive.[31]

Russian control over the rebellion has solidified since August 2014, after which the rebels were integrated into an overall command structure, following orders from Russian military handlers.[32] Notably, the Russian state did not solely gain influence through military and financial support. A string of assassinations has befallen independent-minded and anti-oligarchic rebel leaders, which could not be traced to the Ukrainian military.[33] These assassinations came after evidence surfaced of Russian meddling in the Donbass general elections in October 2014.[34] The communist party in the Donetsk People's Republic (not to be confused with the aforementioned communist party in Ukraine proper) was not allowed to participate, supposedly for technical reasons. When its leader, Boris Litvinov, challenged this decision, he received a phone-call from Russian state adviser Borodai, who told him to drop his objections and remain loyal, emphasizing Russian support for the rebels. The Donbass insurgents have hero status in Russia—and it seems the state preferred not to have leftist and anti-oligarchic ideas spread.

In fact, even the communist party has a very limited progressive agenda, and remains by and large loyal to the rebel leadership—underscoring the very tight control of the Kremlin over the rebels since August 2014. After being denied participation in the elections, Litvinov assured his party that 'there is no need to go into deep opposition,' re-affirming his earlier statement that 'we are not in the opposition, we are the vanguard [of the republic].' In his 130-page review of the Ukrainian left during and after Maidan, the Ukrainian sociologist Volodymyr Ishchenko finds the left to be extremely weak and fractured on both sides of the conflict. Although communist, anti-oligarchic and other leftist ideas are more popular among the rebels, they remain just that, ideas. As Ishchenko writes: "The public activity of the [communist] party for almost the whole year, according to the official web-site, consisted exclusively of ritualistic activities on symbolic communist dates, *subbotniki* and the reconstruction of *pioneer* and *Komsomol* youth organizations. The party clearly exists only to support communist identity but not to engage in communist politics."[35]

The 'left' battalions operate in a similar vein. By far the most progressive brigade is Prizrak—whose commander was assassinated, ostensibly with separatist involvement—and even they were willing to postpone progressive politics in favor of 'unity against the aggressor.' As the head of Prizrak's political department put it: "this is not a social revolution but a national-liberation war of the Donbass peoples, greater Novorossiya peoples and those in Ukraine who disagree with principles of political intolerance."[36] Notably, Novorossiya was a former imperial province of the Russian empire stretching over much of Southern and Eastern Ukraine, whose revival as a concept is an obvious sign of Russian nationalism. As for the 'political intolerance', quite ironically, Prizrak has tolerated the admittance of Russian Neo-Nazis in their battalion, underscoring the level of political sacrifice that progressive elements within the uprising were willing to make in favor of 'unity.'[37]

Yet Russia has also been reigning in some of the ultranationalist rebel leaders. As Shaun Walker wrote for the *Guardian*: "those who disagree with the uneasy peace on all sides are being sidelined. Andrei Purgin, one of the original ideologues of the Donetsk People's Republic, who represented the territory at the Minsk negotiations, was sacked from his position in the leadership last month and spent four days under arrest. In an interview in Donetsk, Purgin evaded a direct answer as to the reason behind his arrest, but said he disagreed with the ceasefire. ... Purgin said he believed a criminal case could be launched against him, and his movements were being tracked by the separatist authorities he led until recently."[38] Purgin is not the only rebel leader to have publicly lamented the Minsk agreement; many wish to secure the entire Donbass, especially the city of Mariupol where crucial supplies and access to a seaport are located. But Russia's main interests require a cessation of war.

Neutral status for Ukraine can be established through the Minsk accords, by giving Donbass veto power over NATO membership within a federalized Ukraine. The military base in Crimea was already secured in March 2014, and Putin has prevented loss of face by saving the rebellion from sure defeat. Indeed, Merkel and Hollande both praised Putin for pressuring the rebel leadership to accept the Minsk II accords.[39] As the ICG documented, separatists have consistently complained that their Russian military handlers have strictly enforced the ceasefire orders.[40] Analysts on both sides have therefore suggested that the occasional spikes in violence are attempts to pressure Kiev politically, to implement the Minsk accords for example, reminding Ukraine that the Russia is still willing to use its military force.[41]

We can thus establish that Russian support for the Donbass rebellion was and remains very substantial—and that the new proto-states are essentially ruled from the Kremlin. Nevertheless, it is quite a stretch that countless media were reporting a 'Russian invasion,' or an impending one, by uncritically copying statements and 'classified intelligence' from US, Kiev and NATO sources. Indeed, comparisons with actual invasions might be enlightening. The first gulf war, for example, involved nearly a million troops on the side of Kuwait, about 700,000 of them from the US. In fact, the number of Russian troops in Donbass is comparable to the US military presence in Iraq *after* the 'full withdrawal' in 2011. Admittedly, the scale of the Ukraine conflict was smaller, but the vast majority of rebel fighters have at all times been locals. As such, many accusations from Kiev and NATO have been extremely misleading. When a Russian convoy of trucks sent highly necessary humanitarian aid across the border, Western politicians cried foul about a "direct invasion".[42] An extremely grave misrepresentation, considering that several Western journalists were allowed to inspect the trucks and only found bottles of water and boxes with sleeping bags.[43]

In the end of August 2014, accusations of an impending Russian invasion further intensified, this time supported by satellite images straight from the Pentagon. This was a curious development, since a mission of the OSCE, who had been monitoring the border since the 6th of August, had only seen large groups of unarmed men pass the border.[44] It should be clear that an all-out invasion, as opposed to an incursion or covert support, is not something that can just happen unnoticed. Putin tried to make this point clear by assuring EU commissioner Manuel Barroso over the phone that "if I want to, I can take Kiev in two weeks."[45] Many Western media subsequently spun this remark as an open threat to take the city of Kiev. On the 1st of September 2014, a dozen US intelligence veterans sent an open letter to Chancellor Merkel.[46] They warned that "the [US] "intelligence" [about Ukraine] seems to be of the same dubious, politically "fixed" kind used 12 years ago to "justify" the U.S.-led attack on Iraq."[47] These veterans were not alone. In public testimony in the French parliament, Director of Military Intelligence Christophe Gomart proclaimed that:

> NATO had announced that Russia would invade Ukraine, whereas according to our information, nothing supported this hypothesis—indeed, we observed that the Russians had not deployed command centers or a supply chain, notably military hospitals, that would allow for a military invasion, and reserve units had not moved at all. Subsequent events proved us right, because if some Russian soldiers were indeed seen in Ukraine, it was more a maneuver aiming to exert pressure on Ukrainian President Poroshenko than an attempted invasion.[48]

He explained that "the real problem with NATO is that US intelligence is preponderant there, whereas French intelligence is only more or less taken into account."

A similar thing happened at the start of March 2015, when the war activities were winding down and the Minsk II accords were starting to take hold. Philip Breedlove, Supreme

Allied Commander of NATO, took to the stage and told a press conference that the rebels had just been supplied with "well over a thousand combat vehicles, Russian combat forces, some of their most sophisticated air defense, battalions of artillery." He emphasized that "it is not getting better. It is getting worse every day." Two days later, an extensive article appeared in *Der Spiegel*, which revealed that several high ranking German intelligence officers considered these statements "dangerous propaganda."[49] And this was not the first time this happened either. In fact, these exaggerated statements intensified each time peace was in reach. "NATO in the past has always announced a new Russian offensive just as, from our point of view, the time had come for cautious optimism," a German parliamentarian told *Der Spiegel*. NATO has always been a US-dominated organization, leading some to conclude that the Americans were hijacking the peace effort. In addition, *Der Spiegel* reported that:

> Berlin officials have noticed that, following the visit of American politicians or military leaders in Kiev, Ukrainian officials are much more bellicose and optimistic about the Ukrainian military's ability to win the conflict on the battlefield. "We then have to laboriously bring the Ukrainians back onto the course of negotiations," said one Berlin official.[50]

The fact that the United States has continuously been pushing for war is crucial. We noted earlier that Bloomberg View considered the US embassy to be a 'center of power' in Ukraine; that Geoffrey Pyatt met every two weeks with President Poroshenko to give him 'firm' orders; that important ministerial and even defense appointments were 'vetted' by Washington. Indeed, several foreigners have been appointed in important governmental positions, including former Georgian president Mikheil Saakashvili and several of his close associates—hardline hawks who provoked war with Russia in 2008, and have extensive ties with neocon circles in Washington.[51] Furthermore, working directly under Joe Biden for US affairs in Ukraine is the Assistant Secretary of State for European and Eurasian Affairs, Victoria Nuland. A characteristic figure of the continuity in US foreign policy making, Nuland had also served as the principal deputy foreign policy adviser to Vice President Dick Cheney, among those chiefly responsible for the 2003 invasion of Iraq. She's also married to the neo-con Robert Kagan, who co-founded the Project for a New American Century (PNAC), a think tank in favor of a "Reaganite policy of military strength and moral clarity." Ten out of twenty-five co-founders of PNAC went on to serve under the Bush administration, including Dick Cheney, Donald Rumsfeld and Paul Wolfowitz.

US influence could help to explain why President Poroshenko has made such half-hearted attempts at peace. According to pro-government sources, in March 2014 a deal was arranged in Vienna between pro-Russian oligarch Dmytro Firtash and then presidential candidate Petro Poroshenko, where they agreed that Firtash's backing would be conditional upon securing peace in the Donbass.[52] This deal was obviously not made out of charity, but with material interests in mind. Firtash, as well as Akhmetov, have loads of assets in the Donbass that have been ravaged by the war, enabling other oligarchs to overtake their influence. Nevertheless, peace is certainly in the interest of Ukraine, and has enough support among the wider population to be achieved without major electoral losses (or even with electoral gains, depending on your interpretation of the polls).[53] It is therefore striking that so little progress has been made.

At the time of the meeting in Vienna, Dmytro Firtash was facing extradition to the United States on bribery charges by the FBI, for which he was already forced to pay $125 million in bail. From the very start, the oligarch claimed the charges were fake. On the 30th of April 2015, a regional court in Vienna largely confirmed his accusation.[54] The Austrian judge Christoph Bauer ruled in Firtash's favor, because the charges concerned "at least partially politically motivated accusations." But not only was the prosecution selective, "there just wasn't sufficient proof." Concerning the bribery witnesses, the US Justice Department consistently refused to provide the requested information, nor was the department responding to questions. In fact, the Austrian judge had strong doubts "whether these witnesses even existed."

A third person was present in Vienna when Poroshenko and Firtash made their deal: Vitaly Klitschko, the most popular candidate in the polls, who pulled out of the presidential race in support of Petro Poroshenko right after this meeting. Let us revisit what Victoria Nuland thought of Klitchko one month earlier: "I don't think Klitsch should go into the government. I don't think it's necessary, I don't think it's a good idea." Rather, she thought that "Yats is the guy." Nuland was undoubtedly aware of the support Klitschko received from the pro-Russian oligarch Firtash and might have assessed Yatsenyuk as more willing to take stronger anti-Russian stances. If indeed so, this assessment would prove to be correct. On the 10th of September 2014—five days after Poroshenko signed the first Minsk accords—Yatsenyuk founded his new People's Front party, in direct opposition to the peace accords.

There were, however, some positive signs for a US détente in Ukraine that year. Notably, in a complete break with his past approach—avoiding diplomatic relations with Russia—Obama called Putin on January 14, 2016 to discuss Minsk II.[55] In April, Victoria Nuland reportedly even pressured Ukrainian officials to implement the accords.[56] She had also flown all the way to Kiev to oversee the July 2015 vote on the first reading of the decentralization bill, which passed with Nuland and Pyatt attending the session in the Ukrainian parliament. This has led some observers to blame the far-right—who staged a violent protest in front of parliament the day of the vote, as previously mentioned—for the indefinite delay of the bill.[57] Nevertheless, if the US support for the Minsk accords was genuine, there surely hasn't been much resolve. In 2016, during his annual September address to the Ukrainian parliament, Poroshenko publicly turned Minsk II on its head by stating:

> We have convinced our western allies and partners that any political settlement [such as constitutional amendments and local elections in rebel-held territories] must be preceded by apparent and undeniable progress on security issues: a sustainable ceasefire, withdrawal of Russian troops and equipment from the occupied territories, disarmament of militants and their family—and finally the restoration of our control over our own border.[58]

Of course, the accords clearly stipulate the exact reverse timeline. Poroshenko is simply reiterating his refusal, among other obligations, to make the constitutional amendments that should have been implemented already by December 31, 2015. As for the "western allies" that supposedly agree with this, Poroshenko met with the US secretary of defense just two days later, where he was rewarded with a bilateral partner concept, which pledged continued military support for Ukraine.[59] A few days later, Ukraine also received another billion-dollar tranche from the IMF—which, as Michael Hudson notes, has been in violation of their own rules by lending to a country at war.[60] Poroshenko visited Washington around the same time, making several high-profile speeches and securing another billion-dollar loan from the US government.[61] On September 22, 2016 US Vice President Joe Biden re-affirmed that he was still spending two to three hours a week on the phone with his Ukrainian counterparts.[62] He also slyly noted that Poroshenko needed to ensure that the Europeans wouldn't blame him for the failure of Minsk II, because "you have to understand: everybody's willing to blame the victim."[63]

We do not have to rely solely on circumstantial evidence to demonstrate US support for Poroshenko's stance on Minsk. Biden himself articulated the same position nine months earlier—reversing the Minsk time-line, and subsequently blaming Russia for the lack in progress—in his address to the Ukrainian parliament on December 9, 2015:

While there has been some progress in deescalating the violence, there can be no sanctions relief unless and until Russia meets all of its commitments under the Minsk Agreement. (Applause).

... Heavy weapons must be withdrawn from the frontlines. The OSCE must be granted full, unencumbered access. Russia must press the separatists to hold elections according to Ukrainian law and OSCE standards and disavow the illegal election that's just taken place [Biden thus endorses Poroshenko's position on the local elections, and even seems to be uninformed about the cancellation of elections in rebel-held teritorries, in accordance with the Normandy Four agreement] ... Hostages held by Russia and its proxies must be returned. Russian troops must leave. The Ukrainian side of the border must be returned to Ukrainian control. *Unless all—if they do all of that, and only if they do, Ukraine also has a responsibility it still has to fulfill* —including amnesty for those who have not committed capital offenses; granting devolved administration to the Donbass. [note here also Biden's endorsement for limiting the amnesty law in violation of Minsk II] ... *That only happens if Russia lives up to its commitments, if Russia does its part. If it does, then you must follow through with yours.* [emphasis mine]

Notably, there have been divisions within the Obama administration over Ukraine. The US president certainly gave in to a lot of anti-Russian rhetoric, but he also continually emphasized Russia's weakness, favoring a more measured response. He had few allies in this approach. In his memoirs, senior defense official Derek Chollet describes a high-level discussion on the provision of lethal aid to the Kiev administration: "this was one of the few occasions I can recall in the Obama administration in which just about every senior official was for doing something that the president opposed."[64] In fact, such opposition ran much deeper than simple face-to-face discussions. A batch of e-mails from the former NATO supreme commandor Phillip Breedlove—released by the website DC leaks, the authenticity of which was confirmed by two of Breedlove's interlocutors—revealed far-reaching efforts to "fashion a NATO strategy to leverage, cajole, convince or coerce the US to react."[65] As senior advisor to the Atlantic Council, Harlan Ullman, remarked: "Given Obama's instruction to you not to start a war, this may be a tough sell."[66]

The e-mails show Breedlove reaching out to a number of high-level officials, including Colin Powell and his NATO predecessor Wesley Clark, seeking council on "how to work this personally with the POTUS [President of the United States]," who needed to approve of any lethal aid sent to Ukraine.[67] Ullman advised Breedlove to reach out to Joe Biden, because "I know of no better way of getting" to Obama.[68] Indeed, the US vice-president, who was Washington's point-man in Ukraine, actively supported NATO expansion and military interventions in Eastern Europe and the Balkans since the 1990s. As such, he might have been more pliable to listen to hawkish proposals, although we have no record of Breedlove actually reaching out to him.

What the DC Leaks do show is the centrality of a figure named Philip Karber, whose name pops up throughout the e-mail correspondence. He is president of the Potomac Foundation, which openly advocates for NATO expansion and received over $300,000 from George Soros' Open Society Foundation.[69] Karber is also a long-time cold war hawk and among the most discredited of intelligence analysts. A useful summary of his track-record was recently published in *Foreign Policy* by Jeffrey Sachs, a colleague and acquaintance of Karber who felt the need to speak out.[70] Karber's controversies go back to at least the 1970s, when he first published a paper, "The Tactical Revolution in Soviet Doctrine", purporting to uncover a secret Soviet strategy for an unreinforced attack against NATO. An analyst from the Defense Inteligence Agency, among others, had reviewed Karber's citations, only to find that the paper was incompetent if not fraudulent, with quotes either taken out of context or wholly mistranslated. And this was no isolated incident. In another case, Karber made the wild assertion that China had 3000 nuclear weapons—more than ten times the number of other intelligence estimates—based, among other things, on images that turned out to be stage sets from Chinese soap-operas. In fact, the paper was full of such errors, and even managed to cite a long-debunked essay that was plagiarized from an internet forum. In both cases, Karber simply continued repeating his discredited claims throughout the years.[71]

Even as recently as the Ukraine crisis, Karber caused somewhat of a scandal when he forwarded pictures taken in South Ossetia during the 2008 war, as proof of Russian involvement in Donbass. The fraud was quickly uncovered when the pictures found their way to the US press, after having been viewed by a number of Ukrainian and US officials.[72] Yet if Breedlove was unaware of all these controversies, some alarm bells should have certainly rung when Karber mailed the NATO commandor in November 2014, trying to lend credence to the ridiculous notion that the rebels were in possession of a tactical nuclear warhead. This did not seem to discourage Breedlove, however, as he kept forwarding intelligence reports from Karber into "the right places" with the "fingerprints removed."[73]

In the end, Karber and Breedlove failed to convince Obama, who remained steadfast in his refusal to give lethal aid to Kiev. Such presidential engagement with the conflict, however, proved to be an exception. As Bromwich aptly noted in the *London Review of Books*, Obama has been "the world's most important spectator," both on Ukraine and other foreign policy matters.[74] While leaving responsibility in the hands of the State Department, including figures such as Nuland, "the message has got around by now that Obama doesn't particularly want to know things:"

His obliviousness to the Cheney weeds in his policy garden is characteristic and revealing. As Barton Gellman revealed in *Angler*, still the best book about Cheney, the vice president in 2001 was given a free hand to sow the departments and agencies of government with first and second-echelon workers who were fanatically loyal to him. Many of those people are still around; Obama made no effort to scour his government of their influence.[75]

A number of US officials active in Ukraine were fed by Karber's intelligence—including the State Department's representative Victoria Nuland, NATO deputy secretary general Rose Gottemoeller, Ambassador Geoffrey Pyatt and his military attaché, Joseph Hickox.[76] The correspondence revealed a shocking level of incompetence in the US embassy, with social media reports and Pravda news bulletins having to pass as intelligence, google translated and all. As Hickox put it: "we're largely blind."[77]

Karber sought to fill the gap by regularly visiting the front-lines in Donbass. He developed a particularly "intimate" relationship with the oligarch-funded and ultranationalist Dnipro-1 batallion, whom he also visited for Christmas. As he told Breedlove: "The toasts and vodka flow, the women sing the Ukrainian national anthem—no one has a dry eye."[78] As expected, Karber's briefings were consistently alarmist. In February 2015, days after the second Minsk accords were signed, Karber mailed Breedlove to warn about the "prospect of an imminent Ukrainian defensive collapse," the "likely fall of the Poroshenko government" and Russia's "further offensive movement toward Kharkiv, Dnepropetrovsk, and opening a land corridor to Crimea," which would increase the conflict area by more than ten-fold and swallow nearly half of Ukraine.[79]

Despite Karber's fantastical claims, the DC leaks show him to be well-connected beyond US policy circles as well. He regularly mentions meetings with top-officials, such as the Polish and Baltic defense ministers, and even casually adds a two-hour "debriefing session with President Poroshenko."[80] Indeed, such Ukrainian connections started even before Kiev initiated its "Anti-Terrorist Operation" in Donbass, when Philip Karber and former NATO supreme commandor Wesley Clark were invited by the Ukrainian National Security Advisor to share their expertise.[81] In late March and early April 2014, they reported to have participated in 35 meetings with senior Ukrainian officials and military commanders—and going by the hacked e-mail correspondences, this seems to have been the start of a longstanding alliance.[82] No wonder then, that German diplomats often complained about having to "laboriously bring the Ukrainians back onto the course of negotiations."[83]

Notably, Wesley Clark was the one to introduce Karber to Breedlove, which he did with the following lines: "[Karber] was one of the premier strategists who analyzed Soviet intentions and capabilities within the Pentagon ... he was extremely well thought of, and came up with groundbreaking understandings that helped shape our entire strategic approach."[84] Such, apparently, is the reputation Karber deserved for his fraudulent work in the 1970s. Indeed, Jeffrey Lewis still sees many of his intelligence colleagues citing Karber's most discredited works. As he rightly points out:

> there are few professional consequences in Washington for "misunderstandings", especially if you tell someone what he or she wants to hear. Alarmist studies about Soviet doctrine, bizarre estimates of the Chinese nuclear weapons stockpile, and now pictures of Russian brutality — all matters of concern that require no exaggeration — found a ready audience among people who already knew what they wanted to do, and were eager for evidence that would support it. [quotation marks mine, Lewis uses the word "misunderstanding" ironically throughout the text].[85]

Hardly marginal, Karber's research on Soviet forces during the 1970s received consistent funding from Andrew Marshall's Office of Net Assesment, an internal Pentagon think tank providing an "important part of the language spoken by leaders in the higher levels of DOD [Department of Defense]," according to Yale professor Paul Bracken.[86] Notably, Andrew Marshall remained the director of Net Assesment for decades, just recently retiring at the age of 93. Neo-cons such as Dick Cheney, Donald Rumsfeld and Paul Wolfowitz—who used fallacious intelligence derived from torture to invade Iraq in 2003—are often considered to be Marshall's "star protégés."[87] No surprises there. As Kieran Kelly documented in his *Context to the Iraq Genocide*, downright fraudulent and alarmist intelligence has been a useful American trade for decades, and even managed to militarize the Carter presidency by the end of the 1970s.[88] As such, it is no coincidence that such practices have resurfaced in Ukraine.

Endnotes

1   Kramer, A. E. (2014, August 19). Plenty of Room at the Top of Ukraine's Fading Rebellion. Retrieved from http://www.nytimes.com/2014/08/20/world/europe/plenty-of-room-at-the-top-of-ukraines-fading-rebellion.html

2   Shuster, S. (2014, May 12). Meet the Cossack 'Wolves' Doing Russia's Dirty Work in Ukraine. Retrieved from http://time.com/95898/wolves-hundred-ukraine-russia-cossack/

3   Shenfield, S. (2014, April 5). Ukraine: Popular Uprising or Fascist Coup? Retrieved from http://www.stephenshenfield.net/themes/international-relations/164-ukraine-popular-uprising-or-fascist-coup; Shenfield, S. (2015, April 17). Moscow, Kiev, and the West European Far Right. Retrieved from http://stephenshenfield.net/places/russia/current-politics/168-moscow-kiev-and-the-west-european-far-right

4   Walker, S. (2015, July 24). 'We like partisan warfare.' Chechens fighting in Ukraine - on both sides. Retrieved from http://www.theguardian.com/world/2015/jul/24/chechens-fighting-in-ukraine-on-both-sides

5   Franchetti, M. (2014, June 8). Pinned to the ground by blizzard of bullets. Retrieved from http://www.thesundaytimes.co.uk/sto/news/

world_news/Ukraine/article1420283.ece; Chivers, C. J., & Sneider, N. (2014, May 03). Behind the Masks in Ukraine, Many Faces of Rebellion. Retrieved from http://www.nytimes.com/2014/05/04/world/europe/behind-the-masks-in-ukraine-many-faces-of-rebellion.html?_r=1; Gessen, K. (2014, September 11). Why not kill them all? Retrieved from http://www.lrb.co.uk/v36/n17/keith-gessen/why-not-kill-them-all; Judah, T. (2014, April 28). Ukraine: Hate in Progress. Retrieved February 16, 2016, from http://www.nybooks.com/daily/2014/04/28/ukraine-hate-progress/

6 EU:n tiedustelujohtaja: Venäjä ei ole asemoitunut sotilaallisesti Ukrainaan. (2014, April 14). Retrieved from http://yle.fi/uutiset/eun_tiedustelujohtaja_venaja_ei_ole_asemoitunut_sotilaallisesti_ukrainaan/7190544

7 Ukraine rebels snub Putin call to delay vote. (2014, May 8). Retrieved from http://www.aljazeera.com/news/europe/2014/05/ukraine-rebels-snub-putin-call-delay-vote-20145884017392321.html

8 Kramer, A. E. (2014, May 23). Putin Indicates He'll Respect Result of Ukrainian Election. Retrieved from http://www.nytimes.com/2014/05/24/world/europe/putin-indicates-hell-respect-result-of-ukrainian-election.html; RIA Novosti: Lavrov: Moscow Recognizes Parliamentary Election Results in Ukraine. (2014, October 27). Retrieved from http://russialist.org/ria-novosti-lavrov-moscow-recognizes-parliamentary-election-results-in-ukraine/

9 Higgins, A., Gordon, M. R., & Kramer, A. E. (2014, April 20). Photos Link Masked Men in East Ukraine to Russia. Retrieved from http://www.nytimes.com/2014/04/21/world/europe/photos-link-masked-men-in-east-ukraine-to-russia.html?_r=2

10 humanrightsinvestigations.org (2014, April 22). Evidence of undercover Russian troops in Ukraine debunked. Retrieved from http://humanrightsinvestigations.org/2014/04/22/evidence-of-undercover-russian-troops-in-ukraine-debunked/

11 Parry, R. (2014, April 23). NYT Retracts Russian-Photo Scoop. Retrieved from http://consortiumnews.com/2014/04/23/nyt-retracts-russian-photo-scoop/

12 Boyd-Barrett, O. (2016). Western Mainstream Media and the Ukraine Crisis: A Study in Conflict Propaganda. Routledge.

13 Esipova, N., & Ray, J. (2016, May 05). Information Wars: Ukraine and the West vs. Russia and the Rest. Retrieved from http://hir.harvard.edu/information-wars-ukraine-west-vs-russia-rest/

14 Judah, T. (2014, September 2). Ukraine: A Catastrophic Defeat. Retrieved from http://www.nybooks.com/daily/2014/09/05/ukraine-catastrophic-defeat/

15	The Russian soldiers were supposedly fighting in Ukraine during their holidays, as an alternative to the beach. Donbass Insurgent Leader Confirms: Thousands of Russian army soldiers fighting in east Ukraine. (2014, August 28). Retrieved from https://www.youtube.com/watch?v=wsEoR8TtLek; The army of the Lugansk and Donetsk People's Republics has 20,000 fighters - Gubarev. (2014, July 9). Retrieved from http://tass.ru/en/world/739790; Foster, H., & Tatyana Goryachova, Special for USA TODAY. (2014, July 12). Ukraine's next battle is Donetsk, but no bombs, please. Retrieved from http://www.usatoday.com/story/news/world/2014/07/12/ukraine-donetsk-separatists/12506719/
16	Grove, T. (2014, August 28). Exclusive - Over 100 Russian soldiers killed in single Ukraine battle - Russian rights activists. Retrieved from http://uk.reuters.com/article/uk-ukraine-crisis-russia-casualties-idUKKBN0GS20H20140828
17	Black, J. L., & Johns, M. (Eds.). (2016). The Return of the Cold War: Ukraine, The West and Russia. Routledge.
18	Walker, S. (2015, December 17). Putin admits Russian military presence in Ukraine for first time. Retrieved from http://www.theguardian.com/world/2015/dec/17/vladimir-putin-admits-russian-military-presence-ukraine
19	Black, J. L., & Johns, M. (Eds.). (2016). The Return of the Cold War: Ukraine, The West and Russia. Routledge.
20	Interior lines concerns a military strategy whereby troops can maneuver very quickly from one front to another, enabling a small army to defeat a larger army.
21	Ferguson, J., & Jenzen-Jones, N. R. (2014). Raising Red Flags: An Examination of Arms & Munitions in the Ongoing Conflict in Ukraine (No. 3). Research Report, p. 86.
22	Black, J. L., & Johns, M. (Eds.). (2016). The Return of the Cold War: Ukraine, The West and Russia. Routledge.
23	No Russian Troops in Ukraine says Kiev General. (2015, February 1). Retrieved from https://www.youtube.com/watch?v=T0x0mnrq9j4; Ukraine has evidence of Russian military presence in Donbass. (2015, January 29). Retrieved from http://www.ukrinform.net/rubric-ukrnews/1809163-ukraine_has_evidence_of_russian_military_presence_in_donbas_328608.html
24	OSCE SMM doesn't confirm presence of Russian troops in Donbass, sees only 'fighters from outside the region' (2016, September 09). Retrieved from http://en.interfax.com.ua/news/general/369129.html
25	Ukraine: The Line (Rep.). (2016, July 18). Retrieved from International Crisis Group website: https://d2071andvip0wj.cloudfront.net/ukraine-

	the-line.pdf
26	SIPRI Yearbook 2015 Summary: Armaments, Disarmament and International Security (Rep.). (2015, October 1), p. 5. Retrieved https://www.sipri.org/sites/default/files/2016-03/YB-15-Summary-EN.pdf
27	Robinson, P. (2016). Russia's role in the war in Donbass, and the threat to European security. European Politics and Society, 1-16.
28	Russia and the Separatists in Eastern Ukraine (Rep.). (2016, February 5). Retrieved from International Crisis Group website: https://www.crisisgroup.org/europe-central-asia/eastern-europe/ukraine/russia-and-separatists-eastern-ukraine
29	Ukraine: The Line (Rep.). (2016, July 18). Retrieved from International Crisis Group website: https://d2071andvip0wj.cloudfront.net/ukraine-the-line.pdf
30	Walker, S. (2015, October 01). As Russia enters war in Syria, conflict in Ukraine begins to wind down. Retrieved from http://www.theguardian.com/world/2015/oct/01/as-russia-enters-war-in-syria-conflict-in-ukraine-begins-to-wind-down
31	Ukraine: The Line (Rep.). (2016, July 18), pp. 9-10. Retrieved from International Crisis Group website: https://d2071andvip0wj.cloudfront.net/ukraine-the-line.pdf
32	Katchanovski, I. (2016). The Separatist War in Donbass: A Violent Break-up of Ukraine?. European Politics and Society, 1-17; Ukraine: The Line (Rep.). (2016, July 18). Retrieved from International Crisis Group website: https://d2071andvip0wj.cloudfront.net/ukraine-the-line.pdf
33	Carroll, O. (2015, May 24). Ukraine crisis: The last days of Aleksey Mozgovoi, rebel hero of the 'Ghost' battalion - killed in an ambush. Retrieved from http://www.independent.co.uk/news/world/europe/ukraine-crisis-the-last-days-of-aleksey-mozgovoi-rebel-hero-of-the-ghost-battalion-killed-in-an-10273837.html; Kirilov, D., & Dergachov, V. (2015, December 12). «Батя» не доехал до свадьбы. Retrieved from http://www.gazeta.ru/politics/2015/12/12_a_7962323.shtml#!photo=0
34	Luhn, A. (2014, November 07). Is Eastern Ukraine Becoming a People's Republic or Puppet State? Retrieved from http://www.thenation.com/article/eastern-ukraine-becoming-peoples-republic-or-puppet-state/
35	Ishchenko, V. (2016, January 22). The Ukrainian Left during and after the Maidan Protests, p. 90. Retrieved from https://www.academia.edu/20445056/The_Ukrainian_Left_during_and_after_the_Maidan_Protests
36	Ibid, p. 81.

37 Ibid, p. 79.
38 Walker, S. (2015, October 01). As Russia enters war in Syria, conflict in Ukraine begins to wind down. Retrieved from http://www.theguardian.com/world/2015/oct/01/as-russia-enters-war-in-syria-conflict-in-ukraine-begins-to-wind-down
39 Меркель: Путин убедил ополченцев согласиться на перемирие. (2015, February 12). Retrieved September 29, 2016, from http://www.vz.ru/news/2015/2/12/729288.html
40 Russia and the Separatists in Eastern Ukraine (Rep.). (2016, February 5). Retrieved from International Crisis Group website: https://www.crisisgroup.org/europe-central-asia/eastern-europe/ukraine/russia-and-separatists-eastern-ukraine
41 Ukraine: The Line (Rep.). (2016, July 18). Retrieved from International Crisis Group website: https://d2071andvip0wj.cloudfront.net/ukraine-the-line.pdf
42 Flounders, S. (2014, August 28). Russian trucks deliver food and aid - and leave. Retrieved from http://www.workers.org/articles/2014/08/28/russian-trucks-deliver-food-aid-leave/
43 Ukraine crisis: BBC finds Russian aid trucks 'almost empty' (2014, August 15). Retrieved from http://www.bbc.com/news/world-europe-28799627; Walker, S. (2014, August 15). Aid convoy stops short of border as Russian military vehicles enter Ukraine. Retrieved from http://www.theguardian.com/world/2014/aug/14/russian-military-vehicles-enter-ukraine-aid-convoy-stops-short-border
44 OSCE. (2014, August 13). Weekly update from the OSCE Observer Mission at the Russian Checkpoints Gukovo and Donetsk, for the period 6–12 August 2014. Retrieved from http://www.osce.org/om/122613; OSCE. (2014, September 3). Weekly update from the OSCE Observer Mission at the Russian Checkpoints Gukovo and Donetsk, 28 August until 08:00, 3 September 2014. Retrieved from http://www.osce.org/om/123151
45 Ushakov, Y. (2014, September 2). Vladimir Putin's '2 weeks to Kiev' taken out of context. Retrieved from http://web.archive.org/web/20141010101036/http://articles.economictimes.indiatimes.com/2014-09-02/news/53479851_1_eastern-ukraine-pro-russian-rebels-crimea
46 Veteran Intelligence Professionals for Sanity (VIPS). (2014, September 1). Warning Merkel on Russian 'Invasion' Intel. Retrieved from http://consortiumnews.com/2014/09/01/warning-merkel-on-russian-invasion-intel/
47 Ibid.
48 Hugues, S. (2015, April 14). French officials debunk NATO warnings

of Russian invasion of Ukraine. Retrieved from http://www.wsws.org/en/articles/2015/04/14/fren-a14.html
49 Breedlove's Bellicosity: Berlin Alarmed by Aggressive NATO Stance on Ukraine. (2015, March 6). Retrieved from http://www.spiegel.de/international/world/germany-concerned-about-aggressive-nato-stance-on-ukraine-a-1022193.html
50 Ibid.
51 See the chapter: Seeing Beyond the Imperial Divide.
52 Korotkov, D. (2015, May 1). Суд над Фирташем: венская пощечина Вашингтону. Retrieved from http://vesti-ukr.com/strana/98517-sud-nad-firtashem-venskaja-powechina-vashingtonu
53 A KIIS poll from September 2015, for example, indicated that the vast majority of Ukrainians wanted the "continuation of negotiations and a peaceful resolution" to the conflict. At the same time, only 27 percent trusted the Minsk Accords. Socio-Political Situation in Ukraine: September 2015. (2015, October 5). Retrieved from http://www.kiis.com.ua/?lang=eng&cat=reports&id=548&page=1
In addition, while trust in almost every government institution has dropped to dismal figures, nearly half of Ukrainians say they trust the Ukrainian armed forces (a third distrust them). Indeed, many volunteers have collected donations for their equipment. Trust in Social Institutions and Social Groups. (2016, January 15). Retrieved from http://www.kiis.com.ua/?lang=eng&cat=reports&id=579&page=2
54 Herszenhorn, D. M. (2015, April 30). Judge Rebuffs U.S. in Rejecting Extradition of Ukraine Billionaire. Retrieved from http://www.nytimes.com/2015/05/01/world/europe/dmitry-v-firtash-extradition.html?_r=0
55 Bhadrakumar, M. K. (2016, January 14). Obama changes tack on Russia, calls up Putin. Retrieved from http://atimes.com/2016/01/obama-changes-tack-on-russia-calls-up-putin/
56 Кредиты в обмен на Минск. Апрельские тезисы Виктории Нуланд. (2016, April 26). Retrieved from http://strana.ua/articles/analysis/10496-kredity-v-obmen-na-minsk-aprelskie-tezisy-viktorii-nuland.html
57 Golinkin, L. (2016, December 05). The Ukrainian Far Right-and the Danger It Poses. Retrieved from https://www.thenation.com/article/the-ukrainian-far-right-and-the-danger-it-poses/
58 Crooke, A. (2016, September 20). Washington's Hawks Push New Cold War. Retrieved from https://consortiumnews.com/2016/09/20/washingtons-hawks-push-new-cold-war/ ; Cohen, S. (2016, September 07). More Lost Opportunities to Diminish the New Cold War. Retrieved

	October 01, 2016, from https://www.thenation.com/article/more-lost-opportunities-to-diminish-the-new-cold-war/
59	Secretary Meets With Ukrainian Defense Minister in London. (2016, September 08). Retrieved from http://www.defense.gov/News/Article/Article/937766/secretary-meets-with-ukrainian-defense-minister-in-london
60	Michael, B. (2015, December 20). The IMF Changes its Rules to Isolate China and Russia. Retrieved from http://michael-hudson.com/2015/12/the-imf-changes-its-rules-to-isolate-china-and-russia/
61	Rampton, R., & Crosby, A. (2016, September 21). Biden warns Ukraine on reforms, says EU sanctions on Russia at risk. Retrieved from http://af.reuters.com/article/worldNews/idAFKCN11S051
62	Ibid.
63	Ibid.
64	Luce, D., De, & Standish, R. (2016, October 30). What Will Ukraine Do Without Uncle Joe? Retrieved from https://foreignpolicy.com/2016/10/30/what-will-ukraine-do-without-joe-biden-putin-war-kiev-clinton-trump/
65	Fang, L., & Jilani, Z. (2016, July 01). Hacked Emails Reveal NATO General Plotting Against Obama on Russia Policy. Retrieved from https://theintercept.com/2016/07/01/nato-general-emails/; Schult, C., & Wiegrefe, K. (2016, July 28). Dangerous Propaganda: Network Close to NATO Military Leader Fueled Ukraine Conflict. Retrieved from http://www.spiegel.de/international/world/breedlove-network-sought-weapons-deliveries-for-ukraine-a-1104837.html
66	Ibid.
67	Ibid.
68	Ibid.
69	Grants are listed in Potomac's tax returns available at Pro Publica. The Potomac Foundation. (n.d.). Retrieved from https://projects.propublica.org/nonprofits/organizations/541468870
70	Lewis, J. (2015, February 19). Say It Ain't So, Phil. Retrieved from https://foreignpolicy.com/2015/02/19/say-it-aint-so-phil-ukraine-russia-open-source-analysis/
71	Ibid.
72	Ibid.
73	Conversation of P. Breedlove with Phillip Karber. (2016, April 10). Retrieved from http://dcleaks.com/index.php/conversation-of-p-breedlove-with-phillip-karber/
74	Bromwich, D. (2014, July 3). The World's Most Important Spectator. Retrieved from http://www.lrb.co.uk/v36/n13/david-bromwich/the-worlds-most-important-spectator

75 Ibid.
76 Conversation of P. Breedlove with Phillip Karber. (2016, April 10). Retrieved from http://dcleaks.com/index.php/conversation-of-p-breedlove-with-phillip-karber/
77 Ibid.
78 Ibid; Schult, C., & Wiegrefe, K. (2016, July 28). Dangerous Propaganda: Network Close to NATO Military Leader Fueled Ukraine Conflict. Retrieved from http://www.spiegel.de/international/world/breedlove-network-sought-weapons-deliveries-for-ukraine-a-1104837.html
79 Conversation of P. Breedlove with Phillip Karber. (2016, April 10). Retrieved from http://dcleaks.com/index.php/conversation-of-p-breedlove-with-phillip-karber/
80 Ibid.
81 Gordon, M. R. (2014, April 16). General and Former Defense Official Urge Nonlethal Military Aid for Ukraine. Retrieved from https://www.nytimes.com/2014/04/16/world/general-and-former-defense-official-urge-nonlethal-military-aid-for-ukraine.html
82 Clark, W., & Karber, P. (2014, April 8). Interim Report #1. Retrieved from https://www.documentcloud.org/documents/1114174-clark-karber-report-with-appendix.html
83 Breedlove's Bellicosity: Berlin Alarmed by Aggressive NATO Stance on Ukraine. (2015, March 6). Retrieved from http://www.spiegel.de/international/world/germany-concerned-about-aggressive-nato-stance-on-ukraine-a-1022193.html
84 Conversation of P. Breedlove with Phillip Karber. (2016, April 10). Retrieved from http://dcleaks.com/index.php/conversation-of-p-breedlove-with-phillip-karber/
85 Lewis, J. (2015, February 19). Say It Ain't So, Phil. Retrieved from https://foreignpolicy.com/2015/02/19/say-it-aint-so-phil-ukraine-russia-open-source-analysis/
86 Ibid; Bracken, P. (2006). Net Assessment: A Practical Guide. Parameters, 36(1), 90.
87 Mcgray, D. (2003, February 1). The Marshall Plan. Retrieved from https://www.wired.com/2003/02/marshall/
88 Kelly, K. R. (2012). The context of the Iraq genocide (Unpublished master's thesis). University, Palmerston North, New Zealand, pp. 72-74, 195-199. Retrieved from https://ongenocide.files.wordpress.com/2012/02/context-of-iraq-genocide.pdf

| Chapter Eighteen |

WESTERN MILITARY DOCTRINE AND THE NORMALIZATION OF WAR CRIMES

The United States was very closely involved with the 'Anti-Terrorist Operation' in Ukraine. Directly after the operation was announced, CIA director John Brennan visited Kiev in early April 2014.[1] According to German intelligence sources, the military effort was already aided by dozens of CIA advisers who helped to set up a "functioning security structure" in Ukraine.[2] In addition, hundreds of mercenaries from the American private military contractor, Blackwater, infamous for widespread torture in Iraq, would soon be sent to the east according to another reported German intelligence briefing.[3] There was also overt military support for the Kiev regime. The US has given $3 billion in loan guarantees and $1.1 billion in non-lethal defense assistance since February 2014.[4] Obama also ordered a team of Pentagon advisers to "shape and establish an enduring program for future U.S. efforts to support the Ukrainian military through subject-matter expert teams and long-term advisers."[5] Canada also sent $5 million in defense equipment and pledged another $49 million dollars for the information war with Russia.[6] Furthermore, Lithuania supplied Ukrainian troops with 150 tons of ammunition.[7]

But the war effort was not limited to individual countries. At the September 5, 2014, NATO summit in Wales, the alliance emphasized that: "NATO and Ukraine will continue to promote the development of greater interoperability between Ukrainian and NATO forces, including through continued regular Ukrainian participation in NATO exercises."[8] The first exercise was held the same month in Lviv, Ukraine as a continuation of training exercises that first started under the Yushchenko presidency.[9] In addition, inter alia, NATO "will launch substantial new programs with a focus on command, control and communications, logistics and standardization, cyber defense, military career transition, and strategic communications. ... [In addition,] allies are reinforcing their advisory presence at the NATO offices in Kiev. Allies have taken note of Ukraine's requests for military-technical assistance, and many Allies are providing additional support to Ukraine on a bilateral basis."[10]

Ukraine's defense minister stated during a press conference that "lethal assistance" was being supplied by five NATO countries. "We reached agreements in closed talks, without media, about ... those weapons that we currently need. (...) I have no right to disclose any specific country we reached that agreement with. But the fact is that those weapons are already on the way to us—that's absolutely true, I can officially tell you."[11] The statement was subsequently denied by several NATO countries, including the United States. This underlines the fact that Kiev—which has an entire state apparatus to fight its war—is less dependent on external support than the rebels, who had regular Russian troops fighting on their side. Nevertheless, the differences in the level of foreign support are largely a reflection of the necessities on the ground, as well as the larger importance of the conflict to the Russian state.

The former is aptly illustrated by the fact that Ukraine continued to illegally export weapons to South-Sudan during the war in Donbass.[12] Indeed, the country has been South-Sudan's principal military supplier after an international embargo was announced in 2004, in the midst of severe human-rights violations.[13] In 2017, the UN World Food Programme (WFP) actually declared a famine in South-Sudan—the first time the agency was forced to make such a dire announcement anywhere in the world since 2011—caused by what the head of the WFP called a "man-made" disaster of war.[14] This is no isolated case. Between 2014-16—according to the most recent SIPRI data—Ukraine was the 11th largest exporter of military equipment in the world.[15] As such, in 2016, a pro-Ukrainian volunteer who gathered supplies for batallions in Dobass complained that: "This year alone, Ukraine has exported 12 units of the weapon most demanded on the front, the 122-mm howitzer D-30, as well as Mi-24 and Mi-29 helicopters; and then Ukraine was begging for newer weapons from the West."[16]

Considering the overwhelming dominance of the United States in Ukrainian politics and its continued supply of military and intelligence advisers, it seems reasonable to suggest that Ukraine's war strategy is heavily influenced by Washington. For one, the United States has more experience with counter-insurgency warfare than any other country on the planet. In this sense, it is relevant to consider standard US military doctrines. Starting with the most recent major war initiated by the United States (the 2003 invasion of Iraq), we find the application of the 'shock and awe' strategy. The term was coined by the aforementioned Harlan Ullman, senior advisor to the Atlantic Council, in a dense tome publish by the Pentagon-funded National Defense University:

> Shock and Awe are actions that create fears, dangers and destruction that are incomprehensible to the people at large, specific elements/sectors of the threat society, or the leadership. Nature in the form of tornadoes, hurricanes, earthquakes, floods, uncontrolled fires, famine, and disease can engender Shock and Awe. The ultimate military application of Shock and Awe was the use of two atomic weapons against Japan in WW2.
>
> (…) [Possible targets] could include means of communication, transportation, food production, water supply, and other aspects of infrastructure.

(...) It would be vitally important to give the appearance that there are no safe havens from attack, and that any target may be attacked at any time with impunity and force.[17]

The widespread targeting of civilian infrastructure continued well after the invasion of Iraq, when the war turned into a counter-insurgency operation. The British-American coalition also used numerous banned weapons, such as depleted uranium and—as has Kiev in the Donbass—cluster munitions and incendiary weapons.[18] As Kieran Kelly extensively documented in his *Context to the Iraq Genocide*, the deliberate destruction of entire societies has been inherent to nearly all major US wars— with mortality counts running in the millions in Korea, Indo-China and Iraq—the vast majority of whom were civilians.[19] In an extensive historical review, political scientist Robert Pape concludes that:

> Over more than seventy-five years, the record of air power is replete with efforts to alter the behavior of states by attacking or threatening to attack large numbers of civilians. The incontrovertible conclusion from these campaigns is that air attack does not cause citizens to turn against their government. (...) In fact, in the more than thirty major strategic air campaigns that have thus far been waged, air power has never driven the masses into the streets to demand anything.
>
> (...) Although bombing economic structures can weaken an opponent's military capabilities in long wars, the first effects are generally felt by civilians. Since nearly all military and governmental facilities have backup power generation, the loss of electric power mainly shuts down public utilities (water pumping and purification systems), residential users (food

refrigeration), and general manufacturing in the economy. Since the military generally has first call on oil, the effects of oil shortages fall mainly on civilians, cutting the fuel available for heating and civilian transportation (food distribution). Destroying rail and road bridges throughout the country further degrades the food distribution system.

(…) Electric power grids, internal transportation networks, and dams were destroyed in Korea; electric power grids, oil refining, and internal transportation were also wrecked in Vietnam; and electric power, oil refining, and internal transportation were demolished in Iraq. In none of these cases, however, did civilian pressure induce governments to surrender. The key reason is that air attack against civilian infrastructure is even less effective than direct punishment in stimulating disruptive behaviour.[20]

According to the US State Department, as of November 2015, there were 300 US troops deployed to train regular forces in Ukraine.[21] $265 million had already been spent on the training and equipment. Luckily, the US Congress had passed an amendment that "limits arms, training, and other assistance to the neo-Nazi Ukrainian militia, the Azov Battalion." An investigation by *The Daily Beast*, however, found that this was far from guaranteed.[22] US Captain Modugno admitted that "When it comes to vetting and the Ukrainian government, the most I can tell you is that we are training at the request of the government and where these guys come from and where they go—it is their decision not ours." Another spokesman from the US State Department admitted: "It's a mishmash of folks: volunteers, soldiers, war heroes, Maidan veterans—I mean I couldn't tell you, you know, short of investigating the background of each guy." The article goes on to report that: "in an interview with *The Daily Beast,* Sgt.

Ivan Kharkiv of the Azov battalion talks about his battalion's experience with U.S. trainers and U.S. volunteers quite fondly, even mentioning U.S. volunteer engineers and medics that are still currently assisting them." The US has also become closely involved with the training of Ukrainian police forces which, as previously mentioned, have incorporated neo-Nazi Azov fighters all the way to its top ranks.[23] Furthermore, Texas Rangers and US Special Forces have been assigned to help militarize new Ukrainian SWAT police forces, which would reportedly give preference to former soldiers in their recruitment practices.[24]

The United States, however, is not the only country active in Ukraine. The BBC announced in 2014 that dozens of British soldiers were training Ukrainian forces, and David Cameron later stated that another 75 military advisers had been sent to Kiev.[25] Furthermore, another 200 Canadian troops were involved in training missions and "a [separate] contingent of military police is working in Kiev mentoring counterparts there," the Canadian *Globe and Mail* reported.[26] Notably, neither the UK nor Canada has even attempted to address the problem of training far-right battalions. In fact, in mid-December 2015, the US Congress decided to scrap the amendment that limited training of the Azov battalion. A US official told *The Nation* that this was done under pressure from the Pentagon.[27] This decision accompanied a huge spending bill for fiscal year 2016, which contained "$64 billion for overseas contingency operations." Part of this would be spend to "reinforce European countries facing Russian aggression."[28]

In the context of the engagement of some of these battalions in torture, abduction and summary executions, it might be relevant to consider another historical pattern. Namely, the United States has never genuinely worried about the human rights record of its trainees. A pertinent example is the School of the Americas (SOA)—where US forces trained over 64.000 Latin American soldiers in counterinsurgency, psychological warfare and torture.[29] As Blakeley notes, US support for "repression is evident in training manuals used at SOA that advocated torture and murder, and in additional training materials used by US security and intelligence agencies during the Cold War."[30] Indeed, William Brownfield, the US official in charge of the police training mission in Ukraine, has his own dubious history concerning human rights in Latin America, both in Venezuela and Colombia. During his time as US ambassador to the latter country, for example, he defended "serious war crimes by the Colombian military" as some unfortunate "bumps in the road."[31]

Indeed, such disregard for human rights has been both global and systemic. Chomsky and Herman already "reported back in 1979 [that], of 35 countries using torture on an administrative basis in the late 1970s, 26 were clients of the United States."[32] Unfortunately, this was no coincidence. Numerous studies have found that U.S. aid flows disproportionately to the worst violators of fundamental human rights.[33] Statistical analysis also found strong correlations between graduates of US training programs and subsequent practitioners of torture.[34] Another study specifically demonstrated that the more foreign police aid given by the US, the more brutal and less democratic were the police institutions.[35]

Admittedly, most of these research efforts are somewhat dated and in need of renewal. As such, two studies published in November and December of 2016 are highly revealing. Firstly, Dandlin demonstrated that—with the exception of small states that are "woefully unimportant"—US aid continued to flow disproportionally to the worse violators of human rights.[36] More importantly, such bias was evident even when focusing exclusively on US allies, which received more aid when they engaged in more repression. In other words, US officials are not just indifferent to human rights violations, but actually "reward such actions and incentivize the behavior further, as repressing domestic unrest or latent dissent is helpful to the US when the state in question is a national security asset."[37] This hypothesis was confirmed by Sandholtz, who demonstrated that state repression consistently worsened *after* receipt of US aid.[38] In fact, "US military aid is associated with declines in human rights even during a period when human rights performance has been improving on average."[39] Finally, although Sandholtz and Dandlin did not focus specifically on direct training, an extensive review by Nick Turse of US training missions in Africa indicates a similar pattern. After listing some of the worse abuses by US-trained soldiers in Mali, Cameroon and Chad, he summarizes that:

> The U.S. carried out such [training] missions in Mauritania ("abusive treatment, arbitrary arrests"), Morocco ("excessive force to quell peaceful protests, resulting in hundreds of injuries; torture and other abuses by the security forces"), Niger ("reports that security forces beat and abused civilians"), Senegal ("some reports that the government or its agents committed arbitrary or unlawful killings"), Tunisia ("security forces committed human rights abuses"), and Uganda ("unlawful killings, torture, and other abuse of suspects and detainees"). Meanwhile, ... exercises were held in Senegal in 2011 ("reports of physical abuse and torture"), Mauritania in 2013 ("authorities arbitrarily arrested and detained protesters, presidential opponents, and journalists"), Niger in 2014 ("some reports the government or its agents committed arbitrary or unlawful killings") (...) [training missions were also conducted] in Algeria, where, according to the State Department, "Impunity remained a problem," and Kenya, where there were "abuses by the security forces, including unlawful killings, forced disappearances, torture, rape, and use of excessive force."[40]

Endnotes

1. Mason, J., Loney, J., & Beech, E. (2014, April 14). CIA Director John Brennan Visits Ukraine Amid Crisis. Retrieved from http://www.huffingtonpost.com/2014/04/14/john-brennan-ukraine_n_5147869.

2 html Original from Reuters Lambeck, M., & Rackow, A. (2014, April 5). CIA & FBI: Agenten beraten Übergangsregierung in Kiew. Retrieved from http://www.bild.de/politik/ausland/nachrichtendienste-usa/dutzende-agenten-von-cia-und-fbi-beraten-kiew-35807724.bild.html

3 Scahill, J. (2011). *Blackwater: The rise of the world's most powerful mercenary army.* Profile Books.; Einsatz gegen Separatisten: Ukrainische Armee bekommt offenbar Unterstützung von US-Söldnern. (2014, May 11). Retrieved from http://www.spiegel.de/politik/ausland/ukraine-krise-400-us-soeldner-von-academi-kaempfen-gegen-separatisten-a-968745.html

4 Medynsky, I. (2016, February). U.S. Military Assistance to Ukraine under Obama and Beyond. Retrieved from http://kennankyiv.org/wp-content/uploads/2016/04/Medynskyi_Agora_V16_final-2.pdf; Formation of a new Government opens possibilities for providing additional financial assistance to Ukraine—meeting of the President of Ukraine with the U.S. Vice President. (2016, March 31). Retrieved from http://www.president.gov.ua/en/news/formuvannya-novogo-uryadu-vidkrivaye-mozhlivosti-dlya-vidile-36932; USAID Announces U.S. Issuance of $1 Billion Loan Guarantee to the Government of Ukraine. (2016, September 30). Retrieved from https://www.usaid.gov/news-information/press-releases/sep-30-2016-usaid-announces-us-issuance-1-billion-loan-guarantee-government-ukraine

5 Ybarra, M. (2014, July 22). Obama orders Pentagon advisers to Ukraine to fend off Putin-backed rebels. Retrieved from http://www.washingtontimes.com/news/2014/jul/22/pentagon-team-dispatched-to-ukraine-amid-crisis-wi/

6 Pugliese, D. (2014, September 20). No safeguards stopping Canadian equipment from falling into wrong hands in Ukraine, opposition MPs say. Retrieved from http://news.nationalpost.com/news/canada/no-safeguards-stopping-canadian-equipment-from-falling-into-wrong-hands-in-ukraine-opposition-mps-say; Brewster, M. (2016, January 7). Instructing Ukrainian troops a wake-up call for Canadian soldiers. Retrieved from http://www.theglobeandmail.com/news/national/instructing-ukrainian-troops-a-wake-up-call-for-canadian-trainers/article28048695/

7 Lithuania Sends Ammo To Ukraine. (2016, September 3). Retrieved from http://www.rferl.org/a/lithuania-sends-ammunition-ukraine/27965377.html

8 Nato.int. (2014, September 5). Wales Summit Declaration issued by the Heads of State and Government participating in the meeting of the North Atlantic Council in Wales. Retrieved from http://www.nato.int/

9 cps/en/natohq/official_texts_112964.htm; Nato.int. (2014, September 4). Joint Statement of the NATO-Ukraine Commission. Retrieved from http://www.nato.int/cps/en/natohq/news_112695.htm Mackinnon, M., & Mackrael, K. (2014, September 3). NATO to take part in joint exercises with Ukrainian army. Retrieved from http://www.theglobeandmail.com/news/world/nato-to-take-part-in-joint-exercises-with-ukrainian-army/article20332348/; Hahn, G. (2016, January 21). The Russian-American 'Reset', NATO Expansion, and the Making of the Ukrainian Crisis. Retrieved from http://gordonhahn.com/2016/01/21/report-the-russian-american-reset-nato-expansion-and-the-making-of-the-ukrainian-crisis/#_ftn1

10 Nato.int. (2014, September 4). Joint Statement of the NATO-Ukraine Commission. Retrieved from http://www.nato.int/cps/en/natohq/news_112695.htm

11 Sukhotski, K., Balmforth, R., & Heneghan, T. (2014, September 14). NATO countries have begun arms deliveries to Ukraine: Defense minister. Retrieved from http://www.reuters.com/article/us-ukraine-crisis-heletey-idUSKBN0H90PP20140914

12 UN: Zero tolerance for states who flout Arms Trade Treaty obligations. (2016, August 22). Retrieved from https://www.amnesty.org/en/press-releases/2016/08/un-zero-tolerance-for-states-who-flout-arms-trade-treaty-obligations/

13 LeBrun, E. (2012, April). Reaching for the gun: Arms flows and holdings in South Sudan (Rep.). Retrieved http://www.smallarmssurveysudan.org/fileadmin/docs/issue-briefs/HSBA-IB-19-Arms-flows-and-holdings-South-Sudan.pdf

14 Famine declared in South Sudan. (2017, February 20). Retrieved from http://www.radionz.co.nz/news/world/324971/famine-declared-in-south-sudan

15 TIV of arms exports from the top 50 largest exporters, 2014-2015. (n.d.). Retrieved from http://armstrade.sipri.org/armstrade/html/export_toplist.php

16 Nemtsova, A. (2016, November 18). Ukraine's Merchant of Death in South Sudan. Retrieved from http://www.thedailybeast.com/articles/2016/11/18/ukraine-s-merchant-of-death-in-south-sudan.html

17 Ullman, H. K., Wade, J. P., Edney, L. A., Franks, F. M., Horner, C. A., Howe, J. T., & Brendley, K. (1996). *Shock and awe: Achieving rapid dominance*. National Defense University, Washington DC, p. xxvii, 83, 110-111. Ullman credits himself as "the primary creator of the doctrine of 'shock and awe." Ullman, Harlan. (n.d.). Retrieved from http://www.atlanticcouncil.org/about/experts/list/harlan-ullman#fullbio

18 U.S. Using Cluster Munitions In Iraq. (2003, April 01). Retrieved from https://www.hrw.org/news/2003/04/01/us-using-cluster-

munitions-iraq; U.S. official admits phosphorus used as weapon in Iraq. (2005, November 16). Retrieved from http://www.cbc.ca/news/world/u-s-official-admits-phosphorus-used-as-weapon-in-iraq-1.557818; Jahmail, D. (2013, March 15). Iraq: War's legacy of cancer. Retrieved from http://www.aljazeera.com/indepth/features/2013/03/2013315171951838638.html

19 Kelly, K. R. (2012). The context of the Iraq genocide (Unpublished master's thesis). University, Palmerston North, New Zealand. Retrieved from https://ongenocide.files.wordpress.com/2012/02/context-of-iraq-genocide.pdf

20 Pape, R. A. (2014). *Bombing to win: Air power and coercion in war.* Cornell University Press, pp. 68-69.

21 US to Begin Training Ukraine's Active-Duty Military. (2015, September 16). Retrieved from http://www.military.com/daily-news/2015/09/16/us-to-begin-training-ukraines-active-duty-military.html

22 Epstein, J. (2015, July 4). Is America Training Neonazis in Ukraine? Officially no, but no one in the U.S. government seem to know for sure. Retrieved from http://www.thedailybeast.com/articles/2015/07/04/is-the-u-s-training-neo-nazis-in-ukraine.html

23 Kozloff, N. (2017, January 4). Maidan Year Three: Revolution Comes Full Circle Amidst Police Reform, U.S.-Trained Right Wing SWAT Force and Former Venezuela Ambassador. Retrieved from http://www.huffingtonpost.com/nikolas-kozloff/maidan-year-three-revolut_b_13960996.html

24 Ibid.

25 British Infantry In Ukraine Training Mission. (2014, February 24). Retrieved from http://news.sky.com/story/1433447/british-infantry-in-ukraine-training-mission

26 Brewster, M. (2016, January 7). Instructing Ukrainian troops a wake-up call for Canadian soldiers. Retrieved from http://www.theglobeandmail.com/news/national/instructing-ukrainian-troops-a-wake-up-call-for-canadian-trainers/article28048695/; Walkom, T. (2015, February 25). Toronto Star writer: Canada and U.S. stumbling toward confrontation with Russia. Retrieved from Walkom, T. (2015, February 24). Canada quietly tiptoes into Ukraine-Russia war. Retrieved from https://web.archive.org/web/20150225015408/http://www.thestar.com/news/canada/2015/02/24/canada-quietly-tiptoes-into-ukraine-russia-war-walkom.html

27 Carden, J. (2016, January 14). Congress Has Removed a Ban on Funding Neo-Nazis From Its Year-End Spending Bill. Retrieved from http://www.thenation.com/article/congress-has-removed-a-ban-on-

	funding-neo-nazis-from-its-year-end-spending-bill/
28	Ibid.
29	The list of graduates includes a long list of dictators. They are all recorded in the following database. SOA Grads. (n.d.). Retrieved from http://www.soaw.org/about-the-soawhinsec/soawhinsec-grads
30	Blakeley, R. (2006). Still training to torture? US training of military forces from Latin America. *Third World Quarterly*, 27(8), 1439-1461, p. 2.
31	Kozloff, N. (2017, January 4). Maidan Year Three: Revolution Comes Full Circle Amidst Police Reform, U.S.-Trained Right Wing SWAT Force and Former Venezuela Ambassador. Retrieved from http://www.huffingtonpost.com/nikolas-kozloff/maidan-year-three-revolut_b_13960996.html
32	Herman, E. S. (2001, September 15). Folks Out There Have a "Distaste of Western Civilization and Cultural Values." Global Research. Retrieved January 5, 2015, from http://www.globalresearch.ca/articles/HER109A.html
33	Schoultz, L. (1981). U. S. Foreign Policy and Human Rights Violations in Latin America: A Comparative Analysis of Foreign Aid Distributions. *Comparative Politics,* 13(2), 149; Carleton, D., & Stohl, M. (1985). The Foreign Policy of Human Rights: Rhetoric and Reality from Jimmy Carter to Ronald Reagan. *Human Rights Quarterly,* 7(2), 205; Regan, P. M. (1995). U. S. Economic Aid and Political Repression: An Empirical Evaluation of U. S. Foreign Policy. *Political Research Quarterly,* 48(3), 613; Stohl, M., Carleton, D., & Johnson, S. E. (1984). Human Rights and U.S. Foreign Assistance from Nixon to Carter. *Journal of Peace Research,* 21(3), 215-226.
34	Mccoy, K. E. (2005). Trained to Torture? The Human Rights Effects of Military Training at the School of the Americas. *Latin American Perspectives,* 32(6), 47-64.
35	Huggins, M. K. (1998). *Political policing: the United States and Latin America.* Durham: Duke University Press.
36	Sandlin, E. W. (2016). Competing Concerns: Balancing Human Rights and National Security in US Economic Aid Allocation. *Human Rights Review,* 17(4), 439-462, p. 457.
37	Ibid, 459.
38	Sandholtz, W. (2016). United States Military Assistance and Human Rights. *Human Rights Quarterly,* 38(4), 1070-1101.
39	Ibid, 1099.
40	Turse, N. (2015, September 10). Nothing Succeeds Like Failure. Retrieved from http://www.tomdispatch.com/blog/176042/tomgram:_nick_turse,_nothing_succeeds_like_failure

| Chapter Nineteen |

SEEING BEYOND THE IMPERIAL DIVIDE

The work of Zbigniew Brzezinski offers more clarity on the meaning of this development of recent years.[1] He is one of the most influential American policy planners of the last few decades, and is considered an unofficial foreign policy adviser of Barack Obama, who described Brzezinski as a mentor.[2] In 1997, he wrote his magnum opus *The Grand Chessboard*, where he describes how America can remain the "sole global superpower". He explains that there are several "geopolitical pivots" which are key: "their geography, ... gives them a special role either in denying access to important areas or in denying resources to a significant player ... In some cases, a geopolitical pivot may act as a defensive shield for a vital state or even a region ... Ukraine, Azerbaijan, South Korea, Turkey, and Iran play the role of critically important geopolitical pivots."[3] Brzezinski is also convinced that "Eurasia is ... the chessboard on which the struggle for global primacy continues to be played."[4] Russia is subsequently described as a "black hole" that should be made subservient to the security policy of NATO and economic institutions like the World Bank and IMF. At a certain point, he even suggests that Russia should be cut in three parts, resulting in a "loosely confederated Russia—composed of a European Russia, a Siberian Republic, and a Far Eastern Republic."[5]

The 2014 NATO summit in Wales tried to push Russia further into the corner. "NATO's door will remain open to all European democracies", they attested.[6] Georgia, Montenegro, Macedonia and Bosnia and Herzegovina were specifically mentioned. The fact that "NATO and Ukraine will [also] continue to promote the development of greater interoperability between Ukrainian and NATO forces," has already been mentioned.[7] Finally a Rapid Reaction Force was formed composed of 4000 NATO troops that now patrol the Baltic States. This has a tense relation with the 1997 NATO-Russia Founding Act, in which NATO promised not to deploy any permanent troops in new member states—using the mobility of the Rapid Reaction Force as a loophole. James Carden, former adviser of the American State Department, argues that since this small force cannot possibly stop a Russian invasion, the Rapid Reaction Force is rather being used as a pretext to further militarize the Russian border.[8] NATO is indeed talking about a "preparation of infrastructure, prepositioning of equipment and supplies, and designation of specific bases."[9] In February 2016, US Secretary of Defense Ash Carter proclaimed:

> We are reinforcing our posture in Europe to support our NATO allies in the face of Russia's aggression. In Pentagon parlance, this is called the European Reassurance Initiative and after requesting about $800 million for last year, this year we're more than quadrupling it for a total of $3.4 billion in 2017.
>
> That will fund a lot of things: more rotational US forces in Europe, more training and exercising with our allies, more preposition and war-fighting gear and infrastructure improvements to support all this.
>
> And when combined with US forces already in and assigned to Europe—which are also substantial—all of this together by the end of 2017 will let us rapidly form a highly capable combined arms ground force that can respond across that theater, if necessary.[10]

Unfortunately, Brzezinski was not alone in his imperial ambitions. For one, the joint vision of the American Department of Defense until 2020 "emphasizes full-spectrum dominance ... [which] means the ability of U.S. forces, operating alone or with allies, to defeat any adversary and control any situation across the range of military operations."[11] Indeed, the most recent National Defense Panel Review states that the United States should now be prepared to "fight in any number of regions in overlapping time frames: on the Korean peninsula, in the East or South China Sea, South Asia, in the Middle East, the Trans-Sahel, Sub-Saharan Africa, in Europe, and possibly elsewhere."[12]

This level of militarism was echoed in the September 2016 report *The Future of the Army,* where the influential Atlantic Council argued that the US should prepare for the possibility of "the next big war'—involving very capable adversaries, high levels of death and destruction, and perhaps hundreds of thousands of US troops"—naming Russia and China repeatedly as potential opponents. In an October 2016 speech Mark Milley, the US Army Chief of Staff, even proclaimed that war between nation states in the near future "is almost guaranteed," also repeatedly hinting at Russia and China. In a blunt warning against a potential "high-end enemy," Milley adds that "those who try to oppose the United States ... we will stop you and we will beat you harder than you've ever been beaten before." Notably, Obama's 2015 National Security Strategy emphasizes that "The United States will use military force, unilaterally if necessary ... to defend its core interests," later defined as including "a strong, innovative, and growing U.S. economy in an open international economic system that promotes opportunity and prosperity."[13]

Ever since 2002, NATO has been trying to remove Russia's nuclear deterrent with a missile defense shield.[14] For years they have claimed that it was aimed against Iran, but now Western politicians are talking in clear language. For one, the Polish minister of defense recently asserted that developments in Ukraine have urged them to speed up their development of the missile defense system.[15] In another case, American Senator

Bob Corker recently proposed a bill that would bind Obama to "prevent further Russian aggression" by, among things, "Accelerating implementation of European and NATO missile defense efforts."[16] This missile defense shield is only capable of intercepting around 60 nuclear warheads, a minuscule fraction of the total amount of nuclear weapons held by Russia. The shield therefore can only be used effectively as an *offensive weapon*. For decades the Soviet Union and the United States have been trying to attain a so-called first-strike capability, meaning the capacity to neutralize all your opponent's nuclear warheads in one surprise attack.[17] In the prestigious *Foreign Affairs* journal of the Council on Foreign Relations, one of the most influential think tanks in America, Lieber and Press wrote in 2006 that America would for the first time in 50 years reach nuclear primacy, because of the "precipitous decline of Russia's arsenal, and the glacial pace of modernization of China's nuclear forces."[18] They asserted that "If the United States launched a nuclear attack against Russia (or China), the targeted country would be left with a tiny surviving arsenal—if any at all. At that point, even a relatively modest or inefficient missile-defense system might well be enough to protect against any retaliatory strikes, because the devastated enemy would have so few warheads and decoys left."[19]

Indeed, in December 2001, the United States unilaterally terminated the Anti-Ballistic Missile Treaty (ABMT) that it had signed 30 years earlier with the Soviet Union.[20] The ABM systems are designed to intercept ballistic missile-delivered nuclear weapons. Under the treaty, each party was limited to a maximum of two ABM complexes, which were subsequently limited to 100 anti-ballistic missiles each. At the same time, the United States started developing so-called Nuclear Bunker Busters, capable of destroying underground bunkers containing terrorists— or Russian nukes—without causing an enormous, albeit still significant, nuclear fallout. These are low-yield nuclear weapons that—according to its critics, which include senior US Defense officials—blur the distinction between nuclear and conventional warfare.[21] The development of these weapons officially ceased in

2005, but according to the prestigious Jane's Information Group there is evidence that the program continued under a different name.[22] In fact, in September 2014, President Obama shocked the world by announcing an enormous modernization program of its nuclear arsenal. With a price ticket of $1 trillion over the next 30 years, the program is "comparable to spending for procurement of new strategic systems in the 1980s under President Ronald Reagan," according to a study by the James Martin Center for Nonproliferation Studies.[23] The nuclear bunker buster remains unmentioned and Obama is planning only to improve the existing arsenal in order to uphold his promise not to develop new nuclear weapons. Nevertheless, as *The New York Times* reports:

> Critics, including a number of former Obama administration officials, look at the same set of facts and see a very different future. The explosive innards of the revitalized weapons may not be entirely new, they argue, but the smaller yields and better targeting can make the arms more tempting to use—even to use first, rather than in retaliation.
>
> ... The insider critiques soon focused on individual weapons, starting with the B61 Model 12. The administration's plan was to merge four old B61 models into a single version that greatly reduced their range of destructive power. It would have a "dial-a-yield" feature whose lowest setting was only 2 percent as powerful as the bomb dropped on Hiroshima in 1945.
>
> The plan seemed reasonable, critics said, until attention fell on the bomb's new tail section and steerable fins. The Federation of American Scientists, a Washington research group, argued that the high accuracy and low destructive settings meant military commanders might press to use the bomb in an attack, knowing

the radioactive fallout and collateral damage would be limited.[24]

The B61 Model 12 has already entered the production engineering phase and is scheduled to enter full-scale production by 2020.[25] Already back in 2008, several high-ranking NATO officials pressed for 'preventive' nuclear attacks as an integral strategy against Iran, even though it has long been proven—even by the US intelligence community—that the country is not developing any nuclear weapons.[26] In September 2016, the Obama administration seemed unwilling to rule out a first strike, with senior officials specifically mentioning China, Russia and North Korea.[27] In March 2017, the reputable Bulletin of Atomic Scientists reviewed the modernization program to conclude that it "'has implemented revolutionary new technologies that will vastly increase the targeting capability of the US ballistic missile arsenal. This increase in capability is astonishing—boosting the overall killing power of existing US ballistic missile forces by a factor of roughly three—and it creates exactly what one would expect to see, if a nuclear-armed state were planning to have the capacity to fight and win a nuclear war by disarming enemies with a surprise first strike."[28]

Younger generations might look on these activities as pointless military posturing. Nevertheless, as Peter Kuznick and Oliver Stone extensively documented in *The Untold History of the United States*, the world has come very close to nuclear catastrophe—and very often at that. The atom bomb has never been gathering dust in military silos. Rather, the United States has been using the nuclear weapons threat continuously—like a crook uses a gun to rob a store—you don't have to pull the trigger to make a weapon useful. President Nixon explained it like this: "I call it the madman theory, Bob. I want the North Vietnamese to believe I've reached the point where I might do anything to stop the war. We'll just slip the word to them that, 'for god's sake, you know Nixon is obsessed about Communists. We can't restrain him when he's angry—and he has his hand on the nuclear button.'"[29]

Nixon mirrored his practise after Eisenhower, who threatened the Chinese with nuclear weapons during the Korean war.[30]

Of course, these threats were hardly hypothetical. The president before him, Harry Truman, had actually dropped two nuclear bombs on Japan. Contrary to popular belief, literally every single US military leader found it to be "of no material assistance in our war against Japan," and rather "adopted an ethical standard common to the barbarians of the Dark Ages."[31] Indeed, it was the entry of the Red Army, famous for defeating the Nazis, that was cited by Japanese government officials as the reason for unconditional surrender. This is confirmed by a study conducted by the U.S. War Department in January 1946, which found "little mention ... of the use of the atomic bomb by the United States in the discussions leading up to the ... decision ... it [is] almost a certainty that the Japanese would have capitulated upon the entry of Russia into the war."[32] Truman simply wanted to show the world—and the Soviet Union in particular—that the US was not constrained by humanitarian concerns in its quest for global domination. Early documents show that Germany was initially also considered as a target, but that "comparatively flimsy wooden houses" in some Japanese cities would better demonstrate the destructive power of the atomic bomb.[33] In addition, "the possibility of eliminating a large fraction of the Fire Force of a Japanese town [in the initial blast] ... is attractive and realistic ... the probability of a devastating fire, spreading well beyond the limits of the blast damage, will be greatly increased."[34]

Obama's modernization program would supposedly lead to a reduction of nuclear weapons after thirty years' time. Yet this eventual reduction is completely dependent on the political will of multiple subsequent presidents, therefore a very uncertain prospect. Indeed, one could argue that the program violates the spirit of the New Strategic Arms Reduction Treaty (START)—a ten-year agreement between Russia and the United States to limit their nuclear arsenal to no more than 1,550 deployed warheads—which was signed in 2010. As Andy Weber, former assistant secretary of defence for nuclear, chemical, and biological defence programs from 2009 to 2014, explained in an interview: "It doesn't violate the treaty because there's a loophole in the treaty called the bomber counting rule ... So each of our 60-ish bombers only counts as one warhead, even though they can carry up to 20 of these air launch cruise missiles each."[35] Notably, already back in 2007, Putin vocally expressed his frustration at a G8 press conference:

> An arms race really is unfolding. Well, was it we who withdrew from the ABM Treaty? We must react to what our partners do. We already told them two years ago, "don't do this ... You are destroying the system of international security. You must understand that you are forcing us to take retaliatory steps." ... Then we heard about them developing low-yield nuclear weapons and they are continuing to develop these charges.
> ... [They] lower the threshold for using nuclear weapons, and thereby put humankind on the brink of nuclear catastrophe. But they are not listening to us. We are saying: do not deploy weapons in space. We don't want to do that. No, it continues: "whoever is not with us is against us". What is that? Is it a dialogue or a search for compromise? The entire dialogue can be summed up by: whoever is not with us is against us.
> ... We implemented the CFE, the Conventional Armed Forces in Europe Treaty [the treaty signed by the former head of the Soviet Union Gorbachev, which aims to demilitarize Europe]. ... And in response we get bases and a missile defense system in Europe. So what should we do?
> You talked about public opinion. Public opinion in Russia is in favor of us ensuring our security. Where can you find a public in favor of

the idea that we must completely disarm, and then perhaps, according to theorists such as Zbignew Brzezinski, that we must divide our territory into three or four parts.[36]

Since that time, Russia has announced new nuclear modernization programs of its own and also engaged in dangerous nuclear posturing.[37] Now that the first missile-defense installation has become operational in Romania, with a second under construction in Poland, Russia has placed nuclear-capable ballistic missiles in Kaliningrad and within range of Poland—seemingly threatening to strike.[38] Since the Ukraine crisis, both NATO and Russia have been holding massive military exercises with nuclear-capable forces around their borders, at one point simultaneously, mere kilometers away from each other.[39] Such close proximity is unprecedented in cold war history. Indeed, as a wide range of concerned scientists and anti-nuclear organizations note in an open letter to Russian and NATO leaders: "Western media are indignant when Russian planes 'buzz' US ships: They don't mention that those very ships were within appx 70Km of St Petersburg," the second largest city in Russia.[40]

Formal channels of communication between NATO and Russian militaries have all but seized to exist, and so has scientific co-operation in nuclear defense.[41] This is especially dangerous because both countries still maintain their nuclear weapons on 'hair-trigger alert,' which allows for a fifteen minute window to launch nuclear missiles if anything is detected on the radar systems; a policy that has repeatedly threatened global catastrophe.[42] In 1983, for example, such a threat was evaded because one Russian official, Stanislav Petrov, refused to notify his superiors when six missiles appeared on his screen; which turned out to be a glitch in the computer system.[43] *There have been hundreds of such false alarm cases.*[44] According to estimates from the Bulletin of Atomic Scientists, the time required for Russia's technical nuclear launch procedures is some six to ten minutes—leaving even less time, mere minutes, for human deliberation. The scientists warn that, in the face of a US first strike threat, "Russian leadership would seem to have little choice but to pre-delegate nuclear launch authority to lower levels of command."[45] As such, the terrifying reality is that an increasingly large amount of fingers will be resting on the nuclear button. And while the United States continues to expand its vastly superior nuclear capabilities, China is now also considering the creation of "hair trigger alert" systems to protect against a first-strike, bringing the world another step closer to nuclear catastrophe.[46]

The reputable *Bulletin of Atomic Scientists* has now put their doomsday clock on two and half minutes to midnight, worse than it was during the Cuban missile crisis and representing a historical low point.[47] At that time, by President Kennedy's own assessment, odds of a global nuclear holocaust might have been as high as 50 percent. And as Chomsky expertly documented, unlike Stanislav Petrov, Kennedy decided to make that reckless toin-coss; when he struck down a Soviet settlement proposal that he himself admitted "would look like a very fair trade" to "any other rational man."[48] Many western citizens find it hard to imagine that anyone would perceive NATO as a threat, because we regard ourselves as peace-loving citizens. But even this is in itself a doubtful statement. A worldwide survey by the American Gallup Center found that half of US and Canadian citizens found military attacks against citizens, i.e. war-crimes, justifiable.[49] This was the highest rate in the world—followed by Europe and Sub-Saharan Africa—where one-fifth supported war crimes. Furthermore, recent research indicates that the chance is higher that an American would support a military intervention in Ukraine if he can't point the country out on a map.[50] This could also explain why 30 percent of Republican voters and 19 percent of Democratic voters supported bombing Agrabah, a fictional country in the Disney movie Aladdin.[50] More importantly, however, the relevance of public opinion is doubtful. Research of the Princeton political scientist Martin Gilens, who compared over 1800 policy proposals over 20 years with public opinion polls, concluded that "the preferences of the average American appear to have only a minuscule, near-zero, statistically non-significant impact upon public policy."[52] The American historian William Blum summarizes America's post-WW2 foreign policy quite succinctly:

> The United States of America has …
>
> 1. Attempted to overthrow more than 50 governments, most of which were democratically-elected.
>
> 2. Attempted to suppress a populist or nationalist movement in 20 countries.
>
> 3. Grossly interfered in democratic elections in at least 30 countries.
>
> 4. Dropped bombs on the people of more than 30 countries.
> 5. Attempted to assassinate more than 50 foreign leaders.[53]

When a Gallup poll asked the world's citizens in 2013 which country was "the greatest threat to world peace," the United States was chosen by far the greatest.[54] And of all these countries, Russia picked the US most frequently. Some will subscribe this threat perception to effective Russian propaganda, but there is certainly some reality to the matter. In the 20th century alone, Russia experienced two devastating invasions from Western countries, with many millions killed in each one of them. Even the lowest death toll of the two—the 1917-1922 civil war with foreign intervention on the side of the Tsarist forces—outnumbers the total amount of people killed in *both* World Wars in Britain, France and the United States *taken together*. More recently, Western financial institutions had propped up the Yeltsin regime in the 90s, who defended IMF reform packages by, among other things, assaulting an elected parliament with tanks, explosives and automatic machine guns.[55] Russia expert and emeritus professor at Princeton, Stephen Cohen, summarized the flaws of the pro-Western Yeltsin presidency quite succinctly:

> economic "shock therapy" and oligarchic looting of essential state assets, which destroyed tens of millions of Russian lives; armed destruction of a popularly elected Parliament and imposition of a "presidential" Constitution, which dealt a crippling blow to democratization and now empowers Putin; brutal war in tiny Chechnya, which gave rise to terrorists in Russia's North Caucasus; rigging of his own re-election in 1996; and leaving behind, in 1999, his approval ratings in single digits, a disintegrating country laden with weapons of mass destruction.[56]

The Russian economist Sergey Glazyev, who resigned from his ministerial post under Yeltsin and now advises Putin, though he also opposed the latter for most of his political career, argued that economic 'shock therapy' during the 90s amounted to genocide:

> Since 1992, Russia has experienced a steady tendency of depopulation, characterized by a 1.5-1.7-times excess of deaths over births. ... Russia's overall demographic losses for those years... are estimated at 8 million people, of which approximately 3 million died prematurely and 5 million were not born.... The rate of annual population loss during the mid-1990s was more than double the rate of loss during the period of Stalinist repression and mass famine in the first half of the 1930s.[57]

After Putin gained the presidency on December 31, 1999,

he made an informal deal with the Russian oligarchs—he would leave their immense wealth intact if they wouldn't meddle in political affairs. Oligarchs who supported the liberal pro-Western opposition—Berezovsky, Gusinsky and Khodorkovsky—were either exiled or imprisoned. Mikhail Khodorkovsky—once the richest man in Russia—was imprisoned for a total of 10 years, and his Yukos oil company, with assets the size of Iraq, nationalized. As Marshall Goldman explains: "Arresting rich businessmen, even billionaires, is no longer a novelty in Russia or elsewhere. But in Russia they are arrested by masked men armed with machine guns, and they are denied bail. Those who are not jailed are increasingly pressured to accept *siloviki* [government-backed agents] as partners or return ownership to the state, lest their corporations be stripped of their value."[58]

To be entirely clear, Putin has never been a socialist—and Russia remains one of the most unequal countries in the world.[59] Nevertheless, by reining in the worst excesses of the Yeltsin regime—which shrank the economy by 26 percent—and then enjoying a period of historically high energy prices, the country was stabilized and a growth of 433 percent established in 15 years' time, according to the World Bank.[60] Despite the persisting inequalities, the poverty rate declined from 40 percent in 1999 to 11 percent in 2013, as documented by the CIA World Fact Book.[61] Moreover, the 'middle class,' defined by the World Bank as those living on more than $10 a day, grew from 30 to 60 percent of the population between 2001 and 2010, while life expectancy was raised by five years between 2000 and 2014.[62] In addition, IMF statistics show that under Putin, the level of public debt went from 89 percent to just 12 percent of GDP in 2014.[63] No wonder that, despite his authoritarian rule, the approval ratings of Putin—as measured by the American Gallup Center—are, at 83%, as high as ever.[64]

High popularity polls are not uncommon among authoritarian regimes, but they are not universal either. Indeed, Putin himself experienced a low of 54 percent in 2012 and 2013, following two years of mass protests against him. The Russian president actually overcame his dwindling popularity because of the Ukraine crisis. Indeed, 74% of the Russian population backed the annexation of Crimea.[65] Different figures have been found in other polls, but always a comfortable majority.[66] It is exactly the provocations of NATO, coupled with its endless hypocritical condemnations, that the Russian state media abuses to stir up nationalism, and distract the population from serious problems, such as the worsening of wealth inequality, with the 7th highest Gini-coefficient in the world; the second-highest incarceration rate, with an estimated 256 people that have been prosecuted for their views; the fourth highest military expenditure as a percentage of GDP, and the second largest volume of weapon exports.[67]

Putin is, in fact, a wartime politician. He became acting president after Yeltsin resigned on December 31,1999—and won his elections on the back of a brutal assault on Chechnya, finishing what Yeltsin had started in 1994. The Chechens had already endured centuries of oppression. Like the Crimean Tatars, they were deported wholesale under Stalin. An estimated third of them died in overcrowded trucks heading for labor camps in Kazakhstan. After Yeltsin's invasion failed to defeat the Chechen drive for self-determination—having killed between 40,000 and 100,000 people in a region of 1.3 million—a referendum on independence was agreed upon, to be held in Chechnya on the 31st of December 2001.[68] This agreement, however, would soon be terminated. In September 1999, apartment buildings were bombed in Moscow, killing over 200 people. The attack was never claimed, and while there are strong indications that the Russian secret services were involved, a determination on this matter is beyond the purview of this book.[69] An answer to the question of culpability, however, is unnecessary to determine the moral bankruptcy of the Russian response.[70]

Like the Donbass in Ukraine, Chechnya was cut off from all gas and electricity supplies from its parent country, right in the middle of winter.[71] At the same time, the Russian air force bombarded Chechen towns, sparing no civilian targets—including schools, hospitals, market places, manufacturing plants and even buses carrying refugees.[72] In fact, refugees fleeing the violence—

mostly women and children—often used 'safe corridors' set up by the Russian military, only to be slaughtered on those very roads.[73] On the other hand, Chechen men were rounded up and held in camps—supposedly to filter out terrorists—where rape, torture and abuse was rampant.[74] In November 2004, two years after the official military operations had ended, Tony Wood wrote:

> There can be no greater indictment of Putin's rule than the present condition of Chechnya. Grozny's population has been reduced to around 200,000—half its size in 1989—who now eke out an existence amid the moonscape of bomb craters and ruins their city has become. According to UNHCR figures, some 160,000 displaced Chechens remained within the warzone by 2002, while another 160,000 were living in refugee camps in Ingushetia. The latter figure has declined somewhat since—a Médecins Sans Frontières report of August 2004 estimated that around 50,000 Chechen refugees remained in Ingushetia—thanks to the Kremlin's policy of closing down camps and prohibiting the construction of housing for refugees there. Those forced back to Chechnya live on the brink of starvation, moving from one bombed-out cellar to another, avoiding the routine terror of zachistki and the checkpoints manned by hooded soldiers, where women have to pay bribes of $10 to avoid their daughters being raped, and men aged 15–65 are taken away to 'filtration camps' or simply made to disappear. The Russian human rights organization Memorial, which covers only a third of Chechnya, reported that between January 2002 and August 2004, some 1,254 people were abducted by federal forces, of whom 757 are still missing.[75]

In this respect, it is notable how much outrage followed the imprisonment of the pro-Western oligarch Khodorkovsky in 2003—although many argued that it was a selective prosecution, no-one actually doubted the criminal origins of his wealth—compared to the havoc wreaked on the people of Chechnya. Condemnation of Khodorkovsky's trial was universal in the West—from the White House, to the president of the European parliament and the German head of state. To prevent a similar fate for Russian oligarch Boris Berezovsky, the UK even granted him political asylum from 2003 onwards. However, before Russia started prosecuting oligarchs, opposed the invasion of Iraq and backed the Syrian regime of Assad—relations had been much warmer. In fact, as universal as was the condemnation of Khodorkovsky's prosecution, so was Western praise for Putin as he rained terror upon the people of Chechnya. As Tony Wood writes:

> In September 2001, while state-sanctioned murders were being committed with impunity in Chechnya, Putin received a standing ovation in the Bundestag; in the summer of 2002, Chirac endorsed the Russian view of the 'anti-terrorist operation', and he and Schroeder reiterated their support at Sochi in August 2004. ...
> Putin wasted no time in linking Chechnya to the wider battle against Islamic extremism, and gave the US permission to plant forward bases across Central Asia, its former sphere of influence, as a quid pro quo for Washington's approval for war in Chechnya. The Bush administration has responded with the requisite silence.[76]

In fact, 'requisite silence' is quite an understatement. In June 2001, George Bush famously told the press that "I looked the man [Putin] in the eye. I found him to be very straight forward and trustworthy and we had a very good dialogue. I was able to get a sense of his soul. He's a man deeply committed to his country and the best interests of his country and I appreciate very much the frank dialogue and that's the beginning of a very constructive relationship."[77] The stance of UK prime-minister Tony Blair was hardly different. Asked by the *Guardian* whether it is "the right response to terrorism to raze a city like Grozny to a pile of rubble," Blair responded in kind: "Well, they have been taking their action for the reasons they've set out because of the terrorism that has happened in Chechnya."[78] Just like Yeltsin's first assault in 1996, Putin's war on Chechnya was accompanied by a continued stream of funds from the World Bank and IMF.[79] In addition, US President Bill "Clinton ordered the Pentagon to rush Moscow state of the art night-vision and communications equipment for Russian helicopters being used against insurgents in the Caucasus [referring to Chechnya]." The White House assured the readers of the *Toronto Sun* that the equipment was only being used "to combat terrorism."[80] A German agent later told Reuters News Agency that Western secret services—including the US, German, French and British—also "provided Moscow with intelligence on Chechen rebels."[81]

This history underscores the fact that Russia, in many respects, does not differ too much from the West. Indeed, the United States has by far the biggest military budget, the world's highest incarceration rate and the largest volume of arms exports, often selling to the same clients as Russia—including Iraq, Afghanistan, Israel and the United Arab Emirates, among others.[82] As Sakwa notes: "this is not a second Cold War. Russia is neither a consistent ideological nor strategic foe. Instead, cooperation has continued over Afghanistan—the Northern Distribution Network across Russia continued to channel 40 per cent of supplies and personnel to and from Afghanistan throughout the Ukraine crisis—and in the Middle East, and there have even been signs of cooperation over Syria in the face of the Islamic State".[83] The latter eventually collapsed during the battle of Aleppo, over one-sided condemnations by US officials of otherwise serious Russian and Syrian war crimes. These condemnations were not only hypocritical historically, but especially disingenious considering the simultaneous US backing of an almost identical siege on Mosul, Iraq. [83] Clearly, the difference in foreign policy primarily concerns the pursuit of global hegemony—the drive for which lies squarely in the United States and Western Europe—indeed, one could argue, has done so for centuries.

Even during the entire Cold War, when Soviet world dominance was supposedly imminent, the issue of hegemony had always been quite clear. Soviet military expenditures reached its absolute peak in 1988. Regardless, NATO's military budget was still more than twice the size of that of the Warsaw pact countries.[85] The disparities were even larger on other parameters. A study by Ruth Leger Sivard, which analyzed 125 military conflicts between 1946 and 1981—95 percent of which occurred in the global south, involving foreign forces in most cases—found "western powers accounting for 79 percent of the interventions, communist for 6 percent."[86] All the communist interventions were enacted around their borders, with the exception of Cuba, which supported multiple African liberation wars against European colonial powers. Another study of military interventions between 1946 and 1989 found that the major Western powers—France, the US and UK—accounted for 147 interventions, while China and the Soviet Union accounted for 46.[87] Incidentally, a study of 69 armed conflicts during (roughly) the same period confirmed that the chance of a foreign intervention increased 100-fold based on the existence of oil and gas interests.[88] On the number of foreign bases, the balance was even more skewed. The Soviet Union counted a few dozen bases, mainly in Eastern Europe, while in December 1970, the US Senate Subcommittee on Security Agreements and Commitments Abroad pointed out that the U.S. global military presence reached over 3,000 foreign military bases "virtually surrounding both the Soviet Union and Communist China."[89]

In terms of economic power, the disparities were incredibly vast at the start of the Cold War, when the United States controlled half of the global economy while the Soviet Union had barely survived a genocidal invasion by Nazi Germany. Nevertheless, even at the most favourable data point in 1975, the Soviet economy remained but 59 percent of that of the US—and the disparities between their allies were even greater.[90] Indeed, in terms of soft power, a Defence Monitor report in 1980 traced Soviet influence on a country-by-country basis since World War 2, concluding that its power peaked in the late 1950s and by 1979 "the Soviets were influencing only 6 percent of the world's population and 5 percent of the world's G.N.P., exclusive of the Soviet Union."[91]

Now, have these parameters changed? The answer is a resounding yes. Russia's only remaining mutual defence alliance—in any way comparable to agreements stipulated in NATO—is the Collective Security Treaty Organization (CSTO). Its signatories are the post-Soviet states of Russia, Armenia, Belarus, Kazakhstan, Kyrgyztan and Tajikistan. Joint military exercises are held yearly in the framework of the agreement—similar to the crucial article 5 principle of the NATO alliance—that aggression against one signatory would be perceived as an aggression against all. Admittedly, even this comparison is not entirely fair. In 2014, for example, there were still US, German and French military bases on the territory of CSTO signatories, while the equivalent of Russian bases on NATO soil would be completely unthinkable.[92] Nevertheless, this only affirms my point. The combined CSTO military budget as of 2014 is not even one-tenth the size of NATO's.[93]

Even comparing NATO with the Shanghai Cooperation Organization (SCO)—a loose (military) co-operation that also includes China—the NATO budget remains more than three times as large.[94] I want to emphasize; this is hardly a fair comparison. Complementary alliances would surely account for countries such as Australia, Canada and Japan, on the side of NATO. Indeed, these countries—along with almost the entirety of the Southern American continent, among others—have actual mutual defence agreements with the United States, similar to NATO's article 5. Regardless, an extensive study of military interventions between 1990 and 2005, found that three major NATO powers—France, the UK and US—were responsible for 89 interventions, while China and Russia accounted for just 11.[95] Furthermore, the number of SCO foreign military bases runs in single digits, while the exact number of foreign NATO bases is not even known—though all estimates put it well over a 1000, a figure that might understate the number of foreign US bases, alone.[96] Furthermore, as Nick Turse reports: "In 2015, according to Special Operations Command spokesman Ken McGraw, U.S. Special Operations forces deployed to a record-shattering 147 countries –75% of the nations on the planet... On any day of the year, in fact, America's most elite troops can be found in 70 to 90 nations."[97] Perhaps most telling, the last published US intelligence budget (2010)—which includes both analytical and operational agencies—was substantially larger than that of the entire Russian military establishment.[98] These agencies are always shrouded in secrecy, but a major Senate committee investigation into CIA activities during the Cold War—initiated after the Watergate scandals—helps to reveal the scale of such undertakings. Over the 14 years reviewed, the committee found 900 major operations and 3000 minor operations from this single agency.[99]

Economic comparisons bring similar figures. The total GDP of CSTO countries constitute less than twelve percent of the NATO-zone economy. Despite all of the column inches spent on the rise of China, economic disparities remain vast there too. Comparing NATO economies with the signatories of the SCO—again, a much less binding security co-operation—the SCO countries still constitute but 59 percent of the NATO-zone's GDP.[100] These comparisons also ignore the production of manufactured goods. Russia is largely a supplier of raw materials to Europe—an obvious sign that its integration into the global economy has come from an inferior position.[101] Despite all the cries about Europe's dependence on Russian gas, the fact remains that the Russian Federation is dependent for over 50 percent of its exports on the European Union, making the dependence mutual at least.

Indeed, it is no secret that the Russian economy was

harshly hit in the wake of the (still limited) sanctions over Ukraine: by 2015, the country faced over $100 billion in capital flight, the ruble's value sank by a third and the Russian economy contracted by 3.7%.[102] Probably most damaging to the Russian economy was the simultanuous drop in global energy prices, which only underlines the country's economic vulnerability and international dependence.[103] In fact, there is substantial evidence to suggest that the price-drop was driven by the United States and Saudi-Arabia in the first place—in a bid to damage their geopolitical rivals.[104] Russian counter-sanctions, however, seemed to barely have any effect. The Eurozone actually experienced its best economic performance in almost a decade, with 14 consecutive quarters of growth.[105] The overall share of EU imports in Russia's trade figures also remained stable despite the counter-sanctions.[106] Of course, some EU sectors did suffer under a Russian embargo; particularily agricultural exports, which dropped by nearly €5 billion in the first year.[107] Nevertheless, this decrease was also caused by the flailing Russian economy, as agricultural products outside of the embargo's scope also faced sharp export-drops due to the lower Russian demand.[108] Moreover, the EU's agricultural sector was able to find alternative markets in the wake of Russia's economic crisis, and overall agri-food exports to non-EU countries actually increased by nearly six percent in the first year.[109]

Clearly, Russia is not the senior partner in its trade relations with the European Union; even a study from the Russian Academy of Sciences seems to admit this much. The article estimated the long-term adverse impact of sanctions on the Russian economy at 8-10% of GDP, contrasted by some 0.5% of GDP for the EU.[110] Finally, as for China, even though the country has made much progress, the primary sectors of its economy still produce low-technology goods, and substantial parts of its production lines are owned by Western multinational corporations. No wonder that Russia's per capita GDP is less than half that of the United States—and China's but a quarter.[111] As Professor Chomsky observes, American power has been declining since the Second World War, when it controlled half of the global economy, yet it remains firmly in place. As a March 2017 review of the US foreign policy establishment confirmed, this view is widely shared in the highest corridors of power.[112] In this context, Chomsky offers guidance to understand the Western response to the annexation of Crimea:

> Columnist Thanassis Cambanis summarizes the core issue succinctly in *The Boston Globe*: "Putin's annexation of the Crimea is a break in the order that America and its allies have come to rely on since the end of the Cold War—namely, one in which major powers only intervene militarily when they have an international consensus on their side, or failing that, when they're not crossing a rival power's red lines."
>
> This era's most extreme international crime, the United States-United Kingdom invasion of Iraq, was therefore not a break in world order—because, after failing to gain international support, the aggressors didn't cross Russian or Chinese red lines.
>
> In contrast, Putin's takeover of the Crimea and his ambitions in Ukraine cross American red lines.
>
> Therefore "Obama is focused on isolating Putin's Russia by cutting off its economic and political ties to the outside world, limiting its expansionist ambitions in its own neighborhood and effectively making it a pariah state," Peter Baker reports in *The New York Times*.
>
> American red lines, in short, are firmly placed at Russia's borders. Therefore Russian ambitions "in its own neighborhood" violate world order and create crises. ...
>
> ... The U.S. invasion of Indochina, like the invasion of Iraq, crossed no red lines, nor have many other U.S. depredations worldwide. To

repeat the crucial point: Adversaries are sometimes permitted to have red lines, but at their borders, where America's red lines are also located. If an adversary has "expansionist ambitions in its own neighborhood," crossing U.S. red lines, the world faces a crisis.[113]

In this context, the recent speculations about an impending Russian annexation of Ukraine—and even Poland and the Baltic States—is patently absurd. Even general Petr Pavel, chairman of the NATO Military Committee, recently admitted that no intelligence assessments indicate that Russia is preparing to invade the Baltic states.[114] Furthermore, if Russia had wished to annex Ukraine proper, the perfect opportunity to do so surfaced in the spring of 2014. On March 1st, the Ukrainian president Yanukovych ostensibly send a letter to Vladimir Putin, asking for a Russian military intervention: "The country is in the grip of outright terror and violence driven by the West. ... People are persecuted on political and language grounds. In this context, I appeal to the President of Russia Vladimir V. Putin to use the armed forces of the Russian Federation to re-establish the rule of law, peace, order, stability and to protect the people of Ukraine"[115] to invade Ukraine proper—at the invitation of its own de jure president—as well as the most opportune moment militarily, since Ukraine's security apparatus was completely disintegrating. Yet only Crimea, home to a crucial Russian military base, was annexed. In addition, plenty of pretexts arose for the annexation of rebel-controlled territories in the Donbass. After the independence referendum in May 2014, the rebel leadership asked repeatedly to join Russia, a request that was never honoured.[116]

Indeed, it is much more likely that the Donbass will transform into another 'frozen conflict' area. After the disintegration of the Soviet Union, some artificial Soviet borders were challenged, leading to civil war and the creation of small de-facto states within the parent countries of Georgia, Moldova and Azerbaijan. In the cases of Abkhazia, South Ossetia, and

Transnistria, these de-facto states became highly dependent on the Russian state for both security and funding. The secessionist regions have often been portrayed—like the Donbass uprising—as a cynical Russian ploy divorced from local realities. However, a peer-reviewed multi-year study of the three de-facto states, including extensive surveys, suggests otherwise.[117] They all have a presence of Russian peace keeping forces—as stipulated in agreements signed by the parent states—whose *permanent* presence is supported by an overwhelming majority of Abkhazian and South Ossetian citizens, while half of Transnistrian residents support a continued Russian military presence. The vast majority of all secessionist republics have trust in the Russian leadership. Asked about the future of their republics, barely anyone was interested in re-integration with its parent country. Most Abkhazians chose independence, followed by accession to Russia. An overwhelming 81 percent of South Ossetians wished to join Russia, while 16 percent favoured independence. Half of Transnistrians picked accession to Russia and a third preferred independence. In the case of Transnistria, there have been two referenda on independence in 1991 and 2006, both of which passed with an overwhelming majority. The second even asked explicitly: 'Do you support the course towards independence for the Transnistrian Moldovan Republic and its subsequent free unification with the Russian Federation?' On a 78 per cent turnout, 97 per cent voted in favour.[118] Obviously, if Putin wanted to restore the former Soviet Union in its full glory, these republics would be the first places to start. Nevertheless, none of these secessionist states have been annexed. In fact, a recently published book by William Hill, who served two spells as head of the Organisation for Security and Cooperation in Europe (OSCE) Mission to Moldova in1999-2006, reveals that Russia was hardly an obstacle to resolving these conflicts. A review summarizes some of the most pertinent issues:

> The author challenges the stereotype that Russia maintained the conflicts in the Black Sea region

in a frozen state in order to project its influence in the new post-Soviet states. Hill makes his point by stressing that notwithstanding the deep differences with other OSCE states on some individual policy issues, Russia was apparently willing to work cooperatively with other OSCE states, including the United States, even on the territory of the former USSR. The book gives very interesting examples of Russia's collaborative stance on Transdniestrian conflict issues such as the replacement of the controversial commander of the 14th Russian army General Alexandr Lebed, the significant reduction of Russian military presence from the region, withdrawal of the stockpiles of ammunition and several Moscow initiatives to broker power-sharing agreements in 1996, 2001 and 2003. It is implicit in Hill's argument that Russian initiatives were quite reasonable and copied the EU approaches in the Balkans. In particular, the controversial power-sharing agreement produced by Putin's close associate Dmitry Kozak in fact grew out of the initiative of Moldovan president Vladimir Voronin and was supported by other mediators from Ukraine and the OSCE.

Another important finding of the book is the author's acknowledgement that Western capitals displayed insufficient sensitivity toward Russia and denied her an independent diplomatic and political role in the region that had once been hers exclusively. This lack of sensitivity becomes particularly controversial given that in the 1990s [under Yeltsin] the Western partners chose not to deal with conflicts in the post-Soviet space and even encouraged Russia to play a major role in the conflicts in the Caucasus and Transnistria. The problem of Russia being denied agency is also outlined when the author stresses that Russia–NATO problems were not caused by the very fact of its enlargement, but by the fact that Moscow was prevented from meaningfully participating in or influencing decisions of the most important political and security questions in Europe.[119]

Notably, in Russia's effort to resolve the 'frozen conflicts,' even popular claims to independence remained unrecognized for nearly two decades—and in the case of Transnistria to this very day. Abkhazia and South Ossetia—both on internationally recognized territory of Georgia—were only recognized by Moscow in 2008, after an attempt by Georgian president Mikheil Saakashvili to seize South Ossetia by force.[120] Both sides committed war crimes—including the use of cluster munitions—and the Russian counter-offensive also temporarily occupied Georgia proper, though the latter happened only briefly and on a small scale. It seems that Russia wanted to send a message—especially since Georgia had applied for NATO membership shortly before its aggression against South-Ossetia. In addition, Saakashvili received extensive military aid from the United States, including about 150 military advisers whose role in the conflict remains unexamined. Rather than strength, however, these Russian moves showed increasing desperation. As US President Obama remarked after the annexation of Crimea: "Russia is a regional power that is threatening some of its immediate neighbors—not out of strength but out of weakness. ... The fact that Russia felt it had to go in militarily and lay bare these violations of international law indicates less influence, not more."[121] Indeed, it is exactly Russia's weakness that forces it to become a "profoundly conservative power" which seeks to "maintain the status quo." As Professor Sakwa explains:

> Russia under Putin had been the opposite of a land-grabbing state. ... In October 2004 Putin

achieved a definitive agreement with China over their 4,400-kilometre-long border, in exchange for the transfer of several major islands in the Ussuri River to Chinese jurisdiction. In September 2010 agreement was finally reached with Norway over the long-contested maritime delineation of the Barents Sea, agreeing to a split down the middle, which turned out to grant Norway the bulk of the energy resources. Under Putin agreement was finally reached over the borders with Estonia and Latvia, although both retained popular aspirations to have part of Russia's neighbouring Pskov region restored to them, which had been part of the interwar republics. Putin even offered to return to the 1956 agreement with Japan and to restore two of the four Kurile Islands (Northern Territories) to that country. Admittedly, these were the two smallest, but in mathematical terms honours would be even. … Russia under Putin is a profoundly conservative power and its actions are designed to maintain the status quo, hence the effort Moscow put into ratifying its existing borders. It was the West that was perceived to be the revisionist power.[122]

The failure of Western diplomacy in Ukraine was severe. The crimes of Kiev were legitimized by western political and military support.[123] NATO praised Kiev for its "restraint" while the American ambassador Jen Psaki even defended Yatsenyuk's use of the term "subhumans" to refer to Russians.[124] Presidential aides told *The New York Times* in April 2014 that "Mr. Obama has concluded that even if there is a resolution to the current standoff over Crimea and eastern Ukraine, he will never have a constructive relationship with Mr. Putin."[125]

This cold war mentality escalated further when the MH17 passenger plane with 298 people on board was shot down. Sanctions against Russia were immediately put in place even though little of what had happened was actually known at the time. A CIA source of investigative journalist Robert Parry said the agency was, among other scenarios, considering a failed assassination attempt on Putin by radical elements in the Kiev regime.[126] The Russian presidential plane looked a lot like MH17 and was scheduled to fly over Eastern Ukraine around that time, although the source dried up and later research points in different directions. German intelligence, for example, claimed to have 'unambiguous findings' proving the rebels shot down MH17 with a captured BUK missile from the Ukrainian military.[127] On the other hand, an open source Bellingcat investigation claimed to have conclusive evidence that the plane was shot down by the rebels with a Russian-supplied BUK missile.[128] The official investigation came to the same conclusion.

Clearly, assessing all the evidence is beyond the purview of this book. Nevertheless, there seems to be a western consensus on the fact that the crash involved an accident and that Russian actions at worst had been criminally reckless.[129] On the other hand, little was said about the fact that the downing of MH17 happened in the context of a brutal war that was killing the population of the Donbass region in far greater numbers. Indeed, this is why the rebels were shooting at airplanes in the first place. Preceding the international tragedy, seventeen Ukrainian military aircrafts had already been shot down—including two fighter jets the very day before MH17—leading multiple civilian airlines to avoid the Donbass airspace.[130] Indeed, the official investigation also noted that there was sufficient reason to close off the air-space for civilian flights above Eastern Ukraine, something Kiev failed to do. The cynicism of the sanctions is obvious given the historical precedent. Chomsky gives a pertinent example:

> Every literate person, and certainly every editor and commentator, instantly recalled another case when a plane was shot down with comparable loss of life: Iran Air 655 with 290 killed, including

66 children, shot down in Iranian airspace in a clearly identified commercial air route. The crime was not carried out "with U.S. support," nor has its agent ever been uncertain. It was the guided-missile cruiser *USS Vincennes*, operating in Iranian waters in the Persian Gulf.

The commander of a nearby U.S. vessel, David Carlson, wrote in the U.S. Naval Proceedings that he "wondered aloud in disbelief" as "'The *Vincennes* announced her intentions" to attack what was clearly a civilian aircraft. He speculated that "Robo Cruiser," as the *Vincennes* was called because of its aggressive behavior, "felt a need to prove the viability of Aegis (the sophisticated anti-aircraft system on the cruiser) in the Persian Gulf, and that they hankered for the opportunity to show their stuff."

Two years later, the commander of the *Vincennes* and the officer in charge of anti-air warfare were given the Legion of Merit award for "exceptionally meritorious conduct in the performance of outstanding service" and for the "calm and professional atmosphere" during the period of the destruction of the Iranian Airbus. The incident was not mentioned in the award.

President Reagan blamed the Iranians and defended the actions of the warship, which "followed standing orders and widely publicized procedures, firing to protect itself against possible attack." His successor, Bush I, proclaimed that "I will never apologize for the United States —I don't care what the facts are ... I'm not an apologize-for-America kind of guy."

... We know why Ukrainians and Russians are in their own countries, but one might ask what exactly the *Vincennes* was doing in Iranian waters. The answer is simple. It was defending Washington's great friend Saddam Hussein in his murderous aggression against Iran. For the victims, the shoot-down was no small matter. It was a major factor in Iran's recognition that it could not fight on any longer, according to historian Dilip Hiro.[131]

Despite the obvious double standards, Western leaders were eager to use the suffering of the MH17 victims to push Russia into a corner. A case was made for sanctions, despite an extensive study by the political scientist Robert A. Pape—which examined 115 sanctions regimes and came to a success rate of 4 percent.[132] He added that sanctions are "more likely to enhance the nationalist legitimacy of rulers than to undermine it."[133] The anger of the population, quite understandably, turns towards the imposers of the sanctions rather than their own government. This was especially predictable in Russo-Western relations, which have a long history of animosity. The September 2016 Russian election results seem to confirm this.[134] Putin's United Russia party gained its biggest majority to date—obtaining over three-quarters of the seats in parliament, granting it the ability to change the Russian constitution. On the other hand, the three pro-Western parties combined only managed to garner four percent of the popular vote. Thus, even a united pro-western front would not have passed the five percent threshold to enter parliament. As Stephen Cohen notes, "The pro-western, liberal, political movement in Russia is dead—and was killed by Washington."[135] The remaining opposition is, in fact, more nationalist than Putin.

Endnotes

1 Scott, P. D. (2009, August 11). The Real Grand Chessboard and the Profiteers of War. Retrieved from http://www.globalresearch.ca/the-real-grand-chessboard-and-the-profiteers-of-war/14672

2   Hauke, R. V. (2008, August 26). Die Welt als Schachbrett—Der neue Kalte Krieg des Obama-Beraters Zbigniew Brzezinski. Retrieved from http://www.hintergrund.de/20080826235/politik/welt/die-welt-als-schachbrett-der-neue-kalte-krieg-des-obama-beraters-zbigniew-brzezinski.html#_ftnref; Obama: I've learned an immense amount from Dr. Brzezinski. (2008, March 13). Retrieved from https://www.youtube.com/watch?v=ASlETEx0T-I

3   Brzezinski, Z. (1997). *The Grand Chessboard: American Primacy and its Geostrategic Imperatives.* New York, NY: BasicBooks, p. 41

4   Ibid, p. 31

5   Ibid, p. 202

6   Wales Summit Declaration issued by the Heads of State and Government participating in the meeting of the North Atlantic Council in Wales. (2014, September 5). Retrieved from http://www.nato.int/cps/en/natohq/official_texts_112964.htm

7   Joint Statement of the NATO-Ukraine Commission. (2014, September 4). Retrieved from http://www.nato.int/cps/en/natohq/news_112695.htm

8   Carden, J. (2014, September 08). The 2014 NATO Summit: Giving War a Chance. Retrieved from http://www.thenation.com/article/181521/2014-nato-summit-giving-war-chance

9   Wales Summit Declaration issued by the Heads of State and Government participating in the meeting of the North Atlantic Council in Wales. (2014, September 5). Retrieved from http://www.nato.int/cps/en/natohq/official_texts_112964.htm

10 Carter, A. (2016, February 2). Remarks by Secretary Carter on the Budget at the Economic Club of Washington, D.C. Retrieved from http://www.defense.gov/News/News-Transcripts/Transcript-View/Article/648901/remarks-by-secretary-carter-on-the-budget-at-the-economic-club-of-washington-dc

11 Garamone, J. (2000, June 02). Joint Vision 2020 Emphasizes Full-spectrum Dominance. Retrieved from http://archive.defense.gov/news/newsarticle.aspx?id=45289

12 Perry, W. J., & Abizaid, J. P. (2014). Ensuring a Strong US Defense for the Future: The National Defense Panel Review of the 2014 Quadrennial Defense Review. United States Inst. of Peace, Washington, DC, p. 2

13 National Security Strategy (Rep.). (2015, February). Retrieved https://www.whitehouse.gov/sites/default/files/docs/2015_national_security_strategy.pdf, p. 2, 8

14 Ballistic missile defence. (2016, February 9). Retrieved from http://www.nato.int/cps/en/natolive/topics_49635.htm

15 Goettig, M., & Shalal, A. (2014, March 20). Poland speeds up missile

	defence plan amid Ukraine crisis. Retrieved from http://uk.reuters.com/article/uk-poland-defence-idUKBREA2J26K20140320
16	S. S. 2277, 113th Cong. (2014). Retrieved from https://www.gpo.gov/fdsys/pkg/BILLS-113s2277is/html/BILLS-113s2277is.htm
17	From Counterforce to Minimal Deterrence: A New Nuclear Policy on the Path Toward Eliminating Nuclear Weapons. (n.d.). Retrieved from http://fas.org/pub-reports/counterforce-minimal-deterrence-new-nuclear-policy-path-toward-eliminating-nuclear-weapons/
18	Membership Roster. (2016, February 12). Retrieved from http://www.cfr.org/about/membership/roster.html; Lieber, K. A., & Press, D. G. (2006). The Rise of U.S. Nuclear Primacy. *Foreign Affairs*, 85(2), 42. Retrieved from https://www.foreignaffairs.com/articles/united-states/2006-03-01/rise-us-nuclear-primacy, p. 42
19	Ibid., p. 52
20	ABM Treaty Withdrawal Neither Necessary nor Prudent. (2001, December 13). Retrieved from http://www.armscontrol.org/node/2515
21	Koplow, D. A. (2010). Death by moderation: the US military's quest for useable weapons. Cambridge University Press, p. 123.
22	US dumps bunker-buster—or not? (2015, November 17). Retrieved from http://web.archive.org/web/20071022215958/http:/janes.com/defence/news/jid/jid051117_1_n.shtml
23	Cited in Chomsky, N. (2014, August 06). As Hiroshima Day dawns, why are we still tempting nuclear fate? Retrieved from http://www.theguardian.com/commentisfree/2014/aug/06/hiroshima-day-nuclear-weapons-cold-war-usa-bomb
24	Broad, W. J., & Sanger, D. E. (2016, January 11). As U.S. Modernizes Nuclear Weapons, 'Smaller' Leaves Some Uneasy. Retrieved from http://www.nytimes.com/2016/01/12/science/as-us-modernizes-nuclear-weapons-smaller-leaves-some-uneasy.html
25	Ziezulewicz, B. G. (2016, August 02). B61-12 life extension program receives NNSA approval. Retrieved from http://www.upi.com/Business_News/Security-Industry/2016/08/02/B61-12-life-extension-program-receives-NNSA-approval/3261470147434/
26	Traynor, I. (2008, January 22). Pre-emptive nuclear strike a key option, Nato told. Retrieved from http://www.theguardian.com/world/2008/jan/22/nato.nuclear; The Iran Nuclear Straw Man. (2015, July 17). Retrieved from http://www.counterpunch.org/2015/07/17/the-iran-nuclear-straw-man/
27	Sanger, D. E., & Broad, W. J. (2016, September 05). Obama Unlikely to Vow No First Use of Nuclear Weapons. Retrieved from http://www.nytimes.com/2016/09/06/science/obama-unlikely-to-vow-no-first-use-of-nuclear-weapons.html?_r=0

28 Kristensen, H. M., McKinzie, M., & Postol, T. A. (2017, March 02). How US nuclear force modernization is undermining strategic stability: The burst-height compensating super-fuze. Retrieved from http://thebulletin.org/how-us-nuclear-force-modernization-undermining-strategic-stability-burst-height-compensating-super10578

29 Stone, O., & Kuznick, P. (2013). *The untold history of the United States.* Simon and Schuster, p. 466.

30 Ibid.

31 American Military Leaders Urge President Truman not to Drop the Atomic Bomb. (2010). Retrieved from http://www.colorado.edu/AmStudies/lewis/2010/atomicdec.htm

32 Stone, O., & Kuznick, P. (2013). *The untold history of the United States.* Simon and Schuster, pp. 293-294.

33 Wellerstein, Alex (2012, August 8). The Height of the Bomb. Retrieved from http://blog.nuclearsecrecy.com/2012/08/08/the-height-of-the-bomb/;

34 Ibid.

35 Raphael, T. J. (2016, January 15). Why President Obama is moving ahead with the biggest modernization of US nuclear weapons in decades. Retrieved from http://www.pri.org/stories/2016-01-15/why-president-obama-moving-ahead-biggest-modernization-us-nuclear-weapons-decades

36 Putin, V. (2007, June 8). TLAXCALA : Putin sagt—Pressekonferenz im Anschluß an den G 8 Gipfel. Retrieved from http://www.tlaxcala.es/pp.asp?reference=3039; Hauke, R. V. (2008, August 26). Die Welt als Schachbrett—Der neue Kalte Krieg des Obama-Beraters Zbigniew Brzezinski. Retrieved from http://www.hintergrund.de/20080826235/politik/welt/die-welt-als-schachbrett-der-neue-kalte-krieg-des-obama-beraters-zbigniew-brzezinski.html#_ftnref

37 Kristensen, H. M., & Norris, R. S. (2017, February 28). Russian nuclear forces, 2017. Bulletin of the Atomic Scientists, 73(2), 115-126

38 Reals, T. (2016, November 21). Russia responds to NATO advance with missiles in its Europe enclave. Retrieved from http://www.cbsnews.com/news/russia-s-400-iskander-ballistic-missile-systems-kaliningrad-countermeasures-nato/

39 Hallam, J. *et al.* (2016, December 11). Letter on the need for urgent measures to avert a nuclear war. Retrieved from http://www.defenddemocracy.press/letter-on-the-need-for-urgent-measures-to-avert-a-nuclear-war/

40 Ibid.

41 Cohen, J. (2016, November 11). Commentary: The number one reason to fix U.S.-Russia relations. Retrieved from http://www.reuters.com/

	article/us-russia-nuclear-commentary-idUSKBN1351SD
42	Ibid.
43	Westberg, G. (2016, May 23). Close calls: We were closer to nuclear destruction than we knew. Retrieved from https://peaceandhealthblog.com/2016/05/23/close-calls/
44	Chomsky, N. (2012, October 15). Cuban missile crisis: how the US played Russian roulette with nuclear war. Retrieved from https://www.theguardian.com/commentisfree/2012/oct/15/cuban-missile-crisis-russian-roulette
45	Kristensen, H. M., McKinzie, M., & Postol, T. A. (2017, March 02). How US nuclear force modernization is undermining strategic stability: The burst-height compensating super-fuze. Retrieved from http://thebulletin.org/how-us-nuclear-force-modernization-undermining-strategic-stability-burst-height-compensating-super10578
46	Cohen, J. (2016, November 11). Commentary: The number one reason to fix U.S.-Russia relations. Retrieved from http://www.reuters.com/article/us-russia-nuclear-commentary-idUSKBN1351SD
47	It is two and a half minutes to midnight. (2017, January 26). Retrieved from http://thebulletin.org/clock/2017
48	Chomsky, N. (2012, October 15). Cuban missile crisis: how the US played Russian roulette with nuclear war. Retrieved from https://www.theguardian.com/commentisfree/2012/oct/15/cuban-missile-crisis-russian-roulette
49	Views of Violence. (n.d.). Retrieved from http://www.gallup.com/poll/157067/views-violence.aspx
50	Dropp, K., Kertzer, J., & Zeitzoff, T. (2014, April 7). The less Americans know about Ukraine's location, the more they want U.S. to intervene. Retrieved from https://www.washingtonpost.com/news/monkey-cage/wp/2014/04/07/the-less-americans-know-about-ukraines-location-the-more-they-want-u-s-to-intervene/
51	Johnson, M. E. (2015, December 18). Poll: 30% of Republicans want to bomb a fictional Disney country. Retrieved from http://www.motherjones.com/politics/2015/12/poll-30-republicans-want-bomb-fictional-disney-country
52	Gilens, M., & Page, B. I. (2014). Testing Theories of American Politics: Elites, Interest Groups, and Average Citizens. Perspect. Polit. Perspectives on Politics, 12(03), 564-581. Retrieved from http://journals.cambridge.org/action/displayAbstract?fromPage=online&aid=9354310, p. 575
53	Blum, W. (2011, July 28). The Anti-Empire Report #96. Retrieved from http://williamblum.org/aer/read/96 The list is mostly drawn from his Blum, W. (2003). *Killing hope: US military and CIA interventions*

	since World War II. Zed Books. And Blum, W. (2006). *Rogue state: a guide to the world's only superpower*. Zed Books.
54	End of Year Survey 2013: Global Results. (2013, December 30). Retrieved from http://www.wingia.com/en/services/about_the_end_of_year_survey/global_results/7/33/
55	Klein, N. (2007). *The shock doctrine: The rise of disaster capitalism*. Macmillan.
56	Cohen, S. F. (2014, February 12). Distorting Russia: How the American media misrepresent Putin, Sochi and Ukraine. Retrieved from http://www.thenation.com/article/178344/distorting-russia
57	Cited in Kelly, K. R. (2012). The context of the Iraq genocide (Unpublished master's thesis). University, Palmerston North, New Zealand, p. 53. Retrieved from https://ongenocide.files.wordpress.com/2012/02/context-of-iraq-genocide.pdf
58	Goldman, M. I. (2004). Putin and the Oligarchs. *Foreign Affairs*. New York, 83(6), 33-44.
59	Hemment, J. (2009). Soviet-Style Neoliberalism? *Problems of Post-Communism*,56(6), 36-50.
60	World Bank. (n.d.). GDP per capita, PPP (current international $). Retrieved from http://data.worldbank.org/indicator/NY.GDP.PCAP.PP.CD
61	CIA, E. (2001). The world factbook 2001. Central Intelligence Agency, Washington, DC; CIA, E. (2015). The world factbook 2015. Central Intelligence Agency, Washington, DC.
62	Breslow, J. M. (2015, January 23). Retrieved from http://www.pbs.org/wgbh/frontline/article/inequality-and-the-putin-economy-inside-the-numbers/; Russian Federation. (n.d.). Retrieved from http://data.worldbank.org/country/russian-federation
63	Abbas, A. S., Belhocine, N., ElGanainy, A. A., & Horton, M. A. (2010, November 1). A Historical Public Debt Database. Retrieved from https://www.imf.org/external/pubs/cat/longres.aspx?sk=24332.0; Abbas, S. M., Belhocine, N., ElGanainy, A. A., & Horton, M. (2010). A historical public debt database. IMF Working Papers, 1-26.
64	Ray, J., & Esipova, N. (2014, July 18). Russian Approval of Putin Soars to Highest Level in Years. Retrieved from http://www.gallup.com/poll/173597/russian-approval-putin-soars-highest-level-years.aspx
65	More Russians Support Annexation of Crimea, Poll Shows. (2014, September 2). Retrieved from http://www.themoscowtimes.com/news/article/more-russians-support-annexation-of-crimea-poll-shows/506247.html
66	Notably, support for the Russian incursion in Donbass was much lower, which helps to explain why Putin has been denying the extent

	of Russian involvement for so long. Podosenov, S. (2014, November 25). Россияне ждут новой донбасской войны. Retrieved from http://www.gazeta.ru/politics/2014/11/24_a_6313609.shtml
67	For the GINI-coefficient consult Shorrocks, A., Davies, J., & Lluberas, R. (2016, November). Global Wealth Databook 2016, pp. 106-109. Retrieved http://publications.credit-suisse.com/tasks/render/file/index.cfm?fileid=AD6F2B43-B17B-345E-E20A1A254A3E24A5; for changes in wealth inequality since 2000 consult Shorrocks, A., Davies, J., & Lluberas, R. (2016, November). Global Wealth Report 2014, p. 33. Retrieved https://publications.credit-suisse.com/tasks/render/file/?fileID=60931FDE-A2D2-F568-B041B58C5EA591A4; for incarceration rates consult BBC. (n.d.). World Prison Populations. Retrieved from http://news.bbc.co.uk/2/shared/spl/hi/uk/06/prisons/html/nn2page1.stm; Davydov, V. (2015, December 10). List of political prisoners in the Russian Federation (Rep.). Retrieved http://www.inostrannyi-agent.org/files/list-of-political-prisoners-eng-10dec15-small.pdf; for arms expenditure data consult the SIPRI database.
68	Wood, T. (2004). The case for Chechnya. *New Left Review,* NLR 30. Retrieved from http://newleftreview.org/II/30/tony-wood-the-case-for-chechnya
69	Ahmed, Nafeez Mosaddeq, The Smashing of Chechnya—An International Irrelevance: A Case Study of the Role of Human Rights in Western Foreign Policy, Islamic Human Rights Commission, London, April 1999.
70	Ibid.
71	Ibid.
72	Ibid.
73	Ibid.
74	Ibid.
75	Wood, T. (2004). The case for Chechnya. *New Left Review,* NLR 30. Retrieved from http://newleftreview.org/II/30/tony-wood-the-case-for-chechnya
76	Ibid., p. 34
77	Wyatt, C. (2001, June 16). Retrieved from http://news.bbc.co.uk/2/hi/europe/1392791.stm
78	Ahmed, Nafeez Mosaddeq, The Smashing of Chechnya—An International Irrelevance: A Case Study of the Role of Human Rights in Western Foreign Policy, Islamic Human Rights Commission, London, April 1999.
79	Ibid.
80	Ibid.
81	Ibid.

82	SIPRI's databases. (n.d.). Retrieved from http://www.sipri.org/databases
83	Sakwa, R. (2014). *Frontline Ukraine: Crisis in the Borderlands.* IB Tauris, p. 36.
84	Cockburn, P. (2016, October 21). Compare the coverage of Mosul and East Aleppo and it tells you a lot about the propaganda we consume. Retrieved from http://www.independent.co.uk/voices/iraq-syria-aleppo-mosul-patrick-cockburn-propaganda-we-consume-a7373951.html
85	SIPRI's databases. (n.d.). Retrieved from http://www.sipri.org/databases
86	Ruth Leger Sivard, World Military and Social Expenditures 1981, Leesburg, VA: World Priorities, 1981, p. 8. Cited in Chomsky, N. (2013). *The Footnotes For: Understanding Power: The Indispensible Chomsky.* Chapter 2. The New Press, p. 2. Retrieved from http://www.understandingpower.com/files/AllChaps.pdf
87	Pickering, J., & Kisangani, E. F. (2009). The International Military Intervention dataset: An updated resource for conflict scholars. Journal of peace research,46(4), 589-599.
88	Bove, V., Gleditsch, K. S., & Sekeris, P. G. (2015). "Oil above Water" Economic Interdependence and Third-party Intervention. *Journal of Conflict Resolution*, 0022002714567952.
89	Senate Subcommittee on Security Agreements and Commitments Abroad, Security Agreements and Commitments Abroad, Report to the Senate Foreign Relations Committee, December 21, 1970, 91st Congress, 2nd Session, Washington: U.S. Government Printing Office, 1970, C.I.S.# 70-S382-17, p. 3. Cited in Chomsky, N. (2013). *The Footnotes For: Understanding Power: The Indispensible Chomsky.* Chapter 2. The New Press, p. 2. Retrieved from http://www.understandingpower.com/files/AllChaps.pdf
90	Mearsheimer, J. J. (2001). *The Tragedy of Great Power Politics.* WW Norton & Company, p. 74.
91	Center for Defense Information, "Soviet Geopolitical Momentum: Myth or Menace? Trends of Soviet Influence Around the World From 1945 to 1980," *Defense Monitor,* January 1980, p. 5. Cited in Chomsky, N. (2013). *The Footnotes For: Understanding Power: The Indispensible Chomsky.* Chapter 2. The New Press, p. 2. Retrieved from http://www.understandingpower.com/files/AllChaps.pdf
92	Germany To Shut Uzbek Base. (2016, February 18). Retrieved from http://www.rferl.org/content/uzbekistan-germany-to-shut-base-last-western-in-central-asia/27308248.html
93	SIPRI's databases. (n.d.). Retrieved from http://www.sipri.org/

	databases
94	Ibid.
95	Pickering, J., & Kisangani, E. F. (2009). The International Military Intervention dataset: An updated resource for conflict scholars. *Journal of peace research,* 46(4), 589-599.
96	Turse, N. (2011, January 9). The Pentagon's Planet of Bases. Retrieved from http://www.tomdispatch.com/blog/175338/; Kucera, J. (2011, January 9). At Press Conference, Putin Forgets About Military Bases in Armenia, Moldova, Abkhazia... Retrieved from http://www.eurasianet.org/node/71416 China has no foreign military bases, nor do other SCO members.
97	Turse, N. (2015, october 25). Nick Turse, Success, Failure, and the "Finest Warriors Who Ever Went Into Combat". Retrieved from http://www.tomdispatch.com/blog/176060/tomgram%3A_nick_turse,_success,_failure,_and_the_%22finest_warriors_who_ever_went_into_combat%22/
98	DNI Releases Budget Figure for 2010 National Intelligence Program. (2010, October 28). Retrieved from https://fas.org/irp/news/2010/10/dni102810.html; DOD Releases Military Intelligence Program 2010 Topline Budget. (2010, October 28). Retrieved from https://fas.org/irp/news/2010/10/dod102810.html; SIPRI's databases. (n.d.). Retrieved from http://www.sipri.org/databases
99	Hahn, N. S. C. (2007). Neoliberal imperialism and Pan-African resistance,. *Journal of World-Systems Research*, 13(2), 142-178.
100	World Bank Data.
101	Morozov, V. (2015). *Russia's Postcolonial Identity: A Subaltern Empire in a Eurocentric World*. New York: Palgrave Macmillan, pp. 67-102.
102	Harris, J. (2015). The Confict in Ukraine: Between Two Worlds, p. 21. Retrieved from https://www.academia.edu/30107213/The_Conflict_in_Ukraine_Between_Two_Worlds.docx
103	Morozov, V. (2015). *Russia's postcolonial identity: a subaltern empire in a eurocentric world*. New York: Palgrave Macmillan, pp. 67-102.
104	Ahmed, N. (2015, May 8). The US-Saudi war with OPEC to prolong oil's dying empire. Retrieved from http://www.middleeasteye.net/columns/us-saudi-war-opec-prolong-oil-s-dying-empire-222413845; Klare, M. (2015, November 12). The Geopolitics of Tumbling Oil Prices. Retrieved from http://therealnews.com/t2/index.php?option=com_content&task=view&id=31&Itemid=74&jumival=12752. Interestingly, in the leaked march 2014 minutes from DC leaks, we can also read the following: "Soros then mentioned his idea [that] US sanctions should involve the freezing of the dollar denominated assets of Russian banks and the strategic release of reserves to depress the price of oil

for the next 90 days." We can also read the US ambassador noting that "Secretary Kerry would be interested to hear GS's views on the situation directly, upon return from his trip." Incidentally, Kerry also handled the diplomatic negotiations with Saudi-Arabia and implied, in relation to the drop in oil prices, that they were attempting to hurt the Russian economy (see Ahmed 2015). GS Ukraine Visit. (2014, March), pp. 1, 28. Retrieved from http://soros.dcleaks.com/view?div=europe

105 Giles, C. (2017, February 6). Eurozone economy quietly outshines the US. Retrieved from https://www.ft.com/content/0bbc026a-ea12-11e6-967b-c88452263daf

106 Gros, D., & Mustilli, F. (2016, July 05). The Effects of Sanctions and Counter-Sanctions on EU-Russian Trade Flows. Retrieved from https://www.ceps.eu/publications/effects-sanctions-and-counter-sanctions-eu-russian-trade-flows

107 Russian import embargo: EU export development until July 2015. (2015, September 25). Retrieved from http://ec.europa.eu/agriculture/sites/agriculture/files/russian-import-ban/pdf/2015-09-22-russian-import-ban_en.pdf

108 Szczepański, M. (2015, October). Economic impact on the EU of sanctions over Ukraine conflict, pp. 7-8. Retrieved from http://www.europarl.europa.eu/RegData/etudes/BRIE/2015/569020/EPRS_BRI(2015)569020_EN.pdf

109 Russian import embargo: EU export development until July 2015. (2015, September 25). Retrieved from http://ec.europa.eu/agriculture/sites/agriculture/files/russian-import-ban/pdf/2015-09-22-russian-import-ban_en.pdf

110 Shirov, A. A., Yantovskiy, A. A., & Potapenko, V. V. (2015, February 20). Estimating potential effect of sanctions on economic development in Russia and EU. Retrieved from http://worldeconomicsassociation.net/russia/wp-content/uploads/sites/20/2015/02/Sanstions_fin4_eng.pdf

111 World Bank data.

112 Chomsky, N. (2014, May 1). The Politics of Red Lines: Putin's takeover of Crimea scares U.S. leaders because it challenges America's global dominance. Retrieved from https://chomsky.info/20140501/

113 Muller, R., Hovet, J., & MacSwan, A. (2016, June 20). NATO commander sees no imminent Russian threat to Baltics. Retrieved from http://www.reuters.com/article/us-nato-russia-pavel-idUSKCN0Z616T

114 Charbonneau, L. (2014, March 03). Russia: Yanukovych asked Putin to use force to save Ukraine. Retrieved from http://www.reuters.com/article/us-ukraine-crisis-un-idUSBREA2224720140304

115 Hunt, E. (2017, March 13). The American Empire Isn't in Decline.

Retrieved from https://www.jacobinmag.com/2017/03/obama-trump-mattis-united-states-empire/

116 Robinson, M., & Prentice, A. (2014, May 13). Rebels appeal to join Russia after east Ukraine referendum. Retrieved from http://www.reuters.com/article/us-ukraine-crisis-idUSBREA400LI20140513

117 O'Loughlin, J., Kolossov, V., & Toal, G. (2014). Inside the post-Soviet de facto states: a comparison of attitudes in Abkhazia, Nagorny Karabakh, South Ossetia, and Transnistria. *Eurasian Geography and Economics*, 55(5), 423-456.

118 Sakwa, R. (2014). *Frontline Ukraine: crisis in the borderlands.* IB Tauris, p. 121.

119 Samokhvalov, V. (2014). Russia, the Near Abroad and the West: Lessons from the Moldova-Transdniestria Conflict. *Europe-Asia Studies,* 66(6), pp. 1021-1022.

120 Klußmann, U. (2009, June 15). A Shattered Dream in Georgia: EU Probe Creates Burden for Saakashvili. Retrieved from http://www.spiegel.de/international/world/a-shattered-dream-in-georgia-eu-probe-creates-burden-for-saakashvili-a-630543.html

121 Wilson, S. (2014, March 25). Obama dismisses Russia as 'regional power' acting out of weakness. Retrieved from https://www.washingtonpost.com/world/national-security/obama-dismisses-russia-as-regional-power-acting-out-of-weakness/2014/03/25/1e5a678e-b439-11e3-b899-20667de76985_story.html

122 Sakwa, R. (2014). *Frontline Ukraine: crisis in the borderlands.* IB Tauris, pp. 122-123.

123 Pugliese, D. (2014, September 20). No safeguards stopping Canadian equipment from falling into wrong hands in Ukraine, opposition MPs say. Retrieved from http://news.nationalpost.com/2014/09/20/no-safeguards-stopping-canadian-equipment-from-falling-into-wrong-hands-in-ukraine-opposition-mps-say/; Harper, S. (2014, August 7). Statement by the Prime Minister of Canada announcing security assistance to Ukraine. Retrieved from http://web.archive.org/web/20150324220432/http://pm.gc.ca/eng/news/2014/08/07/statement-prime-minister-canada-announcing-security-assistance-ukraine; Rampton, R., Mason, J., & Stonestreet, J. (2014, June 04). Obama says Poroshenko a wise choice for Ukraine, pledges aid. Retrieved from http://www.reuters.com/article/2014/06/04/us-ukraine-crisis-obama-idUSKBN0EF0P020140604; Nato.int. (2014, September 4). NATO leaders pledge support to Ukraine at Wales Summit. Retrieved from http://www.nato.int/cps/en/natohq/news_112459.htm; Sukhotski, K., Balmforth, R., & Heneghan, T.

(2014, September 14). NATO countries have begun arms deliveries to Ukraine: Defense minister. Retrieved from http://www.reuters.com/article/us-ukraine-crisis-heletey-idUSKBN0H90PP20140914

124 Spaki, J. (2014, June 16). Daily Press Briefing: June 16, 2014. Retrieved from http://www.state.gov/r/pa/prs/dpb/2014/06/227650.htm#UKRAINE

125 Baker, P. (2014, April 19). In Cold War Echo, Obama Strategy Writes Off Putin. Retrieved from http://www.nytimes.com/2014/04/20/world/europe/in-cold-war-echo-obama-strategy-writes-off-putin.html

126 Parry, R. (2014, August 8). Was Putin Targeted for Mid-Air Assassination? Retrieved from http://consortiumnews.com/2014/08/08/was-putin-targeted-for-mid-air-assassination/

127 Gude, H., & Schmid, F. (2014, October 19). Deadly Ukraine Crash: German Intelligence Claims Pro-Russian Separatists Downed MH17. Retrieved from http://www.spiegel.de/international/europe/german-intelligence-blames-pro-russian-separatists-for-mh17-downing-a-997972.html

128 Higgins, E. (2015, October 08). MH17—The Open Source Evidence. Retrieved from https://www.bellingcat.com/news/uk-and-europe/2015/10/08/mh17-the-open-source-evidence/

129 Bennett, B. (2014, July 22). U.S. officials believe attack against Malaysian plane was mistake. Retrieved from http://www.latimes.com/world/europe/la-fg-ukraine-intelligence-us-20140722-story.html

130 Troianovski, A., Alpert, L. I., & Lee, C. E. (2014, July 23). Tragedy Fails to Quiet Ukraine. Retrieved from http://www.wsj.com/articles/pro-russia-rebels-down-two-ukrainian-warplanes-ukraine-army-says-1406117307?mod=WSJ_hp_LEFTTopStories

131 Chomsky, N. (2014, August 14). Outrage. Retrieved from https://chomsky.info/20140814/

132 Pape, R. A. (1997). Why economic sanctions do not work. International Security, 22(2), 90-136.

133 Ibid., p. 107

134 Doctorow, G. (2016, September 20). Making sense of the Russian parliamentary elections of 18 September 2016: A first attempt. Retrieved from http://usforeignpolicy.blogs.lalibre.be/archive/2016/09/20/making-sense-of-the-russian-parliamentary-elections-of-18-se-1153037.html

135 Cohen, S. (2016, September 21). Who Is Making American Foreign Policy-the President or the War Party? Retrieved from https://www.thenation.com/article/who-is-making-american-foreign-policy-the-president-or-the-war-party/

| Chapter Twenty |

DIVISIONS ON THE WESTERN FRONT?

US Secretary of State John Kerry indicated multiple times that there had been disagreements with the EU over the extent of the sanctions regime against Russia.[1] The US eventually even sent a special envoy to convince European countries to take a tougher stance.[2] At this point, it is relevant to return one last time to the leaked phone call between Victoria Nuland and US ambassador Geoffrey Pyatt, where they more or less handpicked the interim government of Ukraine. We noted how Nuland didn't "think Klitsch should go into the government." However, what I have failed to mention before, is that Vitaly Klitschko was closely aligned with Germany. He spoke the language fluently, had met with several German ministers and was even decorated by the German federal government in 2010 for his efforts to improve German-Ukrainian ties. Indeed, these ties were hardly a secret, Klitschko's UDAR party listed Angela Merkel's Christian Democratic Union as a partner on its website. The US intelligence contractor Stratfor explains:

> All the traditional German parties—including the Christian Democratic Union, Social Democratic Party, the Christian Social Union, the Free Democratic Party, the Greens and The Left—have foundations that get funding from the German federal budget and work internationally to strengthen ties to Germany, promote democracy

and strengthen civil society. The two largest political foundations are the Friedrich Ebert Foundation (affiliated with the Social Democratic Party) and the Konrad Adenauer Foundation (affiliated with the Christian Democratic Union), which jointly receive around 250 million euros (around $345 million) annually from the federal government. And while all the German political foundations have programs in Ukraine, the Konrad Adenauer Foundation is the most active. It has the strongest ties to the Ukrainian opposition, particularly the Ukrainian Democratic Alliance for Reform led by Vitaly Klitschko, members of which as recently as November participated in events organized by the Konrad Adenauer Foundation.[3]

It seems clear that, throughout the Ukraine conflict, US and EU agendas have differed. We have seen German and French intelligence officers disagreeing with US 'propaganda,' and even leaking this to the press. The schism is perhaps best demonstrated by the fact that the United States has been absent from all peace negotiations, starting with Yanukovych during Maidan and continuing later with Minsk I and II. In the leaked call with the US ambassador, Victoria Nuland expressed her contempt for Europe very clearly when she told Pyatt, "you know, Fuck the EU." This antagonism between the EU and the United States underlies a fundamental reality: European economies are deeply intertwined with Russia's.[4] As of 2013, the total trade between the two power blocs equaled approximately $330 billion, nearly ten times the size of the US-Russia trade volume. The European Union accounts for roughly half of Russia's imports and exports, and is easily its largest trading partner. Russian exports, in turn, consist mainly of fuel and energy, which are crucial for the functioning of European economies. In fact, these energy relations pre-date the end of the Cold War and even the Perestroika reforms under Gorbachev. The most important pipeline supplying Western Europe with Russian gas was built in the early 80s, despite heavy protest from the Reagan administration, which then included US sanctions against Western Europe.[5] The head of Stratfor—a private intelligence contractor once dubbed the 'shadow CIA' by *Barron* magazine for its close co-operation with the agency—described US policy in relation to the Ukraine crisis as follows:

> For all of the last 100 years Americans have pursued a very consistent foreign policy. Its main goal: to not allow any state to amass too much power in Europe. First, the United States sought to prevent Germany from dominating Europe, then it sought to prevent the USSR from strengthening its influence.
>
> The essence of this policy is as follows: to maintain as long as possible a balance of power in Europe, helping the weaker party, and if the balance is about to be significantly disrupted—to intervene at the last moment. And so, in the case of the First World War, the United States intervened only after the abdication of Nicholas II in 1917, to prevent Germany from gaining ground. And during WWII, the US opened a second front only very late (in June 1944), after it became clear that the Russians were prevailing over the Germans. [This strategy was most explicitly articulated by soon-to-be president Truman in 1941, when he proposed: "If we see that Germany is winning we ought to help Russia and if Russia is winning we ought to help Germany, and that way let them kill as many as possible.]"
>
> What is more, the most dangerous potential alliance, from the perspective of the United States, was considered to be an alliance between Russia and Germany. This would be an alliance

of German technology and capital with Russian natural and human resources.[6]

Nevertheless, to avoid the danger of exaggerating the rift and in order to properly asses its meaning, it's important to point out that the United States has always favored a strong European Union, to be closely aligned with the US agenda. After WW2, the alliance was considered an important market for American corporations and served to overcome animosities, not insignificant after WW2, in the anti-Soviet camp. During the Cold war, Western Europe was heavily reliant on American troops, so US influence was not in jeopardy. To strengthen and maintain its position vis-a-vis the EU, the United States later pushed for the accession of strongly NATO-aligned states, such as the UK, Poland and the Baltic States. Incidentally, French President de Gaulle had publicly vetoed British accession into the EEC in 1963, the predecessor of the EU, provoking the fury of US President Kennedy, who subsequently threatened to withdraw his troops from Europe.[7] De Gaulle called his bluff, and became all the more convinced that Britain was the United States' "Trojan Horse." Only after de Gaulle left office ten years later, was Britain admitted into the EEC. De Gaulle's suspicions proved largely correct: Britain remained closely aligned with the United States both in the financial and security sphere. With regard to Ukraine, it was the only European country to openly train military forces. It is no coincidence that in July 2015, Barack Obama intervened in the British referendum debate, telling the BBC that "having the UK in the European Union gives us much greater confidence about the strength of the transatlantic union."[8]

Another notable 'fifth columnist,' to use de Gaulle's terminology, is the Netherlands. It was extensively praised in a leaked cable from the US ambassador for steering European policy towards the US agenda, among other things.[9] Indeed, Frans Timmermans, the Dutch minister of foreign affairs, joined in on the Cold war rhetoric during the Ukraine crisis with especially notable phrases, given the normally subdued and secular style of

Dutch politics. "Today there is an unholy alliance of anti-EU and anti-American sentiments," he preached in Arlington, USA. But Putin will know that "Our Alliance—as embodied by NATO—is strong."[10] In an extended interview on national television, he told the Dutch people to prepare themselves for an arms race; to get ready for an economic war that could drag the economy back into a recession, one that had barely even passed.[11]

Notably, Europe's Eastern Partnership initiative—which led to the association agreement with Ukraine, and also includes the post-Soviet states of Armenia, Azerbaijan, Belarus, Georgia and Moldova—was designed and proposed by the Polish and Swedish ministers of foreign affairs in 2008, Carl Bildt and Radoslaw Sikorski.[12] Both are fiercely anti-Russian, going so far as to make comparisons between Russia and Nazi-Germany, which were then echoed by several senior US and British politicians, such as Hillary Clinton and David Cameron.[13] In fact, Carl Bildt was one of the founding members of the Committee for the Liberation of Iraq, advocating for the 2003 invasion alongside senior US neo-cons. Sikorski, on the other hand, has lived for years in the United States and the United Kingdom. He's been a British citizen for nearly 20 years, with his citizenship only revoked in 2006 upon becoming minister of defense in Poland. During his time at Oxford, he was taught by the same tutor as former US president Bill Clinton, and was admitted to the same exclusive student society as British prime minister David Cameron. His wife, Anne Applebaum, is an American citizen and journalist. We see a similar pattern in the Baltic States. The current president of Estonia, Toomas Hendrik Ilves, lived most of his life in the United States. He worked for nearly ten years at Radio Free Europe, which was funded by the CIA for 17 years until it was taken over by the US Congress. Valdas Adamkus, the former president of Lithuania, who ruled for ten years, has worked for the US government for 28 years, serving in the Environmental Protection Agency and before that as a senior officer within a US military intelligence unit. Lastly, the former president of Latvia, Vaira Vīķe-Freiberga, who was also re-elected for a second term, was brought up in

Canada. Obviously, the ties of these Eastern European leaders to North America are very strong, and their states have all been at the forefront in "countering the Russian aggression."

In fact, emeritus professor of international relations, Kees van der Pijl, convincingly argues that Europe's Eastern Partnership Initiative was a mediating instruments for the United States "and never was a 'European' endeavour outside the purview of Washington."[14] He documents substantial parallels between the EU agreements and a US State Department intervention blueprint, which was developed by two officials working under Condoleezza Rice, one of whom was a former ambassador in Kiev. The plan targeted 'weaker states' in crisis (including those with ethnic divisions) for far-reaching neoliberal overhauls, in order to "change the very social fabric of a nation."[15] The targeted state would 'share' its 'sovereignty' by signing "a voluntary agreement between recognized national political authorities and an external actor such as another state or a regional or international organization."[16] As van der Pijl explains, "if Brzezinski had drawn the broad contours of a geopolitical reordering of Europe and the post-Soviet sphere, this was the operationalisation of that grand strategy with the help of a hands-on rulebook."[17]

It is no coincidence that the eastward expansion of Europe has always been strongly favored by Washington. Zbigniew Brzezinski, the Democratic Party's leading geopolitical thinker, considered the EU "the Eurasian bridgehead for American power and the potential springboard for the democratic global system's expansion into Eurasia."[18] He explained: "The essential point regarding NATO expansion is that it is a process integrally connected with Europe's own expansion.... Ultimately at stake in this effort is America's long-range role in Europe. A new Europe is still taking shape, and if that new Europe is to remain geopolitically a part of the "Euro-Atlantic" space, the expansion of NATO is essential."[19] Associate professor Gordon Hahn calculated that the new EU member states had taken an average of five years and eight months to accede to NATO, after their first EU association agreement came into force.[20] This process was faster than EU membership. Furthermore, Professor Sakwa notes that since the Lisbon treaty came into effect in 2009—despite having been voted down by referenda in the Netherlands and France—"acceding countries are now required to align their defense and security policy with that of NATO, resulting in the effective "militarization" of the EU."[21] In the case of Ukraine—where EU membership is not in the cards—the US Assistant Secretary of Defense for International Security Affairs, Elissa Slotkin, stated that the Ukrainian army will be interoperable with NATO forces by 2020.[22] As UCLA professor Perry Anderson observes:

> Expansion to the East was piloted by Washington: in every case, the former Soviet satellites were incorporated into NATO, under US command, before they were admitted to the EU. Poland, Hungary and the Czech Republic had joined NATO already in 1999, five years before entry into the Union; Bulgaria and Romania in 2004, three years before entry; even Slovakia, Slovenia and the Baltics, a gratuitous month—just to rub in the symbolic point?—before entry (planning for the Baltics started in 1998). Croatia, Macedonia and Albania are next in line for the same sequence.[23]

The rift between the different European blocs had already become apparent in 2003 over the decision to invade Iraq, which was opposed by Belgium, Germany and France—half of the original members of the EEC. Indeed, the alliance between France and Germany was the very goal of the EEC when it was founded in 1957. In an interview on Dutch television, US secretary of Defense Donald Rumsfeld defended the Iraq invasion:

> Now, you're thinking of Europe as Germany and France. I don't. I think that's old Europe. If you look at the entire NATO Europe today, the center of gravity is shifting to the east. And there are a lot

of new members. And if you just take the list of all the members of NATO and all of those who have been invited in recently—what is it? Twenty-six, something like that?—you're right. Germany has been a problem, and France has been a problem. ... But you look at vast numbers of other countries in Europe. They're not with France and Germany on this, they're with the United States.[24]

Thus, it seems that the head of Stratfor touches upon an elemental reality. Namely, the war in Ukraine serves to keep the EU in line with the wider US agenda. We have seen that, since the Ukraine crisis, the existence and expansion of the NATO alliance has found new legitimation—which remains a pivotal organization for US influence over the EU. Germany and France were also successfully pressured to sanction Russia, even if these remain limited. In addition, the two countries allowed NATO to deploy troops in the Baltic States and to continue EU membership invitations to post-soviet countries. Furthermore, the TTIP negotiations started to prominently feature shale gas exports from the US, reflecting the lifting of a US exports ban.[25] Although American shale gas can hardly replace the entire Russian supply, it will help to make the EU further dependent on the United States, while further isolating Russia. In addition, Germany is now facing a lot of pressure from Eastern Europe to drop its plans for building the Nord Stream 2 pipeline, which would bypass Ukraine as a transit-country for Russian gas, thus depriving the country of its transit fees.[26] The Ukrainian conflict has also sharpened the boundaries of acceptable discourse within Germany, as the intelligentsia has popularized a new pejorative slur, "Putin-versteher," to refer to anyone diverging from the standard anti-Russian line.[27]

Nevertheless, some nuance is definitely necessary. The statement of the Stratfor intelligence analyst—that the US intends to prevent a German-Russian alliance—is obviously a hyperbole, and might say more about the Cold War mindset of US policymakers than actual realities on the ground. Clearly, the widespread worries that were triggered by the election of Donald Trump—particularly about his perceived disinterest in NATO and his preference for normalizing relations with Russia—confirmed that the European intelligentsia has its own interest in perpetuating the cold-war paradigm. Indeed, the EU, and Germany in particular, had spent years supporting pro-Western political factions in Ukraine, despite the polarized state of the country. Furthermore, the EU consistently refused to even talk to Russia in relation to the association agreement, until it was forced to by the specter of war. It was also the EU who refused to provide substantial funds for the reforms embedded in the association agreement, which forced Ukraine to turn to the IMF after Maidan. Internal communications of European officials show they considered the IMF loans and the EU association agreement as part of one package, which was indeed the very reason Yanukovych postponed signing it.[28]

The merging of Western agendas have also been pronounced in the global sphere. What remains perhaps most telling is that Russia, as well as the other BRICS countries, were excluded from both major intercontinental trade agreements involving the EU—TTIP and TISA. It seems that France and Germany are just as committed to extending the Western frontier, but are simply more cautious about damaging their economic relations with Russia. Indeed, Jerry Harris documented in detail how such corporate links limited the extent of possible sanctions, even within the United States.[29] Although US defense contractors have repeatedly bragged to their investors about surging markets in the wake of new hostilities with Russia, they also quietly flip-flopped once to protect their interests.[30] When Congress banned the purchase of Russian rockets, necessary for launching military and intelligence satellites, Boeing and Lockheed Martin started lobbying against the legislation—even with the aid of then-Director of National Intelligence and fierce anti-Russian hawk, James Clapper Jr.[31] As a member of the House Armed Services Committee rightly noted: "some of our biggest defense companies are lobbying on behalf of the Russians. That's a strange position for the defense industry to have."[32]

Clearly, if corporate interests can momentarily turn James Clapper Jr. into a dove, it is no surprise that the much deeper economic links between Russia and the European Union invoked further restrictions on their jingoism. This has evidently little to do with some fundamental divide. Incidentally, Professor Anderson was also skeptical about German and French resistance to the invasion of Iraq, the previous 'major' transatlantic rift.

> Chirac and Schröder [respectively the former French and German heads of state] had a domestic interest in countering the invasion. Each judged their electorates well, and gained substantially — Schröder securing re-election—from their stance. On the other hand, American will was not to be trifled with. So each compensated in deeds for what they proclaimed in words, opposing the war in public, while colluding with it *sub rosa*. Behind closed doors in Washington, France's ambassador Jean-David Levitte—currently diplomatic adviser to Sarkozy—gave the White House a green light for the war, provided it was on the basis of the first generic UN Resolution 1441, as Cheney urged, without returning to the Security Council for the second explicit authorization to attack which Blair wanted, that would force France to veto it. In ciphers from Baghdad, German intelligence agents provided the Pentagon with targets and coordinates for the first US missiles to hit the city, in the downpour of Shock and Awe. Once the ground war began, France provided airspace for USAF missions to Iraq (passage Chirac had denied Reagan's bombing of Libya), and Germany the key transport hub for the campaign. Both countries voted for the UN resolution ratifying the US occupation of Iraq, and lost no time recognizing the client regime patched together

by Washington. ... As for the EU, its choice of a new president of the Commission in 2004 could not have been more symbolic: the Portuguese ruler who hosted Bush, Blair and Aznar at the Azores summit on 16 March 2003 that issued the ultimatum for the assault on Iraq.[33]

Thus, we have seen that European policy—including that of the German and French—quite consistently adapts to American designs, whether on Russia or Iraq. Most crucially, in deciding Russia's place in the post-Cold War order in 1989, Western agendas had converged yet again. Thus we return one more time to the settlement of Eastern Germany and the future of NATO. A balanced account of this diplomatic episode was written by Mary Elise Sarotte, published as an afterward to her Princeton University Press study on post-Cold War Europe, an adapted version of which was published in the pro-establishment journal *Foreign Affairs*.[34] Based on primary documents, most of them recently declassified, she shows that a promise had indeed been made. In the words of US Secretary of State James Baker: "NATO's jurisdiction would not shift one inch eastward from its present position." The West German chancellor elaborated that "such a statement must refer not just to [East Germany], but rather be of a general nature. For example, the Soviet Union needs the security of knowing that Hungary, if it has a change of government, will not become part of the Western Alliance."[35] Based on repeated assurances of this nature, Gorbachev gave what German Chancellor Hermut Kohl called "the green light" for German reunification: a single economic and monetary union was created.

Nevertheless, US President Bush was not pleased and wished to seize what he saw as an opportunity to advance on the Soviets. "To hell with that!," he told the German Chancellor. "We prevailed, they didn't. We can't let the Soviets clutch victory from the jaws of defeat." As Bush sought to claim his Cold war victory, his aims suddenly became more feasible. The Soviet Union's economy was collapsing, and a strategy arose to "bribe the soviets out." West Germany gave fifteen billion Deutsche marks to the Soviet government—and this is how, in essence, the limits on NATO expansion were both promised and later unpromised—not on the basis of morality, but due to power dynamics in the negotiation process. Sarotte elaborates:

> In May 1990, Jack Matlock, the U.S. ambassador to Moscow, reported that Gorbachev was starting to look "less like a man in control and more [like] an embattled leader." The "signs of crisis," he wrote in a cable from Moscow, "are legion: Sharply rising crime rates, proliferating anti-regime demonstrations, burgeoning separatist movements, deteriorating economic performance . . . and a slow, uncertain transfer of power from party to state and from the center to the periphery."
>
> Moscow would have a hard time addressing these domestic problems without the help of foreign aid and credit, which meant that it might be willing to compromise. The question was whether West Germany could provide such assistance in a manner that would allow Gorbachev to avoid looking as though he was being bribed into accepting a reunified Germany in NATO with no meaningful restrictions on the alliance's movement eastward.
>
> Kohl accomplished this difficult task in two bursts: first, in a bilateral meeting with Gorbachev in July 1990, and then, in a set of emotional follow-up phone calls in September 1990. Gorbachev ultimately gave his assent to a united Germany in NATO in exchange for face-saving measures, such as a four-year grace period for removing Soviet troops and some restrictions on both NATO troops and nuclear weapons on former East German territory. He also received

12 billion deutsche marks to construct housing for the withdrawing Soviet troops and another three billion in interest-free credit. What he did not receive were any formal guarantees against NATO expansion.[36]

Another MIT study by Joshua R. Itzkowitz Shifrinson suggests, however, that this chain of events does actually suggest an agreement against NATO expansion.[37] Although it is true that no formal guarantees were issued, this is fairly standard practice in international diplomacy, especially so during the Cold War. For example, even the infamous Cuban missile crisis was resolved through an informal agreement. Shifrinson documents how American and West German officials quite consistently gave the impression that a deal against NATO expansion was actually on the table, all the way until the final reunification of Germany. As such, the formal agreement that no non-German troops would be deployed in Eastern Germany could be understood as a confirmation of such a broader informal understanding.

Shifrinson shows, moreover, that US policymakers were consciously deceitful, privately making plans for US and NATO dominance in the region while suggesting otherwise during the negotiations. Such deceit was no small matter. Then U.S. National Security Adviser Brent Scowcroft recognized that a reunified Germany within NATO would be "the Soviet Union's worst nightmare" and "rip the heart out of the Soviet security system."[38] US assessments even considered the possibility that the Soviet Union would trigger a "World War III scenario" to prevent this outcome.[39] As Gorbachev told Kohl during the negotiations, "When you say that NATO would disintegrate without Germany, this also applies to the Warsaw Pact."[40]

Whatever the exact nature of the broken promise, however, both Shifrinson and Sarotte agree that Gorbachev had proposed a way out of this Cold War dynamic: the formation of a pan-European security arrangement. The United States, which knew some West Europeans might have feared German reunification, made sure this never happened. Bush communicated with his Western European counterparts, assuring French President Mitterand in a letter that "it is difficult to visualize how a European collective security arrangement including Eastern Europe, and perhaps even the Soviet Union, would have the capability to deter threats to Western Europe." Sarotte continues:

> As it happened, the next month, Gorbachev proposed just such a pan-European arrangement, one in which a united Germany would join both NATO and the Warsaw Pact, thus creating one massive security institution. Gorbachev even raised the idea of having the Soviet Union join NATO. "You say that NATO is not directed against us, that it is simply a security structure that is adapting to new realities," Gorbachev told Baker in May, according to Soviet records. "Therefore, we propose to join NATO." Baker refused to consider such a notion, replying dismissively, "Pan-European security is a dream."
>
> … By design, Russia was left on the periphery of a post–Cold War Europe. A young KGB officer serving in East Germany in 1989 offered his own recollection of the era in an interview a decade later, in which he remembered returning to Moscow full of bitterness at how "the Soviet Union had lost its position in Europe." His name was Vladimir Putin, and he would one day have the power to act on that bitterness.[41]

This history underscores the obvious anti-Russian nature of NATO-expansion, which was also the very founding goal of the security alliance. Indeed, Tsygankov documented the persistence of Russophobia in US policy circles throughout the post-cold war period and the continued refusal to offer Russia NATO membership, as the country was portrayed as an eternal expansionist threat. The latter was often explicitly seized upon by the "entrepreneurs who lobbied for NATO expansion," as they "argued that it was essential to contain Russia, rather than merely improve security in Europe."[42]

Endnotes

1   U.S. Department of State. (2015, April 29). Secretary Kerry Delivers Remarks With EU High Representative Mogherini. Retrieved from https://www.youtube.com/watch?v=ALoA4svY3po
2   Deutsche Wirtschafts Nachrichten. (2015, December 5). US-Sonderbeauftragter soll EU bei Russland-Sanktionen auf Linie bringen. Retrieved from http://deutsche-wirtschafts-nachrichten.de/2015/12/05/us-sonderbeauftragter-soll-eu-bei-russland-sanktionen-auf-linie-bringen/
3   German Involvement With the Ukrainian Opposition. (2013, December 12). Retrieved from https://www.stratfor.com/analysis/german-involvement-ukrainian-opposition
4   Who will threatened sanctions hit most? US-EU-Russia trade in numbers. (2014, March 4). Retrieved from https://www.rt.com/business/us-eu-russia-sanctions-590/
5   Wikipedia. (n.d.). Urengoy–Pomary–Uzhgorod pipeline. Retrieved from https://en.wikipedia.org/wiki/Urengoy–Pomary–Uzhgorod_pipeline; Greer, B. I., & Russell, J. L. (1982). European Reliance on Soviet Gas Exports: The Yamburg-Urengoi Natural Gas Project. The Energy Journal, 3(3), 15-37.; Hogselius, P., Åberg, A., & Kaijser, A. (2013). Natural Gas in Cold War Europe: The Making of a Critical Infrastructure. In The Making of Europe's Critical Infrastructure (pp. 27-61). Palgrave Macmillan UK.
6   Chernenko, E., & Gabuev, A. (2015, January 17). 'In Ukraine, U.S interests are incompatible with the interests of the Russian Federation' Stratfor chief George Friedman on the roots of the Ukraine crisis. Retrieved from http://us-russia.org/2902-in-ukraine-us-interests-are-incompatible-with-the-interests-of-the-russian-federation-stratfor-chief-george-friedman-on-the-roots-of-the-ukraine-crisis.html
7   Trachtenberg, M. (Ed.). (2003). *Between Empire and Alliance: America and Europe during the Cold War*. Rowman & Littlefield Publishers, p. 106.
8   BBC. (2015, July 24). Obama urges UK to stay in European Union. Retrieved from http://www.bbc.com/news/uk-politics-33647154

9	US embassy cables: Why Holland is so important to US. (2010, December 15). Retrieved from http://www.theguardian.com/world/us-embassy-cables-documents/38987
10	Timmermans, F. (2014, April 30). Toespraak minister Timmermans bij Arlington: Finding Leo Lichten - A Tribute to our Liberators. Retrieved from https://www.rijksoverheid.nl/documenten/toespraken/2014/04/30/toespraak-minister-timmermans-arlington-finding-leo-lichten-a-tribute-to-our-liberators
11	Eén op Eén. (2014, May 13). Frans Timmermans. Retrieved from http://www.npo.nl/een-op-een/13-05-2014/KN_1657805
12	Playing East against West. (2013, November 23). Retrieved from http://www.economist.com/news/europe/21590585-success-eastern-partnership-depends-ukraine-playing-east-against-west
13	Judah, B. (2014, October 19). Putin's Coup. Retrieved from http://www.politico.com/magazine/story/2014/10/vladimir-putins-coup-112025; Kakabadze, D., & Allnut, L. (2008, October 3). Carl Bildt Persona Non Grata In Russia? Retrieved from http://www.rferl.org/content/Swedish_FM_Persona_Non_Grata_In_Russia_/1293795.html; Jones, O. (2014, September 03). David Cameron and the cynicism of comparing Putin to Hitler. Retrieved from http://www.theguardian.com/commentisfree/2014/sep/03/david-cameron-cynicism-comparing-vladimir-putin-adolf-hitler-ukraine; Ruckur, P. (2014, March 5). Hillary Clinton says Putin's actions are like 'what Hitler did back in the '30s'. Retrieved from https://www.washingtonpost.com/news/post-politics/wp/2014/03/05/hillary-clinton-says-putins-action-are-like-what-hitler-did-back-in-the-30s/
14	Pijl, K., Van der. (2016, June). Capitalist Discipline and the Three Cold Wars, p. 34. Retrieved from http://www.academia.edu/26566085/Capitalist_Discipline_and_the_Three_Cold_Wars
15	Cited in ibid, p. 37.
16	Cited in ibid, p. 34.
17	Cited in ibid, p. 33.
18	Brzezinski, Z. (1998). *The Grand Chessboard: American primacy and its geostrategic imperatives.* Basic Books, p. 74.
19	Ibid, pp. 79-80.
20	Hahn, G. (2016, January 21). The Russian-American 'Reset', NATO Expansion, and the Making of the Ukrainian Crisis. Retrieved from http://gordonhahn.com/2016/01/21/report-the-russian-american-reset-nato-expansion-and-the-making-of-the-ukrainian-crisis/#_ftn1
21	Sakwa, R. (2015, September 21). The New Atlanticism: An Alternative Atlantic Security System. Retrieved from http://eng.globalaffairs.ru/number/The-New-Atlanticism-17695

22	U.S. to provide aid to Ukrainian Armed Forces to ensure NATO interoperability. (2015, November 6). Retrieved from http://en.interfax.com.ua/news/general/302007.html
23	Anderson, P. (2009). *The New Old World*. Verso Books, p. 69.
24	Secretary Rumsfeld Briefs at the Foreign Press Center. (2003, January 22). Retrieved from http://web.archive.org/web/20100302014308/http://www.defense.gov/transcripts/transcript.aspx?transcriptid=1330
25	Klein, N. (2014, April 10). Why US fracking companies are licking their lips over Ukraine. Retrieved from http://www.theguardian.com/commentisfree/2014/apr/10/us-fracking-companies-climate-change-crisis-shock-doctrine; Smedley, T. (2015, August 05). TTIP: What does the transatlantic trade deal mean for renewable energy? Retrieved from http://www.theguardian.com/public-leaders-network/2015/aug/05/ttip-free-trade-deal-renewable-energy-transatlantic-partnership-eu-us
26	Jakóbik, W. (2016, February 16). Time is on the side of Nord Stream 2's opponents. Retrieved from http://neweasterneurope.eu/articles-and-commentary/1890-time-is-on-the-side-of-nord-stream-2-s-opponents
27	Doctorow, G. (2016, December 25). German Resistance to Russia Detente. Retrieved from http://www.strategic-culture.org/news/2016/12/25/german-resistance-russia-detente.html
28	Mast, J., Beunders, S., Beek, B., Van, & Ploeg, C., De. (2016, April 04). Hoe de overheid intern communiceert over het associatieverdrag met Oekraïne. Retrieved from https://www.ftm.nl/artikelen/overheid-intern-associatieverdag
29	Harris, J. (2016). *Global Capitalism and the Crisis of Democracy*, Edition: First, Chapter: The Conflict in Ukraine: Between Two Worlds, Publisher: Clarity Press, pp.143-165.
30	Fang, L. (2016, August 19). U.S. Defense Contractors Tell Investors Russian Threat Is Great for Business. Retrieved from https://theintercept.com/2016/08/19/nato-weapons-industry/
31	Harris, J. (2016). *Global Capitalism and the Crisis of Democracy*, Edition: First, Chapter: The Conflict in Ukraine: Between Two Worlds, Publisher: Clarity Press, pp.143-165, p. 161.
32	Ibid, p. 161.
33	Anderson, P. (2009). *The New Old World.* Verso Books, pp. 71-72.
34	Sarotte, M. E. (2014). A Broken Promise?. *Foreign Affairs*, 93(5), 90-97.
35	Cited in ibid. We have very few quotes of the actual closed-door negotiations with Gorbachev. Therefore, interpretation is necessarily dependent on statements made between Western officials about the talks. That also goes for this quote. More of such evidence on the nature of the negotiations are also offered by Shifrinson (2016).

36 Ibid.
37 Shifrinson, J. R. I. (2016). Deal or no deal? The end of the cold war and the US offer to limit Nato expansion. International Security, 40(4), 7-44.
38 Cited in ibid, p. 20.
39 Cited in ibid, p.20.
40 Cited in ibid, p. 28.
41 Sarotte, M. E. (2014). A Broken Promise?. *Foreign Affairs*, 93(5), 90-97.
42 Tsygankov, A. P. (2013). The Russia-NATO mistrust: Ethnophobia and the double expansion to contain "the Russian Bear". *Communist and Post-Communist Studies*, 46(1), 179-188, p. 187.

| Chapter Twenty-One |

COLD WAR POLITICS IN THE AGE OF TRUMP

Despite NATO's anti-Russian tendencies, we have also seen that Vladimir Putin is not interested in challenging Western imperialism. Rather, Russia wants its 'rightful place' as a regional power in a multi-polar world. It is no coincidence that Russian officials regularly defend their actions by pointing to the similarities in Western doctrines.[1] In fact, it is exactly this co-operative stance that has won Putin a level of sympathy in some elite circles within the US.

Although Trump has posed himself as an anti-establishment figure, his cabinet has become by far the richest in history—with factions of Big Oil, Wall Street, the Military Industrial Complex and the far-right especially well represented.[2] Henry Kissinger was advising Trump during the formation of his cabinet; an effort supported by a number of neocon officials from the Bush administration, such as Dick Cheney, Robert Gates, Condoleeza Rice and Stephen Hadley.[3] All of these figures endorsed Trump's most 'pro-Russian' cabinet pick: multi-millionaire and former CEO of ExxonMobil, now Secretary of State, Rex Tillerson. The man had previously secured an agreement with Russia over a $300 billion oil drilling operation in the Arctic; was decorated in 2013 with the Russian Order of Friendship by Putin, and was against the anti-Russian sanctions in the wake of the Ukraine crisis. Notably, the whole idea of appointing Tillerson was pushed by the aforementioned neo-cons in the first place—not Trump, and all of them have corporate ties to ExxonMobil.[4] So does Tillerson's close friend, James Baker, who served in the Reagan and Bush senior administrations.

It is no coincidence that some realists have been voicing doubts about the US stance towards Russia from the very start of the conflict in Ukraine. Henry Kissinger, for example, urged co-operation with Russia in the *Washington Post* as early as March 2014.[5] Mearsheimer, on the other hand, argued in *Foreign Affairs* that NATO triggered the crisis and that the US should focus on 'containing' China, rather than a decaying power such as Russia.[6] Indeed, the European sanctions over Ukraine forced Russia to diversify its energy relations, leading to its signing a major 30-year $400-billion gas deal with China—two countries that are still mending their ties after decades of hostility.[7]

After his inauguration, Trump spared no time in announcing new, largely unprovoked sanctions against Iran, which also included two Chinese companies and three Chinese individuals.[8] According to *The New York Times*, the administration had even planned to raid an Iranian navy ship residing in international waters—potentially the start of actual military confrontations—a plan that was fortunately cancelled after it leaked.[9] Trump has stacked his administration with anti-Iran and anti-China hawks, whose rhetoric is steering towards a clear pro-war line.[10] In fact, one of Trump's closest advisors, the far-right extremist Steve Bannon, was on the radio in March 2016 predicting that: "we're going to war in the South China Sea in five to 10 years."[11] Trump is rapidly accelerating a process that started under Obama, the former president who oversaw the militarization of China's borders in his grand "pivot to Asia."[12]

These militaristic stances also threaten a détente with Russia itself, since Russia has alliances with both China and Iran through, among other affiliations, the aforementioned Shanghai Co-operation Organization. According to senior US, European and Arab officials, Trump has already been attempting to sway Russia into breaking with Iran.[13] Yet the Kremlin has made it clear that it's not willing to sacrifice its relations on the altar of American threat-diplomacy. The chairman of the International

Affairs Committee of Russia's Federation Council, Konstantin Kosachev, for example, argued that "along with the new team's anti-Chinese initiatives, it [anti-Iranian moves] could have a strong negative influence on Russian-American relations."[14]

Trump's first overtures towards Russia have also been underwhelming. While massive military buildup and NATO military exercises continued around Russia's borders, Trump offered to make the removal of sanctions dependent on an agreement over the reduction in nuclear stockpiles. Not only does this proposal ignore the vast disparities in conventional military power, such negotiations would necessarily be limited if the missile-defense shields are not on the table. The President's recent remarks about nuclear weapons don't spark confidence in good-faith negotiations either. Trump has repeatedly claimed that the START nuclear treaty with Russia was a 'bad deal' for the US—something he reportedly also told Putin during their first phone call—pronounced himself ready for an 'arms race' and favored "unpredictability" in his use of nuclear weapons, not unlike Nixon's madman theory.[15] Unsurprisingly then, Trump's nuclear offer was met with a swift rebuke from the Russian state. More precisely, Russia was willing to negotiate nuclear agreements, but not with the sanctions used as leverage.[16]

To add insult to injury, the second 'pro-Russian' Trump appointment, National Security advisor Michael Flynn, reportedly favored NATO expansion in Montenegro.[17] Flynn's advice might very well be adopted by the Trump administration, despite the fact that more Montenegro citizens consider NATO a threat rather than a protection, according to a 2017 Gallup poll.[18] Indeed, although much has been made about Trump's supposed anti-NATO stance, such commentaries necessarily quote him out of context. Trump has actually been very consistent and explicit about his stance on NATO: the other side of the Atlantic needs to start paying up.[19] Trump's off the cuff remarks about potentially leaving the alliance were always explicitly used as leverage to achieve that end. EU countries fail to spend at least 2% of their GDP on the military, a target stipulated in NATO agreements and only met by seven out of 28 member states.[20] No wonder that even the anti-Russian and Hawkish Lithuanian Defense Minister, Raimundas Karoblis, concurred that: "Mr. Trump was very right to send messages during the election campaign that Europe needs to invest more in defense ... It's really a wake-up call for all European Union member states."[21] Rather than "abolishing" NATO then, it seems Trump is only further militarizing the alliance. That includes the United States itself. Trump's first federal budget proposal planned to increase military expenditure by a whopping $54 billion, more than 80 percent of the entire Russian military budget![22]

Finally, a number of crucial cabinet-level positions—such as the Secretary of Defense and CIA director—have been filled by fiercely anti-Russian hawks.[23] It is no surprise that both the Russian administration and public looked towards the Trump presidency with a healthy dose of suspicion.[24] Although much has been made of the exchanges between Putin and Trump during the American election campaign, Putin's calling Trump a 'colorful' figure is hardly a resounding endorsement. Putin has also complimented Obama on multiple occasions, as a simple matter of courtesy, and he even made the effort to correct Trump to say he never called the man "brilliant."[25] Nor is it often recognized that there was a broad public debate within Russia on which presidential candidate would be better for the country. If some Russian analysts preferred a Trump presidency, and indeed there were plenty that did, this was often because they considered him the lesser of two evils, an argument that must sound awfully familiar to Clinton supports. Indeed, Trump's endorsements of Putin have been equally exaggerated. As Stephen Cohen rightly notes:

> All Trump has said in this regard is that Putin is "a strong leader" and "smart" and that it would be good "to cooperate with Russia" These are empirically true statements. They pale in comparison with, for example, the warm words of FDR about Stalin, Nixon about Brezhnev, and particularly President Clinton about Russian

President Boris Yeltsin, whom he compared favorably with George Washington, Abraham Lincoln, and FDR. Only against the backdrop of unrelenting US media demonizing of Putin could Trump's "praise" be considered "lavish." Unlike virtually every other mainstream American politician and media outlet, Trump simply refused to vilify Putin—as in declining to characterize him as "a killer," for which there is also no evidence.[26]

Yet whether US-Russian relations improve is not solely dependent upon the Trump cabinet. Equally important is the level of elite opposition to any kind of détente, which reached a fever pitch as Obama was poised to leave office. US intelligence agencies, in a concerted effort with the US media establishment, attempted to discredit Trump's legitimacy by arguing that "Russia hacked the U.S. election."[27] Such rhetorical framing has caused half of Clinton voters to believe that Russia actually tampered with the vote tallies, a claim that none of even the most extreme propagandists has dared to make explicitly.[28] Ironically, however, serious election fraud has occurred quite systemically in the United States, through the voter disenfranchisement strategies of the Republican Party. There is overwhelming evidence to suggest that the Republicans would not have won the 2000, 2004 and 2016 Presidential elections without these efforts.[29]

The integrity of US elections is hardly the concern of the US deep state which nonetheless, more specifically, peddled the story that Russia hacked and subsequently leaked e-mails from the Democratic National Committee (DNC), supposedly to swing the elections in Trump's favor. The leaks were actually authentic, and it is certainly notable that the content, some of it explicitly about the integrity of the *primary* elections, received much less attention than the sourcing of the DNC e-mails.[30] Nor was much attention paid to an investigation by *Politico*, which found that the Ukrainian embassy had, among other things, co-operated extensively with the DNC in an investigation of Trump's campaign manager, Paul

Manafort.[31] Indeed, Manafort was compelled to resign over the revelations; just like the four DNC officials who were implicated in the leaked e-mails. Yet US government responses were markedly different in both cases. After the DNC leaks, Obama expelled 35 Russian diplomats; shut down two of their real estate compounds; sanctioned two Russian intelligence agencies, including some of its officials; threatened taking covert actions against Russia; called the hack an act of 'armed conflict' and delivered the message over a Red-phone system that was initially established for nuclear emergencies; the first time Obama had ever used the line.[32] Yet the Ukrainian meddling—admittedly, less serious than a hacking operation—passed without as much as a comment from the US government. Overall, however, it is unlikely that either of these cases made a big difference. As Chomsky rightly observes:

> Much of the world must be astonished—if they are not collapsing in laughter—while watching the performances in high places and in media concerning Russian efforts to influence an American election, a familiar US government specialty as far back as we choose to trace the practice. There is, however, merit in the claim that this case is different in character: By US standards, the Russian efforts are so meager as to barely elicit notice.[33]

Indeed, such double standards become obvious even when considering one of the tamer cases of US election meddling: the re-election of Boris Yeltsin in 1996, Russia.[34] His election campaign was secretly guided by a number of US advisers, revealed only after the fact in *Time* magazine.[35] Among other things, these US consultants urged Yeltsin to aggressively use his leverage over state-run media so that "Russia's television became a virtual arm of the Yeltsin campaign."[36] The Russian president also received a major $10.2 billion loan-guarantee from the IMF starting 1996, with some $4 billion paid out during the first year.[37] The cash injection allowed Yeltsin to pay some $2.8 billion in back wages and to temporarily raise social spending in the run-up to the elections. *The New York Times* further writes that: "In announcing the three-year loan, [IMF representative] Mr. Camdessus put the Russian electorate on notice that the fund would cut off the money if the Communists came to power and abandoned the reforms."[38] Even these efforts, however, failed to sufficiently boost Yeltsin's popularity, which is why he reverted to large-scale vote-rigging on the day of the elections. European and US officials subsequently pressured the OSCE to hide its findings of massive electoral fraud. This was revealed only 15 years later by the former head of the OSCE's monitoring mission in Russia, Michael Meadowcroft.[39] So it happened that Yeltsin miraculously overcame his single-digit approval ratings at the start of the campaign. Clearly, the publication of some authentic e-mails from a party office would have been the least of anyone's concerns in 1996 Russia.

Notably, both Wikileaks and independent US intelligence veterans have contested the truthfulness of the Russian hack story, to say nothing of its limited relevance.[40] The Veteran Intelligence Professionals for Sanity (VIPS) argue that the e-mails must have come from an insider leak, rather than a hacking operation.[41] This was echoed by former UK ambassador Craig Murray, who even claims to know the identity of the US official that leaked the e-mails.[42] According to VIPS, the NSA has the capability to trace and publish precise and conclusive evidence for a hacking operation, "without any danger to sources and methods."[43] Indeed, that is exactly what the US government did when, in 2014, it published a 56-page indictment of a team of Chinese hackers, all of whom were accused by name.[44] For now, however, all of the supplied evidence concerning Russia has been either circumstantial, hearsay or "classified."[45] In its highly publicized report, the Office of the Director of National Intelligence—with input from the CIA, FBI and NSA (the latter most important agency expressed a lower "moderate confidence" in the claims)—presented only conclusions, assessments and statements, rather than any new evidence. This was duly noted even by some of Putin's fiercest opponents, and especially notable since the White House promised to make "as much of it public as they possibly can."[46]

In fact, the report's annex on Russia Today was about as long as the main section dealing with the Russian hacking claims. The annex was also embarrassingly dated, stemming from 2012, and managed to name a show that had been off the air for two years. (Incidentally, the show's host used her air time to denounce the annexation of Crimea).[47] Ironically, the US agencies also repeated the long-debunked and exaggerated claims made by Russia Today about its audience reach, peddled by the channel to justify its funding from the Russian state. As a September 2015 investigation by the *Daily Beast* pointed out:

> Of the top 100 most-watched over five years, 81 percent—344 million views—went to videos of natural disasters, accidents, crime, and natural phenomena. RT's political news videos, featuring the content by which it seeks to shape Western opinion and thus justify its existence, accounted for a mere 1 percent of its total YouTube exposure, with fewer than 4 million views. ...
>
> RT Documentary, cited as one of the brand's least popular YouTube channels, got an average of 200 to 300 views per video in 2013. The Daily Beast found that now, only about 100 of RT Documentary's videos have had more than 10,000 views. Many of the most-watched are part of a graphic birthing series called "newborn Russia."
> [A leaked 2013 report of the now defunct RT-competitor, RIA Novosti, documented that performance on cable television was hardly better, concluding that] ... 'RT names its competitors the news channels CNN, Fox, BBC, CNBC, MSNBC, Sky and also channels funded by governments —Al Jazeera and CCTV, ... But compared to the leading news channels on the distribution network, RT does not bear comparison with the others on the sizes of the audiences claimed—the

others are watched by tens of millions of people a day, and RT by tens of thousands."

RT's ratings in Europe and the United States seem to have improved significantly since that time, easily surpassing Al Jazeera—the network that was demonized and bombed during the Afghanistan and Iraq invasions, and whose US office shut down in 2016—but RT remains far behind all top domestic news channels.[48]

Like Al Jazeera, the channel offers much needed alternative perspectives.[49] If you take a look at the US intelligence annex on Russia Today, for example, it mentions a whole range of supposedly sinister topics that are completely legitimate to report on: "allege[d] widespread infringements of civil liberties, police brutality, and drone use ... criticism of the US economic system, US currency policy, alleged Wall Street greed, and the US national debt ... RT runs anti-fracking programming, highlighting environmental issues and the impacts on public health."[50] Notably, the report also wrongly claims that RT served as a pro-Trump outlet. Some examples of RT programme-names can easily dispel this notion:

> "Dictator Trump Threatens Free Speech," "Why Trump's Cabinet Is a Basket of Deplorables," "How Trump Could Bring on the Crash of 2016," "Does Trump Mean the End of the Internet as We Know It?," "Why Trump's Win Is a Koch Coup Against Our Democracy" and "Is Donald Trump the Master of BS?"—to name a few.[51]

There was only one candidate who received fairly consistent favorable coverage, Bernie Sanders.[52] This is quite remarkable considering some of Sanders' official policy positions: "to temper Russian aggression, we must freeze Russian government assets all over the world, and encourage international corporations with huge investments in Russia to divest from that nation's increasingly hostile political aims.

… The United States must collaborate to create a unified stance with our international allies in order to effectively address Russian aggression."[53] Clearly, RT is anti-establishment above anything else, and some of its hosts are among the most reputable of Western dissidents, such as the former *New York Times* war correspondent Chris Hedges, who resigned after being formally reprimanded by his newspaper for critiquing the invasion of Iraq—not inside the *NYT*, but during a speech he gave on a college campus.[54]

All of this did not stop Western media from hysterical reporting about "Russian propaganda." In January 2017, for example, *The New York Times* mentioned "Russian" or "Kremlin propaganda" more than once a day on average, including in five front-page stories.[55] The most viral article, however, was published by the *Washington Post* in November 2016, titled "Russian Propaganda Effort Helped Spread 'Fake News' During Election, Experts Say." The article claims that "stories planted or promoted by the disinformation campaign were viewed more than 213 million times."[56] The problem? Nearly all of these news sites had no link to the Russian state whatsoever. The list was compiled by an anonymous internet group, PropOrNot, and included nearly any medium—from left to right—that challenged the dominant narrative pushed by NATO. As Greenwald and Norton noted: "Basically, everyone who isn't comfortably within the centrist Hillary Clinton/Jeb Bush spectrum is guilty."[57] The *Post* eventually recognized that it could not "vouch for the validity of PropOrNot's findings," but this correction was not promoted— not even by as much as a tweet from the writer—and therefore failed to reach a significant, let alone mass audience.[58]

Notably, one US senator's office had aided PropOrNot in publicizing its story because, as one spokesman put it, "there has been bipartisan interest in these kind of Russian efforts, including interference in elections, for some time now."[59] Indeed, similar to Ukraine, in December 2016 the senate passed a "Countering Foreign Propaganda and Disinformation Act," which allocated an additional $160 million to address both "state and non-state propaganda and disinformation efforts aimed at undermining

United States national security interests."⁶⁰ This comes on top of other US propaganda efforts which, as I've already noted, had been outspending known Russian programs by a factor of 200 to one.⁶¹ Not coincidentally, the new 2016 bill was introduced by two senators well connected to Ukraine and the Ukrainian UCCA lobby within the United States. Similar to the Western backing of Israel, it seems security ties have a led to a cross-fertilization of repressive strategies.⁶²

The narrative of losing an information war against Russia has firmly taken hold across the entire Western world. Indeed, the European Union and Germany announced new counter-propaganda programs of their own.⁶³ Both sides of the Atlantic are also considering censorship of "fake news" on social media to counter supposed 'filter bubbles' and 'echo chambers' where opposing views would be absent. Yet there is very little evidence to support this theory, apart for some sections within the ideological fringes.⁶⁴ An extensive study by Alcott and Genskow estimates that the average "fake news" story reaches about 1.2 percent of Americans, only half of whom believe them.⁶⁵ That makes the recent "fake news" phenomenon about as prevalent as holocaust denial in 1994 USA, and significantly less relevant than a whole range of other historical conspiracy theories.⁶⁶ This is not to say that "fake news" was irrelevant for the election campaign; half of Trump voters, for example, believed the published Podesta e-mails talked about pedophilia and human-trafficking (something never promoted by Russia Today, incidentally).⁶⁷ Yet the real question is why Trump was able to win the elections with a quarter of eligible voters voting for him; fewer votes than both McCain and Romney received in 2008 and 2012 respectively. Nor are Trump's lies about millions of illegal voters so different from Reagan's rhetoric about "crack babies" and "super predators" (the latter was also embraced by Hillary Clinton), or his denial of the aids epidemic.⁶⁸

Perhaps more importantly, however, censorship of "fake news" will not be neutral or objective. Not only is the whole issue being put on the agenda primarily by the extreme center—which, as shown, peddles more than enough "fake news" of their own—

government links to social media censorship have been extensively documented, and will likely have a tremendous impact on the interpretation and implementation of "fake news" guidelines.[69] In fact, Facebook has already announced a test-run for such a policy in the United States, in partnership with the International Fact-Checking Network (IFCN), whose funders include all the usual suspects: the National Endowment for Democracy, the Open Society Foundation and the Omidyar Network, among others.[70] With the exception of Climate Feedback, all of the US-based IFCN signatories have been discredited by selection bias, erroneous fact-checking or a lack of rigorous standards.[71]

To its credit, PolitiFact acknowledges the inevitability of human error, subjectivity and that "reasonable people can disagree" with its rulings.[72] Indeed, even the IFCN signatories have regularly disagreed amongst each other (and PolitiFact once even with itself).[73] Yet this begs the question why PolitiFact would want to be the co-arbiter on what nearly two billion Facebook users deserve to see—that's one in four people across the globe, half of whom use the network for consuming news.[74] Facebook is not planning to censor stories outright, but rather to reduce their traffic by lowering them in people's newsfeed. There are indications that this has already happened to Craig Murray, the former UK ambassador who testified that he knew the alleged leaker of the DNC mails, who saw his Facebook and Twitter traffic make a sudden and steep drop in December 2016.[75]

There have also been widespread allegations of Russian ties to political parties in Europe, including hysteria over the potential integrity of the 2017 elections in France, Germany, the Netherlands and potentially Italy.[76] This is mainly because there are serious contenders in favor of easing relations with Russia.[77] US intelligence agencies have even announced an investigation into Russian infiltration efforts inside the European Union.[78] Indeed, according to the *Washington Post*, among others, we have already seen such Russian meddling during the 2016 Dutch consultative referendum, which saw two-thirds of voters reject the EU association agreement with Ukraine. The agreement has already been ratified by the lower house of parliament regardless of the no-vote, although it did lead to negotiations on the interpretation of a number of political clauses. This included a guarantee that the agreement "does not contain an obligation for the Union or its Member States to provide collective security guarantees or other military aid or assistance to Ukraine."[79]

Once the referendum campaign started, foreign funds did indeed get involved, but these were not coming from Russia. George Soros' Open Society Foundation (OSF), for example, publicly invested 200.000 euros in the yes campaign.[80] The aforementioned leaked OSF documents actually suggest the figure to be 700,000 euros, which would match the total amount of subsidies offered by the Dutch state for each side of the campaign.[81] The Ukrainian state and civil society also joined in a major concerted effort, which one official called the "largest informational campaign in the history of our independence."[82] As an example, Myroshnychenko mentions the creation of a campaign website that got three million views, in a country of just 17 million.[83] Another Ukrainian official earlier elaborated on a "variety of pre-election campaigns" by the Foreign ministry, stating that "there will be campaigns in social networks. There will also be public campaigns. I do not know the size of the billboards, but they will also be part of the campaign. There are going to be cultural events, information campaigns and 'interpersonal contacts' with the involvement of opinion leaders and stars of show business."[84]

On the other hand, a *NYT* investigation into Russian meddling efforts was unable to unearth anything noteworthy. The article therefore sensationalized its finding that at least two individual Russians—one of whom actually grew up in Donbass, has a Ukrainian passport and made a career in Kiev, albeit with some ties to the Russian establishment—had actively campaigned in the "Ukrainian team" of the Dutch Socialist Party, advocating a strongly pro-Kremlin line.[85] These mere two (!) individuals were then absurdly credited with having "tilted a Dutch vote." As the article itself, however, was also forced to admit: "no one has yet come up with concrete evidence that the Russian state, rather than individual Russians, is working to skew the election, and many wonder why Moscow would even bother trying to do so."[86]

So how exactly does this justify the *Post's* headline claiming "the Dutch just showed the world how Russia influences Western European elections"? Anne Applebaum—wife of the aforementioned Radoslaw Sikorski, who was responsible for Europe's Eastern Partnership Initiative, something the *Post* fails to mention—cites a poll to support her argument:

> 59 percent of those who voted against the treaty listed, as an important motivation, the fact that Ukraine is corrupt; 19 percent believed that Ukraine was responsible for the crash of MH-17, the plane that Russian separatists shot down over Ukraine in 2014 [with 193 Dutch citizens on board]; 34 percent believed that the treaty would guarantee Ukraine's membership in the European Union. Of those three points, the second two are certainly false. The first, while true, is hardly a rational argument against a treaty designed to reduce corruption in Ukraine.[87]

More extensive research by the Foundation for Dutch Electoral Research (SKON) confirmed that the two most cited motivations for a no vote were corruption and potential EU membership.[88] Yet there are still some major problems with Applebaum's assertions. Firstly, the notion that the treaty has been ineffective in tackling corruption is not just promoted by "Russian propaganda channels," but even by the European Court of Auditors itself.[89] This is clearly no proof of Russian influence; nor is the fear of potential EU membership. I did a brief survey of some Russia Today articles during the campaign and found plenty that mentioned very explicitly that the association agreement would not lead to EU membership.[90] This is no surprise, since this distortion has long been propagated by none other than the Ukrainian government itself—to make the agreement sound more attractive to its population—something RT and the Russian government have long had the pleasure of debunking.[91] Indeed, the Dutch No campaigners were citing these very Maidan politicians to prove their claims about EU membership.[92]

Finally, Applebaum's treatment of MH17 is simply a complete distortion. Not only was it among the least (7th) cited motivations for a no vote (the survey allowed for multiple choices), but the option she cites only mentioned "because of MH17."[93] Pertaining to this topic, a media study only found an argument (with a mere 0.6% frequency) that people should vote "no" due to remaining "uncertainties about the attack."[94] This was before the release of the official investigation, a time when even the Dutch state refrained from prematurely identifying the culprits. In fact, the prime minister has remained cautious to this very day, presumably to ensure international co-operation.[95] Furthermore, "because of MH17" could also point to Kiev's failure to close the civil airspace or its role in fueling the war that led to the assault. According to two nationwide surveys, only three percent of Dutch citizens believe the plane was shot down by the Ukrainian military.[96]

Admittedly, some Russian news was occasionally shared by the far-right web-blog *GeenStijl*, which co-initiated the referendum. Yet this was evidently their autonomous choice and highly sporadic and selective—as demonstrated by their claims about EU membership (a share-second among the most cited "no" arguments).[97] Indeed, an investigation into the twitter networks of the five most prominent No campaigners found no noteworthy presence of either Russian trolls, media or government officials.[98] Nor did the No campaigners dominate Dutch media coverage. The aforementioned media study found that *Geenstijl* was the only medium that propagated more arguments for a no vote than vice-versa. Most newspapers were propagating a yes vote in around two-thirds of their argumentative coverage, and so did the most widely read news site of the Netherlands.[99]

Finally, credible surveys showed a fairly consistent two-thirds advantage for a no-vote from the very start of the campaign; and although the turnout was at 32 percent only slightly higher than the legal requirement, opponents of the agreement actually had a lower turnout than proponents.[100] Obviously, a couple of individual Russians and some marginal 'fake news' could not have possibly "tilted" such a huge advantage. Any Russian influence also seems negligible compared to Ukrainian efforts, and especially irrelevant in light of historic US meddling. Probably the most damning statistic on the influence of "Russian propaganda," however, is the amount of public support enjoyed by Putin. Shortly before the referendum, a Pew survey found that 91 percent of Dutch citizens had confidence in Obama "to do the right thing regarding world affairs;" while Putin polled at 14 percent.[101] In fact, although generally less extreme, trends tend to be similar across the NATO zone.[102]

During the Dutch referendum, there was internationalist campaigning for a no vote, some of it in co-operation with Ukrainian leftists, for reasons that should be evident to the reader by now.[103] Predominantly, however, the no campaign was dominated by xenophobic rhetoric, which has been growing at least since the nationalist politician, Pim Fortuyn, was shot in 2002. In the *Washington Post*, Anne Applebaum suggests a link between the prospering of the far right, Putin and the referendum. Yet how this has anything to do with Russia remains elusive, even on a vague ideological level. Putin only made his traditionalist and Christian conservative turn, often cited as the reason for his far-right support in Europe, after his re-election in 2012; long after the rise of the far right.[104]

In the Netherlands, the MH17 disaster has even forced the ultranationalist PVV party to occasionally adopt anti-Russian rhetoric.[105] Admittedly, the PVV is the only Dutch party that gets significant funding from abroad. Yet these come from pro-Israel groups in the United States, the biggest donor being the David Horowitz Freedom Center.[106] Incidentally, Horowitz also sits on the Board of Directors of the US-funded National Endowment for Democracy, alongside none other than Anne Applebaum herself.[107] Yet she somehow has the nerve to blame Putin, without any tangible evidence, for contributing to a Dutch environment which, as she rightly notes, is increasingly reflecting that of "the 1930's."

Much has been made of a supposed alliance between the European far right and the Russian state, but these ties seem to be tactical, opportunistic and limited.[108] Actual funding has only been documented in the case of France's Front National, in the form of an $11 million loan from a private bank owned by a Russian oligarch on good terms with the Kremlin. Notably, a 2017 investigation by German intelligence officers was unable to find any evidence of Russian meddling in the country.[109] Similarly, the UK's foreign minister Boris Johnson admitted that: "We have no evidence the Russians are actually involved in trying to undermine our democratic processes at the moment. We don't actually have that evidence."[110] Indeed, such documentation has been strikingly absent in reporting on the topic; something the authors often recognize themselves. A widely cited 27-page report by the Atlantic Council, for example, tried to spin their lack of tangible proof as, bizarrely, proof of a sinister Russian strategy:

> The web of political networks is hidden and nontransparent by design, making it purposely difficult to expose. Traceable financial links would inevitably make Moscow's enterprise less effective: when ostensibly independent political figures call for closer relations with Russia, the removal of sanctions, or criticize the EU and NATO, it legitimizes the Kremlin's worldview. It is far less effective, from the Kremlin's point of view, to have such statements come from individuals or organizations known to be on the Kremlin's payroll.[111]

In other words, similar to the PropOrNot list, calling for détente with Russia—or even to just "criticize the EU and NATO" at all—is sufficient to be deemed complicit in a grand Russian plot. No wonder that the Atlantic Council report accuses a whole range of parties and individuals of being "the Kremlin's Trojan horses," including leftists such as Die Linke in Germany, Jeremy

Corbin in the UK and Syriza in Greece. In 2014, Lithuanian and Romanian officials even blamed anti-fracking activists of working for Russia, a claim subsequently echoed without evidence by the supreme commander of NATO.[112] Among the organizations involved was Greenpeace, the same NGO so often hailed as a hero for its activism against Russian fossil fuel interests. But since RT runs anti-fracking programs, we are to suppose Greenpeace was indeed guilty of advocacy that "closely resembled known Russian propaganda."[113]

Evidently, the rise of anti-establishment politics within the European Union has reasons beyond Russia, and pointing fingers at a foreign enemy will do little to stop the far right in its tracks. In fact, such fact-free reporting has enabled ultranationalist leaders to flip the script every time they are confronted with their pathological lying.[114] Nor does such framing do any justice to the fact that many 'moderate' pro-NATO and EU parties have been pandering for far-right votes for years, easily outdoing Putin—who has consistently emphasized a multi-ethnic conception of his nation—in their racist rhetoric.[115]

Clearly, reviewing all anti-Russian distortions is beyond the purview of this book, and would make for a fine media study in and of itself.[116] It is notable, however, that the US security establishment was directly fueling the anti-Russian media campaign against Trump. As such, the Breedlove network that plotted against Obama is likely but a taste of the opposition that Trump will face, and it remains to be seen if he can push back against such pressures. Indeed, one of two 'pro-Russian' cabinet-level picks, National Security Advisor Michael Flynn, has already been forced to resign, after intelligence officials leaked that Flynn ostensibly discussed Obama's last round of sanctions with the Russian ambassador before he took office.[117] This was potentially a violation of the Logan Act, an arcane law from 1799 for which no one has ever been prosecuted, that prohibits individuals outside of the administration from influencing foreign governments in disputes with the United States.

Notably, the transcript of the phone call hasn't been released, and one account suggests that Flynn simply said that sanctions would be reviewed upon taking office, only after the Russian ambassador brought it up.[118] If that is a crime, then there are certainly far worse precedents: Nixon sabotaged a peace initiative with Vietnam when he was on the campaign trail; Reagan prevented the release of US hostages in Iran to hijack the re-election of Jimmy Carter; not hideous, but comparable to Flynn, Obama's top Russia adviser, Michael McFaul, visited Moscow on the campaign trail in 2008, for talks with Russian officials.[119] As Eli Lake rightly notes:

> Normally intercepts of U.S. officials and citizens are some of the most tightly held government secrets. This is for good reason. Selectively disclosing details of private conversations monitored by the FBI or NSA gives the permanent state the power to destroy reputations from the cloak of anonymity. This is what police states do.
>
> In the past it was considered scandalous for senior U.S. officials to even request the identities of U.S. officials incidentally monitored by the government (normally they are redacted from intelligence reports). John Bolton's nomination to be U.S. ambassador to the United Nations was derailed in 2006 after the NSA confirmed he had made 10 such requests when he was Undersecretary of State for Arms Control in George W. Bush's first term. The fact that the intercepts of Flynn's conversations with Kislyak appear to have been widely distributed inside the government is a red flag.[120]

Indeed, multiple officials were involved in leaking Flynn's signal intelligence, which is considered one of the most serious felonies under US federal laws pertaining to classified material.[121]

Despite the fact that both Democrats and Republicans have been cheering this on, it is no secret that Obama has relentlessly prosecuted whistleblowers during his administration, more than any other president in history; and for leaks that didn't have such obvious political motivations.[122] In fact, these efforts seem to have been largely successful. Flynn's replacement, Lieutenant General H.R. McMaster, is strongly hawkish on Russia; so are two later key appointments, White House senior director for Russia and Europe, Fiona Hill, and US ambassador to NATO, Richard Grennell.

The leaks didn't stop with Flynn either. Multiple investigations have been opened to scrutinize Trump's ties to Russia, and more anonymous officials leaked their interpretation of signal intelligence to the press, claiming that multiple Trump "associates" have had contact with senior Russian intelligence officials in the year before the elections.[123] The spin was obvious, but it's actually unclear what was discussed and whether the individuals even knew that they were talking with Russian intelligence officials.[124] Indeed, the only individual mentioned is Paul Manafort—a Trump campaign advisor who was discredited by having worked for ousted Ukrainian president Yanukovych. Yet the notion that Manafort is a Russian intelligence asset is certainly dubious, since he urged Yanukovych to sign the EU association agreement and lobbied Americans to support this, according to *The New York Times*.[125]

A number of key figures—including the house speaker Paul Ryan, both Republican and Democratic members of the Senate Intelligence Committee, which gained sweeping powers to investigate the matter, former CIA chief Michael Morell and even the former Director of National Intelligence until January 20th, James Clapper Jr.—affirmed that so far no evidence has been supplied that suggests actual collusion or co-ordination, rather than mere communication, with Russian officials.[126]
Such lack of evidence is especially striking considering the unprecedented attention the matter has received from both the US press and the intelligence community—with large-scale and

ongoing investigations by the FBI and both the House and Senate Intelligence Committees. An extensive *New York Times* article, based on testimony from more anonymous intelligence officials, further describes how "in the Obama administration's last days, White House officials scrambled to spread information about Russian efforts to undermine the presidential election—and about possible contacts between associates of President-elect Donald J. Trump and Russians—across the government."[127] These efforts also significantly widened the scope for possible leaks because "there was a push to process as much raw intelligence as possible into analyses, *and to keep the reports at a relatively low classification level to ensure as wide a readership as possible.*"[128] (emphasis mine).

As several former US ambassadors to Russia—some of them strongly critical of Putin—have already pointed out, while actual collusion would be concerning, mere communication is routine practice and highly encouraged for establishing normal diplomatic relations.[129] Indeed, calls for the resignation of the attorney general Jeff Sessions—which followed quickly on the heels of Michael Flynn's resignation—have been equally misleading. Sessions supposedly "lied under oath" when he said he had not been in contact with the Russians—answering a question that was clearly inquiring into the actual matter of collusion, the reason why Sessions failed to mention a routine meeting with the Russian ambassador in his capacity as a member of the Senate Armed Services Committee.[130] Notably, just days before the Russian controversy broke, Sessions' ministry had dropped a 6-year Department of Justice lawsuit against a discriminatory voter ID law in Texas—i.e., an actual threat to the American electoral system.[131] Needless to say, this story did not receive nearly the same amount of attention, nor did any Democrat call for Sessions' impeachment on this basis. In point of fact, four of Trump's other cabinet-level appointments had made statements in their senate confirmation hearings that were much more misleading than those of Sessions.[132] And these lies pertained to actual issues of concern to the American population—such as Education Secretary de

Vos' financial ties to anti-LGBT groups, and massive improper 'robo-sign' foreclosures of home-owners by Treasury Secretary Mnuchin's former bank.[133]

In the final count, even if some of the worse allegations about the Trump-Russia connection turn out to be true when the investigations are concluded—and any revelations should certainly be treated with the utmost scrutiny in this environment—the premature and highly illegal leaks are clearly an effort to spin an anti-Russian campaign to hijack Trump's détente ambitions. Along with the US withdrawal from the TTIP trade agreement, this was actually one of the few reasonable proposals of the new administration. As such, the anti-Russian frenzy only serves to detract from Trump's massive assault on the dying remnants of the welfare state; his dangerous imperial posturing against China and Iran; his embrace of white nationalism; his denial of human-induced climate change and, in fact, his reckless embrace of a nuclear arms race with Russia itself. As the reputable and long-time Putin-critic Masha Gessen rightly notes: "Russiagate is helping him [Trump]—both by distracting from real, documentable, and documented issues, and by promoting a xenophobic conspiracy theory in the cause of removing a xenophobic conspiracy theorist from office."[134]

Trump himself has also been the target of the neo-McCarthyist and fact-free Kremlin-baiting. During the presidential campaign, the former MI-6 agent Christopher Steele was hired by Trump's Republican and Democrat electoral opponents, to find dirt on their contender. Steele managed to produce a 35-page memorandum with extraordinarily explosive claims: the Russian state would have gathered compromising material, involving sex-videos with prostitutes, to blackmail Trump; the president-elect would have taken bribes from Russian officials; he supposedly even struck a covert a deal with Russia, who would hack the DNC in return for silence over Ukraine. The memo had actually been circulating for weeks in the media, but no one dared to publish such unsubstantiated claims—many basic factual errors have already surfaced—produced by such an obviously partisan operative.[135]

It was only after senior intelligence officials gave the report a veneer of officialdom that the memo exploded in the media. The officials included a two-page summary of the memo in a range of intelligence briefings, which included the President and the President-elect, a fact they subsequently leaked to CNN who dramatically covered the "breaking news."[136] Of course, it was only a matter of time until one of the media channels, in this case Buzzfeed, decided to publish the whole memo and to rake in six million views; with the minor caveat (not even in the title) that "allegations are unverified, and the report contains errors."[137] As *The New York Times* rightly noted: "the decision of top intelligence officials to give the president, the president-elect and the so-called Gang of Eight—Republican and Democratic leaders of Congress and the intelligence committees—what they know to be unverified, defamatory material was extremely unusual."[138]

One senior official later admitted to *NBC News* that the two-page summary wasn't even seen by Trump, but simply included in the annex of a thick document, as an example of unvetted "disinformation" that they didn't get to during the oral briefing.[139] Yet this explanation obviously skirts the fact that the briefing, and specifically the inclusion of the defamatory memo, was leaked to CNN and therefore able to make countless media headlines. By all appearances, that is the primary reason it was included in the first place. Indeed, when the story died down after a month, anonymous officials leaked signal intelligence yet again, claiming to have "corroborated some of the communications detailed in a 35-page dossier."[140] The problem is that these corroborations seem to be entirely irrelevant factoids since, as they themselves admit, "none of the newly learned information relates to the salacious allegations in the dossier."[141] More specifically, they found that some of the conversations between Russian individuals detailed in the document took place on the time and place mentioned, but whether the actual content of the dialogues was accurate they wouldn't say. As Ivan Katchanovski rightly observes about the memo:

> This published document has all features of kompromat [compromising material, sometimes authentic selective leaking but often outright forgery]. Such kompromat is often used in Ukraine [and Russia] during the presidential elections. It was beyond [the] realm of possibility for a private investigator or his/her team working for the Democratic Party to make numerous anonymous top government and business insiders in Russia and the Trump campaign ... reveal over [such a] short period of time ... all [of this] ... secret information, which all just happens to be highly damaging to Trump['s] presidential campaign.[142]

Indeed, with the battle lines of the new cold war shaking, a similar struggle is unfolding inside Ukraine—and the earliest signs are not particularly hopeful. After Trump's election, the pro-Western oligarch, Viktor Pinchuk, published a proposal to essentially follow the Minsk Accords, guarantee Ukraine's international neutrality and postpone negotiations on Crimea's status for 15-20 years.[143] His reasonable suggestion was met with widespread and virulent criticism by Ukraine's 'totalitarian' movements, and the Security Service of Ukraine subsequently opened an investigation against Pinchuk for "encroachment on the territorial integrity and inviolability of Ukraine."[144] Thus, even the pro-Western multi-billionaire was forced to cave in, later publishing a piece in *Ukrainska Pravda* where he retracted the bulk of his proposal—claiming to have been misinterpreted in his earlier piece, which was supposedly cut and edited for an American audience by the *Wall Street Journal*.[145]

By the end of January 2017, just nine days after the inauguration of Donald Trump, the Donbass conflict escalated again into full-scale war, for the first time since the signing of Minsk II. The OSCE even reported the heaviest shelling it had observed since the very start of the conflict in 2014.[146] On the 1st of February, Deputy Defense minister Ihor Pavlovsky told the Ukrainian media that "as of today, despite everything, meter by meter, step by step, whenever possible our boys have been advancing."[147] His remarks echoed earlier front-line reports about a "creeping offensive" by the Ukrainian military.[148] Although Pavlovsky was careful to accuse the rebels of provoking such "advanc[es]," the German newspaper *Süddeutsche Zeitung* reported that German officials blame Kiev for the escalations.[149] In fact, this seems to be acknowledged even by Ukrainian intelligence. Several sources told *Ukrainska Pravda* that the major January-February escalation followed the seizure of a strategically important rebel position by Ukrainian forces.[150] In other words, Kiev, not the rebels, was responsible yet again for one of the most serious escalations of war.

Notably, some of Trump's fiercest opponents within the United States also supported the offensive. On New Year's Eve, Republican senators Lindsey Graham and John McCain—two of the most outspoken anti-Russian hawks—visited Ukrainian troops on the front lines in Donbass. Footage has emerged of Graham, standing alongside President Poroshenko, inciting the soldiers to renew the war: "Your fight is our fight, 2017 will be the year of offense. All of us will go back to Washington and we will push the case against Russia. Enough of a Russian aggression. It is time for them to pay a heavier price."[151] McCain subsequently assured the troops that such an offensive would be successful: "I believe you will win. I am convinced you will win and we will do everything we can to provide you with what you need to win."[152]

It goes without saying that no one will investigate whether this constituted a violation of the 1799 Logan Act. Yet the German officials made the obvious observation that Poroshenko—and by extension figures such as McCain and Graham—was probably trying to hijack Trump's deténte ambitions.[153] Indeed, this was not without success. On February 1st, Trump's newly appointed UN envoy, Nikki Haley, attended her first open briefing session in the UN Security Council, where she made a "clear and strong condemnation of Russian actions."[154] EU states quickly followed suit, unanimously vowing to continue their sanctions against Russia until the Ukrainian conflict had resolved.[155]

The January-February offensive, however, was only partially successful in stoking the flames. Although Haley spent most of her UN speech in condemnation, she also emphasized that "we do want to better our relations with Russia;"[156] and that she wasn't seeking to turn this into a routine, as her predecessor under Obama did. The Russian UN envoy, Vitaly Churkin, claimed to notice "a tangible change of tone … friendly enough, with the allowances for the circumstances and the subject."[157] I wouldn't have been particularly convinced of Haley's détente gesture myself, if it wasn't for her taking the initiative to visit Churkin the next day. After meeting at his residence, a Russian spokesman said that "both sides expressed the intention to cooperate tightly within the United Nations in accordance with their respective capitals' intentions."[158] Trump himself refused to blame Russia during a Fox interview, by arguing (wrongly) that it was unclear if anyone controlled the rebels.[159] A White House statement, summarizing Trump's call with President Poroshenko, refrained from assigning culpability for the recent hostilities. Trump's offer for a new nuclear agreement, which was rejected, also de-linked the sanctions against Russia from the Minsk accords and Crimea. Nevertheless, several senior officials in his administration have affirmed that sanctions would stay linked to their initial pretexts, and as the new McCarthyist smears increasingly took a hold on US discourse, so did Trump himself. A later White House statement re-affirmed that sanctions would stay in place until Crimea was returned to Ukraine.[160]

If the Trump administration sticks to that line, this means the first round of sanctions—which are the least extensive ones—will likely stay in place. In fact, by March 2017, government insiders suggested to *The New York Times* that Trump had decided to shelve his entire détente project for the time being, as the administration continued to face heat over its supposed Russia connection.[161] As the President put it at a press conference after Flynn's resignation: "It would be unpopular for a politician to make a deal … It would be much easier for me to be so tough—the tougher I am on Russia, the better."[162]

This stance is certainly unfortunate; with figures such as Nuland gone, the dynamics in Ukraine had been shifting. After Trump was inaugurated, negotiations with Russia, the rebels and European officials intensified, according to officials close to Poroshenko.[163] Although they argued that "major concessions" could be made towards Russia, their suggestions mostly seemed in line with the earlier signed Minsk accords. Furthermore, although Poroshenko harshly attacked Pinchuk after his first détente proposal in the *Wall Street Journal*, some reports have suggested that the piece was published in co-operation with the Ukrainian administration, in order to test public support for potential concessions.[164]

Clearly, subsequent developments showed that Poroshenko would struggle to overcome the virulent nationalism he himself helped to create, and the January hostilities further indicate that multiple strategies were enacted simultaneously. The fact that negotiations seemed to have continued, however, was reason for cautious optimism. Indeed, on January 11th 2017, the Ukrainian Cabinet finally adopted an Action Plan to ease mobility for Donbass citizens crossing the conflict zone, improve the flow of humanitarian goods into rebel-held territory, and increase government services close to the contact line, even if only in government-held territory.[165] This was highly necessary and still far too little. Just one month later UNICEF announced that the number of Ukrainian children in urgent need of humanitarian assistance had doubled in one year's time, to one million in February 2017.[166] Poverty figures have become deeply troubling throughout Ukraine. A march 2017 Gallup poll found that nearly half of Ukrainians (46%) experienced times in the past year ''when they did not have enough money for food for themselves or their families—the highest figure Gallup had ever recorded for Ukraine."[167] The same global survey also found that 42 percent of Ukrainians now say they are suffering—a category based on people's rating of both their current and future lives as below four out of ten—the third highest percentage in the entire world, only behind Haiti and South-Sudan.[168]

This leaves the most optimistic short-term scenario for Ukraine to be stable nationalist and authoritarian rule, combined with harsh foreign debt dependence. Some seem to prefer all-out war. Clearly, from a historical point of view, there seems to be little reason for rejoicing either way. The main movements of Ukraine—Maidan and Anti-Maidan—found themselves caught in an old, albeit unequal, imperialist rivalry. So it happens that the fate of the country is largely decided in the back rooms of Moscow, Washington and Berlin, rather than on the streets of Kiev and Donetsk. That is not to say that Ukrainians have had no agency themselves. On the contrary, some chose to seize the rising tide of the new cold war, and grass-roots mobilization got caught in its own nationalist competition. If only the protestors had taken an independent course, who knows what the future could have held. Perhaps that is the lesson of the Ukrainian tragedy.

Endnotes

1 Morozov, V. (2015). Russia's postcolonial identity: a subaltern empire in a eurocentric world. New York: Palgrave Macmillan, pp. 103-134.
2 Ahmed, N. (2017, February 14). How the Trump regime was manufactured by a war inside the Deep State. Retrieved from https://medium.com/insurge-intelligence/how-the-trump-regime-was-manufactured-by-a-war-inside-the-deep-state-f9e757071c70
3 Johnson, E. (2016, December 12). Cheney emerges as surprise Trump surrogate. Retrieved from http://www.politico.com/story/2016/12/dick-cheney-trump-surrogate-232746; Buncombe, A. (2016, December 27). Henry Kissinger has 'advised Donald Trump to accept' Crimea as part of Russia. Retrieved from http://www.independent.co.uk/news/people/henry-kissinger-russia-trump-crimea-advises-latest-ukraine-a7497646.html
4 Schleiffer, T., Labott, E., & Krieg, G. (2017, December 13). GOP heavyweights with ties to Exxon pushed Tillerson. Retrieved from http://edition.cnn.com/2016/12/13/politics/rex-tillerson-robert-gates-condoleezza-rice/
5 Kissinger, H. (2014, March 5). To settle the Ukraine crisis, start at the end. Retrieved from https://www.washingtonpost.com/opinions/henry-kissinger-to-settle-the-ukraine-crisis-start-at-the-

	end/2014/03/05/46dad868-a496-11e3-8466-d34c451760b9_story. html?utm_term=.7826a526644a; Kissinger, H., & Heilbrunn, J. (2015, August 19). The Interview: Henry Kissinger. Retrieved from http://nationalinterest.org/feature/the-interview-henry-kissinger-13615
6	Mearsheimer, J. J. (2014, August 18). Why the Ukraine Crisis Is the West's Fault. Retrieved from https://www.foreignaffairs.com/articles/russia-fsu/2014-08-18/why-ukraine-crisis-west-s-fault
7	Paton, J., & Guo, A. (2014, November 09). Russia, China Add to $400 Billion Gas Deal With Accord. Retrieved from https://www.bloomberg.com/news/articles/2014-11-10/russia-china-add-to-400-billion-gas-deal-with-accord
8	Johnson, A. (2017, February 07). On Iran, SPLC's 'Extremist' Is NPR's 'Expert.' Retrieved from http://fair.org/home/on-iran-splcs-extremist-is-nprs-expert/; Jilani, Z., & Emmons, A. (2017, February 02). Press Secretary Sean Spicer Falsely Accuses Iran of Attacking U.S. Navy Vessel, an Act of War. Retrieved from https://theintercept.com/2017/02/02/press-secretary-sean-spicer-falsely-accuses-iran-of-attacking-u-s-navy-vessel-an-act-of-war/; Aleem, Z. (2017, February 06). Trump's new sanctions targeted Iran. So why is China angry about them? Retrieved from http://www.vox.com/world/2017/2/6/14522040/iran-sanctions0china
9	Hassan, M. (2017, March 1). Trump's "moderate" defense secretary has already brought us to the brink of war. Retrieved from https://theintercept.com/2017/03/01/trumps-moderate-defense-secretary-has-already-brought-us-to-the-brink-of-war/
10	Marston, H. (2017, January 23). Trump Has Nothing to Offer Asia Except Threats. Retrieved from https://foreignpolicy.com/2017/01/23/trump-has-nothing-to-offer-asia-except-threats/
11	Haas, B. (2017, February 01). Steve Bannon: 'We're going to war in the South China Sea ... no doubt' Retrieved from https://www.theguardian.com/us-news/2017/feb/02/steve-bannon-donald-trump-war-south-china-sea-no-doubt
12	Pilger, J. (2016, December 1). The coming war on China. Retrieved from https://newint.org/features/2016/12/01/the-coming-war-on-china/
13	Larison, D. (2017, February 6). Pushing Russia to Break with Iran Is Unlikely to Succeed. Retrieved from http://www.theamericanconservative.com/larison/pushing-russia-to-break-with-iran-is-unlikely-to-succeed/
14	Ibid.
15	Holland, S. (2017, February 24). Trump wants to make sure U.S. nuclear arsenal at 'top of the pack' Retrieved from http://www.reuters.com/article/us-usa-trump-exclusive-idUSKBN1622IF; Williams, K.

B. (2017, February 09). Trump denounced arms-reduction treaty in Putin call: report. Retrieved from http://thehill.com/policy/national-security/318733-trump-denounced-arms-reduction-treaty-in-putin-call-report; Legum, J. (2016, September 12). 9 terrifying things Donald Trump has publicly said about nuclear weapons. Retrieved from https://thinkprogress.org/9-terrifying-things-donald-trump-has-publicly-said-about-nuclear-weapons-99f6290bc32a#.31h90prf8. Greg Grandin argues that Trump actually fits a Kissinger doctrine of unpredictability. Kissinger was of course Secretary of State under Nixon. Grandin, G. (2016, December 10). Mad Men: Trump May Be the Perfect Vehicle for Kissinger's Philosophy. Retrieved from https://www.thenation.com/article/mad-men-trump-may-be-the-perfect-vehicle-for-kissingers-philosophy/

16 Russian Official Rejects Trump Offer To Lift Sanctions For Nuclear Arms Deal. (2017, January 17). Retrieved from http://www.rferl.org/a/ryabkov-rejects-trump-offer-lift-sanctions-in-deal-curb-nuclear-arms/28238248.html

17 Hanna, A. (2017, February 6). Flynn to recommend Trump back NATO membership for Montenegro. Retrieved from http://www.politico.com/story/2017/02/trump-nato-montenegro-michael-flynn-234697

18 Most NATO Members in Eastern Europe See It as Protection. (2017, February 10). Retrieved from http://www.gallup.com/poll/203819/nato-members-eastern-europe-protection.aspx

19 Gore, D. (2016, May 11). What's Trump's Position on NATO? Retrieved from http://www.factcheck.org/2016/05/whats-trumps-position-on-nato/

20 The UK, Estonia, Poland, france, Greece, Turkey and the United States according to the most recent (2015) SIPRI data. SIPRI Military Expenditure Database (n.d.). Retrieved from https://www.sipri.org/databases/milex

21 Simenas, D. (2017, February 06). One NATO Member Thinks Trump Is Right. Retrieved from https://www.bloomberg.com/politics/articles/2017-02-06/trump-is-right-says-baltic-nato-member-shattering-spending-goal. Trump continued to insist on increases in European defense spending after his inauguration, both publicly and in phone-calls with his European counterparts. Liptak, K. (2017, February 7). Trump salutes NATO with vow of strong support. Retrieved from http://edition.cnn.com/2017/02/06/politics/trump-nato-centcom/; Palmeri, T., Dawsey, J., Vogel, K. P., & Toosi, N. (2017, February 8). Trump's faux-pas diplomacy. Retrieved from http://www.politico.com/story/2017/02/trump-foreign-leaders-phone-calls-234770

22 Emmons, A. (2017, February 27). Trump's Proposed Increase in U.S.

	Defense Spending Would Be 80 Percent of Russia's Entire Military Budget. Retrieved from https://theintercept.com/2017/02/27/trumps-proposed-increase-in-u-s-defense-spending-would-be-80-percent-of-russias-entire-military-budget/
23	Team Trump on Russia: Words and Actions. (2017, February 21). Retrieved from https://www.russiamatters.org/analysis/team-trump-russia-words-and-actions
24	Doctorow, G. (2017, January 22). Letter from Moscow: how the Trump inauguration is being viewed in Russia. Retrieved from http://usforeignpolicy.blogs.lalibre.be/archive/2017/01/22/letter-from-moscow-how-the-trump-inauguration-is-being-viewe-1154970.html; Pukhov, R. (2016, November 11). Russia Isn't Actually That Happy About Trump's Victory. Retrieved from https://www.nytimes.com/2016/11/11/opinion/russia-isnt-actually-that-happy-about-trumps-victory.html?_r=3; Ryan, D. (2017, February 14). An end to bromance: Russia's in love with Trump, right? Not as much as you think. Retrieved from http://www.salon.com/2017/02/11/an-end-to-bromance-russias-in-love-with-trump-right-not-as-much-as-you-think/
25	Qiu, L. (2016, September 8). Did Putin call Trump brilliant? Retrieved from http://www.politifact.com/truth-o-meter/statements/2016/sep/08/donald-trump/did-vladimir-putin-call-trump-brilliant/
26	Cohen, S. (2017, February 16). Kremlin-Baiting President Trump (Without Facts) Must Stop. Retrieved from https://www.thenation.com/article/kremlin-baiting-president-trump-without-facts-must-stop/. Putin is of course guilty of massive war-crimes, but the reference of him being a "killer" normally refers to accusations that he personally ordered the killing of numerous opposition politicians and journalists. There is indeed no evidence for this. In one case the allegations were even overturned by the ruling of a US Attorney for the District of Columbia, after a joint investigation with the FBI and Washington's Metropolitan Police Department. Robinson, P. (2016, October 29). Case closed. Retrieved from https://irrussianality.wordpress.com/2016/10/29/case-closed/. A nuanced treatment of the assassination allegations—and a whole host of other Putin mythologies—was recently offered by a Russian-born journalist in the Guardian. Gessen, K. (2017, February 22). Killer, kleptocrat, genius, spy: the many myths of Vladimir Putin. Retrieved from https://www.theguardian.com/world/2017/feb/22/vladimir-putin-killer-genius-kleptocrat-spy-myths. For a more systemic scrutiny of killing allegations consult Kriukov, F. (2008, February 16). An Audit of the Committee to Protect Journalists Claims. Retrieved from http://fkriuk.blogspot.nl/2008/02/audit-of-committee-to-protect.html For an

overview of some of the most deranged conspiracy theories recently promoted by Western journalists consult Greenwald, G. (2017, March 07). Leading Putin Critic Warns of Xenophobic Conspiracy Theories Drowning U.S. Discourse and Helping Trump. Retrieved from https://theintercept.com/2017/03/07/leading-putin-critic-warns-of-xenophobic-conspiracy-theories-drowning-u-s-discourse-and-helping-trump/ Finally, two-thirds of Russians support Putin's perceived anti-corruption efforts and respect for individual liberties, significantly higher than under Yeltsin. Poushter, J. (2015, June 10). 2. Russian Public Opinion: Putin Praised, West Panned. Retrieved from http://www.pewglobal.org/2015/06/10/2-russian-public-opinion-putin-praised-west-panned/. For more (somewhat old but still fairly timely) analysis on the state of Russian democracy consult Petro, N. (2006, February 24). Russian democracy: a reply to Mischa Gabowitsch. Retrieved from https://www.opendemocracy.net/globalization-institutions_government/russia_reply_3299.jsp.

27   Greenwald, G. (2016, December 29). The Guardian's Summary of Julian Assange's Interview Went Viral and Was Completely False. Retrieved from https://theintercept.com/2016/12/29/the-guardians-summary-of-julian-assanges-interview-went-viral-and-was-completely-false/

28   Frankovic, K. (2016, December 27). Belief in conspiracies largely depends on political identity. Retrieved from https://today.yougov.com/news/2016/12/27/belief-conspiracies-largely-depends-political-iden/

29   A literature review concerning 2000 and 2004 is provided by Ahmed, N. M. (2005). The war on truth: 9/11, disinformation, and the anatomy of terrorism. Northampton, MA: Olive Branch Press; The 2016 elections are dealt with in Palast, G. (2016, November 11). The Election was Stolen—Here's How... Retrieved from http://www.gregpalast.com/election-stolen-heres/

30   Sainato, M. (2017, February 09). DNC Chair Candidate Tom Perez Admits Democratic Primaries Were Rigged. Retrieved from http://observer.com/2017/02/dnc-chair-candidate-tom-perez-admits-democratic-primaries-rigged/

31   Vogel, K. P., & Stern, D. (2017, January 11). Ukrainian efforts to sabotage Trump backfire. Retrieved from http://www.politico.com/story/2017/01/ukraine-sabotage-trump-backfire-233446

32   Sanger, D. E. (2016, December 29). Obama Strikes Back at Russia for Election Hacking. Retrieved from https://www.nytimes.com/2016/12/29/us/politics/russia-election-hacking-sanctions.html?_r=0; Arkin, W. M., Dilanian, K., & McFadden, C. (2016, December 19). What Obama said to Putin on the Red Phone about the election

hacks. Retrieved from http://www.nbcnews.com/news/us-news/what-obama-said-putin-red-phone-about-election-hack-n697116; Korte, G. (2016, December 16). Obama threatens retaliation against Russia for election hacking. Retrieved from http://www.usatoday.com/story/news/politics/2016/12/15/obama-threatens-retaliation-against-russia-election-hacking/95501584/

33 Polychroniou, C. J. (2017, January 19). Noam Chomsky on the Long History of US Meddling in Foreign Elections. Retrieved from http://www.truth-out.org/opinion/item/39159-noam-chomsky-on-the-long-history-of-us-meddling-in-foreign-elections

34 An extensive account of the US meddling is offered by Guillory, S. (2017, March 13). Dermokratiya, USA. Retrieved from https://www.jacobinmag.com/2017/03/russia-us-clinton-boris-yeltsin-elections-interference-trump/

35 Kramer, M. (1996, July 15). Rescuing Boris. Retrieved from http://content.time.com/time/subscriber/article/0,33009,984833-1,00.html

36 Ibid.

37 Gordon, M. R. (1996, February 22). Russia and I.M.F. agree on a loan for $10.2 billion. Retrieved from http://www.nytimes.com/1996/02/23/world/russia-and-imf-agree-on-a-loan-for-10.2-billion.html

38 Ibid.

39 Zaitchik, A., & Ames, M. (2011, December 9). How The West Helped Invent Russia's Election Fraud: OSCE Whistleblower Exposes 1996 Whitewash. Retrieved from http://exiledonline.com/how-the-west-helped-invent-russias-election-fraud-osce-whistleblower-exposes-1996-whitewash/

40 Another decent review of the evidence was offered by investigative journalist Parry, R. (2017, March 08). Fresh Doubts about Russian 'Hacking' Retrieved from https://consortiumnews.com/2017/03/08/fresh-doubts-about-russian-hacking/

41 Binney, W., Gravel, M., Johnson, L., Mcgovern, R., Murray, E., & Wiebe, K. (2016, December 12). US Intel Vets Dispute Russia Hacking Claims. Retrieved from https://consortiumnews.com/2016/12/12/us-intel-vets-dispute-russia-hacking-claims/

42 Murray, C. (2016, December 11). The CIA's Absence of Conviction. Retrieved from https://www.craigmurray.org.uk/archives/2016/12/cias-absence-conviction/

43 Binney, W., Gravel, M., Johnson, L., Mcgovern, R., Murray, E., & Wiebe, K. (2016, December 12). US Intel Vets Dispute Russia Hacking Claims. Retrieved from https://consortiumnews.com/2016/12/12/us-intel-vets-dispute-russia-hacking-claims/

44 Biddle, S. (2016, December 14). Here's the Public Evidence Russia

Hacked the DNC - It's Not Enough. Retrieved from https://theintercept.com/2016/12/14/heres-the-public-evidence-russia-hacked-the-dnc-its-not-enough/

45 Ibid.

46 Fabian, J. (2017, January 05). Obama receives classified report on Russian hacking. Retrieved from http://thehill.com/homenews/administration/312804-obama-receives-classified-report-on-russian-hacking-report; Gessen, M. (2017, September 1). Russia, Trump & Flawed Intelligence. Retrieved from http://www.nybooks.com/daily/2017/01/09/russia-trump-election-flawed-intelligence/; Rothrock, K. (2017, January 7). American Unintelligence on Russia (Op-ed). Retrieved from https://themoscowtimes.com/articles/american-unintelligence-on-russia-op-ed-56746

47 Martin, A. (2017, January 6). Abby Martin Responds to Exploitation by NY Times. Retrieved from http://mediaroots.org/abby-martin-responds-to-exploitation-by-ny-times/

48 Simonyan, M. (2015, September 24). So this is 'Putin's propaganda TV'? A look at how RT's chief editor responds to evidence that the network is a political failure. Retrieved from https://meduza.io/en/feature/2015/09/24/so-this-is-putin-s-propaganda-tv; RT watched by 70mn viewers weekly, half of them daily—Ipsos survey. (2016, March 10). Retrieved from https://www.rt.com/news/335123-rt-viewership-ipsos-study/; 23, 2. J. (2015, June 29). Did Bush Really Want to Bomb Al Jazeera? Retrieved from https://www.thenation.com/article/did-bush-really-want-bomb-al-jazeera/

49 I assume the reader naturally understands the obvious disclaimer that RT is one-sided and should be consumed critically and complemented with other perspectives. Of course, the quality of the programmes also varies significantly and the channel regularly hosts both radical left and far-right commentators.

50 Background to "Assessing Russian Activities and Intentions in Recent US Elections": The Analytic Process and Cyber Incident Attribution (Rep.). (2017), pp. 7-8. Retrieved from https://www.dni.gov/files/documents/ICA_2017_01.pdf.

51 Ryan, D. (2017, January 10). RT America Was Not 'Pro-Trump' Retrieved from https://www.thenation.com/article/rt-america-was-not-pro-trump/

52 Pitney, N. (2016, July 27). Putin's State Media Have Definitely Picked A Side In The U.S. Presidential Race. Retrieved from http://www.huffingtonpost.com/entry/russia-media-clinton-trump-putin_us_5797dd56e4b02d5d5ed359bc; Ryan, D. (2017, January 10). RT America Was Not 'Pro-Trump' Retrieved from https://www.thenation.

53   com/article/rt-america-was-not-pro-trump/
     Bernie Sanders on Russia. (n.d.). Retrieved from http://feelthebern. org/bernie-sanders-on-russia/
54   Schaeffer, F. (2011, February 23). An American Prophet (Chris Hedges) Is Vindicated. Retrieved from http://www.huffingtonpost. com/frank-schaeffer/american-patriots-would-k_b_827000.html
55   Lexis Nexis Power Search: (Russ! w/10 propagan!) or (krem! w/10 propagan!) for January 1, 2017 to January 31, 2017.
56   Timberg, C. (2016, November 24). Russian propaganda effort helped spread 'fake news' during election, experts say. Retrieved from https://www.washingtonpost.com/business/economy/russian-propaganda-effort-helped-spread-fake-news-during-election-experts-say/2016/11/24/793903b6-8a40-4ca9-b712-716af66098fe_story.html?utm_term=.dd9e1f6dde50
57   Norton, B., & Greenwald, G. (2016, November 26). Washington Post Disgracefully Promotes a McCarthyite Blacklist From a New, Hidden, and Very Shady Group. Retrieved from https://theintercept.com/2016/11/26/washington-post-disgracefully-promotes-a-mccarthyite-blacklist-from-a-new-hidden-and-very-shady-group/
58   Greenwald, G. (2017, January 04). WashPost Is Richly Rewarded for False News About Russia Threat While Public Is Deceived. Retrieved from https://theintercept.com/2017/01/04/washpost-is-richly-rewarded-for-false-news-about-russia-threat-while-public-is-deceived/
59   Chen, A. (2016, December 02). The Propaganda About Russian Propaganda. Retrieved from http://www.newyorker.com/news/newsdesk/the-propaganda-about-russian-propaganda
60   Strether, L. (2017, January 03). Does the "Countering Foreign Propaganda and Disinformation Act" Apply to American Independent or Alternative Media? Retrieved from http://www.nakedcapitalism.com/2017/01/100755.html
61   Johnson, A. (2015, April 14). Reporting on Russia's Troll Army, Western Media Forget West's Much Bigger, Sophisticated Troll Army. Retrieved from http://fair.org/home/reporting-on-russias-troll-army-western-media-forget-wests-much-bigger-sophisticated-troll-army/
62   Abunimah, A. (2014). The battle for justice in Palestine. Chicago, IL: Haymarket Books.
63   Boffey, D., & Rankin, J. (2017, January 23). EU escalates its campaign against Russian propaganda. Retrieved from https://www.theguardian.com/world/2017/jan/23/eu-escalates-campaign-russian-propaganda; Troianovski, A. (2015, April 17). Germany Seeks to Counter Russian 'Propaganda' in Baltics. Retrieved from https://www.wsj.com/articles/germany-seeks-to-counter-russian-propaganda-in-baltics-1429294362

64   A 2016 Pew survey found that only one-fifth of Twitter and Facebook users considered the political views in their online network similar to their own: Bruns Professor, Creative Industries, Queensland University of Technology, A. (2017, February 13). Echo Chamber? What Echo Chamber? Retrieved from https://theconversation.com/echo-chamber-what-echo-chamber-69293. Another Pew survey found similar percentages two years earlier, with only two percent saying posts were "always or nearly always" convergent with their views. This percentage was somewhat higher on the ideological extremes—especially among "consistent conservatives," nearly half of which had their views regularily confirmed on Facebook; yet they also tend to rely heavily on one conventional medium, Fox News. Mitchell, A., Gottfried, J., Kiley, J., & Matsa, K. E. (2014, October 20). Section 2: Social Media, Political News and Ideology. Retrieved from http://www.journalism.org/2014/10/21/section-2-social-media-political-news-and-ideology/. Indeed, a study comparing offline and online media segregation between "liberals" and "conservatives" found both to be low, even higher in national newspapers than on the internet. Combined with the fact that social media is less trusted and relied upon as a primary source than conventional media, the 'echo chamber' theory just cannot hold. Gentzkow, M., & Shapiro, J. (2011). Ideological Segregation Online and Offline. Quarterly Journal of Economics,126(4), 1799-1839. doi:10.3386/w15916

65   Ibid.

66   Ibid.

67   Frankovic, K. (2017, February 18). Belief in conspiracies largely depends on political identity. Retrieved from https://today.yougov.com/news/2016/12/27/belief-conspiracies-largely-depends-political-iden/

68   Stahl, R. M. (2016, December 14). The Fallacy of Post-Truth. Retrieved from https://www.jacobinmag.com/2016/12/post-truth-fake-news-trump-clinton-election-russia/

69   Greenwald, G. (2016, September 12). Facebook Is Collaborating With the Israeli Government to Determine What Should Be Censored. Retrieved from https://theintercept.com/2016/09/12/facebook-is-collaborating-with-the-israeli-government-to-determine-what-should-be-censored/; How Twitter and Facebook Censor Content Without Telling Anyone. (2014, November 24). Retrieved from https://motherboard.vice.com/en_us/article/how-twitter-and-facebook-censor-content-without-telling-anyone

70   About the International Fact-Checking Network. (2017, February 15). Retrieved from http://www.poynter.org/about-the-international-fact-

	checking-network/
71	Uscinski, J. E. (2015). The Epistemology of Fact Checking (Is Still Naive): Rejoinder to Amazeen. Critical Review,27(2), 243-252; Marietta, M., Barker, D. C., & Bowser, T. (2015). Fact-Checking Polarized Politics: Does The Fact-Check Industry Provide Consistent Guidance on Disputed Realities? The Forum,13(4), 577-596; The Daily Mail Snopes Story And Fact Checking The Fact Checkers. Retrieved from http://www.forbes.com/sites/kalevleetaru/2016/12/22/the-daily-mail-snopes-story-and-fact-checking-the-fact-checkers/#6f4128841e02; Fair.org also published multiple critiques each for the fact-checking publications of Politifact, ABC news, the Washington Post, Factcheck.org and the Associated Press, available on their website. Finally, Marietta *et al.* found a bias for the frequency in fact-checking senators who are on the ideological extremes, both left and right: Marietta, M., Barker, D. C., & Bowser, T. (2015). Fact-Checking Polarized Politics: Does The Fact-Check Industry Provide Consistent Guidance on Disputed Realities? The Forum,13(4).
72	Uscinski, J. E. (2015). The Epistemology of Fact Checking (Is Still Naive): Rejoinder to Amazeen. Critical Review,27(2), 243-252, p. 249.
73	Ibid, p. 246; Marietta, M., Barker, D. C., & Bowser, T. (2015). Fact-Checking Polarized Politics: Does The Fact-Check Industry Provide Consistent Guidance on Disputed Realities? The Forum,13(4), 577-596.
74	Newman, N., Fletcher, R., Levy, A., & Nielson, R. (2016). Reuters institute digital news report 2016 (Rep.). University of Oxford. Retrieved from https://reutersinstitute.politics.ox.ac.uk/sites/default/files/Digital-News-Report-2016.pdf.
75	Murray, C. (2016, December 08). Twitter and Facebook Censorship and Mainstream Media Denial. Retrieved from https://www.craigmurray.org.uk/archives/2016/12/twitter-facebook-censorship-mainstream-media-denial/
76	Russian Meddling and Europe's Elections. (2016, December 19). Retrieved from https://www.nytimes.com/2016/12/19/opinion/russian-meddling-and-europes-elections.html
77	As Robinson notes, the frequently used label "pro-Russian" is quite damaging in this regard. Robinson, P. (2016, November 09). 'Pro-Russian' wins election. Retrieved from https://irrussianality.wordpress.com/2016/11/09/pro-russian-wins-election/
78	Foster, P. (2016, January 16). Russia accused of clandestine funding of European parties as US conducts major review of Vladimir Putin's strategy. Retrieved from http://www.telegraph.co.uk/news/worldnews/europe/russia/12103602/America-to-investigate-Russian-meddling-in-EU.html

79 European Council Conclusions on Ukraine (15 December 2016) (Rep.). (2016). Brussels: European Council, p. 4. Retrieved from http://www.consilium.europa.eu/en/meetings/european-council/2016/12/15-euco-conclusions-ukraine/

80 Hekster, K. (2016, January 22). Amerikaanse miljardair sponsort 'ja'-campagne Oekraïne-referendum. Retrieved from http://nos.nl/artikel/2082091-amerikaanse-miljardair-sponsort-ja-campagne-oekraine-referendum.html

81 Schram Bauke Schram (1993) is sinds april 2016 online redacteur bij Elsevier Volg Bauke Schram:, B. (2016, August 17). Wat is het Soros-lek? Vier vragen over zijn politieke investeringen. Retrieved from http://www.elsevier.nl/economie/achtergrond/2016/08/wat-is-sorosleaks-vier-vragen-over-de-documenten-341846/; Verdeling subsidie. (2016, June 24). Retrieved from https://www.referendumcommissie.nl/subsidie/inhoud/subsidieregeling/verdeling-subsidie

82 Yermolenko, V. (2016, April 11). Seven consequences of the Dutch referendum. Retrieved from http://www.eurozine.com/seven-consequences-of-the-dutch-referendum/

83 Ibid.

84 Ukraine Prepares to Campaign for Association Agreement Vote in the Netherlands. (2016, January 20). Retrieved from http://www.uawire.org/news/ukraine-prepares-to-campaign-for-association-agreement-vote-in-the-netherlands#

85 Modderkolk, H., & Kreling, T. (2017, February 25). Deze man is volgens de NY Times een verlengstuk van het Kremlin. 'Fake news', zegt hij zelf. Retrieved from http://www.volkskrant.nl/buitenland/is-deze-man-onderdeel-van-de-lange-arm-van-het-kremlin~a4467422/

86 Higgins, A. (2017, February 16). Fake News, Fake Ukrainians: How a Group of Russians Tilted a Dutch Vote. Retrieved from https://www.nytimes.com/2017/02/16/world/europe/russia-ukraine-fake-news-dutch-vote.html The NYT also cites some "fake news" that would have supposedly tilted the results of the referendum, yet the article fails to provide any concrete evidence on the audience reach and impact. The writer claims, for example, that "Russian sympathizers in the Netherlands, including members of Mr. Van Bommel's Ukrainian team, have labored tirelessly to promote implausible alternative theories for the downing of the Boeing jet carrying Malaysia Airlines Flight 17." As I show later in this chapter, however, opinion polls demonstrate that barely anyone in the Netherlands believed these theories. Another such example is the fake video—apparently emanating from a trolling center in St. Petersburg—that purported to show the Azov battalion threatening Dutch voters with a terrorist attack in case of a "no."

However, even when the no-campaigning GeenStijl web-blog—whose slogan literally says "biased, baseless and needlessly hurtful"—posted the video; they also included the video rebuttal from the actual Azov battalion, and called the threat-video potentially a "bad-joke" from the yes-campaign. Obviously, other Dutch media simply seized on the video as an example of Russian propaganda. The impact of such "fake news" on the referendum result was likely insignificant, and it certainly didn't register in any of the polls. Rossem, V. (2016, January 19). WTF. Gewapende Oekrainers bedreigen GeenPeil. Retrieved from http://www.geenstijl.nl/mt/archieven/2016/01/vrienden_van_verhofstadt_maken_wraakvideo_tegen_geenpeil.html

87 Applebaum, A. (2016, April 08). The Dutch just showed the world how Russia influences Western European elections. Retrieved from https://www.washingtonpost.com/opinions/russias-influence-in-western-elections/2016/04/08/b427602a-fcf1-11e5-886f-a037dba38301_story.html

88 Kristof, K., Klingeren, M., Van, Kolk, H., Van der, Meer, T., Van der, & Steenvoorden, E. (2016). Het Oekraïne-referendum: Nationaal Referendum Onderzoek 2016 (Rep.). Stichting KiezersOnderzoek Nederland. Retrieved from http://www.ru.nl/publish/pages/813323/web_96646_onderzoeksrapport_nro_2016nw.pdf

89 See the chapter Condoning Corruption

90 5 EU states block Ukraine's membership prospects—report. (2016, April 2). Retrieved from https://www.rt.com/news/338095-eu-oppose-ukraine-membership/; Ukraine should never join EU—Dutch Prime Minister. (2016, March 31). Retrieved from https://www.rt.com/news/337950-ukraine-eu-dutch-pm-referendum/; 3 in 4 Dutch voters oppose EU association agreement with Ukraine—poll. (2016, January 9). Retrieved from https://www.rt.com/news/328403-dutch-poll-ukraine-association/;

91 'Dating that will never end in marriage': Medvedev describes Ukraine's chances in EU. (2014, December 15). Retrieved from https://www.rt.com/politics/214431-russian-medvedev-ukraine-european/

92 Associatieverdrag draait wél om EU-lidmaatschap. (2016, February 14). Retrieved from http://oekrainee.eu/associatieverdrag-draait-wel-om-eu-lidmaatschap/; Rossem, V. (2015, November 23). Premier Oekraine: 'Oekraine wordt EU-lidstaat!' Retrieved from http://www.geenstijl.nl/mt/archieven/2015/11/premier_oekraine_oekraine_word.html

93 Nederlanders over het associatieverdrag met Oekraïne. (2016, April 1). Retrieved from http://content1d.omroep.nl/urishieldv2/l27m4b343dc6272617570058a8a561000000.00c78c2b28f6db0472c1900ba3f5d67c/nos/docs/050416_ipsos.pdf

94	Veghel, T., Van. (2016). Het referendum dat de journalistiek niet wilde: Een onderzoek naar de berichtgeving over het Oekraïne-referendum (Unpublished master's thesis). Erasmus University Rotterdam, p. 55. Retrieved from https://www.villamedia.nl/docs/130916_oekrainierefscriptie_ThijnvanVeghel.pdf
95	Weissink, A. (2016, September 28). MH17-onderzoek wijst op Russische medeplichtigheid. Retrieved from https://fd.nl/economie-politiek/1169297/raket-mh17-kwam-uit-gebied-pro-russische-rebellen
96	Hond, M., De. (2015, August 2). De Stemming van 2 augustus 2015. Retrieved from http://tpo.nl/wp-content/uploads/2015/08/2015-08-02.pdf
97	Veghel, T., Van. (2016). Het referendum dat de journalistiek niet wilde: Een onderzoek naar de berichtgeving over het Oekraïne-referendum (Unpublished master's thesis). Erasmus University Rotterdam, p. 54. Retrieved from https://www.villamedia.nl/docs/130916_oekrainierefscriptie_ThijnvanVeghel.pdf
98	Broer, T. (2016, March 21). In opdracht van Vrij Nederland onderzocht Twitterspecialist Thomas Boeschoten de beïnvloeding van GeenPeil... Retrieved from https://www.vn.nl/geenpeil-nuttige-twitteriodioten-poetin/
99	Veghel (2016), p. 56.
100	Kanne, P. (2016). Het Oekraïne-referendum en de peilingen. Clou,78, 28-29. Retrieved from http://www.ioresearch.nl/Portals/0/clou%2078%20%20juli_2016_28-29_complot.pdf; Kristof, K., Klingeren, M., Van, Kolk, H., Van der, Meer, T., Van der, & Steenvoorden, E. (2016). Het Oekraïne-referendum: Nationaal Referendum Onderzoek 2016 (Rep.). Stichting KiezersOnderzoek Nederland. Retrieved from http://www.ru.nl/publish/pages/813323/web_96646_onderzoeksrapport_nro_2016nw.pdf
101	Mitchell, T. (2016, June 29). 2. Obama's international image remains strong in Europe and Asia. Retrieved February 18, 2017, from http://www.pewglobal.org/2016/06/29/2-obamas-international-image-remains-strong-in-europe-and-asia/
102	Ibid; A later survey found that public opinion in four NATO countries—Greece, Turkey, Slovenia and Bulgaria—was drifting towards Russia, but this rather proves the point that Russian propaganda is not a key factor. These countries have had their own unique developments that has lead them in this direction; in contrast to all the other NATO countries equally exposed to Russian propaganda. Champion, M. (2017, February 17). Four NATO Nations Would Pick Russia to Defend Them If Threatened: Poll. Retrieved February 17, 2017, from

> https://www.bloomberg.com/politics/articles/2017-02-17/melania-trump-s-slovenia-would-pick-russian-over-u-s-protection

103 Staal, J. (2016, April 30). Unfriendly Terrain. Retrieved from https://www.jacobinmag.com/2016/04/netherlands-dutch-right-geert-wilders-freedom-party/

104 Morozov, V. (2015). Russia's postcolonial identity: a subaltern empire in a eurocentric world. New York: Palgrave Macmillan, pp. 103-134. Furthermore, the argument that Western attention for Russia's Christian conservatism, although a very serious problem, is a distinctly homonationalist phenomenon has been convincingly made by a number of authors. LeBlanc, F. (2013). Sporting homonationalism: Russian homophobia, imaginative geographies and the 2014 Sochi Olympic games. In Sociology Association of Aotearoa New Zealand Annual Conference, Auckland, NZ; Bennetts, M. (2014, February 5). Russia's anti-gay law is wrong—but so is some of the criticism from the west. Retrieved from https://www.theguardian.com/commentisfree/2014/feb/05/russia-anti-gay-law-criticism-playing-into-putin-hands; LGBT Rights in Russia and our Western Fantasies. (2013, August 9). Retrieved from https://howupsetting.com/2013/08/09/lgbt-rights-in-russia-and-our-western-fantasies/

105 Weezel, M. V. (2014, July 25). De PVV laat zich van zijn anti-Poetin kant zien. Was Wilders op vakantie of heeft hij na de dag van nationa... Retrieved from https://www.vn.nl/wilders-nu-ook-tegen-poetin/

106 Moerman, T. (2016, November 30). Dit is waarom DENK buitenlandse subsidie voor politieke partijen wil stoppen. Retrieved from https://www.businessinsider.nl/dit-waarom-denk-buitenlandse-subsidie-voor-politieke-partijen-wil-stoppen/

107 National Endowment for Democracy Adds Three to Board of Directors Skaggs, Applebaum, Horowitz begin three-year term. (2016, January 20). Retrieved from http://www.ned.org/national-endowment-for-democracy-adds-three-to-board-of-directors-skaggs-applebaum-horowitz-begin-three-year-term/

108 Most major anti-establishment parties, especially those on the far-right, have occasionally visited fora and congresses in Russia, yet these were mostly attended by marginal figures in the country's political scene. There are some exceptions, of course, but the simple fact that a government is willing to meet with parties that favor détente—as well as to offer them some occasional air-time on marginal state-media channels—does not somehow prove major Russian influence or control. It only proves the most predictable of diplomatic policies one could possibly imagine. As for the ideological overlap, this seems to be mostly limited to Christian conservatism and traditionalism. The influence of fascist

ideologues such as Dugin seem to be grossly exaggerated. For analysis on Putin, Dugin and Eurasianism consult Schmidt, M. (2005). Is Putin Pursuing a Policy of Eurasianism? Demokratizatsiya: The Journal of Post-Soviet Democratization,13(1), 87-100; Hahn, G. (2015, May 19). Myths about Putin's Ideology Refuse to Die. Retrieved from http://russia-insider.com/en/2015/01/17/2495; Robinson, P. (2017, January 14). The Russian soul and the toxic West. Retrieved from https://irrussianality.wordpress.com/2017/01/14/the-russian-soul-and-the-toxic-west/; Robinson, P. (2016, October 06). Stolypin. Retrieved from https://irrussianality.wordpress.com/2016/10/06/stolypin/; Robinson, P. (2016, December 01). Don't mention the war. Retrieved from https://irrussianality.wordpress.com/2016/12/01/dont-mention-the-war/

109   King, E. (2017, February 07). German intelligence finds no evidence of Russian meddling. Retrieved from http://www.politico.eu/article/german-intelligence-finds-no-evidence-of-russian-meddling/

110   Wintour, P., & Slawson, N. (2017, March 12). Boris Johnson: Russia has ability to disrupt UK politics with hacking. Retrieved from https://www.theguardian.com/uk-news/2017/mar/12/british-democracy-at-risk-from-russian-hackers-says-gchq

111   Polyakova, A., Laruelle, M., Meister, S., Barnett, N., & Sikorski, R. (2016, November). The Kremlin's Trojan Horses (Rep.), p. 4. Retrieved http://www.atlanticcouncil.org/images/publications/The_Kremlins_Trojan_Horses_web_1213_second_edition.pdf

112   Radnitz, S. (2016, February 13). Europe's Extremists Are Not Putin's Fault. Retrieved from http://foreignpolicy.com/2016/02/13/europes-extremists-are-not-putins-fault/

113   The Telegraph argued that there was Russian meddling in the Dutch consultative referendum because anonymous government "sources said arguments deployed in support of the referendum "closely resembled" known Russian propaganda." Foster, P. (2016, January 16). Russia accused of clandestine funding of European parties as US conducts major review of Vladimir Putin's strategy. Retrieved from http://www.telegraph.co.uk/news/worldnews/europe/russia/12103602/America-to-investigate-Russian-meddling-in-EU.html

114   Easley, J. (2016, September 25). Trump Becomes The Biggest Liar In US Political History By Lying Once Every 3 Minutes. Retrieved from http://www.politicususa.com/2016/09/25/trump-biggest-liar-political-history-lying-3-minutes.html

115   In fact, Trump's Islamohobic rhetoric and policies, such as the visa ban on seven muslim-majority countries, are another liability for the Russian state. Home to an estimated 20 million Muslim citizens (fifteen percent of the population) and counting a number of muslim-

majority countries as important allies, Russia clearly needs to preserve its multi-confessional and multi-ethnic identity. In sharp contrast to the Trump administration, for example, the Russian state facilitates the practice of Islamic jurisprudence in Chechnya, and allowed its capital Grosny to host an estimated million-strong demonstration against the Je Suis Charlie movement that swept Western Europe. Senior government officials, including Putin himself, regularly visit mosques, pay their respects to Islamic holidays; and Islam is positively portrayed in Russian schoolbooks. This is not to say that the country does not have its own serious problems with islamophobia, yet the government response is markedly different from Western Europe and the United States, where anti-Islamic sentiments are often actively and explicitly fueled by senior government officials. Dobrovolskiy, D. A., & Headly, T. (2016, April 26). Islamophobia: What America can Learn from Russia. Retrieved from https://intpolicydigest.org/2016/04/26/islamophobia-what-america-can-learn-from-russia/; Sharkov, D. (2017, February 04). Why Putin won't comment on Trump's new travel ban. Retrieved from http://europe.newsweek.com/why-russia-has-not-condemned-trumps-immigration-ban-550227?rm=eu; Mackinnon, M. (2012, September 06). In rebuilt Grozny, an awkward peace with Russia. Retrieved from http://www.theglobeandmail.com/news/world/in-rebuilt-grozny-an-awkward-peace-with-russia/article552926/. For more on white nationalism and Putin consult endnote 108 and Robinson, P. (2016, December 04). Guilt by association. Retrieved from https://irrussianality.wordpress.com/2016/12/04/guilt-by-association/comment-page-1/

116   One minor study was undertaken by Tsygankov, A. P. (2015, August 23). Nobody loves Russia: how western media have perpetuated the myth of Putin's 'neo-Soviet autocracy' Retrieved from http://blogs.lse.ac.uk/europpblog/2015/08/17/nobody-loves-russia-how-western-media-have-perpetuated-the-myth-of-putins-neo-soviet-autocracy/. Some more recent examples of fallacious reporting (far from exhaustive) include Robinson, P. (2016, October 19). Drifting towards authoritarianism, or not. Retrieved from https://irrussianality.wordpress.com/2016/10/19/drifting-towards-authoritarianism-or-not/; Greenwald, G. (2017, January 04). WashPost Is Richly Rewarded for False News About Russia Threat While Public Is Deceived. Retrieved from https://theintercept.com/2017/01/04/washpost-is-richly-rewarded-for-false-news-about-russia-threat-while-public-is-deceived/; Greenwald, G. (2016, December 09). A Clinton Fan Manufactured Fake News That MSNBC Personalities Spread to Discredit WikiLeaks Docs. Retrieved from https://theintercept.

com/2016/12/09/a-clinton-fan-manufactured-fake-news-that-msnbc-personalities-spread-to-discredit-wikileaks-docs/

117 There are multiple interpretations on why he finally resigned and what motivated the officials to leak the information. I find the anti-Russian narrative the most convincing. See the next endnote and Giraldi, P. (2017, February 16). More About Russia and Less About Flynn? Retrieved from http://www.theamericanconservative.com/articles/more-about-russia-and-less-about-flynn/

118 Lake, E. (2017, February 14). The Political Assassination of Michael Flynn. Retrieved from https://www.bloomberg.com/view/articles/2017-02-14/the-political-assassination-of-michael-flynn?utm_campaign=buffer&utm_content=buffere4d72&utm_medium=social&utm_source=twitter.com

119 Cohen, S. (2017, February 16). Kremlin-Baiting President Trump (Without Facts) Must Stop. Retrieved from https://www.thenation.com/article/kremlin-baiting-president-trump-without-facts-must-stop/; Farrell, J. A. (2016, December 31). Nixon's Vietnam Treachery. Retrieved from https://www.nytimes.com/2016/12/31/opinion/sunday/nixons-vietnam-treachery.html; Ruiz-Marrero, C. (2014, October 29). The October Surprise Was Real. Retrieved from http://www.counterpunch.org/2014/07/11/the-october-surprise-was-real/; Rosenberg., P. (2014, June 7). Ronald Reagan "treason" amnesia: GOP hypocrites forget their hero negotiated with terrorists. He was just really bad at it. Retrieved from http://www.salon.com/2014/06/07/ronald_reagan_treason_amnesia_gop_hypocrites_forget_their_hero_negotiated_with_terrorists_he_was_just_really_bad_at_it/

120 Lake, E. (2017, February 14). The Political Assassination of Michael Flynn. Retrieved from https://www.bloomberg.com/view/articles/2017-02-14/the-political-assassination-of-michael-flynn?utm_campaign=buffer&utm_content=buffere4d72&utm_medium=social&utm_source=twitter.com

121 Greenwald, G. (2017, February 14). The Leakers Who Exposed Gen. Flynn's Lie Committed Serious - and Wholly Justified - Felonies. Retrieved from https://theintercept.com/2017/02/14/the-leakers-who-exposed-gen-flynns-lie-committed-serious-and-wholly-justified-felonies/

122 Ibid.

123 Schmidt, M. S., Apuzzo, M., & Mazzetti, M. (2017, February 14). Trump Campaign Aides Had Repeated Contacts With Russian Intelligence. Retrieved from https://www.nytimes.com/2017/02/14/us/politics/russia-intelligence-communications-trump.html?hp&action=click&pgtype=Homepage&clickSource=story-heading&module=span-

ab-top-region&region=top-news&WT.nav=top-news

124 Galeotti, M. (2017, February 15). The NYT story on "Trump associates" and Russian spooks: some questions. Retrieved from https://inmoscowsshadows.wordpress.com/2017/02/15/the-nyt-story-on-trump-associates-and-russian-spooks-some-questions/

125 Myers, S. L., & Kramer, A. (2016, July 31). How Paul Manafort Wielded Power in Ukraine Before Advising Donald Trump. Retrieved from https://www.nytimes.com/2016/08/01/us/paul-manafort-ukraine-donald-trump.html?_r=0

126 Holt, L., Hunt, K., Welker, K., & Todd, C. (2017, February 28). Speaker Ryan hasn't been shown any evidence of American collusion with Russia during campaign. Retrieved from http://www.nbcnews.com/politics/donald-trump/ryan-shown-no-evidence-any-americans-colluded-russia-during-campaign-n726691; Watkins, A. (2017, March 9). Inside The Investigation To Get To The Bottom Of Russia's Role In The Election. Retrieved from https://www.buzzfeed.com/alimwatkins/the-people-investigating-russias-role-in-the-election-worry?utm_term=.csp50mDL8#.htv1x4A5V; Ross, B., Meek, J. G., & Mosk, M. (2017, March 9). 'No evidence' Trump campaign aides recruited by Russia, former spy chief says. Retrieved from http://abcnews.go.com/Politics/top-spy-chief-evidence-trump-campaign-aides-recruited/story?id=46013305; Greenwald, G. (2017, March 16). Key Democratic Officials Now Warning Base Not to Expect Evidence of Trump/Russia Collusion. Retrieved from https://theintercept.com/2017/03/16/key-democratic-officials-now-warning-base-not-to-expect-evidence-of-trumprussia-collusion/

127 Rosenberg, M., Goldman, A., & Schmidt, M. S. (2017, March 01). Obama Administration Rushed to Preserve Intelligence of Russian Election Hacking. Retrieved from https://www.nytimes.com/2017/03/01/us/politics/obama-trump-russia-election-hacking.html

128 Ibid.

129 Matlock, J. (2017, March 4). Contacts with Russian Embassy. Retrieved from http://jackmatlock.com/2017/03/contacts-with-russian-embassy/; Easley, J. (2017, March 11). Diplomats warn of Russia hysteria. Retrieved from http://thehill.com/homenews/administration/323479-diplomats-warn-of-russia-hysteria

130 Novak, J. (2017, March 02). Jeff Sessions should absolutely not resign over these bogus Russia allegations. Retrieved from http://www.cnbc.com/2017/03/02/no-jeff-sessions-shouldnt-resign.html

131 Fernandez, M., & Lichtblau, E. (2017, February 27). Justice Dept. Drops a Key Objection to a Texas Voter ID Law. Retrieved from

	https://www.nytimes.com/2017/02/27/us/justice-dept-will-drop-a-key-objection-to-a-texas-voter-id-law.html
132	Gessen, M. (2017, March 6). Russia: The Conspiracy Trap. Retrieved from http://www.nybooks.com/daily/2017/03/06/trump-russia-conspiracy-trap/
133	Ibid.
134	Ibid.
135	Greenwald, G. (2017, January 11). The Deep State Goes to War With President-Elect, Using Unverified Claims, as Democrats Cheer. Retrieved from https://theintercept.com/2017/01/11/the-deep-state-goes-to-war-with-president-elect-using-unverified-claims-as-dems-cheer/
136	Ibid.
137	Bensinger, K., Elder, M., & Schoofs, M. (2017, January 11). These Reports Allege Trump Has Deep Ties To Russia. Retrieved from https://www.buzzfeed.com/kenbensinger/these-reports-allege-trump-has-deep-ties-to-russia?utm_term=.qszNyOdWR#.xkBEkDobR
138	Shane, S., Goldman, A., & Rosenberg, M. (2017, January 10). Trump Received Unsubstantiated Report That Russia Had Damaging Information About Him. Retrieved from https://www.nytimes.com/2017/01/10/us/politics/donald-trump-russia-intelligence.html
139	Arkin, W. M., McFadden, C., Eremenko, A., & Smith, E. (2017, January 11). Trump wasn't told about unverified Russia memo during intel briefing. Retrieved from http://www.nbcnews.com/news/world/trump-cites-nazi-germany-rejects-dossier-alleged-russia-dealings-n705586
140	Sciutto, J., & Perez, E. (2017, February 10). US investigators corroborate some aspects of the Russia dossier. Retrieved from http://edition.cnn.com/2017/02/10/politics/russia-dossier-update/index.html
141	Ibid.
142	Katchanovski, I. (2017, January 10). Facebook. Retrieved from https://www.facebook.com/ivan.katchanovski/posts/1474909339205614. Interestingly, the similarity to post-Soviet Kompromat was even noted in one New York Times article: Taub, A. (2017, January 15). 'Kompromat' and the Danger of Doubt and Confusion in a Democracy. Retrieved from https://www.nytimes.com/2017/01/15/world/europe/kompromat-donald-trump-russia-democracy.html?action=click&contentCollection=Europe&module=RelatedCoverage®ion=EndOfArticle&pgtype=article. Katchanovski's analysis regarding the accuracy of the memo has also been shared by a range of security experts, who argue that such far-ranging sources and collection of sensitive intelligence is utterly implausible, even if Steele had been the current head of the CIA. In fact, even the co-director of Steele's private intelligence firm

articulated this position. Hope, B., Rothfeld, M., & Cullison, A. (2017, January 11). Christopher Steele, Ex-British Intelligence Officer, Said to Have Prepared Dossier on Trump. Retrieved from https://www.wsj.com/articles/christopher-steele-ex-british-intelligence-officer-said-to-have-prepared-dossier-on-trump-1484162553; Galeotti, M. (2017, January 11). The Trump Dossier: dynamite or disinformation? Retrieved from http://raamoprusland.nl/dossiers/het-kremlin/418-the-trump-dossier-dynamite-or-disinformation

143   Pinchuk, V. (2016, December 29). Ukraine Must Make Painful Compromises for Peace With Russia. Retrieved from https://www.wsj.com/articles/ukraine-must-make-painful-compromises-for-peace-with-russia-1483053902

144   Analysis and source provided by Katchanovski, I. (2017, January 25). Facebook. Retrieved from https://www.facebook.com/ivan.katchanovski/posts/1489739087722639

145   Webb, I. (2017, February 6). Kiev Is Fueling the War in Eastern Ukraine, Too. Retrieved from https://foreignpolicy.com/2017/02/06/its-not-just-putin-fueling-war-in-ukraine-trump-donbas/

146   Ibid.

147   Kiev admits advancing on rebels in east Ukrainian town 'meter by meter' (2017, February 1). Retrieved from https://www.rt.com/news/375892-kiev-advance-rebels-position/

148   Miller, C. (2017, January 30). Anxious Ukraine Risks Escalation In 'Creeping Offensive' Retrieved from http://www.rferl.org/a/ukraine-russia-creeping-offensive-escalation-fighting/28268104.html

149   Braun, S. (2017, January 30). Kiews Kalkül. Retrieved from http://www.sueddeutsche.de/politik/ostukraine-kiews-kalkuel-1.3356319#redirectedFromLandingpage

150   Стало відомо, з чого почалося загострення в Авдіївці. (2017, February 3). Retrieved from http://www.pravda.com.ua/news/2017/02/3/7134334/

151   Nicholas, M. (2017, February 2). McCain and Graham visited Ukraine's Front Line, told Leadership to go on Offensive. Retrieved from http://macedoniaonline.eu/content/view/31180/53/

152   bid.

153   Braun, S. (2017, January 30). Kiews Kalkül. Retrieved from http://www.sueddeutsche.de/politik/ostukraine-kiews-kalkuel-1.3356319#redirectedFromLandingpage

154   Sengupta, S. (2017, February 2). Trump's U.N. Envoy, Nikki Haley, Condemns Russia's 'Aggressive Actions' in Ukraine. Retrieved from https://www.nytimes.com/2017/02/02/world/europe/nikki-haley-trump-ukraine-russia-putin.html; Mercuris, A. (2017, February 5).

	Trump administration fails to back Ukraine. Retrieved from http://theduran.com/trump-administration-declines-support-ukraine/
155	EU Vows to Stick to Russia Sanctions Despite Trump's Bid for Detente. (2017, February 6). Retrieved from https://www.nytimes.com/reuters/2017/02/06/world/europe/06reuters-ukraine-crisis-russia-eu.html
156	Mercouris, A. (2017, February 06). Trump administration fails to back Ukraine. Retrieved from http://theduran.com/trump-administration-declines-support-ukraine/
157	Ibid.
158	Ibid.
159	Davis, J. H. (2017, February 6). Trump Seems to Side With Russia in Comments on Ukraine. Retrieved from https://www.nytimes.com/2017/02/06/us/politics/ukraine-trump-putin-separatists-poroshenko.html
160	Sanctions imposed for Crimea occupation to remain, - White House. (2017, February 09). Retrieved from http://112.international/politics/sanctions-imposed-for-crimea-occupation-to-remain-white-house-13917.html
161	Trump Wary of Russian Deal; New Advisers Urge Tougher Stand. (2017, March 04). Retrieved from https://www.nytimes.com/aponline/2017/03/04/us/politics/ap-us-trump-russia.html?_r=0 On the other hand, Stephen Cohen argues there are some signs that the détente efforts have been going on more quietly, rather than being abandoned. Cohen, S. F. (2017, March 15). While Neo-McCarthyism Spreads, US-Russian Détente May Be Unfolding. Retrieved from https://www.thenation.com/article/while-neo-mccarthyism-spreads-us-russian-detente-may-be-unfolding/
162	Ibid.
163	Grytsenko, O., & Sukhov, O. (2017, February 13). Rumor mill goes into overdrive over prospect of secret peace deal with Kremlin. Retrieved from https://www.kyivpost.com/ukraine-politics/rumor-mill-goes-overdrive-prospect-secret-peace-deal-kremlin.html
164	Ibid.
165	UNHCR welcomes Action Plan toward Donbas territories beyond gov't control. (2017, January 24). Retrieved from https://www.unian.info/society/1740311-unhcr-welcomes-action-plan-toward-donbas-territories-beyond-govt-control.html
166	One million Ukrainian children now need aid as number doubles over past year—UNICEF. (2017, February 17). Retrieved from http://www.un.org/apps/news/story.asp?NewsID=56193#.WLBzum8rKHt
167	Lyons, L. (2017, March 23). South Sudan, Haiti and Ukraine

Lead World in Suffering. Retrieved from http://www.gallup.com/poll/206891/south-sudan-haiti-ukraine-lead-world-suffering.aspx?g_source=World&g_medium=newsfeed&g_campaign=tiles

168 Ibid.

GLOSSARY OF ACRONYMS

ABMT	Anti-Ballistic Missile Treaty
ARES	Armament Research Services
BBC	British Broadcasting Corporation
BRICS	Brazil, Russia, India, China, South-Africa
CEO	Chief Executive Officer
CIA	Central Intelligence Agency
CIS	Commonwealth of Independent States
CISFTA	Commonwealth of Independent States Free Trade Agreement
CNN	Cable News Network
CSDP	Common Security and Defense Policy
CSLR	Center for Social and Labour Research
CSTO	Collective Security Treaty Organization
DCFTA	Deep and Comprehensive Free Trade Area
DIA	Defense Intelligence Agency
DNC	Democratic National Committee
EBRD	European Bank for Reconstruction and Development
EDA	European Defense Agency
EEC	European Economic Community

EEU	Eurasian Economic Union
ESDI	European Security and Defense Identity
EU	European Union
FBI	Federal Bureau of Investigation
FDI	Foreign Direct Investment
FSB	Federal Security Service of the Russian Federation
GDP	Gross domestic product
GNP	Gross national product
ICG	International Crisis Group
ICRC	International Committee of the Red Cross
IFCN	International Fact-Checking Network
IMF	International Monetary Fund
INTERPOL	International Criminal Police Organization
IRF	International Renaissance Foundation
KGB	Committee for State Security
KHPG	Kharkiv Human Rights Protection Group
KIIS	Kiev International Institute of Sociology
KKK	Klu Klux Klan
LGBT	lesbian, gay, bisexual, and transgender
MAUP	Interregional Academy of Personnel Management
MH17	Malaysia Airlines-flight 17
MI-6	Military Intelligence, Section 6
MIT	Massachusetts Institute of Technology
MP	Member of Parliament

NABU	National Anti-Corruption Bureau of Ukraine
NATO	North-Atlantic Treaty Organization
NED	National Endowment for Democracy
NGO	Non-governmental Organization
NSA	National Security Agency
NYT	New York Times
OCCRP	Organized Crime and Corruption Reporting Project
OSCE	Organization for Security and Co-operation in Europe
OSF	Open Society Foundation
OSW	The Centre for Eastern Studies
OUN	Organization of Ukrainian Nationalists
PVV	Party for Freedom
R&D	Research & Development
RT	Russia Today
SBU	Security Service of Ukraine
SCO	Shanghai Co-operation Organization
SIPRI	Stockholm International Peace Research Institute
SOA	School of the Americas
SS	Schutzstaffel
START	Strategic Arms Reduction Treaty
TISA	Trade in Services Agreement
TTIP	Transatlantic Trade and Investment Partnership
UCCA	Ukrainian Congress Committee of America
UCLA	University of California, Los Angeles

UDAR	Ukrainian Democratic Alliance for Reform
UK	United Kingdom
UN	United Nations
UNA	Ukrainian National Assembly
UNDP	United Nations Development Program
UNHCR	United Nations High Commissioner for Refugees
UNICEF	United Nations International Children's Emergency Fund
UNSC	United Nations Security Council
UNWFP	United Nations World Food Program
UPA	Ukrainian Insurgent Army
US	United States
USA	United States of America
USAF	United States Air Force
USAID	United States Agency for International Development
USD	United States Dollar
USSR	Union of Soviet Socialist Republics
VIPS	Veteran Intelligence Professionals for Sanity
WIIW	Vienna Institute for International Economic Studies
WNISEF	Western NIS Enterprise Fund

INDEX

A

Afghanistan, 252, 303
Aidar battalion, 139, 164
Akhmetov, Rinat, 49, 95, 208
Amnesty International, 139, 172
Anti-BallisticMissile Treaty
    (ABMT), 239, 243
Applebaum, Anne, 281, 310-311
Armament Research Services
    (ARES), 140, 201
Avakov, Arsen, 155, 164, 172
Azerbaijan, 236, 259, 281
Azov battalion, 138, 158, 165, 228-229

B

Baltic States, 61, 89, 237, 258, 281
Bandera, Stepan, 21-22, 26, 29, 60
Belarus, 13, 104, 142, 254, 281
Bellant, Russ, 60-61
Biden, Joe, 80, 91-92, 95-96, 210-212
Biletskiy, Andriy, 158, 166
Breedlove, Philip, 206, 212-215
BRICS, 69, 285
Brzezinski, Zbigniew, 70, 74, 236, 244, 282
Bulatov, Dmitriy, 31
Bulletin of Atomic Scientists, 241, 244-245
Bush, George H. W., 9, 61, 264, 287-288, 290

Bush, George W., 208, 251, 295

C

Cameron, David, 229, 281
Canada, 61-62, 224, 229, 245, 254
Carter, Jimmy, 216, 313
Center for Social and Labour
    Research (CSLR), 18, 21, 128, 143, 183-184
Central Intelligence Agency (CIA), 56, 60, 224, 255, 263, 281, 298, 301, 314
Chang, Ha-Joon, 72, 90
Chechnya, 138, 198, 249-252, 336n115
Chemerys, Volodymyr, 174
Cheney, Dick, 208, 214, 216, 286, 295
China, 69, 74, 92, 238-239, 241, 245, 253-256, 262, 296
Chomsky, Noam, 167, 230, 245, 256-257, 263, 300
Chornovol, Tatyana, 31
Clapper JR, James, 285, 314
Clinton, Bill, 47, 252, 281, 298
Clinton, Hillary, 16, 47, 281, 299, 305, 337n116
Cohen, Stephen, 247, 265, 298
Collective Security Treaty Organization (CSTO), 254-255
Commonwealth of Independent
    States Free Trade Agreement
    (CISFTA), 107-108

Communist Party of Ukraine, 171, 175, 180
Council of Europe, 38, 130
Crimea, 10, 91, 115-119, 120n12, 123, 127, 198, 249, 257, 261-262, 320
Crimean Tatars, 118-119

D

DC Leaks, 57, 212, 214, 273n104
De Gaulle, Charles, 280
Defense Intelligence Agency (DIA), 213
Democratic National Committee (DNC), 299-300
demographics and polling:
   electoral, 14-15, 22, 94-96, 158, 178-180
   ethno-linguistic 12-15, 117-118, 128, 176-177
   in Crimea, 117-119, 120n12
   in Donbass 124-131, 141-142, 152n54, 154, 198-200, 202
   on Anti-Maidan, 115, 128-129
   on Maidan 18, 21, 32-33, 178
   on media 176-177
   on peace 137, 221n53
   on the far-right 21-22, 26, 158, 183, 185
   on the Orange Revolution 54-55
   socio-economic 16, 18, 75, 77, 97, 130-131, 177-178, 183-185
Donbass. See under demographics and polling; Minsk process, the
Dudin, Vitaliy, 110, 180, 194

E

Eastern Partnership initiative, 281-282
Eurasian Economic Union (EEU), 16, 104, 106, 178
European Commission, 57, 206
European Court of Auditors, 97, 308
European Economic Community (EEC), 280, 283
European parliament, 59, 251
European Union:
   general, 23, 38, 40, 89-90, 104, 166-167, 178, 198, 255-256, span 278-286, 305-312
   association agreement with Ukraine, 16-17, 69, 97, 106, 111, 127, 180, 281-282, 285, 307-309 (See also neoliberalization of the Ukrainian)

F

fake news, 304-306, 330n64, 332n86
Federal Bureau of Investigation (FBI), 46, 208, 301, 313, 315, 325n26
Federal Security Service of the Russian Federation (FSB), 66n31, 123
Firtash, Dmytro, 49, 208-209
Flynn, Michael, 297, 312-314, 321
Foreign Affairs (journal), 239, 287, 296
France, 60, 193, 206, 252-254, 280, 283-287, 290, 311
Front National, 166, 311

G

Gallup, 17, 95, 117, 178, 199, 245-246, 248, 297, 321
Georgia, 107, 199, 236, 259, 261
Germany:
   general, 251-252, 254, 279-280, 283-287, 305-306, 311-312
   Nazi, 22, 60, 254, 279

East, 9, 287-290
Ukraine relations, 13, 22,
    58, 62, 142, 182, 193, 207,
    263, 277-278, 284-285,
    319
Gessen, Keith, 155, 140, 325n26
Gessen, Masha, 316
Glazyev, Sergey, 125, 247
Gorbachev, Mikhail, 9-10, 287-290
Guardian, 204, 252, 325n26
Guiliano, Elise, 128-130

H

Hahn, Gordon, 29, 38, 164, 282
Hollande, Francois, 205
Human Rights Watch, 139-140

I

International Monetary Fund (IMF):
    general, 17, 48, 71-74, 98,
        110, 210, 246, 252, 285,
        300-301
    US influence on, 69-70, 79-81,
        236
    See also neoliberalization
    of the Ukrainian
International Committee of the Red
    Cross (ICRC), 142-143
International Crisis Group (ICG),
    126, 154, 166, 195-196, 202-
    205
Iran, 236, 238, 241, 264-265, 296,
    313
Iraq, 205-206, 216, 226-228, 251-
    253, 257, 281, 283, 286- 287,
    303-304
Ishchenko, Volodymyr, 32, 183,
    203

J

Japan, 10, 60, 69, 110, 242, 254,
    262
Jaresko, Natalie, 91-93

K

Karber, Philip, 212-216
Katchanovski, Ivan, 26, 37, 117,
    126, 130, 145, 174-175, 191,
    318
Kennedy, John F., 245, 280
Kerry, John, 91-92, 274n104, 277
Kharkiv Human Rights Protection
    Group (KHPG), 174, 182
Kiev International Institute of Soci-
    ology (KIIS), 26, 75, 124,
    127, 130, 141, 176-178, 180
Kissinger, Henry, 295-296, 324n15
Klitschko, Vitali, 62-63, 209, 277-
    278
Kolomoyskyi, Igor, 47-48, 50, 92,
    95, 176
Kotsaba, Ruslan, 173
Kravchuk, Leonid, 24, 75
Kravchuk, Oleksandr, 76-77, 79,
    106,
Kudelia, Serhiy, 97, 125-126, 128-
    129, 154

L

Leshchenko, Serhiy, 49, 94, 182
London Review of Books, 140, 155,
    198, 213
Lutsenko, Yuriy, 96

M

Maidan. See under demographics
    and polling
Maidan killings, 30-31, 37-39, 40
Manafort, Paul, 300, 314
MAUP (Interregional Academy of
    Personnel Management),
    23-25
McCain, John, 61, 305, 319
media:
    Ukrainian, 45, 49, 56, 171-177
    Western, 9, 199, 205-206,
        244, 299-300, 304-312,

317, 330n64, 332n86, 337n116
Russian, 174-177, 199
(See also Russia Today)
Merkel, Angela, 205, 277
MH17, 263-265, 309-310
military aid:
    Russian, 124, 198-202, 205-207
    Western, 212-213, 215, 224-226, 228-231, 237, 252
military draft, 137, 163, 173, 184
Minsk process, the:
    general, 167, 221n53
    ceasefires and, 145, 164, 166, 176, 191, 202-205, 318-319
    humanitarian crisis and, 141-143, 191-192, 195, 321
    federalization and, 58, 127-128, 163, 183, 192-195, 205
    local elections and, 192- 193
    US influence on, 206-211, 214-215, 278, 320
    Russian influence on, 193, 196, 200, 202-205
Muraya, Dean, 97

N

Nalivaichenko, Valentyn Oleksandrovych, 87
National Anti-Corruption Bureau of Ukraine (NABU), 96-97
National Endowment for Democracy (NED), 56, 58, 61, 306, 311
North Atlantic Treaty Organization (NATO):
    general, 69,258, 281, 310-312, 314, 335n102
    expansion, 9-10, 212, 236, 261, 282-284, 287-291, 297
    Ukraine relations, 17-18, 47, 111, 178, 205-207, 212-215, 224-225, 237, 283
    military expenditure, 253-255, 297-298
    Missile Defense System, 238-239, 241, 243-245, 297
    Russia founding Act, 237
neoliberalization of the Ukrainian:
    budget, 74-75, 131, 195
    financial sector, 76-77
    gas sector, 77-79
    international trade, 104-109
    state enterprises, 91-92
    tax reforms, 79, 88-90, 106
    See also European Union association agreement with Ukraine; International Monetary Fund
Netherlands, 59, 90, 280-281, 283, 306-311
New York Review of Books, 198, 200
New York Times, 9, 36, 62, 126-127, 138, 140, 198-199, 240, 257, 262, 296, 301, 304, 307, 314-315, 317, 320, 332n86, 340n142
Nixon, Richard, 241-242, 298, 313
Normandy Four, 193, 211
Novorossiya, 178, 204
National Security Agency (NSA), 301, 313
Nuland, Victoria, 54, 58, 61-63, 94, 96, 208-209, 214, 277-278

O

Obama, Barack, 9, 209, 211-214, 236, 238, 240-242, 257, 261-262, 280, 296, 300, 315
Odessa, 128-130, 154, 162-163, 165, 178-179
Opposition Bloc, 95-96, 179-180
Organization for Security and Co-operation in Europe

(OSCE), 116, 139-142, 145, 152n53, 171, 202, 206, 211, 260, 301, 319
Organization of Ukrainian Nationalists (OUN), 22, 25-26, 29, 60, 157

P

Party of Regions, 36, 49, 115, 175
Parubiy, Andriy,23, 32, 40, 62, 164, 196
Petro, Nicolai, 108
Pijl, Kees van der, 282
Pinchuk, Viktor, 47, 309, 322
Poland, 13, 21, 39, 58-59, 80, 214, 238, 244, 280-281
PolitiFact, 306, 331n71
Poroshenko Bloc, 80, 94-95, 179, 182
Poroshenko, Petro, 31, 48-50, 63, 80, 95-96, 155, 157, 164, 166, 172, 176, 181-183,192-193, 196, 208-210, 215, 319-321
Prizrak battalion, 204
Putin, Vladimir:
    general, 58, 243, 247-252, 259-263, 265, 291, 295, 297-299, 310-312, 325n26, 335n104, 335n108, 337n115
    on Ukraine, 10, 39, 115, 124, 128, 178, 198, 200, 205-206, 258
Pyatt, Geoffrey, 58, 62-63, 80, 87, 91, 95-96, 209, 214

R

Radical Party, 139, 178
Reagan, Ronald, 56, 60-61, 240, 264, 279, 306, 314
Right Sector, 29-31, 36-38, 40, 118, 129-130, 163-165, 191
Russia. See under military aid; Minsk process, the; Putin, Vladimir; sanctions
Russia Today (RT), 302-304, 308-309
Russiagate, 312-318
Russian propaganda, 167, 246, 304, 308, 332n86, 335n102. See also media

S

Saakashvili, Mikheil, 94, 207, 261
Sakwa, Richard, 252, 261, 283
sanctions:
    Russian, 17, 107-108, 256
    Western:
        against Russia 108, 195, 211, 256, 263, 265, 273n104, 277, 285, 295-297, 311-313, 320
        against Western-Europe, 279
        against Yanukovych, 49, 59
Sarotte, Elise, 287-288, 290
Security Service of Ukraine (SBU), 25, 88, 154
Self-Reliance party, 50, 178
Sessions, Jeff, 315-316
Shanghai Co-operation Organization (SCO), 254-255
Shifrinson, Joshua Itzkowitz, 289-290
Sikorski, Radoslaw, 39, 281
Soros, George, 56-58, 212, 273n104, 307
Soviet Union:
    general, 9-10, 21, 117-118, 242, 245, 253-254, 279, 287-290
    post, 12-16, 24-26, 45, 60-61, 106-107, 110, 126, 131, 157, 171, 199, 254, 258-260, 280-284
Stacks, Graham, 89
Stalin, Joseph, 21, 24-26, 118, 247
Stockholm International Peace Research Institute (SIPRI),

202, 226
Strategic Arms Reduction Treaty (START), 242, 298
Stratfor, 64, 277, 279
Strelkov, Igor, 123-124, 143
Svoboda, 22-23, 29, 40, 63, 163, 166
Syria, 124, 138, 251-252

T

Tillerson, Rex, 296
Tornado battalion, 138-139, 158, 162
Transnistria, 259-261
Truman, Harry S., 242, 279
Trump, Donald, 109, 285, 295-299, 303, 305, 312-321
Turchynov, Oleksandr, 47, 191, 196
Tyahnybok, Oleh, 22-23, 61
Tymoshenko, Yulia, 24, 37, 46, 49, 55, 175

U

Ukrainian Congress Committee of America (UCCA), 60-61, 305
United Nations (UN):
    general, 38, 139-142, 145, 153n54, 67, 320
    Development Program (UNDP), 117, 184
    Security Council (UNSC), 196, 286, 320
    World Food Program (UN WFP), 141, 225
    International Children's Emergency Fund (UNICEF), 141, 322
United Kingdom, 229, 251-252, 255, 257, 280-281, 311-312
United States of America. See under International Monetary Fund; media; military aid; Minsk process, the
US State Department, 49, 59-60, 63, 70, 214, 228
USAID, 56, 92

V

Veteran Intelligence Professionals for Sanity (VIPS), 206, 301
Vienna Institute for International Economic Studies (wiiw), 77-78, 106, 108, 110
Warsaw Pact, 253, 290
Wikileaks, 10, 16, 23, 47-48, 181, 301
World Bank, 69-75, 98
World War 1, 246, 279
World War 2, 10, 26, 60, 167-168, 242, 246, 256, 279

Y

Yanukovych, Viktor, 15-18, 30, 32, 37-39, 49, 175, 314
Yarosh, Dmytro, 38, 40, 130, 165, 191
Yatsenyuk, Arseniy, 47-48, 62-63, 69, 94-96, 109, 155, 158, 209
Yeltsin, Boris, 246-249, 260, 299-301
Yushchenko, Viktor, 14-16, 23-27, 54-55, 61, 157, 225

Made in the USA
Columbia, SC
18 April 2017